D0407545

ENDOWED BY OUR CREATOR

Meyerson, Michael.
Endowed by our creator
: the birth of religious
c2012.
33305225090566
sa   08/28/12

ENDOWED BY OUR CREATOR

The Birth of Religious Freedom in America

MICHAEL I. MEYERSON

Yale

UNIVERSITY PRESS

New Haven & London

Copyright © 2012 by Michael I. Meyerson.
All rights reserved.
This book may not be reproduced, in whole or in part,
including illustrations, in any form (beyond that copying
permitted by Sections 107 and 108 of the US Copyright Law
and except by reviewers for the public press),
without written permission from the publishers.

Yale University Press books may be purchased in quantity
for educational, business, or promotional use.
For information, please e-mail sales.press@yale.edu (US office)
or sales@yaleup.co.uk (UK office).

Designed by James J. Johnson and set in Monotype Dante type by
Duke & Company, Devon, Pennsylvania.
Printed in the United States of America

Library of Congress Cataloging-in-Publication Data

Meyerson, Michael.
Endowed by our creator : the birth of religious freedom
in America / Michael I. Meyerson.
p.   cm.
Includes bibliographical references (p.   ) and index.
ISBN 978-0-300-16632-3 (clothbound : alk. paper) 1. Freedom of
religion—United States. 2. United States. Constitution.
1st Amendment. I. Title.
KF4783.M49 2012
342.7308'52—dc23   2011044463

A catalogue record for this book is available from the British Library.

This paper meets the requirements of ANSI/NISO Z39.48–1992
(Permanence of Paper).
10 9 8 7 6 5 4 3 2 1

To Lesly, William, and Andrew. With love.

CONTENTS

ACKNOWLEDGMENTS

THERE ARE many people to whom I am deeply indebted for their help with this book. First, I want to thank my editor at Yale University Press, Bill Frucht, who has, as always, made the finished product far superior to my original vision. I also want to thank my agent, Geri Thoma, of the Elaine Markson Agency, who helps me present my ideas in a form that an editor would want to read.

Many people gave me assistance, information, and advice throughout my writing of the book. From the University of Baltimore School of Law, a special thanks goes to my secretary extraordinaire, Gloria Joy. This project could not have been completed without the strong support of the superb library staff at the University of Baltimore School of Law. I want to give my warmest thanks to Bijal Shah, Will Tress, Harvey Morrell, Bob Pool, and Elizabeth Rhodes.

I was fortunate to have had two fabulous research assistants, Sarah Ritter and Jonathan Foreman. I want to thank you both for the help you provided and the enthusiasm you brought to your work.

I want to express my appreciation to Dr. Josh Perelman of the National Museum of American Jewish History and Dr. Steve Frank of the National Constitution Center for the time they spent graciously teaching me about their museums' exhibits.

I also want to acknowledge the assistance and guidance from the staff at James Madison's Montpelier and the Center for the Constitution, with special thanks to Michael Quinn and Sean O'Brien. Thanks also go to the staff at Thomas Jefferson's Monticello for research assistance.

I received especially valuable suggestions and critiques from John Ragosta and Alan Gibson. Their comments helped improve the book greatly, though any mistakes that remain are mine alone.

Many people also provided me with emotional support and encouragement throughout this long process. I want to thank Freddie Jeck, Martin Siegel, Neil Kempler, and Adrienne Berger. I also want to thank my parents, Jack and Marian, for all the support they have always shown me as well as for teaching me the value of honest reasoning.

My sons, William and Andrew, have served not only as invaluable sounding boards but also as continual sources of inspiration and joy. Finally I want to thank my wife, Lesly, for everything.

ENDOWED BY OUR CREATOR

"Truth is as essential to history as the soul is to the body."

JOHN LELAND
"The Virginia Chronicle," 1790

Introduction: The Great Seal

ON JULY 4, 1776, shortly after approving the Declaration of Independence, the Continental Congress voted to create a committee to design a "Great Seal"[1] for the newly confederated states: "Resolved, That Dr. Franklin, Mr. J Adams and Mr. Jefferson, be a committee, to bring in a device for a seal for the United States of America."[2]

These three men, Benjamin Franklin, John Adams, and Thomas Jefferson, had just finished serving on the committee that drafted the Declaration of Independence, but their new assignment would prove far more difficult. Rather than using words, they were now asked to create a graphic depiction of their vision for America. Recognizing the challenge of their task, they enlisted the help of a painter, a Swiss immigrant named Pierre Eugène Du Simitière.[3]

Throughout the next month, the members of the committee met as they worked on their individual designs. By August 13, each had produced a proposal.

John Adams wrote his wife that he had proposed a picture entitled "the Choice of Hercules." According to Adams, "The Hero resting on his Clubb. Virtue pointing to her rugged Mountain, on one Hand, and perswading him to ascend. Sloth, glancing at her flowery Paths of Pleasure, wantonly reclining on the Ground, displaying the Charms both of her Eloquence and Person, to seduce him into Vice."[4] Adams did not think highly of his own suggestion. As he wrote to Abigail, "This is too complicated a group for a seal or medal, and it is not original."

Both Franklin and Jefferson proposed biblical imagery. Franklin suggested a picture of Moses standing at the Red Sea with his hand raised, "thereby causing the same to overwhelm Pharaoh who is sitting in an open Chariot, a Crown on his Head and a Sword in his Hand. Rays from a Pillar of Fire in the Clouds reaching to Moses, to express that he acts by Command of the Deity."[5] To accompany the illustration, Franklin offered the motto "Rebellion to Tyrants is Obedience to God."

Jefferson's proposal employed a similar theme. According to Adams, Jefferson suggested, "The Children of Israel in the Wilderness, led by a Cloud by day, and a Pillar of Fire by night."[6] He also proposed that the seal should have a reverse side that would contain a picture of Hengist and Horsa, the leaders of the first Anglo-Saxon settlers in Britain, "whose political principles and form of government we have assumed."

The committee's proposal to Congress, submitted on August 20, largely relied on Du Simitière's idea for its front. This side would consist of a shield with two supporters, "the Goddess Liberty" and "the Goddess Justice," a crest consisting of "the Eye of Providence in a radiant Triangle whose Glory extends over the Shield and beyond the Figures," and a motto, *"e pluribus unum"*—out of many, one.[7] For the reverse, the committee recommended a modification of Franklin's proposal: "Pharaoh sitting in an open Chariot, a Crown on his head and a Sword in his hand passing through the divided Waters of the Red Sea in pursuit of the Israelites: Rays from a Pillar of Fire in the Cloud, expressive of the divine Presence and Command, beaming on Moses who stands on the Shore, and extending his hand over the Sea causes it to overwhelm Pharaoh."[8]

Without recorded discussion, Congress effectively rejected the proposal, voting that it was "to lie on the table."[9] When a seal was finally adopted six years later, the only parts of the committee's suggestion to be retained were the "eye of Providence" and the phrase *e pluribus unum*.[10] Charles Thomson, the secretary of Congress, who created the final seal, placed the eye between an unfinished pyramid and the words *"Annuit Coeptis,"* a Latin phrase he did not define.[11] Historians believe that he took it from Virgil, who wrote, *"Jupiter omnipotens, audacibus annue coeptis"* ("All-powerful Jupiter, favor [my] daring undertakings").[12] Since neither the subject of the phrase "Annuit Coeptis" nor its tense is apparent, it has been variously translated as "It [the Eye of Providence] is favorable to our undertakings," "Providence has favored our undertakings," and "He [God] has favored our undertakings."[13] In his report to Congress, Thomson explained that "the Pyramid signifies strength and duration. The eye over it and the motto allude to the many signal interpositions of providence in favour of the American cause."[14]

The Great Seal that was eventually approved also contained numerous secular references. The first side presents the now-familiar eagle, holding an olive branch in one talon and thirteen arrows in the other, and the motto "e pluribus unum."[15] According to Thomson, the motto referred to the union of the states, and the "Olive Branch and arrows denote the power of peace and war which is exclusively vested in Congress." On the reverse side, at the base of the pyramid, was the year of independence, 1776, in Roman numerals, and underneath that the motto *"Novus Ordo Seclorum"* (A new order of the ages).[16]

As with most analysis of the role of religion in our nation's history, our understanding of religious imagery's significance both in the first committee's proposals and in the final Great Seal has been undermined by the present intellectual environment, which limits discussion to a false dichotomy. In one camp are the "strict separatists," who believe that any form of governmental support of religion, either financial or symbolic, is prohibited by the First Amendment.[17] Opposing them are the "accommodationists," who believe the Constitution permits the government to actively assist and endorse a wide range of religious activities.[18]

Willful blindness dominates contemporary debate over the framing generation's view of religion and government. Each side plays a game in which any piece of evidence that does not fit its opponents' rigid position automatically proves its own extreme perspective. All too often in their recital of American history, separationists either deny the importance of religion or ignore it altogether. Public references to God by Washington, Adams, and, especially, Jefferson and Madison are disparaged as meaningless "ceremonial deism," devoid of religious content. Most biographies of Thomas Jefferson do not even mention his work on the Great Seal.[19] When Bruce S. Feiler, in researching his book *America's Prophet: Moses and the American Story,* first learned about Jefferson's and Franklin's proposals for the Great Seal, he wrote, "This news stunned me. Why hadn't I heard about this before?"[20]

The other side can be equally obtuse. Its advocates ignore the framers' frequent admonitions to ensure that religion and government stay in separate spheres. They insist that the general language of the Declaration of Independence ("our Creator") and Washington's first inaugural address ("Almighty Being") is a reference to their particular faith. They ignore the history of vicious bigotry against Catholics and pretend that the early American definition of "Christian" included Catholics.

Accommodationists often treat any mention of religion or God as proof that the founders intended church and state to be closely allied. James Hutson, for example, in his book *Religion and the Founding of the American Republic,* depicts the story of Jefferson's and Franklin's proposals for the Great Seal as "the power of religion in revolutionary America" on display, since "in the opinion of these two torchbearers of the Enlightenment, nothing less than the story of a biblical miracle would be an appropriate emblem for the confessing countrymen."[21] To others, the story of the Great Seal demonstrates "America's consistent reliance on spiritual principles."[22]

The problem with inferring spiritual content from the biblical proposals is that the same logic would lead to the conclusion that John Adams, with his proposal of Hercules,[23] was endorsing the multiple divinities of ancient Rome and that the entire committee was encouraging a belief in the pagan goddesses Liberty and Justice.[24] In reality, all these references were understood to be allegorical, not theological.[25] Each conveyed a message relating to the fight for freedom and the need for courage, in terms that could be easily understood by Americans and Europeans.

By contrast, the eye of Providence and the phrase "Annuit Coeptis" above the pyramid are undeniably religious, as was Thomson's explanation that they referred to the "many signal interpositions of providence in favour of the American cause."[26] While the nonspecific, ill-defined Latin phrase "Annuit Coeptis," derived from a poem about the Roman god Jupiter, is far more political than sacred, the final design for the seal does indicate, as the historian Derek Davis wrote in *Religion and the Continental Congress*, "the theistic framework in which the Continental Congress sought to have the world understand the creation of the American republic."[27]

Moreover, the willingness to employ explicitly religious references shows that the framers were not afraid of official discussions of religion and did not intend to eliminate religious language from public discourse. Visitors to Madison's home in Montpelier and Jefferson's home in Monticello would have seen numerous religious paintings and sculptures. A list of Madison's pictures includes "Expulsion of Adam & Eve from paradise," "Annunciation of the Virgin," "Crucifixion," and "A descent from the cross"; Jefferson's home contained "The Penitent Magdalen," "the Baptism of Jesus by John," and "Jesus before Pilate," among many others.[28]

The story of the Great Seal, like the full story of religion and the early American government, does not fit neatly into the narratives of either those who argue that the framers created a secular nation that prohibits governmental involvement with religion or those who are convinced history proves that the United States is not merely a religious country but a "Christian" or "Judeo-Christian" nation. Fortunately, we need not be restricted to a binary universe. The framers themselves, after all, did not hold such a narrow worldview. They were capable of sophisticated, multifaceted thinking, and the balance they struck reflects a complexity that modern commentators have often underestimated.

In looking for this balance, we obviously should not expect to find universal agreement among the numerous participants. They did not always agree on the appropriate content of pious governmental language or about the placement of the line between government and religion. Moreover, as the country evolved from separate colonies to confederated states to a nation under the Constitution, these concepts continued to change. Nonetheless, through the efforts of the framing generation, America was able to develop a vibrant and enduring understanding of freedom of religion.

My goal in this book is to tell the story of those who participated in the creation and implementation of the Constitution and First Amendment, and to derive from that history as accurate a picture as possible of the American vision for freedom of religion during the framing period—the time that begins with the drafting of the Constitution, in 1787, and continues through the end of James Madison's presidency, in 1817.[29]

To construct a general picture of the framing generation's theory of freedom of religion, it is essential to consider the complete story, and not to disregard conflicting evidence. According to the English philosopher Robin George Collingwood, intellectual honesty requires that when presented with a fact that is incompatible with a preexisting theory, a person must reexamine both the accuracy of the presumed fact and the validity of the theory.[30] If the theory is contradicted by the evidence, one needs the "intellectual courage" to discard or alter the theory.[31]

Thus, in exploring the American vision for freedom of religion, we must include the views and actions of all those who participated in both the creation and implementation of the Constitution and the First Amendment. For many years, the Supreme Court looked to Thomas Jefferson and James Madison as the prime voices on America's theory of freedom of religion.[32] Some who support closer ties between government and religion have complained that the Court should not rely on these two because "their views on church-state relations were the *least* representative of the founders."[33]

Although theirs are not the only views we should consider, they are especially important precisely because they were atypical; Jefferson and Madison were visionaries as well as leaders. Their battle in Virginia against Patrick Henry's tax to support Christian teachers and in favor of the Virginia Statute for Religious Freedom "played a seminal role in the adoption of the First Amendment and the development of religious freedom."[34] Furthermore, as president, each made numerous decisions, often with the support of Congress, that helped define the scope of that freedom for the new nation.

But the focus on Jefferson and Madison has resulted in a devaluation of the person who probably did the most to create popular support for the national ideal of religious liberty: George Washington.[35] As the first president, he was keenly aware that his actions would establish precedents for the nation, and as he wrote to Madison, "it is devoutly wished on my part, that these precedents may be fixed on true principles."[36] He had seen as commander of the Continental Army that religion could be either a divisive or a unifying force. In Virginia after the war, he saw that the battle over the religious assessment had the potential to "rankle, & perhaps convulse the State."[37]

The myths that surround Washington[38] have made it harder to appreciate his role in establishing a national view of religious liberty. Some commentators, seeking a counterpoint to the views of Jefferson and Madison, try to depict Washington as a proponent of governmental involvement with religion. They argue that "the views that Washington developed differed markedly from Jefferson's 'wall of separation.' Washington's approach was . . . for government to accommodate and even to encourage the practice of religion."[39]

Such analysis understates the nuance and complexity of Washington's views. As president, Washington was careful to use only nonsectarian language when he expressed religious concepts in his official and public communications. He consistently acknowledged the different spheres of religion and civil government. When a group of New England ministers complained that the Constitution contained no explicit "acknowledgement of the only true God and Jesus Christ," Washington answered that it was not the government's responsibility to instruct its citizens as to the "path of true piety," but that "to the guidance of the ministers of the gospel this important object is, perhaps, more properly committed."[40] Acting under the Constitution, he was instrumental in establishing practices in which the national government supported universal religious freedom, kept its distance from religious indoctrination, and yet could publicly acknowledge the value and values of religion.

Another important figure who has been overlooked is the Baptist minister John Leland. Leland was the leading religious figure during the founding period to champion the philosophy of universal religious freedom.[41] He was pivotal in Madison's elections to the Virginia Ratifying Convention in 1788 and to the first House of Representatives in 1789, and was a leading advocate for amending the Constitution to add provisions protecting religious liberty. He was also a close ally of Thomas Jefferson, and he helped lead the fight for disestablishment in Connecticut and Massachusetts.

Most significantly, Leland combined religious fervor with a desire "to exclude religious opinions from the list of objects of legislation."[42] He once wrote that while it saddened him to see people "turn their backs upon public worship, and pursue their labor or recreation in preference to the service of God," still, when he saw "a man with the insignia of his office, arrest a fellow-man for non-attendance on worship, or labor or amusement on Sunday, it strains every fibre of my soul." He often argued that there was no assured path to "heaven without repentance towards God, and faith towards the Lord Jesus,"[43] yet he asserted that "Government should be so fixed, that Pagans, Turks, Jews and Christians, should be equally protected in their rights."[44]

Leland found no contradiction in being a religious person who supported a strict separation of church and state. But others exhibited the opposite tendency; they were less devout but saw religion as beneficial for society. Benjamin Franklin, for example, wrote that he had "some Doubts as to [the] Divinity" of Jesus but added, "I see no harm however in its being believed, if that Belief has the good Consequence as probably it has, of making his Doctrines more respected and better observed."[45]

Thus, the quest to determine the true religious beliefs of Washington, Jefferson, and Madison is largely unrelated to the question of what they considered the proper relationship between government and religion. Their personal piety does not tell us whether they believed governmental involvement in religion would be a force for good or evil.[46]

Just as a focus on the framers' private beliefs diverts attention from the attempt to understand the American vision of freedom of religion, an overemphasis on experiences within the individual states has also distracted many commentators. It is a common misconception, in fact, to fail to recognize that the American vision of religious liberty that was created during the framing period was distinct from the concept that prevailed in the several states.

Under the Articles of Confederation, Congress truly had represented the states. No national philosophy existed apart from that in the component states. The Confederation Congress, like the Continental Congress that preceded it, accepted the consensus view among the states that government should endorse and support the Protestant faith.

The Constitution created a new entity, a national government that was not dependent on the state governments and that was perceived as having a distinct identity. The fundamental paradox of America's history of religion and government is that while the individual states began as narrowly focused, religiously homogeneous communities, the United States was born a pluralistic nation made up of multiple religious groups. The religious diversity of the country, combined with the powerful direction of the early national leaders, permitted the creation of a distinctly American concept of religious freedom. At a time when many of the states still discriminated against Jews, President Washington could write to the Jews in Newport, Rhode Island, that "happily *the Government of the United States,* which gives to bigotry no sanction, to persecution no assistance, requires only that they who live under its protection should demean themselves as good citizens, in giving it on all occasions their effectual support."[47]

Under the leadership of Washington, Jefferson, and Madison, the national government was able "to begin the world anew"[48] and create a revolutionary new understanding of religious liberty. The states followed the national model. In 1790, shortly after the Constitution went into effect, South Carolina removed the requirement that governmental officials be Protestant and eliminated the phrase "so help me God" from its oath of office.[49] As a local historian wrote a few years later, the state acted to "model the constitution of the state in conformity to that of the United States [and] formed a constitution adapted to the new order of things."[50] Other states removed religious test oaths and limitations on religious rights from their constitutions.

Of course, this new American vision was adopted in some states more slowly than in others, and in some not until the First Amendment was applied to the states in the mid-twentieth century.

For the new national government, however, there was a consensus that valued the power of the individual mind and strongly opposed any limitation on personal religious beliefs. "While we are contending for our own liberty," Washington wrote, "we should be very cautious not to violate the rights of conscience in others, ever considering that God alone is the judge of the hearts of men, and to him only in this case they are answerable."[51] American citizens were to have absolute "freedom of conscience"; there were to be no "thought crimes" or required religious oaths, nor could religious expression be punished. Religious conduct was also protected, but could be regulated when it interfered with public order.

The framers most feared divisiveness and sectarian violence and oppression, yet they also believed that religion could be a force for instilling virtue. They believed that if the government was careful, religion could help unify a diverse nation. Many, including most notably George Washington, also personally believed that it was both important and appropriate for the president to lead the nation in prayer and thanksgiving.

To further these aims, the framers viewed governmental action concerning religion with much greater concern than governmental speech. The government was prohibited from penalizing members of minority religions or barring from employment those who did not adhere to a favored religion. Similarly, since the government derived its revenue from all citizens, nonbelievers as well as believers, governmental spending on purely religious activity was to be prohibited.

By contrast, genuine, devout governmental religious speech was to be permitted. But unlike the unrestricted religious speech of the citizenry, the religious speech of the government was to be strictly limited. The critically important aspect of the framing generation's compromise was that only the most general, nonsectarian reference to God was deemed appropriate.

The framers understood from history that religious oppression does not come from a simple belief in God; it arises when a sectarian view of God finds its voice and power in an institution or group that deems itself the sole interpreter of divine will. Accordingly, the framers decided that the American government should not acknowledge religion in a way that favored any particular creed, denomination, or group of denominations. They did not insist on a godless government, and their religious statements were not empty "ceremonial deism." They were not afraid of the public offering of truly religious expression. Yet they strove to find a civil vocabulary that could encompass all people, regardless of their faith.

Though some atheists and other nonbelievers might object to any governmental religious language, it is significant that these people were not to be considered second-class citizens. Not only was their individual liberty of conscience to be safeguarded, but the federal Constitution's prohibition of religious test oaths guaranteed that they were to be considered full members of the American body politic as well. Moreover, the restricted nature of the government's religious vocabulary was broad enough, in Jefferson's words, "to comprehend . . . the Jew and the Gentile, the Christian and Mahometan, the Hindoo, and infidel of every denomination."[52]

Some people have questioned whether the practices and attitudes from the framing generation are truly "suited for the more religiously pluralistic twenty-first century."[53] The American religious landscape is certainly far different from what it was two centuries ago. A 2007 survey revealed that "the United States is on the verge of becoming a minority Protestant country."[54] Protestants make up barely 51 percent of the American population. In a development that would have shocked the framers, Catholics are the largest single American denomination, representing almost 24 percent of the nation. American religious pluralism now includes Mormons, Jehovah's Witnesses, Jews, Muslims, Buddhists, Hindus, and many others, including the unaffiliated, atheists, and agnostics.[55]

It is because we are a pluralistic nation that the framers' understanding of religious liberty remains relevant. Their example teaches us the importance of respecting religious differences. They showed that it is possible to protect individual freedom of conscience while permitting inclusive public religious expression. The framing generation also reminds us that, especially during times of distrust and antagonism, religious acceptance is a fundamental American value. We can learn once more that it is ultimately our decision whether religion will be used to alienate and divide, or to inspire and unify our religiously diverse nation.

CHAPTER 1

Before the Beginning

T HE CREATION of an American understanding of religious freedom began with the widely varied experiences of the thirteen colonies. The colonies were devoutly religious, but they were each, in varying degrees, narrowly sectarian and excluded from full legal, political, and social equality any denomination that did not meet their particular definition of a "true religion." At no time during America's founding was there a "Christian" colony, state, or nation, if the word "Christian" is understood to include Catholics and numerous other disfavored denominations.

In his 1749 novel *The History of Tom Jones: A Foundling,* the British author Henry Fielding illustrates both the narrow-mindedness of the time and the danger for modern readers who mechanically apply modern meanings to historic texts. Fielding's character, Parson Thwackum, declares: "When I mention religion, I mean the Christian religion, and not only the Christian religion but the Protestant religion; and not only the Protestant religion, but the Church of England."[1] This conflating of the specific with the general enabled the dominant religious group in each colony to cloak its restricted perspective in the guise of universalism.

For example, the first charter for the colony of Virginia, in 1606, described one goal of the settlement as the "propagating of Christian

Religion" to the "Infidels and Savages, living in those Parts."[2] This was not understood as an open invitation to diverse interpretations of the "Christian Religion." In an ordinance passed a few months after the charter was written, James I instructed the settlers to train all Virginia residents "in *true religion* and virtue."[3] To ensure that there was no confusion as to what "true religion" meant, the instructions added that settlers were "to employ their utmost care to advance all things appertaining to the Order and Administration of Divine Service according to the form and discipline of the Church of England."

The Second Charter of Virginia, signed May 23, 1609, made clear that the phrase "true religion" excluded Catholics. The charter declared that since a primary goal for the colony was to convert people "unto the true Worship of God and Christian Religion, . . . [it] would be loath that any Person should be permitted to pass that Wee suspected to affect the Superstition of the Chh of Rome."[4]

In 1610, a harsh set of laws known today as "Dale's Code" went into effect. The penalty for blasphemy included inserting a "bodkin," that is, an awl, through the tongue of the offender.[5] Subsequent Virginia laws mandated that ministers "conforme themselves in all thinges according to the cannons of the church of England."[6] Dissenting clerics were exiled: "All nonconformists upon notice of them shall be compelled to depart the collony with all conveniencie."[7] Catholic priests were given even less time to leave the colony, with the law declaring it illegal for "any popish priest . . . to remain above five days after warning given."[8]

In the north, those who settled in Plymouth and Massachusetts had fled England because they believed that the Church of England itself was too similar to the Catholic Church. The Puritans "wanted to get rid of everything they deemed papist and make the Church of England biblical to its core."[9] They were termed "Puritans" because they wanted to "purify" the Church of England of all vestiges of its Catholic heritage. They were preceded in the New World by a group of 102 Puritans who had given up hope of reforming the Church of England and wanted to separate from it entirely. These separatists, also known as "pilgrims," were the ones who landed at Plymouth Rock in 1620.[10]

For a variety of economic and social reasons, the Plymouth Plantation did not exert a strong influence beyond its borders.[11] But the Massachusetts Bay Colony, which subsumed Plymouth in 1690, became a dominant force in the nation's religious and governmental policy from its founding through the American Revolution and beyond.

Massachusetts was founded by its 1620 charter in order "to advance the enlargement of Christian religion."[12] As in the Virginia charter, "Christian" excluded those suspected of believing in the "Superstition of the Chh of Rome." The Massachusetts Puritans, however, took their religious mandate far more strictly than the Virginians did.

The Massachusetts colony was seen by its founders as a holy mission. When John Winthrop, in transit to the new colony aboard the *Arbella* in 1630, declared that they would be "as a city upon a hill," he meant that the rest of the world would watch to see whether they could achieve their goal: "to improve our lives to doe more service to the Lord; the comforte and encrease of the body of Christe, whereof we are members; . . . to serve the Lord and worke out our Salvation under the power and purity of his holy ordinances."[13]

Unlike Virginia, this "city upon a hill" would not be governed by the rules of the Church of England. The Puritans hoped to create a community that had purified its religion of the trappings to which they had long objected. John Cotton, a Puritan minister, explained in 1634 that one of the prime reasons they had crossed the Atlantic was the opportunity to worship according to their precise understanding of the Bible: "It hath been no small inducement to us, to choose rather to remove hither, than to stay there, that we might enjoye the liberty, not of some ordinances of God, but of all and all in purity."[14]

Connecticut was founded on the same strict principles. In 1639, the congregations of the towns of Dorchester, Watertown, and Wethersfield agreed to combine, signing the Fundamental Orders of Connecticut. Believing that "the word of God requires that to mayntayne the peace and union of such a people there should be an orderly and decent Government established according to God," they agreed to confederate "to mayntayne and presearve the liberty and purity of the gospell of our Lord Jesus which we now professe, as also the disciplyne of the Churches, which according to the truth of the said gospell is now practised amongst us."[15]

Purity of religion required that those who differed in their views of the word of God be removed from the body politic. In 1637, Anne Hutchinson, a Puritan preacher, was accused of heresy for criticizing local ministers and ordered exiled from Massachusetts.[16] A group that particularly threatened the established religion was the Baptists, who disagreed most notably with the majority's practice of infant baptism, reserving that rite for believing adults only. In 1644, the colony enacted a law requiring that any person who "shall either openly condemn or oppose the baptizing of Infants [be] sentenced to Banishment."

Baptists who refused to leave Massachusetts were treated with particular harshness. In one celebrated case, three Baptists, John Clarke, Obadiah Holmes, and John Crandall, were arrested on July 20, 1651, for holding religious services in a private home.[17] They were forced to attend Congregational services, where they further infuriated local officials by refusing to remove their hats. For "despising the ordinances of God among us," they were sentenced to be "well whipt."[18] Each prisoner received thirty strokes with a "three-cord whip" until his blood flowed "in little streams down to the waist to soak into the clothing."[19]

The Quakers, founded in 1647 by George Fox, were as despised as the Baptists. The Quakers' behavior was sometimes deliberately provocative, such as "interrupting church services to testify against false worship or going naked to symbolize the condition of their opponents' spiritual state."[20] The Massachusetts General Court, on October 14, 1656, enacted a law to deal with the "cursed sect of haereticks lately risen up in the world, which are commonly called Quakers."[21] Any person found "to have the haeretical opinions of the said Quakers" was to be fined forty shillings for a first offense, for the second offence four pounds, and "for still offending to be imprisoned till banished."[22] Banished Quakers who returned faced still worse treatment. On September 16, 1658, three Quakers, Christopher Holder, John Copeland, and John Rouse, who had ignored the banishment order, each had an ear cut off by Boston's hangman.[23]

The next month, the Massachusetts General Court expressed its frustration that the "pernicious Sect commonly called Quakers" had "not been deterr'd from their impetuous Attempts to undermine our Peace, and hazard our Ruin."[24] The court decreed that anyone convicted of being "of the sect of the Quakers shall be sentenced to be banished upon pain of death." Shortly thereafter, four Quakers, William Robinson, Marmaduke Stephen, Mary Dyer, and William Leddra, were hanged for "rebelliously returning into this jurisdiction"[25]

After a stern rebuke from England, Massachusetts stopped executing Quakers. Still, the religious leaders felt compelled to defend themselves against charges that they were violating liberty of conscience. John Cotton, the leading Puritan minister of the Massachusetts Bay Colony, drew a distinction between persecution "for conscience rightly informed . . . [or] for erroneous and blind conscience."[26] It would certainly be unlawful, he wrote, to persecute those with a "rightly informed" conscience, since that would be as if "Christ himselfe is persecuted." But for those with "erroneous" religious viewpoints, persecution was the only appropriate response, since

> the Word of God in such things is so cleare, that hee cannot but bee convinced in Conscience of the dangerous Errour of his way, after once or twice Admonition, wisely and faithfully dispensed. And then if any one persist, it is not out of Conscience, but against his

Conscience, . . . So that if such a Man after such Admonition shall
still, persift in the Errour of his way, and be therefore punished; He
is not persecuted for Cause of Conscience, but for sinning against
his Owne Conscience.[27]

Nathaniel Ward, a Congregationalist minister in Ipswich, Massachusetts, stated that there was no place in Massachusetts for those
whose religious views were sinful and erroneous.[28] Indeed, Ward
declared that "he had rather the earth should swallow him up quick
[i.e., alive] than he should give a toleration to any opinion against any
truth of God." Ward attacked not only those who believe in "false
religions" but also those who tolerate them: "He that is willing to
tolerate any religion, or discrepant way of religion, besides his own,
unless it be in matters merely indifferent, either doubts of his own or
is not sincere in it."

Ironically, Massachusetts's intolerance led to the creation of one
of the most tolerant colonies, Rhode Island. The leader of this new
colony, Roger Williams, was banished from Massachusetts on November 3, 1635. Among his many offenses against the established religion
was his advocacy of the view that the Ten Commandments should be
seen as consisting of two tables, the first governing people's relationship with God, such as the bans on idolatry and blasphemy, the second
involving social interactions, such as the bans on murder and adultery.
Williams believed that the government had no rightful authority to
exercise control over the purely religious part, preaching that "the
magistrate might not punish a breach of the sabbath nor any other
offence as it was a breach of the first table."

Williams was one of the first residents of the New World to ex-
pound a philosophy of both religious equality and a limited role for
government in religious matters. In fact, he articulated the concept of
a "wall of separation" more than 150 years before Thomas Jefferson.
In 1640, he wrote that initially both Jews and Christians had Edenic
churches, separate from the world, but both permitted "a gap in the

hedge, or wall of separation, between the garden of the church and the wilderness of the world," and in response, "God hath ever broke down the wall itself" and "made his garden a wilderness."[29]

Williams's respect for liberty of conscience extended far beyond Protestants; he desired that "no persons, papists, Jews, Turks, or Indians, be disturbed at their worship." His philosophy reflects what I term the religious basis for freedom of religion. Williams strongly disagreed with those with "Paganish, Jewish, Turkish, or anti-christian consciences," yet he stressed that "they are only to be fought against with that sword which is only (in soul matters) able to conquer, to wit, the sword of God's Spirit, the Word of God."[30] Governmental enforcement of uniformity of religion, he declared, "confounds the civil and religious, denies the principles of Christianity and civility, and that Jesus Christ is come in the flesh."

On March 14, 1644, Williams obtained a patent from Charles I permitting him to establish a government in the Providence Plantations (which eventually grew into the colony of Rhode Island). In 1647, the General Assembly enacted its first code of laws. After listing numerous offenses, the code reiterated Williams's view on the separation of government from religion:

> These are the laws that concern all men and these are the penalties for the transgression thereof which by common consent are ratified and established throughout the whole colony *And otherwise than thus what is herein forbidden, all men may walk as their consciences persuade them every one in the name of his God.* And let the saints of the Most High walk in this colony without molestation in the name of Jehovah their God for ever and ever.[31]

In 1663, Williams obtained a second charter, reaffirming Rhode Island's commitment "to hold forth a livlie experiment" that a civil state could flourish with "a full libertie in religious concernements." Accordingly, the charter decreed that "noe person within the sayd colonye, at any tyme hereafter, shall bee any wise molested, punished, disquieted, or called in question, for any differences in opinione in matters of religion, [who does] not actually disturb the civill peace of our sayd colony."[32]

Despite the sophistication and modernity of Williams's analysis, his writings appear to have faded from public view upon his death in 1683 and to have played no direct role in the formulation of America's concept of religious freedom in the eighteenth century. As the historian Thomas Curry noted, "No library catalogue published in the American colonies listed any of his works."[33] In 1773, Williams's writings were rediscovered by the Massachusetts Baptist preacher Isaac Backus, but still, "principal theorists concerning religious liberty such as Locke, Madison and Jefferson proceeded without apparent influence from Williams's ideas."[34]

Rhode Island eventually pulled back from Williams's ideals. A law that was printed in 1716 barred both Catholics and Jews from voting in the colony. It stated that "all men professing Christianity . . . who acknowledge and are obedient to the civil magistrates, though of different judgments in religious affairs, Roman Catholics only excepted, shall be admitted freemen" with the right to participate in elections.[35]

Another colony founded on principles of religious tolerance would have a much greater influence on American history, though it too would eventually retreat from its founder's vision. William Penn was a Quaker who obtained a charter for what became the Pennsylvania colony in 1681. Penn was a strong believer in religious liberty, declaring that whoever persecuted in the name of religion was "a declared Enemy to God, religion, and the good of human society." Like Roger Williams, Penn believed that governmental intrusions into religious matters "directly invade the Divine Prerogative." He defined liberty of conscience as "the free and uninterrupted exercise of our consciences, in that way of worship, we are most clearly persuaded God requires us to serve him in . . . which being matter of Faith, we sin if we omit." To Penn, liberty of conscience included more than mere belief. It also encompassed the "exercise of ourselves in a visible way of worship, upon our believing it to be indispensibly required at our hands, that if we neglect it for fear or favour of any mortal man, we sin, and incur divine wrath."[36]

In 1682, Penn prepared a "Frame of Government" for Pennsylvania, establishing what some have called "the broadest religious liberty in colonial America."[37] Though excluding atheists from its coverage, the law of Pennsylvania protected the rights of followers of all religions, stating that everyone who would "acknowledge the one Almighty and Eternal God . . . shall in no ways be molested or prejudiced for their religious persuasion or practice in matters of faith and worship, nor shall they be compelled at any time to frequent or maintain any religious worship, place or ministry whatever."[38] This was not total religious equality: all governmental officials and representatives were required to "profess faith in Jesus Christ." The laws also contained prohibitions against "offences against God," including swearing, drunkenness, sodomy, whoredom, stage plays, cards, and dice.[39]

In 1705, Pennsylvania retreated from Penn's idealism and passed a law that barred Catholics as well as Jews from serving in the government. This new law required members of the state assembly to declare that "the invocation or adoration of the Virgin Mary or any other saint, and the sacrifice of the Mass, as they are now used in the Church of Rome, are superstitious and idolatrous."[40] Despite this discrimination, Pennsylvania stayed true to some of Penn's values. The colony never required oaths and never used public revenue to fund churches and clergy.[41]

The Carolinas also trace their beginning to an influential advocate of religious freedom. Their 1669 Fundamental Constitution was drafted primarily by the English philosopher John Locke. Locke had a tremendous influence on many of the leading thinkers of the American revolutionary period. Thomas Jefferson, in particular, was a student of Locke, using Locke's ideas "freely in formulating his own philosophy of the nature of moral man in society, as reflected in the Declaration of Independence and the Virginia Act for Establishing Religious Freedom."[42]

Like Roger Williams, Locke saw the proper role of government as limited to worldly rather than ecclesiastical matters. In his *Letter Concerning Toleration,* Locke wrote that "the whole jurisdiction of the magistrate reaches only to these civil concernments; . . . and that it neither can nor ought in any manner to be extended to the salvation of souls."[43] The civil magistrate, Locke argued, "has no power to enforce by law, either in his own Church, or much less in another, the use of any rites or ceremonies whatsoever in the worship of God." To force people to pray in a way contrary to their consciences "is in effect to command them to offend God."

According to Locke, not only must the government not meddle in religious matters, religious minorities must be included as full members of the body politic: "Neither Pagan nor Mahometan, nor Jew, ought to be excluded from the civil rights of the commonwealth because of his religion." For Locke, religious oppression, not religious dissent, was the true danger to society. He argued, "It is not the diversity of opinions (which cannot be avoided), but the refusal of toleration to those that are of different opinions (which might have been granted), that has produced all the bustles and wars that have been in the Christian world upon account of religion."[44]

But Locke was not prepared to extend religious tolerance completely. He explicitly excluded Catholics, asserting that their loyalty was suspect, since they were pledged to "deliver themselves up to the protection and service of another prince." He also denied toleration to atheists, stating that "promises, covenants, and oaths, which are the bonds of human society, can have no hold" on those who deny the existence of a God.

Much of Locke's philosophy was included in Carolina's Fundamental Constitution.[45] No one was permitted to "disturb, molest, or persecute another for his speculative opinions in religion or his way of worship." Any seven people "agreeing in any religion" could form "a church or profession" as long as they accepted three principles: "there is a God"; "God is publicly to be worshipped"; and that there be "an external way whereby they witness a truth as in the presence of God," whether by laying hands on the bible or holding up the hand "or any other sensible way." Catholics were included in the protections of this initial Fundamental Constitution. Atheists, however, were denied the right to vote and barred from "any place of profit or honor."[46]

In a section of the Fundamental Constitution that Locke did not write, the Church of England was declared the established church of Carolina.[47] According to Article 96, the Church of England "being the only true and orthodox and the national religion of all the King's dominions, is so also of Carolina." Accordingly, "it alone" was to be the beneficiary of public funding for the construction of churches and ministers' salaries.[48]

The Carolinas were divided in the early eighteenth century. South Carolina became a royal colony in 1719, North Carolina in 1729. Both colonies eventually moved away from the ideal of religious equality and toward strengthening the religious establishment. The royal instructions to North Carolina's first governor, George Burrington, directed him to "permit a liberty of conscience to all persons (except papists)."[49] They also required schoolteachers to be members of the Church of England and to obtain "the license of the Lord Bishop of London."[50] A 1741 marriage law limited the right to perform the marriage ceremony to Anglican clergy; if no Anglican clergyman was available, only a civil magistrate could be used. In 1766, after much protest, the clergy of all religions were permitted to perform weddings, provided any fees collected were given to the local Anglican minister.[51]

The South Carolina experience was particularly unsteady: "Periods of tolerance were followed by periods of rigidity, and then the pendulum would swing back again, then again." For example, a 1745 law required that legislators swear on the New Testament. After dissenters objected, the law was changed in 1747 to permit them to take an oath "'according to the form of . . . [their] profession.'"[52]

Jews were permitted to worship in South Carolina, but were barred from holding public office and, in 1721, denied the vote. Catholics, who faced more social hostility than Jews, also were barred from holding public office, though they were not kept from voting until 1759.[53]

Considering the fact that Cecil Calvert, a Catholic, was named the first proprietor for Maryland, one might find it surprising that the colony also discriminated against Catholics in the eighteenth century. In 1633, one year after Calvert had been named proprietor, two boats, the *Ark* and the *Dove,* set sail from England to Maryland with about 200 immigrants. There were both Protestants and Catholics on the boats, with Protestants constituting a slight majority.

Cecil Calvert and his brother, Leonard, whom Cecil selected as governor, attempted to balance the rights of both Protestants and Catholics. They crafted a "Toleration Act" in 1649 that is regarded as a major step forward in the history of religious freedom. Protestants and Catholics alike were protected against being "troubled, Molested or discountenanced for or in respect of his or her religion not in the free exercise thereof." Still, religious freedom was guaranteed only to those "professing to believe in Jesus Christ." The act also imposed capital punishment on those who would "blaspheme God, that is Curse him, or deny our Saviour Jesus Christ to bee the sonne of God, or shall deny the holy Trinity."[54]

Even with these limits, the Toleration Act granted more religious freedom than the colony was willing to accept. Most Maryland Protestants disagreed with the idea of extending "tolerance" to Catholics and never reconciled themselves to living under a "papist" proprietor. Tensions grew worse when, in the name of tolerance, Maryland per-

mitted 300 Puritans to enter the state from Virginia, where they had
been harassed by the established Anglican Church. These Puritans,
barely more accepting of religious diversity than their New England
coreligionists, combined with other Maryland Protestants to oust
Maryland's Catholic leadership. Their efforts succeeded in 1692, when
Maryland was declared a royal colony rather than a proprietorship. A
newly elected assembly quickly rejected Maryland's earlier attempt at
tolerance, terming it a "specious pretence of liberty of conscience."[55]
Instead, the Church of England was declared the established church,
and all Maryland residents, regardless of religious faith, were taxed for
the building of Anglican churches and the maintenance of Anglican
ministers.[56]

Maryland's new government grew increasingly hostile to its
Catholic population. In October 1704, the legislature passed an "Act
to Prevent the Growth of Popery within this Province."[57] This law
forced the closure of Catholic schools and barred Catholics from public worship, permitting worship only in private homes.[58] In 1718, the
legislature expressed its continued frustration that "notwithstanding
all the Measures that have been hitherto taken for preventing the
Growth of Popery within this Province, it is very obvious, that not
only profest Papists still multiply and increase in Number, but that
there are also too great Numbers of others that adhere to and espouse
their Interest, in Opposition to the Protestant Establishment."[59] Accordingly, Catholics were declared "uncapable of giving their Vote,"
in the colony.

Maryland's journey from a Catholic proprietorship to a colony
with an Anglican, anti-Catholic establishment is unique among the
colonies, but New York's experience with established religion was
even more multifarious. New York began as a Dutch colony, New
Amsterdam, and issues of religious intolerance arose long before it
came under English rule. Peter Stuyvesant, the last Dutch governor
of New Amsterdam, tried to expel Jews from the colony. In a letter to

the Dutch West India Company dated September 22, 1654, he urged that "the deceitful race—such hateful enemies and blasphemers of the name of Christ—be not allowed to further infect and trouble this new colony." Partly because the Dutch West India Company included some Jewish shareholders, his request was denied.

Stuyvesant then turned his attention to ridding the colony of Quakers. His proclamation making it a crime to shelter a Quaker led to one of the first declarations of universal religious tolerance in the New World.[60] On December 27, 1657, thirty-one inhabitants of the town of Flushing wrote what has become known as the Flushing Remonstrance, in which they refused to comply with the governor's order. They declared, "The law of love, peace and liberty" extends "to Jews, Turks and Egyptians as they are considered sons of Adam." It was similarly the rule of "our Saviour," according to the Remonstrance, that "whether Presbyterian, Independent, Baptist or Quaker, [we] shall be glad to see anything of God in any of them, desiring to doe unto all men as we desire all men should doe unto us."[61] Stuyvesant called the remonstrance a "seditious, mutinous and detestable letter of defiance,"[62] but was unable to achieve his goal of eliminating Quakers from New York.

The English wrested control of New Amsterdam from the Dutch in 1664 and renamed it New York. They inherited a colony in which Anglicans were a small minority and much of the population belonged to the Dutch Reformed Church.[63] Nonetheless, the royal governor, Benjamin Fletcher, was committed to strengthening the Church of England.[64] He was strongly opposed by the State Assembly, which consisted almost entirely of those he considered "dissenters."[65] After two unsuccessful attempts to persuade the assembly to pass a law naming the Church of England the established church of New York, he managed to obtain a compromise bill, the Ministry Act of 1693. The Ministry Act did not cover the entire state, only New York City and three southern counties, Richmond (Staten Island), Westchester, and

Queens.[66] Moreover, the law did not specify the Church of England as the established church, but simply that there "shall be established a good sufficient Protestant Minister."[67]

The Ministry Act thus left it unclear which church had been established. The law's ambiguity troubled Lewis Morris, an Anglican who was the first American member of the Society for the Propagation of the Gospel in Foreign Parts, a missionary society created in 1701 to strengthen the Church of England in the New World.[68] According to Morris, the Ministry Act had been deliberately drafted to be "very loosely worded which as things stood then when it was made could not be avoided[,] the Dissenters claiming the benefit of it as well as we." Thus, while the governor "never intended to settle a Dissenting Clergy," Morris was forced to concede that the law "will admit a construction in their favor as well as ours."[69]

The issue of whether the Church of England was the only established church was at the heart of a three-decade conflict over control of the Jamaica Church in Queens County. In 1699, the town of Jamaica had paid for construction of a "fine stone Church."[70] By a majority vote at a town meeting, the church and its minister's home were placed under the control of the local Presbyterian minister.

A new Governor, Lord Cornbury, came to office in 1702 and declared that any church funded with public money must, by definition, be part of the Anglican established church. On July 24, 1703, an Anglican minister, the Reverend John Bartow, announced his intent to take over Jamaica Church. The Presbyterian minister, the Reverend John Hubbard, hearing of this plan, entered the church "before the last time ringing" of the church bell and began services before Bartow arrived. In the afternoon, however, Bartow arrived first to begin services. Hubbard and his followers were outraged. They met at a nearby orchard and decided to hold a competing service there. They returned to the church while the Anglican services were still being conducted and began removing chairs for their outdoor service.

According to Bartow, there followed "a shameful disturbance hawling & tugging of seats shoving one the other off, carrying them out & returning again for more."[71] After services ended, Bartow locked the church and handed the key to the sheriff. In what became known as the "Jamaica riot," supporters of Hubbard broke a church window, entered the church, and confiscated the pulpit cushion so that it would be used only by a Presbyterian minister.

For the next several years, physical control of the church passed between the Episcopalians and the Presbyterians. Finally, in 1731, a court ruled that even though Jamaica Church had been built with public funds, it did not belong to the Anglicans but was rightfully controlled by the Presbyterians.[72]

Undoubtedly, New York's establishment was far different from the traditional, narrowly sectarian ones. As the historian Leonard Levy wrote, "The concept of a multiple establishment was understood by and also engaged the attention of the inhabitants of colonial New York. Although New York Anglicans claimed an exclusive establishment of their church, a large number of the colony's population understood the establishment set up by the act of 1693 not as a state preference for one religion or sect over others but as allowing public support for many different churches to be determined by popular vote."[73]

The American colonies thus displayed a broad range of approaches to the establishment of religion. With the possible exception of New York, the colonies that established the Church of England were limited to the South. Maryland was the most northern of the clearly Anglican-established colonies. Once Georgia, chartered in 1732, declared the Church of England its established church in 1758, the five southern-most colonies, Maryland, Virginia, North Carolina, South Carolina, and Georgia, shared a common established religion.[74] The strength of this establishment varied, with North Carolina and Georgia having the weakest centralized church.[75]

In the Mid-Atlantic region, Pennsylvania, Delaware (carved out of three Pennsylvania counties in 1702), and New Jersey (which formally separated from New York in 1738), there was no established church.[76] While New York State north of Westchester County also did not have an established church, as we have seen, the status of establishment in the rest of the state was subject to debate.

In New England, Rhode Island was the only colony without a religious establishment. Massachusetts, Connecticut, and New Hampshire all established the Congregational Church.

That English colonies could establish a religion other than that of the Church of England baffled Anglicans on both sides of the Atlantic. In 1763, an Anglican minister, Henry Caner, wrote to the archbishop of Canterbury to complain after Ezra Stiles, the president of Yale College, stated that "the Congregational Party is the Established Church in new England." Caner wrote, "I cannot sufficiently wonder at their persisting in this mistake when it is so very plain . . . that the Church of England is established in Perpetuity, in all the Territories at that time to England belonging."[77]

This "mistake," however, would never be corrected. Anglicans in New England protested when they were forced to pay to support Congregational ministers, claiming that they were being deprived "not only of the just priviledge we think ourselves entitled to as a branch of that Church established by the laws of England, but even of the Common priviledge allow'd by their Charter."[78] The bishop of London explained that the problem arose because the Crown had acquiesced when the colonies first began publicly funding Congregational ministers and churches. By the 1730s, the bishop said, it was simply too late to "render all their acts relating to Religion as an Establishment there null and void. So that our misfortune is that this matter was not enter'd into twenty or thirty years ago; I mean, that they were not check'd in their first pretensions to act as an Establish'd Church."[79]

Even more galling to the Anglicans was that the New England governments treated Anglicans as similar to, and sometimes worse than, common "dissenters." In 1731, Massachusetts passed a law exempting Quakers from paying taxes for Congregational ministers.[80] Anglicans, however, were exempt only if they lived less than five miles from an Anglican church. Since there were "but few [Anglican] churches (at great distance from each other) in this great country; and the Churchmen being dispersed throughout the whole territory, they are obliged (some of them) to ride 30 or 40 miles to partake of the Holy Sacrament."[81] This meant that most Anglicans still were required to pay for the Congregational ministry, even though Quakers had been exempted. The Anglicans complained to the bishop of London that it was "a most aggravating Circumstance, when the Quakers, with whom we were levell'd in our sufferings, had Obtained that relief by a Law pass'd in their Favour which we applied for with great pains and expense."[82]

Anglicans were not only furious at having been "levell'd" with other dissenters, they, like their English coreligionists, continued to view the New England Congregationalists as "dissenters." Thus, they would complain of being "harassed by seizures of goods for non payment of rates to Dissenting teachers."[83]

The Anglicans were admonished by the Massachusetts lieutenant governor, William Dummer, Jr., a Congregationalist, that they were hurting their plea for tax relief by refusing to acknowledge the proper place of Congregationalists in New England: "I must advise you when you mention the ministers in the Towns, that you give them the character the Laws of this province vest them with,—viz', Ministers, and not Dissenting Teachers, for that gives offence to the Court."[84]

Finally, on July 1, 1742, the Massachusetts General Court passed an act to appease the Anglicans. They were not exempt from religious taxes, but their tax money would be used to support the Anglican Church: "The amount collected shall be delivered to the minister of the church where the professed member regularly attends public worship."[85] Shortly thereafter, Matthias Plant, an Anglican, was able to write to London that "we have erected a fine new church about three miles from where I live. I preach in it every other Sunday."[86]

By that time, all the established religions in the colonies were confronted with a new phenomenon, the First Great Awakening. Generally estimated as beginning around 1735 or a bit earlier and cresting in the early 1740s, the Great Awakening was "a series of proliferating regional religious revivals that coincided with and influenced intense outbreaks of religious fervor in England and Scotland."[87] The Great Awakening split apart many of the traditional denominations. So-called New Lights supported the changes wrought by the revivals; Old Lights resisted the revivals and longed for the status quo.[88]

Historians continue to debate the effect of the Great Awakening on American religion and the political movement that led to the Revolution.[89] But there is little doubt that the spread of a new emotional style of religion, along with the mobility of itinerant preachers, disrupted the relationships between the established religions and colonial governments within individual colonies. The Great Awakening also crossed colonial boundaries and connected religious adherents in different parts of the New World. It "galvanized separation, conflict, and new forms of communal action, and dissipated the elite solidarities upon which deference, force, and persuasion rested."[90]

George Whitefield was one of the most influential ministers of the Great Awakening.[91] In his thirty-four years of ministry, Whitefield is estimated to have preached more than eighteen thousand sermons, averaging more than ten a week.[92] He first arrived in Georgia from England in 1738, and by 1740 had preached in every colony but New Hampshire (which he finally reached in 1754).[93]

Whitefield was a dynamic speaker. According to his friend Benjamin Franklin, "He had a loud and clear voice, and articulated his words and sentences so perfectly that he might be heard and understood at a great distance." During one outdoor sermon, Franklin decided to ascertain how far Whitefield's voice could carry. He walked away from the speaker until his voice was no longer distinct. "Imagining then a semicircle, of which my distance should be the radius, and that it were filled with auditors, to each of whom I allow two square feet, I computed that he might well be heard by more than thirty thousand," Franklin wrote.[94]

Franklin, who made a great deal of money from printing Whitefield's sermons, would often banter with the minister about religion.[95] He told of the time he offered to let Whitefield stay in his accommodations, to which Whitefield replied "that if I made that kind offer for Christ's sake, I should not miss of a reward. And I returned, 'Don't let me be mistaken; it was not for Christ's sake, but for your sake.'" Despite their friendship, Franklin said, "we had no religious connection . . . He used, indeed, sometimes to pray for my conversion, but never had the satisfaction of believing that his prayers were heard. Ours was a mere civil friendship, sincere on both sides, and lasted to his death."[96]

Nonetheless, Franklin was impressed by the religious effect of Whitefield's sermons. He described how the entire community seemed to be moved after listening to Whitefield: "It was wonderful to see the change soon made in the manners of our inhabitants. From being thoughtless or indifferent about religion, it seemed as if all the world were growing religious, so that one could not walk thro' the town in an evening without hearing psalms sung in different families of every street."[97]

One religious trait the two men shared was an abhorrence of sectarian strife. Whitefield gave a sermon attacking the notion that God favored any particular sect: "'Father Abraham, who have you in heaven? Any Episcopalians?' 'No.' 'Any Presbyterians?' 'No.' 'Any Baptists?' 'No.' 'Have you any Methodists, Seceders, or Independents there?' 'No, no.' 'Why, who have you there?' 'We don't know those names here. All who are here are Christians, believers in Christ—men who have overcome by the blood of the Lamb, and the Word of His testimony.'"[98]

When local clergy, partly from fear of competition, stopped letting Whitefield preach in their churches, Franklin helped raise money to erect a building "about the size of Westminster Hall" for his sermons.[99] But reflecting the inclusive view of religion held by both Whitefield and Franklin, the structure was made available without religious discrimination. According to Franklin, the property was "expressly for the use of any preacher of any religious persuasion who might desire to say something to the people at Philadelphia; the design in building not being to accommodate any particular sect, but the inhabitants in general; so that even if the Mufti of Constantinople were to send a missionary to preach Mohammedanism to us, he would find a pulpit at his service."

In naming trustees for the nondenominational religious building, it was decided that no particular group should outnumber any other, "one Church-of-England man, one Presbyterian, one Baptist, one Moravian, etc."[100] At one point, when an opening arose for an additional trustee, there was a fear that the new appointment might cause there to be two members of the same sect. According to Franklin, "At length one mention'd me, with the observation that I was merely an honest man, and of no sect at all, which prevail'd with them to chuse me."

Elsewhere, Whitefield was not as well received as in Philadelphia. A New Jersey Anglican minister, Thomas Bradbury Chandler, warned that his "undutiful and schismatical behaviour" was harmful to the Church of England. Chandler complained that Whitefield and the other Great Awakening ministers (whom he lumped together as "dissenters") were "using all their dexterity and address to gain proselytes from the church. . . . The Dissenters almost to a man are watching every opportunity to promote their cause, and not so much as a negro can fall in their way, but some of them will try to proselyte him."[101]

The threat posed by these religious competitors led to a harsh reaction in Connecticut. The most provocative challenger to the established religion in the colony was James Davenport, a colleague of Whitefield. Davenport traveled throughout the state, criticizing the established ministry. During one sermon, he was reported to have declared that "the greatest Part of the Ministers in this Country were unconverted, and that they were murdering . . . Souls by Thousands and by Millions."[102] According to Connecticut's governor, Joseph Talcott, Davenport's attempt to draw away congregants represented a serious danger to the colony: "His advice to people not to hearken to their Ministers by him condemned, but to go 10 or 20 miles . . . that they had better sett upon private meetings amongst themselves, . . . is a violation and open contempt of Laws of this Coloney, and so aparently tends to the breach the peace of our Religious Sosiaties and subvention of all orders in Church and State."[103] In 1742, to put an end to what the legislature termed "disorderly and irregular practices" that "have a tendency to make divisions and contentions among the people in this colony, and to destroy the ecclesiastical constitution established by the laws of this government," Connecticut outlawed ministers from preaching outside their licensed areas. Moreover, any nonresident of the colony "who shall presume to preach . . . without the desire and license of the settled minister" was to be banished and "sent as a vagrant person, . . . out of the bounds of this colony."[104]

Not surprisingly, one of the first preachers evicted under the law was Davenport himself, whom the Hartford town sheriff, along "with two files of men armed with muskets," placed on a boat to be transported back to his home in Southold, Long Island.[105] Davenport soon returned to Connecticut for what was surely one of the most extraordinary moments of the Great Awakening. On Sunday, March 6, 1743, he and his followers built a giant bonfire on the New London town wharf, where, in an attack on "heresy," they burned the books of orthodox Puritan and Congregationalist writers, including Increase Mather and Charles Chauncy.[106] As the flames rose, Davenport exclaimed: "The souls of the authors of those books, those of them who

are dead, are roasting in the flames of hell . . . the fate of those surviv-
ing, [will] be the same, unless speedy repentance prevent [it]."[107] The
next day, Davenport chose to build another bonfire to attack idolatry. He had his followers collect all but their most modest clothing.
Adherents threw together "Scarlet Cloaks, Velvet Hoods, fine Laces,
and every Thing that had two Colours."[108] Davenport then took off
his "plush breeches" and tossed them on top of the pile. Before the
fire could be lit, a "modest" woman grabbed his breeches and threw
them back at Davenport "with as much indignation, as tho' they had
been the hire of a Wh—— or the Price of a Dog."[109]

Though most of the New Light preachers were not as outrageous
as Davenport, the established churches and their governmental supporters throughout the colonies still felt threatened. Baptists were
treated especially harshly. Although Baptists had lived in colonies
such as Massachusetts and Virginia for many decades, the New Light
Baptists evoked a fresh round of oppression.

In 1752, Massachusetts passed a law making it much more difficult
for New Light Baptists to gain an exemption from the tax supporting the Congregationalist Church. Baptists seeking the exemption
were required to obtain "an endorsement from each of three other
Churches commonly called Anabaptists in this or the neighbouring
provinces to the effect that they conscientiously believe the persons
giving the certificates above referred to be Anabaptists."[110] Because
many of the New Light Baptist churches were not recognized by
the Old Light Baptists, these endorsements were often impossible to
obtain. Furthermore, the very language of the statute was insulting:
"Anabaptist," meaning "re-baptizer," was "on principle offensive" to
Baptists, since they viewed adult baptism as the first true baptism,
rather than a repeat experience.

In 1757, another exemption law was passed, and in the words of the
Baptist minister Isaac Backus, "no tongue nor pen can fully describe
all the evils that were practiced under it." To be exempt from paying

taxes to support the Congregational Church, Baptists were required to procure a "certificate" each year, signed by the minister plus three principal members of the church to which they belonged, attesting that the four signers "verily believe them to be conscientiously of their persuasion, and that they frequently and usually attend public worship in said church on the Lord's days."[111]

Even when Baptists were able to obtain the certificates, local tax collectors often refused to accept them. When the Baptists refused to pay the religious assessment, their property was seized and sold. In one particularly celebrated case, the Baptists of the town of Ashfield were continually harassed. The parish tax collectors seized and sold one Baptist's ten-acre home lot to satisfy a religious assessment of less than four dollars, and sold his father's home, consisting of "twenty acres, containing his orchard and burying-ground" to satisfy a seven-dollar assessment.[112]

Virginia's treatment of the Baptists was even more brutal. Baptist ministers "were beaten and imprisoned; and cruel[ly] taxed."[113] In 1768, three Baptist preachers in the town of Spotsylvania were arrested and told that they would be released if they promised not to preach again in the county for one year and a day. Upon their refusal, they were sent to jail for breach of the peace.[114] When two other Baptist ministers were imprisoned in Chesterfield County in 1770, crowds gathered outside their jail and the ministers continued their "preaching through the grates of their windows."[115]

One Virginian who was especially troubled by the treatment of the Baptists was twenty-two-year-old James Madison. On January 24, 1774, Madison, having graduated from Princeton College, wrote to his close college friend William Bradford of Pennsylvania. He began his letter by contrasting Virginia's and Pennsylvania's approaches to religious diversity: "I want again to breathe your free air. I expect it will mend my constitution and confirm my principles."[116] Madison denounced the "diabolical, hell-conceived principle of persecution.

. . . This vexes me the worst of anything whatever." He described to Bradford the local jailing of several Baptists—"There are at this time in the adjacent country not less than five or six well meaning men in close gaol [jail] for publishing their religious sentiments, which in the main are very orthodox"—and expressed his deep frustration over the religious subjugation: "I have neither patience to hear, talk, or think of anything relative to this matter; for I have squabbled and scolded, abused and ridiculed, so long about it to little purpose, that I am without common patience."[117] Speaking as a Virginian to a friend who lived in a far more hospitable colony, Madison concluded, "So I must beg you to pity me, and pray for liberty of conscience to all."

The differences between Virginia and Pennsylvania were typical of the variation that existed among the colonies. Attitudes toward minority religions ranged from hostility and harassment to general tolerance.

In the second half of the eighteenth century, however, two issues involving England led to a unified response from the colonies. The first was the uproar over the prospect of an "American episcopate," a proposal to send an Anglican bishop across the Atlantic Ocean. The second was Parliament's passage of the Quebec Act, enhancing the rights of Catholics in the Canadian province.

The initial proposal for an American bishop seems to have been made at the very start of the eighteenth century. In 1701, the Society for the Propagation of the Gospel in Foreign Parts was incorporated, and, in addition to sending clergymen to the New World, lobbied to have a bishop "resident in the colonies."[118]

In June 1767, a new request for an "American episcopate" provoked an angry response across colony lines. Thomas Bradbury Chandler, an Anglican minister from New Jersey, raised the issue by publishing a pamphlet, *An Appeal to the Public in behalf of the Church of England in America,* calling for the appointment of an American bishop. His attempts to assure the non-Anglican majority of colonists that appointing a local bishop would neither threaten them nor create a new "establishment" badly misfired. First, he revealed that Anglicans continued to hold a worldview in which those of different religions were "dissenters" rather than pious people worthy of equal respect, writing that "the Episcopate proposed cannot hurt the Dissenters."[119] Next, after denying that the bishop's salary would come from local tax revenues, Chandler wrote, *But should a general tax be laid . . .* supposing we had three Bishops, such a Tax would not amount to more than Four Pence in One Hundred Pounds."

Chandler's pamphlet inaugurated what has been termed "a bitter pamphlet war."[120] Charles Chauncy, the Congregational minister of the First Church in Boston, responded with a warning that an American bishop would be another excuse for Parliament to tax the colonies: "It seems not wholly improbable from what we hear of the unusual tenor of some late parliamentary acts and bills, for raising money on the poor colonies *without their consent,* that provision might be made for the support of these Bishops, if not of all the church clergy also, in the same way."[121]

A New Yorker, William Livingston, then entered the battle. Under the pseudonym "American Whig," he wrote a series of essays for the *New York Gazette,* attacking the proposal and declaring that the appointment of an American bishop would represent "an evil more terrible to every man who sets a proper value either on his liberty, property, or conscience than the so greatly and deservedly obnoxious Stamp Act."[122] Just as the Stamp Act had been successfully defeated by joint colonial action in 1765–66, Livingston believed that what he termed the "ecclesiastical stamp-act" could also be prevented through collaborative action.

He wrote to Samuel Cooper, Sam Adams's pastor in Boston, to urge the recruitment of writers to create a "course of weekly papers" to attack the proposal, which might "prove more effectual in alarming the colonies." As part of the cross-colony mobilization, Livingston noted that "a number of gentlemen will shortly open the ball in Philadelphia. I should be glad [if] the same measure was pursued in Boston."[123]

Among those preparing to "open the ball" in Philadelphia was the Pennsylvanian lawyer John Dickinson. Together with his allies Francis Alison and George Bryan, Dickinson wrote a series of essays under the name "Centinel" to oppose the proposal for an American bishop.[124] Dickinson's most powerful essay expressed a strong opposition to all forms of religious establishments, even, at least implicitly, those in the other colonies.

Writing on May 12, 1768, Dickinson sounded even more like Roger Williams than Pennsylvania's own founder, William Penn.[125] "Religion and Government are certainly very different Things," Dickinson wrote. "While these are kept distinct and apart, the Peace and Welfare of Society is preserved, and the Ends of both answered. But by mixing them together, Feuds, Animosities and Persecutions have been raised, which have deluged the World in Blood, and disgraced human Nature."[126] Looking somewhat askance at the Congregational establishments in New England and the Anglican establishments in the South, Dickinson sounded the call of a proud Pennsylvanian: "In the middle and eastern Governments of North-America, the Legislatures have, with great Wisdom, taken care to keep the Church distinct from the State. . . . Individuals are left at full Liberty to unite themselves into Societies for the public Worship of God, in such a Manner as they judge acceptable to him, and effectual to procure eternal Life and Happiness."

Historians have suggested that there was never a real chance that England would send a bishop to the colonies, yet the controversy helped unite the colonies and encouraged a new discussion on the advisability of established religion.[127] The Quebec Act of 1774 led to an even stronger, and more unified, colonial voice on the intersection of religion and politics.

In response to the Boston Tea Party, Britain enacted several puni-
tive laws in 1774, which George III called "coercive acts," but that
are better known today as the Intolerable Acts.[128] These laws closed
the port of Boston, limited local electoral control in Massachusetts,
permitted royal officials charged with capital crimes in the colony to
be tried in England, and allowed the quartering of troops in private
homes.[129] The Quebec Act, passed by Parliament in June 1774, was
technically not related to the earlier laws, but because of the timing
and the anger it inspired, it was widely considered the fifth of the
Intolerable Acts.

Quebec had been ceded to the British by France in 1763, and in
1774 still had a majority French Catholic population.[130] The Quebec
Act consisted of three main components. The first expanded the
geographic range of Quebec so that it encompassed the area north
and west of the Ohio River, including what became known as the
Northwest Territory.[131] Next, the act authorized the king to appoint
Quebec's governor, legislature, and judges. What was perhaps most
incendiary, though, was the act's protection of the rights of Catholics
in Quebec: "His Majesty's Subjects, professing the Religion of the
Church of Rome, of and in the said Province of Quebec, may have,
hold, and enjoy, the free Exercise of the Religion of the Church of
Rome, subject to the King's Supremacy, . . . and that the Clergy of
the said Church may hold, receive, and enjoy, their accustomed Dues
and Rights, with respect to such Persons only as shall profess the said
Religion."[132] This section guaranteed Catholics the ability to practice
their religion far more freely than in the colonies. The provision referring to "accustomed Dues and Rights" had the added effect of granting
the Catholic Church the power of mandatory tithing, though only
Catholics were legally bound to pay.

An immediate and virulently anti-Catholic colonial outcry followed the passage of the Act. Newspapers in the colonies claimed that
it "establish[ed] popery, slavery and arbitrary power"[133] and would

thereby "CUT OFF ALL THE LIBERTIES OF THE REST OF AMERICA by means of Quebec."[134] When the First Continental Congress convened to decide how the colonies should respond to the Quebec Act and the other Intolerable Acts, this anti-Catholic sentiment would help determine the way the united colonies defined themselves.

CHAPTER 2

A Tolerant, Protestant Nation

THE OPENING of the First Continental Congress marked a
critical early step in the unification of thirteen diverse colonies. The colonists not only began learning how to act in
unison, but also were forced to think about their common interests
and characteristics. Religion was seen as both a unifying force and a
means of accomplishing their goals.

Shortly after the Intolerable Acts became law, the Virginia House
of Burgesses demonstrated its sympathy with the suffering in Boston
by calling for a "Day of Fasting, Humiliation, and Prayer" on June 1,
1774, the day the port of Boston was scheduled to close.[1] Years later,
in his autobiography, Thomas Jefferson wrote irreverently about how
this day of fasting came about. According to Jefferson, he, Patrick
Henry, and a few others decided that they needed help "arousing
our people from the lethargy into which they had fallen as to passing events," and concluded that a call for a day of general fasting and
prayer "would be most likely to call up and alarm their attention."[2] To
draft the resolution, they "rummaged over" previously used language
from Virginia and Massachusetts and "cooked up a resolution." Because
Jefferson and his coauthors felt that they lacked the religious gravitas
needed to introduce the proposal, they agreed to approach a fellow
burgess, Robert Carter Nicholas, "whose grave & religious character

was more in unison with the tone of our resolution and to solicit him to move it."

The following day, Nicholas presented the proposal that the "first day of June be set apart . . . as a day of fasting, humiliation and prayer, devoutly to implore the divine interposition, for averting the heavy calamity which threatens destruction to our civil rights and the evils of civil war; to give us one heart and one mind firmly to oppose, by all just and proper means, every injury to American rights."[3] The House of Burgesses approved the motion, and was subsequently dissolved by the royally appointed Governor, Lord Dunmore.[4]

The next step was to enlist clergy "to perform the ceremonies of the day, and to address to them discourses suited to the occasion."[5] Many ministers were enthusiastic. Landon Carter, a member of the House of Burgesses, reported that his rector used his fast-day sermon to urge listeners to act to "support their Liberties" and instead of concluding with "'God save the King!' he cried out, 'God Preserve all the Just Rights and Liberties of America.'"[6]

Jefferson's plan appears to have succeeded. He wrote: "The effect of the day, through the whole colony, was like a shock of electricity."[7] Among the Virginians heeding the call for a religious observance was George Washington, who recorded his day's activity in his diary: "June 1st 1774. Went to Church & fasted all day."[8]

RELIGION AND THE CONTINENTAL CONGRESS

The other colonies shared Virginia's concern over the Intolerable Acts, and on September 5, 1774, representatives of every colony but Georgia assembled as the First Continental Congress to plan their response.[9] The next day, a motion was made to begin each session with a prayer.[10] A vigorous debate followed. Some of those opposed to the prayer feared that "it would be considered as Enthusiasm & Cant" and worried about "the Hazard of submitting such a Task to the Judgement of any Clergy."[11] Supporters responded by "insisting on the propriety of a Reverence & Submission to the Supreme Being & supplicating his Blessing on every Undertaking."[12]

Some of those who agreed with the general idea of beginning daily sessions with prayers nonetheless opposed the motion on pragmatic grounds that reflected one of the underlying dilemmas facing any attempt to persuade the colonies to work in unison. The colonies as a whole were far more religiously diverse than any individual colony, and the Continental Congress reflected that diversity. Referring to the difficulty of crafting a prayer that could satisfy such a varied assemblage, both John Jay, a Congregationalist from New York, and John Rutledge, an Episcopalian from South Carolina, urged their fellow delegates to defeat the motion. According to John Adams, their concern was that "we were so divided in religious Sentiments, some Episcopalians, some Quakers, some Anabaptists, some Presbyterians and some Congregationalists, . . . that We could not join in the same Act of Worship."[13] John's cousin Sam Adams, a Congregationalist, answered this concern by declaring "he was no Bigot, and could hear a Prayer from a Gentleman of Piety and Virtue, who was at the same Time a Friend to his Country."[14]

To bridge the religious divide, Sam Adams proposed that the prayer be led by a representative of the religion that predominated in the southern colonies: "As many of our warmest Friends are Members of the Church of England, [I] thought it prudent, as well on that as on some other Accounts to move that the Service should be performed by a Clergyman of that Denomination."[15] The cleric he proposed was the Reverend Jacob Duché of Philadelphia.

When Duché arrived the next morning, the delegates had just heard a "horrible Rumour" reporting, incorrectly as it would turn out, a bombardment of Boston by British cannons.[16] Duché, dressed in full clerical garb, read several prayers "in the established Form,"[17] and then turned to Psalm 35, the passage assigned to be read that day by Episcopalians.[18] In light of the rumored attack on Boston, the reading was astonishingly appropriate. As John Adams wrote, "It seemed as if Heaven had ordained that Psalm to be read on that Morning."[19] Psalm 35 begins, "Plead my cause, O Lord, with them that strive with me: fight against them that fight against me."[20] Later in the reading, God is asked, "Let not them that are mine enemies wrongfully rejoice over me: neither let them wink with the eye that hate me without a cause. For they speak not peace: but they devise deceitful matters against them that are quiet in the land." In prescient language, the Psalm asks, "Lord, how long wilt thou look on? Rescue my soul from their destructions."

Reverend Duché then delivered "an extemporary Prayer," which, John Adams told his wife, "filled the bosom of every man present." The prayer began, "O! Lord, our heavenly father, King of Kings and Lord of lords. . . . Look down in mercy, we beseech thee, upon these our American states who have fled to thee from the rod of the oppressor and thrown themselves upon thy gracious protection, desiring henceforth to be dependent only on thee." He pleaded for divine assistance to "defeat the malicious designs of our cruel adversaries." The prayer concluded, "All this we ask in the name and through the merits of Jesus Christ thy son, Our Saviour, Amen."[21]

The Delegates were enthusiastic in their reaction to the prayer. Silas Deane wrote his wife that "it was worth riding One Hundred Mile to hear."[22] Duché preached "with such fervency, purity and sublimity of style and sentiment, and with such an apparent sensibility of the scenes and business before us," Deane added, "that even Quakers shed tears." Pennsylvanian Joseph Reed termed the prayer a "Masterly Stroke of Policy,"[23] and John Adams reported that it "has had an excellent Effect upon every Body here."[24]

The Continental Congress then turned to the tasks before it. On October 14, the delegates voted to approve what has become known as "the Declaration and Resolves of the First Continental Congress."[25]

Unlike the Declaration of Independence, this statement declared that the fundamental rights of the colonial inhabitants were created "by the immutable laws of nature, the principles of the English constitution, and the several charters or compacts."[26] Without claiming to enumerate a complete list of these rights, the statement included "life, liberty and property" and the right of people "to participate in their legislative council" and "peaceably to assemble."[27] The Intolerable Acts, the statement concluded, violated these fundamental rights.

This declaration, while not specifying freedom of religion as a fundamental right, stated that the reason the colonists had convened the Continental Congress was to ensure that "their religion, laws, and liberties, may not be subverted."[28] A separate paragraph was added to address the concerns raised by the Quebec Act. According to the Declaration and Resolves, the Quebec Act had the effect of "establishing the Roman Catholic religion in the province of Quebec, abolishing the equitable system of English laws, and erecting a tyranny there."[29] The Delegates also emphasized their conception that the colonies were Protestant, whereas Quebec was Catholic and thus belonged to a different religion. The Delegates warned that a "great danger" was created "from so total a dissimilarity of Religion, law and government."[30]

Coincidentally, on the evening of the day that the Declaration and Resolves was approved, a confrontation arose concerning both religious rights in Massachusetts and whether the Continental Congress could have any role in protecting religious freedom. Led by Isaac Backus, several Massachusetts Baptist churches voted to petition the Continental Congress to seek redress for the treatment they were suffering at the hands of the Congregational establishment. One of the most noteworthy aspects of this petition was that it was based on the assumption that, in Backus's words, "the Congress was like to have the highest place of civil power over us."[31] He wrote in his diary that the appearance of a potentially supervening authority meant that "now was the most likely time to obtain our religious liberty that we had ever known."[32] Backus's call for protection of religious freedom did not encompass all religions. Rather, he sought relief for Baptists because "as a distinct denomination of Protestants, . . . we have an equal claim to charter-rights with the rest of our fellow-subjects."[33]

After consulting with a supportive group of Quakers from Pennsylvania, Backus decided that going directly to the Continental Congress might "embarrass" the Massachusetts delegation, so he decided to talk to those delegates first.[34] He asked two delegates from Rhode Island, Samuel Ward and Stephen Hopkins, to arrange a meeting. Shortly after the close of the emotional October 14 congressional session approving the Declaration and Resolves, Ward and Hopkins visited the Massachusetts delegates, John Adams, Samuel Adams, Thomas Cushing, and Robert Paine, at their lodgings. Each was invited to return to Carpenter Hall, where the Continental Congress held its sessions, to meet with Backus and James Manning, the president of Providence College (now Brown University).

The meeting began awkwardly. The Massachusetts delegation arrived at six, "supposing it would be only spending an Evening with 2 or 3 Baptist Gentlemen."[35] Instead, as John Adams wrote in his diary, "to my great Surprize [we] found the Hall almost full of People, and a great Number of Quakers seated at the long Table with their broad brimmed Beavers on their Heads."[36] The meeting opened with Manning reading a prepared memorial "considering the unhappy situation of our brethren the Baptists in the province of Massachusetts Bay," which highlighted the seizing of Baptist land in Ashfield to pay for a Congregational minister. The memorial ended with a plea that "according to the dictates of Protestantism, we claim and expect the liberty of worshipping God according to our consciences, not being obliged to support a ministry we cannot attend, whilst we demean ourselves as faithful subjects. These we have an undoubted right to, as men, as Christians, and by charter as inhabitants of Massachusetts Bay."[37]

The Massachusetts delegates greatly resented this discussion. John Adams wrote that he felt "somewhat indignant . . . at seeing our State and her Delegates thus summoned before a self created Trybunal, which was neither legal nor Constitutional."[38] They were also offended by the Pennsylvanian Quaker John Pemberton, who, according to Robert Paine, "bellowed loud on N. England persecution and Hanging the Quakers &c."[39]

The meeting lasted nearly four hours. When Sam Adams argued that the Baptists could avoid the religious tax simply by presenting a certificate, Backus responded, "I cannot give in the certificates they require without implicitly acknowledging that power in man which I believe belongs only to God."[40] To Paine, the Baptists' complaints were trivial: "There was nothing of conscience in the matter; it was only a contending about paying a little money."[41] Paine summarized the Baptists' discussion as consisting of "only this Objection . . . that in Case of legal Trial they must give four pence to the Town Clerk for a copy of this Certificate."[42]

To Backus, the size of the tax was irrelevant to the injustice of its imposition. After all, he argued, the tax on tea that led to the Boston Tea Party was merely "three pence a pound."[43] The Baptists were unable to convince the Massachusetts delegates that their opposition to the certificate was, at heart, based on the same principle as the colonial opposition to the tea tax: both expenses, though small, represented a presumption of an authority that was illegitimate.

The acrimonious discussion continued with John Adams defending the religious practices of his home colony. He stated that the principle of "Liberty of Conscience" actually argued for retaining Massachusetts's system of religious taxation, since any concept of such liberty "would demand indulgence for the tender Consciences of the People of Massachusetts, and allow them to preserve their Laws." The colony's religious laws, he maintained, were "the most mild and equitable Establishment of Religion that was known in the World, if indeed they could be called an Establishment."[44] He concluded by declaring that "we might as well expect a change in the solar system, as to expect they would give up their establishment."[45]

Adams also disagreed with the Baptists on another central point: the role of the Continental Congress in preserving religious freedom. To Adams, this was a matter belonging to the exclusive preserve of the individual colonies. Those gathering in Philadelphia "had no Authority to bind our Constituents to any such Proposals."[46] And on a more pragmatic level, "it would be in vain for Us to enter into any Conferences on such a Subject, for We knew before hand our Constituents would disavow all We could do or say."[47] The meeting ended with the Massachusetts delegates recommending that the Quakers bring their grievances to the Massachusetts General Assembly. Backus reported that they promised to use "their influence toward procuring redress of our grievances."[48]

Despite this seemingly amicable conclusion, by the time that Backus returned to his home colony, the Massachusetts delegation had spread the word that the Baptists and Quakers were traitors to the colonial cause. Robert Paine reported that by bringing their complaints to the Continental Congress "at this critical Time," they had demonstrated "Partiality & Malice."[49] John Adams agreed that the true goal of the meeting had been "to break up the Congress."[50] In the short term, it appeared that the Baptists had hurt their cause; as Paine warned, "We shall not forget this Work of our Brother Esau."[51]

Not surprisingly, when Backus presented his petition to the Massachusetts General Assembly on July 19, 1775, he received little satisfaction. The petition argued that "an entire freedom from being taxed by civil rulers to religious worship, is not a mere favor, from any man or men in the world, but a right and property granted us by God." The petition was debated but, as Backus reported, "other business was crowded in, and nothing more done upon it. Such is the disposition of mankind."[52]

After the contentious October 14 meeting, the Continental Congress took less than two weeks to conclude its work by authorizing five separate documents. The first was the Articles of Association, approved on October 20. Under this agreement, the delegates pledged that the "free Protestant colonies" would act in unison to refuse to import English goods until the Intolerable Acts were lifted.[53] In addition to the Articles of Association, the Continental Congress drafted four letters. On October 21, two messages were approved, a "Circular Letter" to the inhabitants of the colonies and an "Address to the People of Great Britain."

The Circular Letter urged colonists to "humble yourselves, and implore the favour of almighty God" in the ongoing dispute with England.[54] In discussing the Quebec Act, the Circular Letter referred to the inhabitants of the American colonies as being "of another religion" from "the Roman Catholic religion," which allegedly had been established in Quebec. The letter expressed confidence that the English people, as "the defenders of true religion," would assist the colonies and never "take part against their affectionate Protestant brethren in the colonies, in favor of our open and their own secret enemies whose intrigues, for several years past, have been wholly exercised in sapping the foundations of civil and religious liberty."[55]

This hostility to Roman Catholics was even more pronounced in the Address to the People of Great Britain.[56] First, the Continental Congress expressed dismay that the Quebec Act threatened "to reduce the ancient free Protestant colonies" to a state of slavery by establishing Catholicism, a "religion, fraught with sanguinary and impious tenets."[57] The Congress then heightened its own inflammatory, anti-Catholic rhetoric, expressing "astonishment, that a British Parliament should ever consent to establish in that country a religion that has deluged your island in blood, and dispersed impiety, bigotry, persecution, murder and rebellion through every part of the world."[58]

The Continental Congress wrote two additional letters, both approved on the last day the Delegates met, October 26, 1774. In the "Petition of Congress to the King," the Congress once more complained that the Quebec Act had established "the Roman Catholick religion throughout those vast regions, that border on the westerly and northerly boundaries of the free protestant English settlements."[59]

The second letter was an "Address to the Inhabitants of the Province of Quebec," written by John Dickinson.[60] In an act of extraordinary hypocrisy, the delegates informed the Canadians that they were "your unalterable friends" and expressed confidence that the "difference of religion" would not "prejudice you against a hearty amity with us."[61] This paean to religious fellowship ended with an assertion that North Americans should follow the example of the Swiss cantons, in which "Roman Catholic and Protestant States, living in the utmost concord and peace with one another" are able "to defy and defeat every tyrant that has invaded them."[62]

After the First Continental Congress adjourned, anti-Catholic fervor grew throughout the colonies. John Zubly of Georgia decried the Quebec Act as an "endeavour to stir up popish Canadians."[63] A South Carolina minister, Richard Furman, warned that the act created the possibility that "the Popish religion may be established in all the colonies."[64] Most colonists, it seemed, preferred to see the Catholics of Quebec as "secret enemies" rather than as "unalterable friends."

The 1774 "Pope's Day" celebrations, which marked the uncovering of Guy Fawkes's plot to blow up the English Parliament on November 5, 1605, were especially enthusiastic. These annual commemorations generally featured effigies of the pope being tossed into raging bonfires in order, in the words of one supportive colonial newspaper, "to show their abhorrence and detestations of Pope, Pretender and such of their adherents as would overthrow our good old English Constitution."[65] Newport, Rhode Island, featured a special addition to that year's Pope's Day festivities. The locals wanted to demonstrate that they would "by no means sanctify such villainous productions" as the pamphlet, allegedly written by Lord Dartmouth, defending the Quebec Act. Thus, into Providence's bonfire was thrown not merely effigies of "the Devil and Pope," but also "a pamphlet with these words written on the cover: 'L—d Darthmouth's pamphlet in justification of Popery sent over the Colonies.'"[66]

In one of his first major political essays, twenty-year-old Alexander Hamilton joined the anti-Catholic frenzy.[67] On December 15, 1774, he wrote the first in a series of pieces entitled *A Full Vindication of Measures of Congress from Calumnies of their Enemies*.[68] Hamilton declared that it should make one's "blood run cold, to think that an English Parliament should pass an act for the establishment of arbitrary power and popery." If Parliament, he wrote, had truly "been friends to the Protestant cause, they would never have provided such a nursery for its great enemy; they would not have given such encouragement to Popery."

Sam Adams also appealed to religious bigotry. In his March 1775 *Address Of Massachusetts To Mohawk Indians*,[69] a message meant to encourage the formation of a military alliance with the Mohawks, Adams argued that England could not be trusted, because it had "made a law to establish the religion of the Pope in Canada, which lies so near you."[70] The proximity of a Catholic stronghold, Adams wrote, presented a grave danger to the Mohawks: "We much fear some of your children may be induced, instead of worshipping the only true God, to pay *his* dues to images made with their own hands."[71]

Anti-Catholic rhetoric also appears in the most widely read pamphlet of the Revolutionary era, Thomas Paine's *Common Sense*.[72] A large segment of *Common Sense* consists of religious argument, both refuting the notion of the divine right of kings and establishing that a monarchy violates biblical teaching. "The Almighty," Paine wrote, "hath here entered his protest against monarchical government."[73] As the political scientist Rogers M. Smith has written, the "conception of Americans as a distinct people, chosen to serve the Protestant

God's emancipating purposes, forms a major if rather disingenuous theme" of *Common Sense*.[74] For example, Paine writes that the very time period in which Europeans discovered the New World is proof that English control over America "was never the design of Heaven." According to Paine, "The reformation was preceded by the discovery of America, as if the Almighty graciously meant to open a sanctuary to the persecuted in future years, when home should afford neither friendship nor safety."[75]

Paine "appealed to the Protestant ethos of the colonists," not merely with his religious allusions, but also by linking England to Catholicism.[76] Thus, he wrote that "the phrase PARENT OR MOTHER COUNTRY hath been jesuitically adopted by the King and his parasites, with a low papistical design of gaining an unfair bias on the credulous weakness of our minds."[77] Similarly, in attacking the assumption of power by the king, Paine wrote, "a man hath good reason to believe that there is as much of kingcraft as priestcraft in withholding the scripture from the public in popish countries. For monarchy in every instance is the popery of government."[78]

The most notable colonial figure to transcend this sort of religious divisiveness, even when dealing with the fallout from the Quebec Act, was George Washington. When the Second Continental Congress convened in Philadelphia, on May 10, 1775, the Quebec situation was still not resolved. The battles of Lexington and Concord in April had greatly increased the likelihood of a violent split with England, and a strategy was needed for ensuring that Canada would not aid England during the coming conflict. Washington, who was named commander in chief of the Continental Army in June 1775, implemented a strategy that demonstrates a trait that was crucial for both his military career and his tenure as president: his respect for religious diversity and religious freedom.

Washington sent twelve hundred troops north under the command of Benedict Arnold.[79] In his letter of instruction to Arnold,

Washington revealed his capacity to recognize a commonality among those fighting for freedom, a linkage that was frequently overlooked by colonial leaders blinded by religious intolerance:

> I also give it in Charge to you to avoid all Disrespect or Contempt of the Religion of the Country and its Ceremonies—Prudence, Policy, and a true Christian Spirit will lead us to look with Compassion upon their Errors without insulting them—While we are Contending for our own Liberty, we should be very cautious of violating the Rights of Conscience in others; ever considering that God alone is the Judge of the Hearts of Men and to him only in this Case they are answerable.[80]

This is a remarkable statement despite the "note of condescension" in Washington's description of the "Errors" of the Catholic faith.[81] He not only requires "respect" for a religion that he views as different from his own, but also is able to articulate the vision that the Americans' struggle for their "own liberty" was linked to, and thus ought to be consistent with, "the rights of conscience in others."

Washington's religious tolerance is particularly noteworthy, since his opposition to the Quebec Act was founded not only on his patriotic scruples but also on the fact that he claimed ownership of some of the land granted to Quebec by the law.[82] Yet in both his public statements and his private correspondence, Washington refused to employ the anti-Catholic rhetoric of the other colonial leaders.[83]

After Arnold's military campaign in Canada ended in defeat, the Second Continental Congress decided to follow the tone of Washington's message and to send a diplomatic delegation to Canada to try to convince them to join the American cause.[84] On February 15, 1776, Congress appointed a committee that it believed would be acceptable to the Catholics in Canada. The delegation was to be headed by seventy-year-old Benjamin Franklin, who had earned an international reputation for treating people of all religions with respect.[85] Accompanying him were a delegate from Maryland, Samuel Chase, and two prominent Maryland Catholics: Charles Carroll, a leading local politician who would later join the Congress and sign the Declaration of Independence, and his cousin John Carroll, a priest.

Congress instructed the delegation to inform the Quebec Catholics that the Americans "hold sacred the rights of conscience" and would promise the Canadians "the free and undisturbed exercise of their religion."[86] There was only one caveat: "Provided, however, that all other denominations of Christians be equally entitled to hold offices, and enjoy civil privileges, and the free exercise of their religion, and be totally exempt from the payment of any tithes or taxes for the support of any religion."

With this proviso, the Americans were demanding far more religious equality than many of the colonies were prepared to bestow themselves. At least five colonies denied Catholics the right to vote, and many explicitly excluded them from the guarantee of free exercise of religion. Significantly, the American demand for religious equality did not encompass all religions but was limited to "denominations of Christians."

On April 2, 1776, the four-person delegation boarded a sloop to Albany to begin their arduous four-hundred-mile journey from New York to Montreal.[87] Once they arrived, the Reverend John Carroll was sent to speak with the Catholic clergy of the area while the other three set out to negotiate with political leaders. Both sets of meetings were complete failures. To the Americans' apparent surprise, the Canadians were aware of the anti-Catholic messages that had emanated from the First Continental Congress. The predictable reaction to the conflicting addresses of the previous year can be seen in a letter written from Montreal in March 1775.[88] The writer described how the Address to the Inhabitants of the Province of Quebec had been translated into "very tolerable French" and read to a crowd that reacted very positively: "The decent manner in which the religious matters were touched, the encomiums on the French nation flattered the people fond of compliments." Unfortunately, the crowd then asked the translator to translate the Address to the People of Great Britain.

When he came to the description of Catholicism as a religion that "dispersed impiety, bigotry, persecution, murder, and rebellion," the crowd "could not contain their resentment." They were reputed to have exclaimed, "O! The perfidious double-faced congress! Let us bless and obey our benevolent prince, whose humanity is consistent, and extends to all religions; let us abhor all who would seduce us from our loyalty, by acts that would dishonor a Jesuit, and whose addresses, like their resolves, are destructive of their own objects."

The one positive result of the trip serves to illustrate the extraordinary character of Benjamin Franklin. He and the Reverend Carroll had traveled back to New York together, ahead of the rest of the delegation, and forged a bond of friendship and mutual respect. Eight years after their trip together, Franklin made the following notation in his diary: "July 1st.—The Pope's Nuncio called, and acquainted me that the Pope had, on my recommendation, appointed Mr. John Carroll, superior of the Catholic clergy in America, with many of the powers of a bishop; and that probably he would be made a bishop in partibus before the end of the year."[89] Considering that most of the colonies were convulsed in anti-Catholic animus, Franklin's role in helping John Carroll become America's first archbishop is simply remarkable. Franklin was so far ahead of the vast majority of Americans, who willingly joined Alexander Hamilton in attacking "the Popish religion," that he was able develop a relationship with Pope Pius VI such that the pontiff would follow his advice.

An enlightening sidelight to the Quebec Act occurred on June 27, 1775, when New York's Provincial Congress prepared a set of instructions to its delegates to Congress. The document urged the delegates to try to find some way to achieve a compromise with England that would lead to the repeal of the Intolerable Acts.[90] In discussing the Quebec Act, the instructions asserted that the "establishment of Popery" in Quebec threatened the "free enjoyment of the rights of conscience."

An early draft of the instructions also recommended that New York's delegates try to convince the Continental Congress that "all concerns of a religious and ecclesiastical nature, so far as they may be under the cognizance and control of civil authority, ought to remain exclusively with the respective Colony Legislatures." But some in New York's Provincial Congress were unwilling to encourage or endorse any establishment of religion by the colonies. Led by Gouverneur Morris, a New York lawyer who has been termed "among the most religiously tolerant of the Founders,"[91] they deleted the recommendation that religious and ecclesiastical matters be left to the individual colonies and replaced it with a call to end state establishments. The Provincial Congress's final letter of instruction included the following resolution:

> As the free enjoyment of the rights of conscience is of all others the most valuable branch of human liberty, and the indulgence and establishment of popery all along the interior confines of the old Protestant Colonies tends not only to obstruct their growth, but to weaken their security, . . . neither the Parliament of Great Britain, *nor any other earthly legislature or tribunal,* ought or can of right interfere or interpose in anywise howsoever in the religious and ecclesiastical concerns of the colonies.[92]

The New York delegates responded to the Provincial Congress by writing that while they shared the desire to reach a compromise with England, they understood that they were "unrestrained" as to how they should proceed.[93] Nonetheless, John Jay added a fascinating postscript to their response, stating that "we have unanimously agreed to be silent" concerning the instruction's comment on establishment of religion. Jay pointed out that the colonies were deeply divided on religious issues but united politically, and "it would be highly imprudent to run the Risque of dividing them by the Introduction of Disputes foreign to the present Controversy. . . . They are Points about which Mankind will forever differ and therefore should always, and at least in Times like these be kept out of Sight." Not only would the

Continental Congress not address issues of religious freedom, Jay concluded, but "both this and the former Congress have cautiously avoided the least Hint on Subjects of this Kind, all the members concurring in a Desire of burying all Disputes on ecclesiastical Points."

While the Continental Congress generally persisted in "burying all Disputes on ecclesiastical Points," it frequently engaged in religious practices and conveyed religious messages. On July 9, 1776, Congress appointed its first chaplain, the same Jacob Duché who had led the memorable prayer service at the start of the First Continental Congress.[94] But Duché's tenure was brief and disappointing. He resigned after serving less than three months, citing "the state of his health, and his parochial duties."[95] In reality, Duché quit because he opposed the War for Independence.[96] In a peculiar letter to George Washington, he wrote that Congress consisted of a "great majority of illiberal and violent men."[97] He added a touch of religious bigotry, deriding the Catholic delegate Charles Carroll as one of the "dregs of Congress" and complaining that "Maryland no longer sends . . . a protestant Carroll" to Philadelphia.[98] The most inflammatory part of the letter was Duché's suggestion that Washington bypass Congress and seek a peace agreement with England by himself: "Negotiate for America at the Head of your Army."

Washington immediately forwarded the incendiary letter to Congress. John Adams, who previously had praised Duché, wrote to his wife, Abigail, of his disappointment: "Mr. Duché I am sorry to inform you has turned out an Apostate and a Traytor. Poor Man! I pitty his Weakness, and detest his Wickedness."[99]

The men who replaced Duché acquitted themselves far more honorably. On December 21, 1776, Congress appointed two chaplains, George Duffield, a Presbyterian, and William White, an Episcopalian. Each served almost eight years, through the end of the Revolutionary War. Among their regular responsibilities were "offering prayer at each session, preparing and delivering sermons for days of fast,

humiliation, and thanksgiving, [and] assisting in patriotic celebrations."[100] They were also asked to draft one of the congressional proclamations calling for a "day of general thanksgiving."[101] According to
their proclamation, December 30, 1777, was to be a day not merely of
"devout thanksgiving" but also for joining in "a penitent confession
of our sins, and humble supplication for pardon, through the merits
of our Saviour."[102]

The sectarian nature of this proclamation was far from unique for
the Continental Congress. Between June 12, 1775, and October 11, 1782,
Congress appointed a dozen days for fasting, humiliation, and prayer,
on the one hand, or thanksgiving on the other. Many of the accompanying proclamations were decidedly Christian and Trinitarian.[103]

Representative of these is the November 1, 1777, thanksgiving-day
proclamation, drafted by Sam Adams. It begins by declaring "the indispensable duty of all men to adore the superintending providence
of Almighty God."[104] All "the good people" of the United States were
urged to "join the penitent confession of their manifold sins, whereby
they had forfeited every favour, and their humble and earnest supplication that it may please God, through the merits of Jesus Christ,
mercifully to forgive and blot them out of remembrance." In addition
to military success and good harvests, the citizenry was urged to ask
God "to prosper the means of religion for the promotion and enlargement of that kingdom which consisteth 'in righteousness, peace and
joy in the Holy Ghost.'"

These calls for days of fast and thanksgiving were not empty
rituals. On the day of the first fast, all the members of Congress attended two services, one at an Episcopalian church in the morning
and the second at a Presbyterian church in the afternoon.[105] John Adams would later comment that the entire city of Philadelphia took the
fast-day proclamation seriously: "Our Fast has been kept more Strictly
and devoutly than any Sunday was ever observed in [Boston]."[106]

RELIGIOUS LANGUAGE IN THE
DECLARATION OF INDEPENDENCE

In sharp contrast to these fast- and thanksgiving-day proclamations, the Declaration of Independence was carefully crafted to be a religiously inclusive document. The initial committee to draft the Declaration, Thomas Jefferson, John Adams, Benjamin Franklin, Roger Sherman, and Robert Livingston, was appointed by Congress on June 11, 1776.[107] This "Committee of Five" assigned the first draft to Jefferson and Adams. Adams later said that he encouraged Jefferson to do the initial writing for several reasons: "Reason first—You are a Virginian, and a Virginian ought to appear at the head of this business. Reason second—I am obnoxious, suspected, and unpopular. You are very much otherwise. Reason third—You can write ten times better than I can."[108]

The precise chronology of Jefferson's beginning his draft on June 12 and the moment the Committee of Five presented its report to Congress on June 28 is unclear. We know that Jefferson showed his work to both Adams and Franklin, and then to the entire committee. We also know that Adams and Franklin discussed many changes, the most notable being altering the phrase "We hold these truths to be sacred and undeniable," to the far more resonant, "We hold these truths to be self-evident." Unfortunately, there is no record of who suggested which changes, and historians have disagreed on who composed the various phrases that were added to Jefferson's original draft.[109]

Moreover, once the Committee of Five presented its report, the document underwent several days of editing by the entire Congress. The debates over the final language took up "the greater parts of the 2d. 3d. & 4th. days of July"[110] and brought significant alterations. As Adams later described it, "Congress cut off about a quarter of it, as I expected they would; but they obliterated some of the best of it."[111] Because Congress met as a "Committee of the Whole," the discussion was not recorded.[112] Nonetheless, enough documentation exists that we can track the evolution of the language in the Declaration of Independence through three specific moments: Jefferson's original draft; the version presented by the Committee of Five to Congress; and the final version approved on July 4, 1776.[113]

Jefferson's draft began with a religious reference that largely remained in the final version: "When in the course of human events it becomes necessary for a people to advance from that subordination, in which they have hitherto remained and to assume among the powers of the earth, the equal and independent station to which the laws of nature and of nature's god entitle them." The phrase "laws of Nature and of Nature's God" is associated with eighteenth-century Deism, a "rather vague Enlightenment-era belief . . . in a Creator whose divine handiwork was evident in the wonders of nature," but not "a personal God who interceded directly in the daily affairs of mankind."[114]

Jefferson's original draft did not contain the phrase "endowed by their Creator." Instead, he had written: "We hold these Truths to be self evident; *that all Men are created equal and independent; that from that equal Creation they derive Rights inherent and inalienable;* among which are the Preservation of Life, and Liberty, and the Pursuit of Happiness."[115]

When the Committee of Five sent Jefferson's draft to Congress, the language on human rights had been edited into a form which is much closer to its famous final version: "We hold these truths to be self-evident that all men are created equal; that they are endowed by their Creator with inherent & inalienable rights." The theologically ambiguous word "Creator" meshes with a wide range of religious philosophies as well as that of the most orthodox religions in 1776 America. It has been noted that "most Deists referred to 'the Creator.'"[116] Yet the term was also used by Timothy Dwight, a Congregational minister and the president of Yale College, who delivered a sermon stating that the Bible contained "as full a proof, that Christ is the Creator, as that . . . the Creator is God."[117]

Jefferson was generally satisfied with the editing by the Committee of Five. In later weeks, he would send this version to his friends, with the clear expectation that they would find it preferable to the final product produced by Congress. Jefferson agonized over the congressional editing.[118] Throughout the three-day discussion of his work, he walked over to friends and complained, "They are cutting the life out of the paper. They are eliminating my best sentences."[119] He later told Madison that he was "writhing a little under the acrimonious criticisms on some of its parts."[120] Benjamin Franklin offered Jefferson some sympathy. "I have made it a rule," Franklin told him, "whenever in my power, to avoid becoming the draughtsman of papers to be reviewed by a public body."[121]

Among the many changes ultimately made by Congress was the addition of, in the words of the historian Pauline Maier, "two references to God, which were conspicuously missing in Jefferson's draft":[122]

> We, therefore, the Representatives of the United States of America, in General Congress Assembled, *appealing to the Supreme Judge of the world for the rectitude of our intentions,* do, in the Name, and by Authority of the good People of these Colonies, solemnly publish and declare, that these United Colonies are, and of Right ought to be Free and Independent States. . . . And for the support of this Declaration, *with a firm reliance on the protection of divine Providence,* we mutually pledge to each other our Lives, our Fortunes, and our sacred Honor.

It has been said that Congress added these two phrases, "to buttress the argument that God was on the side of American independence."[123] Ashbel Green, a Presbyterian minister who served as chaplain of the United States House of Representatives in the 1790s, viewed Jefferson's failure to include these two references in his original draft as proof that Jefferson was a "bitter reviler of religious sects."[124] In a vituperative attack on Jefferson's religious views, Green emphasized that "we do not owe it to him that our national appeal to arms and declaration of independence, was not made without any recognition of the superintending and all disposing providence of God."[125]

The phrases added by Congress, "appealing to the Supreme Judge of the world" and "protection of divine Providence," are widely interpreted as being more traditionally religious than the earlier two religious references in the Declaration of Independence. They have been said to show that "a biblical God of history who stands in judgment over the world is indicated."[126] It is thus incorrect to say that the final language of the Declaration displays only a Deistic "sense of a distant deity."[127] The very request for "protection," in particular, illustrates a view of an active God who intervenes in human affairs.

Nonetheless, even after the congressional editing, the religious language in the final version of the Declaration of Independence remains inclusive. According to the historian Steven Waldman: "The term *Divine Providence* was one the Deists could accept, because it left the door open for God to work either directly and personally or through the laws of nature."[128] The phrases are not specifically Protestant or Christian; perhaps, as one commentator has asserted, they "derive from Judaism."[129] Most importantly, the final Declaration of Independence presents a public expression of religion that is devout but that recognizes the variety of belief systems. It represents a quintessentially American achievement by being specific enough to be embraceable by those with orthodox religious views but broad enough to permit others to feel included.

RELIGIOUS PROVISIONS IN THE
ARTICLES OF CONFEDERATION

On June 11, 1776, the same day that Congress created the committee to draft the Declaration of Independence, a second committee was selected to draft "a form of a confederation."[130] This committee, which consisted of one delegate from each colony, was led by John Dickinson of Pennsylvania.[131] Dickinson's initial draft for the Articles of Confederation reflected not only Pennsylvania's religious tolerance but also his own experience in opposing the plan for sending an Anglican bishop to America. In 1768, Dickinson had stressed the need "to keep the Church distinct from the State," and in 1776, he tried to implement this belief in the Articles of Confederation. In a section that the historian Jack Rakove has termed "the most innovative of the entire draft," Dickinson attempted to create a national commitment to freedom of religion.[132]

First, he tried to guarantee what is now termed the free exercise of religion: "No person in any Colony living peaceably under the Civil Government, shall be molested or prejudiced in his or her person or Estate for his or her religious persuasion." Next, and even more radically, Dickinson attacked the very concept of establishment of religion. Knowing he could never convince the colonies with established religions to relinquish them, he tried to prevent the creation of any future establishments. Dickinson's proposal stated that no one would be "compelled to frequent or maintain or contribute to maintain any religious Worship, Place of Worship, or Ministry, by any Law or ordinance hereafter to be made in any Colony different from the usual Laws & Customs subsisting at the Commencement of this War." His draft also proposed that no disqualification from office on account of religious persuasion would "hereafter to be made in any Colony" and concluded by declaring that there would be no retreat from the development of full religious equality, "it being the full Intent of these united Colonies that all the Inhabitants thereof respectively of every Sect, Society or religious Denomination shall enjoy under this Confederation, all the Liberties and Priviledges which they have heretofore enjoyed."

Dickinson's fellow delegates had little interest in either a national commitment to freedom of religion or in surrendering any of the individual colonies' recently acquired autonomy. The committee quickly rejected the proposal.[133]

By the time the Articles were finally ratified in 1781, Congress had made numerous changes to Dickinson's draft. The autonomy of the individual states was confirmed by a new article: "Each state retains its sovereignty, freedom, and independence, and every Power, Jurisdiction, and right, which is not by this confederation expressly delegated to the United States, in Congress assembled."

While no protection was given to religious freedom, Congress added one religious reference. The final section of the Articles of Confederation was amended to read: "Whereas it hath pleased the Great Governor of the World to incline the hearts of the legislatures we respectively represent in Congress, to approve of, and to authorize us to ratify the said articles of confederation and perpetual union."[134]

The Articles of Confederation was not the only new governing charter. The Continental Congress declared that "all the powers of government" were to be "exerted, under the authority of the people of the colonies."[135] Accordingly, it voted to approve John Adams's recommendation that any colony lacking a "government sufficient to the exigencies of their affairs" should draft its own constitution and "adopt such government as shall, in the opinion of the representatives of the people, best conduce to the happiness and safety of their constituents in particular, and America in general."[136]

By 1784, Adams's recommendation had been acted on by every colony except Connecticut and Rhode Island.[137] The first colony to complete the task was Virginia.[138]

THE EARLY BATTLE FOR RELIGIOUS FREEDOM IN COLONIAL VIRGINIA

Among the many issues Virginia addressed was the way in which its new Declaration of Rights would deal with religious matters.[139] The question of religious rights had been brought to the state legislature a few years earlier. In response to the rise in popularity of the Baptists, Presbyterians, and other non-Anglican denominations, a bill was introduced in the Virginia House of Burgesses on February 27, 1772, "for extending the Benefit of the several Acts of Toleration to his Majesty's

Protestant Subjects, in this Colony, dissenting from the Church of England."[140] The bill for a new Toleration Act was strongly opposed by the so-called dissenters, since it limited their ability to preach outside a narrow geographic area, barred nighttime services, and required dissenters to keep their church doors open during services.[141]

As tensions with England increased in 1775, the House of Burgesses refashioned itself as a "Colonial Convention," and met in Richmond in July to begin making preparations for war.[142] The revolutionary spirit also caused religious dissenters to become more ambitious. The Baptists filed a petition seeking both an end to the church establishment and a declaration that "all religious societies should be protected in the peaceable enjoyment of their own religious principles and modes of worship."[143]

When that petition was largely ignored, the Baptists sent another, requesting the right to preach to Baptist soldiers serving in the colonial army. This address presented the important, and still novel, argument that people could be of different religions yet share a common political identity; the Baptists stated that "however distinguished from the body of their countrymen by appellations and sentiments of a religious nature, they, nevertheless, considered themselves as members of the same community in respect to matters of a civil nature, and embarked in the same common cause."[144]

Finding it impossible to deny this request made for the benefit of those willing to fight on its behalf, the Colonial Convention agreed to "permit dissenting clergymen to celebrate divine worship, and to preach to the soldiers . . . for the ease of such scrupulous consciences as may not choose to attend divine service as celebrated by the chaplain."[145] This concession has been termed "a bitter pill" for the convention, since the same Baptist preachers who had been thrown in jail a year earlier for illegal preaching were now securing their compatriots' right to conduct the formerly forbidden services.[146]

The Virginia Convention of 1776 faced far greater political challenges than those of the preceding term. On May 15, the convention instructed the Virginia delegates to the Continental Congress to propose a declaration of independence, and also called for a committee to prepare a Declaration of Rights and a new constitution for Virginia.[147]

The lead author of the Declaration of Rights was George Mason.[148] The sixteenth article of his first draft contained a strong endorsement of religious freedom:

> That religion, or the duty we owe to our Creator, and the manner of discharging, can be directed only by reason and conviction, and not by force or violence; and, therefore, that all men should enjoy the fullest toleration in the exercise of religion, according to the dictates of conscience, unpunished and unrestrained by the magistrate, unless, under the color of religion, any man disturb the peace, the happiness, or the safety of society; and that it is the mutual duty of all to practise Christian forbearance, love, and charity towards each other.

When the draft was presented to the Convention, a shy twenty-five-year-old James Madison asked Patrick Henry to introduce a motion to amend article 16—possibly the most important piece of editing in the history of religious freedom. Madison proposed replacing the phrase "all men should enjoy the fullest toleration in the exercise of religion," with "all men are equally entitled to the free exercise of religion."

The difference between "toleration" and "free exercise" was revolutionary. By definition, the word "toleration" implies a favored religion that deigns to grant permission for dissenters to worship. As Thomas Paine would write many years later: "Toleration is not the opposite of Intolerance, but is the counterfeit of it. Both are despotisms. The one assumes to itself the right of withholding Liberty of Conscience, and the other of granting it."[149] The language Madison proposed, by contrast, denied government any initial right over an individual's freedom of religion. According to Madison, it conveyed "an absolute and equal right in all, to the exercise of religion according to the dictates of conscience."[150]

While Madison was able to persuade the Convention to accept this substitution, he was less successful with another part of his amendment. He had proposed adding language that would prevent the government from giving benefits to people because of their specific religious beliefs. His amendment included the clause "no man or class of men, ought, on account of religion to be invested with peculiar emoluments or privileges."[151] Had this been approved, it effectively would have ended the establishment of the Anglican Church in Virginia. The convention, however, was not willing to go that far. When a member of the convention asked Patrick Henry whether the amendment was indeed "designed as a prelude to an attack on the established church," Henry, according to Edmund Randolph, "disclaimed such an object."[152] This section of the proposal was quickly dropped.

Madison's last major amendment involved the conditions under which people could engage in activities connected with their religion. Under the Mason draft, religious activities could be limited if the government found that they "disturb the peace, the happiness, or the safety of society." Madison envisioned a broader protection for religious activity, requiring a much stronger rationale for restricting it; accordingly, he proposed that people should be free to engage in their religious practices, "unless . . . preservation of equal liberty and the existence of the State be manifestly endangered."[153]

The Convention never reached a consensus on whether the Mason or Madison language was the preferable standard for limiting religious practices. The final version contains neither.

The Convention adopted article 16 on June 12, 1776, and it reads as a milestone in the development of religious freedom in America:

> That religion, or the duty which we owe to our Creator, and the manner of discharging it, can be directed only by reason and conviction, not by force or violence, and therefore all men are equally entitled to the free exercise of religion, according to the dictates of conscience; and that it is the mutual duty of all to practise Christian forbearance, love, and charity towards each other.[154]

It is noteworthy that this final version retained Mason's two religious references, one describing "religion, or the duty which we owe to our Creator," and the final statement concerning the "mutual duty of all to practise Christian forbearance, love, and charity towards each other," to which Madison never objected. These statements not only indicate that Virginia was not ready for a total removal of all governmental religious expression, but also reveal the extent to which religious acknowledgments have often accompanied religious freedom. As one commentator has noted, "Unbelievers were expected to practice 'Christian forbearance, love, and charity,' but they were not persecuted for not adhering to the doctrines of the Christian religion."[155]

Passage of the Declaration of Rights fundamentally altered the treatment of minority religions in Virginia. According to the historian Hamilton James Eckenrode, "Prosecution for religious causes ceased. Disabilities on account of religion were removed. . . . Anglicans, Roman Catholics, Evangelicals, Jews, and unbelievers were placed on the same civil footing."[156]

On the other hand, the effect of the Declaration of Rights on the established status of the Anglican Church was much less clear. The Anglicans believed that the establishment continued, while adherents of other denominations viewed the declaration as ending the connection between church and state.[157]

The issue resurfaced when the General Assembly of Virginia, the legislature created by Virginia's new constitution, convened in October 1776. According to Jefferson, who was a member of the House of Delegates, the subsequent two-month battle over the relationship between church and state in Virginia "brought on the severest contests in which I have ever been engaged."[158] Petitions both supporting and opposing the concept of establishment inundated the legislature. The most prominent antiestablishment petition came from the Hanover Presbytery, and announced a kinship with other faiths. The petition called for a guarantee that "all of every religious sect may be protected in full exercise of their several modes of worship."[159]

The Presbyterians also wrote strongly in favor of disestablishment, declaring that "religious establishments are highly injurious to the temporal interests of any community." Their petition proclaimed: "The only proper objects of civil government are the happiness and protection of men in the present state of existence, the security of the life, liberty, and the property of the citizens, and to restrain the vicious and encourage the virtuous by wholesome laws equally extending to every individual." By contrast, "the duty which we owe our Creator and the manner of discharging it can only be directed by reason and conviction and is nowhere cognizable but at the tribunal of the Universal Judge."

Concurrently, Jefferson drafted a bill for repealing "the several laws establishing the . . . Church of England" and prepared an outline of arguments in favor of disestablishment to present to the legislature.[160] Following the language of the Declaration of Independence written only a few months before, he stated that freedom of religion was an "unalienable right" that no person was capable of surrendering. Jefferson's notes showed that he would argue that uniformity in religion was no more necessary than uniformity in philosophy, and that any attempt to achieve religious unanimity would result in "suffoctg. free enqry." Of equal importance, Jefferson argued, such uniformity was unattainable. Noting that millions had been burnt, tortured, fined, and imprisoned because of their religious nonconformity, he observed simply, "yet men differ."

Even though some vestiges of the old establishment remained, Jefferson obtained much of what he wanted. The final bill, approved on December 9, 1776, declared any existing law "which renders criminal the maintaining any opinions in matters of religion, forbearing to repair to church, or the exercising any mode of worship whatsoever" would be of "no validity or force."[161]

The legislature also agreed to exempt "dissenters of whatever denomination" from having to pay taxes for "supporting and maintaining the [Anglican] church as it now is or hereafter may be established
and its ministers." Recognizing that once dissenters were exempt from
taxation to support the church, the resulting assessment imposed on
church members "may be too burthensome," the legislature decided
that, effective January 1, 1777, the fee levied on them should be "suspended . . . until the end of the next session of Assembly." Although it
could not be known at the time, this marked the end of state funding
of religion in Virginia. The suspension was continually extended until
the tax was explicitly eliminated three years later; no religious taxes
were assessed in Virginia after January 1, 1777.[162]

If taxes for a specific church were to be disallowed, proponents of
state support for religion argued, a general assessment, to benefit all
religions, might still be proper. The legislature could not agree on the
wisdom of such a tax and, in rather unusual language, explicitly de-
ferred the issue to a later time: "To the End therefore that so important
a Subject may in no Sort be prejudged, . . . nothing in this Act contained
shall be construed to affect or influence the said Question of a general
Assessment or voluntary Contribution in any respect whatever."[163]

Besides the question of a general assessment, Virginia had taken
advantage of the opportunity presented by the Revolution to commit
itself to a broad understanding of freedom of religion. True, there remained some residual discrimination in favor of the Anglican Church.
For example, only Protestant ministers were licensed to perform marriages, and non-Anglican ministers could perform marriages only
in their own county. No more than four dissenting ministers of any
denomination could be licensed in any county; these limitations did
not apply to Anglican ministers.[164] Similarly, the Anglican Church
retained some unique legal advantages in its ability to possess and
dispose of property.[165]

Nonetheless, adherents of all faiths in Virginia were acknowledged to have the right to exercise their religion freely. The state constitution declared that the right to be treated as an equal member of society was not to depend on one's religion, and people were no longer forced to support a religion with which they disagreed. The other state constitutions that were drafted after Virginia's, however, did not reflect this understanding of freedom of religion.

RELIGIOUS FREEDOM IN THE OTHER STATE CONSTITUTIONS

The next state to enact a constitution was New Jersey, on July 2, 1776. While guaranteeing each citizen the "inestimable privilege of worshipping Almighty God in a manner agreeable to the dictates of his own conscience," New Jersey decreed that only those "professing a belief in the faith of any Protestant sect" were eligible to be "elected into any office of profit or trust."[166] Catholics and Jews were barred.

Delaware drafted its constitution on September 10, 1776. It limited all elected positions, as well as any other "office or place of trust," to Christians. Each officeholder was required to take an oath stating: "I, A. B., do profess faith in God the Father, and in Jesus Christ His only Son, and in the Holy Ghost, one God, blessed for evermore; and I do acknowledge the holy scriptures of the Old and New Testament to be given by divine inspiration."[167]

In Pennsylvania, even Benjamin Franklin was unable to persuade the state's Constitutional Convention to adopt as complete a freedom for religion as Virginia's.[168] Pennsylvania's Provincial Conference met in June 1776 to call a state Constitutional Convention, and on June 21, the attendees voted to require all convention delegates to take a religious oath attesting that they "profess faith in God the Father, and in Jesus Christ his eternal Son, the true God, and in the Holy Spirit, one God blessed for evermore; and . . . acknowledge the Holy Scriptures of the old and new testament to be given by divine inspiration."[169]

Many voiced their objections to the religious oath. Benjamin Rush argued that "no man whose morals were good by walking uprightly amongst his neighbours should be exempted" and that there were "good men who did not believe in the Divinity of the Son of God"—although, he made sure to point out, "I am not one of that class." James Cannon, a mathematics professor who would later serve at the state Constitutional Convention, was far less temperate, assailing those who insisted on a religious oath as "fools, blockheads, self righteous, and zealous bigots."[170]

Surprisingly, when the Pennsylvania Constitutional Convention met in July, the delegates, all of whom had taken the oath, voted initially to delete all references to Christianity in the oath to be required under the new state constitution. This draft simply required officeholders to assert a belief in "one God the Creator and Governor of the Universe."[171] Christopher Marshall, a Quaker who had been "disowned" by the Philadelphia Monthly Meeting of the Society of Friends because of charges that he had produced and distributed counterfeit currency,[172] led the fight to reinstate the Provincial Conference's language. When he saw the new draft oath, he wrote in his diary, "farewell Christianity when Turks, Jews, infidels, & what is worse Deists and Atheists are to make laws for our State."[173]

As the public learned of the draft, strong opposition arose from those who desired a more Christian oath. One essay, written under the name "A Follower of Christ," warned that the oath would remove a "bar against professed Deists, Jews, Mahomedans, and other enemies of Christ" and create "a firmer establishment for Antichrist, and all damnable errors, than the Quebec bill for Popery." The author concluded: "If blasphemers of Christ and the holy blessed Trinity, despisers of Revelation and the holy bible, may be Legislators, Judges, Counsellors and Presidents in Pennsylvania, Wo unto the city! Wo unto the land."[174]

The convention voted to change the oath to require all members of the legislature to assert: "I do believe in one God, the creator and governor of the universe, the rewarder of the good and punisher of the wicked, and I do acknowledge the scriptures of the Old and New Testament to be given by Divine Inspiration." Even though this language effectively limited the assembly to Christians, some in favor of a stronger oath still complained that it did not explicitly mention Christianity or Jesus Christ. Henry Muhlenberg, a German Lutheran preacher, wrote angrily in his diary, "Very well, you smart chief-fabricators with your refined taste, you have acted very cleverly in allowing nothing concerning a Savior of the world and His religion to slip in, . . . Your heathen morality has putrid sources and your wild and tainted flesh abhors the salt of Christian morality."[175]

Benjamin Franklin, as president of the convention, tried unsuccessfully to retain the more inclusive language of the original draft, but, as he lamented, he was "overpower'd by Numbers."[176] He noted that "the Evil of it was the less, as no Inhabitant, nor any Officer of Government" other than members of the Assembly was required to take the oath. He also was able to claim one victory. To defend against the possibility that future legislatures might require stricter religious oaths, he managed to have an additional clause inserted,[177] declaring that "no further or other religious test shall ever hereafter be required of any civil officer or magistrate in this State."[178]

Apart from the oath, the Pennsylvania Constitution of 1776 granted broad protection for religious freedom, covering all religions. Article 2 of the Declaration of Rights stated that "all men have a natural and unalienable right to worship Almighty God according to the dictates of their own consciences and understanding."[179] The declaration further provided that no "man, who acknowledges the being of a God, be justly deprived or abridged of any civil right as a citizen, on account of his religious sentiments or peculiar mode of religious worship." The only group excluded was atheists.

The next state to prepare a constitution was Maryland, and it used the drafting of a new charter to end its establishment of the Church of England. Maryland did reserve the right to impose a "general and equal tax for the support of the Christian religion," but the state legislature never approved such a tax. While not providing full religious equality, Maryland also ended its restrictions on Catholics. The state constitution declared that religious liberty, as well as the right to any public office, would be available to people "professing the Christian religion."[180]

The rest of the southern states quickly enacted their new constitutions. All three states, North Carolina in 1776, Georgia in 1777, and South Carolina in 1778, were far more hostile to Catholics. While granting a general right to worship, each restricted the right of holding political office to Protestants.[181]

Moreover, while North Carolina and Georgia simply ended their establishments, South Carolina replaced its former establishment of the Church of England with a Protestant establishment. The South Carolina Constitution proclaimed: "The Christian Protestant religion shall be deemed, and is hereby constituted and declared to be, the established religion of this State" and mandated a five-point creed for every church wishing to be "esteemed as a church of the established religion of this State."[182]

While New York officially repudiated any religious establishment,[183] John Jay tried to incorporate similar anti-Catholic provisions into the New York state constitution. In March 1777, he proposed that the guarantee of "free toleration of religious profession and worship" exclude "the professors of the religion of the church of Rome, who ought not to hold lands in, or be admitted to a participation of the civil rights enjoyed by the members of this State, until . . . they renounce and believe to be false and wicked, the dangerous and damnable doctrine, that the pope, or any other earthly authority, have power to absolve men from sins."[184]

When his proposal was rejected, Jay tried a more indirect approach, drafting language denying freedom to religions that "encourage licentiousness or [are] used in such manner as to disturb or endanger the safety of the state." Gouverneur Morris, again advocating greater religious freedom, opposed Jay's language because it punished people merely for teaching their religious tenets. Morris proposed compromise language, which the New York convention accepted, limiting the exclusion to bad conduct: "acts of licentiousness" and "practices inconsistent with the peace or safety of this state." The final constitutional language also removed the word "toleration" from the guarantee of religious freedom, substituting protection for "the free exercise and enjoyment of religious profession and worship, without discrimination or preference."

Jay did win one battle for anti-Catholicism. The final New York Constitution barred Catholic immigrants. Immigrants entering the state were required to "renounce all allegiance and subjection to all and every foreign king, prince, potentate, and State in all matters, ecclesiastical as well as civil." Thus, some small role for policing "ecclesiastical" concerns remained in the New York constitution.

Not surprisingly, when Massachusetts prepared its new constitution, it was far more emphatic about preserving a role for government in religious matters. On September 1, 1779, the Massachusetts Constitutional Convention appointed a committee of thirty to draft a constitution and declaration of rights. The committee delegated the drafting to a subcommittee consisting of John Adams, James Bowdoin, and Samuel Adams. Then, according to John Adams, "the sub Committee appointed a Sub sub Committee" assigning him the full task of drafting the document.[185]

Adams retreated to his home in Braintree, where he completed the draft of the entire constitution, except, as he would later report, for the "article relative to religion."[186] Perhaps recognizing the impossibility of reconciling true liberty of conscience with the Massachusetts style of establishment, Adams admitted that he could not draft a provision "consistent with my own sentiments of perfect religious freedom, with any hope of its being adopted by the Convention, so I left it to be battled out in the whole body." He also remarked that he thought "some of the Clergy, or older and graver Persons than myself would be more likely to hit the Taste of the Public."[187] That "older and graver person" turned out to be his cousin Sam, who authored most of the state's constitutional language regarding religion.[188]

After extensive debate and some revision, the convention approved numerous religious provisions.[189] Article II granted broad freedom to practice religion, decreeing that "no subject shall be hurt, molested, or restrained . . . for worshipping God in the manner and season most agreeable to the dictates of his own conscience . . . , provided he doth not disturb the public peace or obstruct others in their religious worship." This was an impressive step for a state whose forebears had executed dissenters who refused to leave the colony.

Nonetheless, Massachusetts's freedom of religion was limited in two ways. First, only Protestants could hold elective office.[190] Jews were excluded by the requirement of an oath attesting "that I believe the Christian religion, and have a firm persuasion of its truth." Catholics who wished to serve were required to renounce the pope and affirm that "no foreign . . . prelate . . . hath, or ought to have, any jurisdiction . . . in any matter, civil, ecclesiastical, or spiritual, within this commonwealth."[191]

Article III, the constitution's other major religious provision, authorized towns to "make suitable provision, at their own expense . . . for the support and maintenance of public Protestant teachers of piety, religion, and morality." Without such funding, many of the proponents of Article III believed, voluntary support for religion would be insufficient. In the words of one member of the Massachusetts convention: "If there is no law to support religion, farewell meeting-houses, farewell ministers, and farewell all religions."[192]

Many of the supporters of Article III claimed that despite the use

of public funds to support a favored religion, Massachusetts's constitution did not create an establishment of religion. This argument is
made in Article III itself, which concludes by declaring "no subordination of any sect or denomination to another shall ever be established by law." A series of newspaper essays written under the name
Hieronymus contended that by not requiring a particular creed, as
the Church of England had done, Massachusetts avoided the "establishment" label: "A religious establishment by law is the establishment
of a particular mode of worshipping God, with rites and ceremonies
peculiar to such mode from which the people are not suffered to
vary."[193] As this argument suggests, even in Massachusetts, the concept of an "establishment" was considered a vestige of colonial times
to be avoided, although its definition was far from clear.

Many other observers, however, saw the public financing of religion as a clear sign of an establishment. John Adams seemed to view
it as "an establishment of Christianity," though one suspects that he
was excluding Catholics from that concept of Christianity.[194] In fact,
the Massachusetts Supreme Court would acknowledge in 1831 that
article 3 was based on the principle that "religious establishment and
public worship ought to be maintained by legal coercion, [and] that
the religion thus to be established and supported ought to be not only
Christianity, but the Protestant Christian religion."[195]

Since the constitution does not specify which Protestant denomination would receive tax money, in its literal language this provision
could be considered the equivalent of a "general assessment."[196] While,
under the previous taxing scheme, public monies were explicitly directed to Congregationalist churches, the 1780 constitution allocated
tax money based on a majority vote in each town.[197] Still, because
Congregationalists made up the majority of most of the state, the
denomination selected as the beneficiary of the public expenditure
"was nearly always a Congregationalist."[198] Moreover, in contrast to
the earlier (at least theoretical) exemptions for Anglicans, Baptists, and

Quakers, Article III required dissenters to pay the tax. For those who belonged to a state-recognized dissenting church, their taxes went to their own pastors. This created obvious problems for Quakers, who did not have ministers, and Baptists, who believed it violated their religion to pay taxes to support even their own ministers.[199] Those who did not go to church at all or who attended an unrecognized church or whose sects were too small to have a minister were required to pay for Congregational ministers.[200] Denominations that arrived after 1780, such as the Methodists, needed to fight long legal battles to obtain state recognition.[201]

Thus, it is not hard to sympathize with Isaac Backus, who declared that the 1780 constitution merely marked "the continuance of the Congregational establishment."[202] He challenged supporters of Article III to consider the issue from a religious dissenter's perspective: "If any suppose that the above article establishes equal religious liberty, let them only change places with us, and empower another denomination to tax them all to religious ministers, and compel them to pay it contrary to their consciences, and then tell them, if they will require the money thus unjustly gathered, they may have it for their own teachers; if not, those who have got it will apply it to support their own party."[203]

Yet Backus was unable to extend his own empathy to all religions. He wrote that he "fully concurred" with the first and last part of Article III.[204] The final part of the Article is an exclusionary provision stating that "every denomination of Christians . . . shall be equally under the protection of the law; and no subordination of any sect or denomination to another shall ever be established by law." The first part of Article III emphasizes the relationship between government and religion: "The happiness of a people and the good order and preservation of civil government essentially depend upon piety, religion, and morality, and . . . these cannot be generally diffused through a community but by the institution of the public worship of God and of the public instructions in piety, religion, and morality." As the historian William McLoughlin wrote, Backus was not able to transcend fully his New England environment. According to McLoughlin, Backus "still believed that the state must encourage religion indirectly. It must acknowledge the truth of the Protestant religion; . . . it must recognize the importance of institutionalized religion as a moral force in society."[205]

A more universal approach can be seen in the writings of Joseph Hawley. Hawley was a member of the Congregational church of Northampton, who refused to take his seat after being elected to the first state Senate under the 1780 constitution.[206] Although the mandated oath accurately encompassed his personal religious beliefs, he wrote to the Senate condemning the religious oath requirement as both "plainly repugnant" to the Constitution's guarantee that "all men are born free and equal" and in violation of the "common right and (as I may say) the natural Franchise of every member of the Commonwealth."[207]

Hawley further argued that the institution of public funding for "the publick worship of God, and for the support and maintenance of publick, protestant teachers . . . is inconsistent with the unalienable rights of conscience."[208] Recognizing the incompatibility between establishment of religion and individual freedom, Hawley pleaded: "Pray give over the impossible (task) of endeavoring to make a religious establishment, (consistent) with the unalienable Rights of Conscience which you can no more effect, with precision and in clear determinate language that you can make a curve line parallel to a straight one."[209]

In 1784, when New Hampshire wrote its constitution, largely copying its religious regulation from the Massachusetts model, the first great experiment in crafting fundamental charters was completed. Together, the states present a complex picture of how the Revolutionary War governments understood the proper relationship between government and religion.

The Church of England, associated with the newly defeated enemy, was no longer established in any state. With New York, Virginia, North Carolina, and Georgia joining the states that never had an establishment, eight states firmly embraced disestablishment as a fundamental principle. Five states had varying degrees of establishment, ranging from Maryland, which permitted, without ever implementing, a tax to benefit Christian churches, to South Carolina, which had established the Christian religion, to the New England states of Massachusetts, Connecticut, and New Hampshire, which maintained establishments that favored Congregational churches.

All states generally allowed people to practice their religions in peace. Rhode Island removed its restriction on Catholic voting by statute in 1783.[210] Most states, however, imposed legal restrictions on non-Protestants. New Jersey, Delaware, North Carolina, Georgia, South Carolina, and Vermont barred Catholics, Jews, and other non-Protestants from serving in the government. Jews, but not Catholics, were excluded from the legislatures of Pennsylvania and Maryland, while South Carolina limited voting rights to those who believed in God. Each state's laws reflected its local concerns and varying degrees of religious homogeneity.

GEORGE WASHINGTON AND
RELIGIOUS FREEDOM IN THE MILITARY

George Washington, on the other hand, was charged with bringing together the full spectrum of America's diverse population. As commander in chief during the Revolutionary War, he was the leader of the only institution that was national in scope.[211] The very nature of military readiness required him to find ways "to keep religious friction at a minimum in the army."[212] Sensitivity to different religions was necessary, as he wrote John Hancock in 1777, so as not "to excite by any act, the smallest uneasiness & jealousy among the Troops."[213]

The need for military cohesion dovetailed with Washington's personal acceptance of religious differences. As many have observed, he appears to have been "one of the very few men of the Revolution who had, in 1775, outgrown or overcome all religious prejudices in religious matters."[214] Both necessity and conviction led Washington to take strong public stands against religious bigotry.

Just as he had instructed Benedict Arnold to "avoid all Disrespect or Contempt" of the Catholicism of the French Canadians, Washington tried to combat anti-Catholic sentiment among his own troops.[215] On November 5, 1775, Washington issued an impassioned order barring soldiers from participating in Pope's Day, which he described as the "ridiculous and childish Custom of burning the Effigy of the pope."[216] In the order, he expressed amazement that "there should be Officers and Soldiers, in this army so void of common sense, as not to see the impropriety of such a step at this Juncture." Especially while trying to solicit Canadian support, Washington wrote, "to be insulting their Religion, is so monstrous, as not to be suffered, or excused."

This order apparently had an effect not only on the military, but on the general population as well. There are no recorded instances of Pope Day celebrations in America after 1775.[217] In his 1908 study *The Irish in the American Revolution,* James Haltigan declared that Pope Day "received its death blow . . . at the hands of the noble Washington."[218]

Another example of Washington's public welcoming of unpopular religions can be seen in his treatment of John Murray, the founder of Universalism in America. Murray had earned the enmity of the orthodox New England clergy by preaching a doctrine of universal salvation.[219] In May 1775, officers of the Rhode Island brigade, led by Major General Nathanael Greene, requested that Murray be named the brigade chaplain. As Murray described it, his selection was opposed by the rest of the military clergy: "the chaplains of the army united in petitioning" Washington not to appoint him.[220] Rather than shun the outcast, Washington had dinner with him and Greene on September

10,[221] and one week later issued a strict order: "The Revd Mr John Murray is appointed Chaplain to the Rhode-Island Regiments and is to be respected as such."[222]

The only religious group General Washington did not fully accept was the Quakers. As a military leader, he was suspicious of their refusal to join the battle against the British. In military orders, he would refer to "the unfriendly Quakers and others Notoriously disaffected to the Cause of American Liberty."[223] He ordered that they be intercepted on their way to their general meeting in Philadelphia and turned back. As he instructed Brigadier General John Lacey, "This is an intercourse that we should by all means endeavour to interrupt, as the plans settled at these meetings are of the pernicious tendency."[224]

Washington's defenders are quick to point out that he could also show kindness to Quakers.[225] For example, when Quakers requested permission to pass through military checkpoints to visit family members who had been exiled to Virginia during the war, Washington approved, noting, "As they seem much distressed, humanity pleads strongly in their behalf."[226] Still he did not believe that Quakers were to be trusted as a group until after the war had ended.

In addition to respecting the religious diversity of those under his command, Washington urged, and sometimes ordered, his soldiers to attend religious services and avoid irreligious and impious behavior. These orders seem to have come from "his belief that religion and public worship were essential to morale among soldiers"[227] as well as his growing sense "that Providence was playing a major role in the progress of the American cause."[228] Several times during the course of the war, he ordered his troops to observe days of thanksgiving. These orders often followed calls by either local governments or the Continental Congress. After Congress called for a day of thanksgiving on December 18, 1777, he ordered: "The Chaplains will properly notice this recommendation, that the day of thanksgiving may be duly observed in the army, agreeably to the intentions of Congress."[229]

Washington also issued several thanksgiving-day proclamations on his own. After France agreed to join the fight against the British, he issued the following statement: "It having pleased the Almighty ruler of the Universe propitiously to defend the Cause of the United American-States and finally by raising us up a powerful Friend among the Princes of the Earth to establish our liberty and Independence upon lasting foundations, it becomes us to set apart a day for gratefully acknowledging the divine Goodness & celebrating the important Event which we owe to his benign Interposition."[230]

Similar orders for thanksgiving days were issued after victories at the battles of Monmouth and Yorktown.[231] In addition, Washington frequently required his troops "to hear divine service from their respective chaplains."[232] In his second general order after he arrived in Cambridge, Massachusetts, to take command of the army, he ordered "all Officers, and Soldiers, not engaged on actual duty, a punctual attendance on divine service, to implore the blessings of heaven upon the means used for our safety and defence."[233] In 1778 at Valley Forge, he ordered all officers to attend "divine Service" every Sunday, in order to "set an Example to their men."[234]

To Washington, irreligious conduct not only was offensive but also risked angering a God whose support was very much needed. In an order forbidding "the foolish, and wicked practice, of profane cursing and swearing," Washington warned: "We can have little hopes of the blessing of Heaven on our Arms, if we insult it by our impiety, and folly."[235] In multiple public communications during the war, Washington actively sought "the blessing of Heaven on our Arms."[236] "The blessing and protection of Heaven are at all times necessary," he wrote, "but especially so in times of public distress and danger."[237] Preparing his soldiers for a major battle in 1776, Washington exhorted his troops: "Let us therefore rely upon the goodness of the Cause, and the aid of the supreme Being, in whose hands Victory is, to animate and encourage us to great and noble Actions."[238]

While much of Washington's public speech during the war was religious in nature, he usually avoided sectarian or Christian language.
In 1777, when Washington repeated Congress's call for the December
18 day of thanksgiving, he quoted only part of the congressional language. He repeated the start of the proclamation that Samuel Adams
had written, but omitted Adams's references to the "merits of Jesus
Christ" and "the Holy Ghost."[239]

Yet there were a few noteworthy examples when General Washington used expressly Christian language in speaking to his troops. In
1776, urging the soldiers to "attend carefully upon religious exercises,"
he declared: "The General hopes and trusts, that every officer, and
man, will endeavour so to live, and act, as becomes a Christian Soldier
defending the dearest Rights and Liberties of his country."[240] In 1778, he
again asked the troops to attend Sunday services and reminded them:
"While we are zealously performing the duties of good Citizens and
soldiers we certainly ought not to be inattentive to the higher duties of
Religion—To the distinguished Character of Patriot, it should be our
highest Glory to add the more distinguished Character of Christian."[241]

Washington's most famous Christian reference came at the end of
one of his final acts as commander in chief. On June 8, 1783, he wrote
a letter, generally referred to as the "Circular Letter," to the governors
of the thirteen states.[242] This was a 4,000-word document, totaling
thirty-six pages when printed as a pamphlet, meant to convince the
individual states of the need to cede more power to a central government.[243] Its genesis, as Washington wrote to Alexander Hamilton,
was Washington's "inclination to contribute my mite in pointing out
the defects of the present constitution" (referring to the Articles of
Confederation).[244]

In the Circular Letter, Washington declared that "it is indispensable to the happiness of the individual States, that there should be
lodged somewhere, a Supreme Power to regulate and govern the general concerns of the Confederated Republic." Additionally, he called

on the governors to repay the monies owed to the veterans, saying it was "more than a common debt, it is a debt of honour."

The lengthy letter closed with this paragraph:

> I now make it my earnest prayer, that God would have you, and the State over which you preside, in his holy protection, that he would incline the hearts of the Citizens to cultivate a spirit of subordination and obedience to Government, to entertain a brotherly affection and love for one another, for their fellow Citizens of the United States at large, and particularly for their brethren who have served in the Field, and finally, that he would most graciously be pleased to dispose us all, to do Justice, to love mercy, and to demean ourselves with that Charity, humility and pacific temper of mind, which were the Characteristicks of the Divine Author of our blessed Religion, and without an humble imitation of whose example in these things, we can never hope to be a happy Nation.

Before analyzing this paragraph, let us consider two different, misleading presentations of the Circular Letter that have been offered in an attempt to render this writing more religious than it was. The more extreme of the two was a nineteenth-century rewriting that added orthodox reverential language from the Episcopal prayer book.[245] Here, with the additional words italicized, is the altered version:

> *Almighty God; We make our* earnest prayer that *Thou wilt keep* the United States in *Thy* Holy protection; that *Thou wilt* incline the hearts of the Citizens to cultivate a spirit of subordination and obedience to Government, and entertain a brotherly affection and love for one another and for their fellow Citizens of the United States at large.
> And finally that *Thou wilt* most graciously be pleased to dispose us all to do justice, to love mercy, and to demean ourselves with that Charity, humility, and pacific temper of mind which were the Characteristics of the Divine Author of our blessed Religion, and without a humble imitation of whose example in these things we can never hope to be a happy nation.
> *Grant our supplication, we beseech Thee, through Jesus Christ our Lord. Amen.*

This ersatz version appears with surprising frequency. It is engraved on a chapel marker in front of St. Paul's Chapel in New York City[246] and is "beautifully illuminated on vellum in nine colors and gold" in the Washington Memorial Chapel at Valley Forge.[247] It is repeatedly used by the United States Senate chaplains as their daily prayer[248] and has been quoted by politicians in an attempt to prove that Washington considered the United States a "Christian Nation."[249] Yet it is a manifestly false version of what Washington wrote.

There is a subtler misuse of the Circular Letter, even from commentators who acknowledge the edited version as "erroneous."[250] These commentators quote Washington's actual language, but insist on separating the final paragraph of the Circular Letter from the rest of the long document and presenting it alone as "Washington's Prayer."[251] The solitary paragraph is offered as a freestanding supplication, "a very real prayer," as authors Michael and Jana Novak describe it.[252]

Such a presentation is misleading for two reasons. First, the paragraph was never offered as a prayer. It was a small part of a completely secular and highly political document. Second, without this context, the meaning of the phrase "I now make it my earnest prayer" is altered. Seen as the beginning of a disconnected statement, that language does indeed appear to be the introduction to a religious invocation. But in its real context, as the close of a thirty-six-page letter, the phrase clearly meant "I hope" or "I wish."

This secular meaning of the word "prayer" was a common component of its eighteenth-century dictionary definition. Samuel Johnson's 1768 dictionary, for example, gives two definitions for "prayer": "Petition to heaven" and an "Entreaty; submissive importunity."[253]

Equally relevant is the fact that Washington often used the word "prayer" in an unquestionably secular context. For example, in attempting to change the depth requirement of a canal to be built by the Potomac River Company from four feet deep to two feet, Washington wrote: "Enclosed you have a petition from the Directors of the potomac Company, which we pray you to lay before the Maryland Assembly . . . The measure prayed for is so reasonable, that we do not conceive there can be any other opposition given to it."[254] Similarly, in rejecting an officer's request for promotion during the Revolutionary War, Washington wrote, "In respect to Lieut. Colo. Dirk, I do not find that there is any necessity for granting the prayer of his Petition."[255]

The misrepresentations about the Circular Letter are part of a broad pattern of exaggerations and falsehoods concerning George Washington and religion. It is not merely the cherry tree fable that became part of American lore: a host of fabricated or exaggerated stories about Washington's public expressions of religion have been introduced into his biography.[256] These misstatements matter because they distract from an honest appraisal of Washington's public statements and prevent a clear understanding of his complicated view of the proper relationship between government and religion. Ironically, they also harm the cause of those who rely on Washington to justify a greater role for government in discussing and encouraging religion, since the misquotations focus attention on the inaccuracies rather than on the language he actually used.

Returning to the real Circular Letter and considering the final paragraph in its proper context, the description of the "humility" of "the Divine Author of our blessed Religion" is "unmistakably a reference to Jesus Christ."[257] The final paragraph of Washington's long missive was deeply pious, a clearly Christian ending to his call to the governors for a stronger national government. Thus, while it is not by any means a "prayer," the statement shows Washington using Christian terminology in a serious, public way to communicate an important political appeal.

Those wishing to draw modern lessons from the Circular Letter, however, must recognize an important caveat. This was the last official utterance in which Washington used Christian terminology. As president, when he used religious discourse in his public communication, he carefully, and without exception, chose inclusive, nonsectarian language.

CONGRESS AND THE AITKEN BIBLE

But in the early 1780s, such circumspection was not considered by Washington, or most of those in government, as necessary or even desirable. The Continental Congress, in particular, did not avoid what the Supreme Court would today term the endorsement or support of religion, most particularly the Protestant religion.

Consider the response of the Continental Congress to calls for help when members of the clergy faced a shortage of Bibles. Before the Revolution, the printing of Bibles was strictly licensed under British law, and licenses had been granted to only three presses, all in England.[258] Thus, there were no printers of Bibles in America. The Revolutionary War created a severe scarcity of Bibles,[259] and in July 1777, three Presbyterian ministers from Philadelphia sent a petition to Congress, "humbly requesting that under your care, & by your encouragement, a Copy of the holy Bible may be printed."[260] A committee consisting of John Adams, Daniel Roberdeau, and Jonathan Bayard Smith was set up to respond.[261] They wrote to several local printers, informing them that "the Congress desire to have a bible printed under their care & by their encouragement" and requested estimates of the cost and time it would take to print them.[262]

The printers' answers indicated that the expense of acquiring sufficient type and paper was prohibitive. In its report to Congress, the committee stated that because "the use of the Bible is so universal, and its importance so great," it recommended that Congress pay "to import 20,000 Bibles from Holland, Scotland, or elsewhere."[263] Though Congress approved the recommendation on September 11, 1777, advancing British troops forced them to evacuate Philadelphia soon after, and no further action was taken on the issue.[264]

A few years later, a Philadelphia printer, Robert Aitken, decided to print his own copies of the Bible and sought congressional assistance. Aitken was well connected, having previously served as the printer for the *Journals of Congress*.[265] He made two specific requests. On January 21, 1781, he requested that his Bibles be said to "be published under the authority of Congress" and that he be formally "commissioned or otherwise appointed & authorized to print and vend Editions of the Sacred Scriptures."[266] Later, on September 9, 1782, he asked Congress to assist him financially by purchasing one-fourth of his stock, or about 2,500 Bibles.[267]

Congress then forwarded a copy of Aitken's Bible to its two chaplains, William White and George Duffield, and asked them "to examine and give their opinion" of the work. The chaplains reported back positively, stating that Aitken's printing of the Bible "is executed with great accuracy as to the sense, and with as few grammatical and typographical errors as could be expected in an undertaking of such magnitude." They also reminded Congress that Aitken had printed the books "at the evident risk of private fortune."[268]

After receiving the chaplains' report, Congress decided not to extend any direct financial assistance but instead to permit Aitken to publicize his Bible as having been officially recommended by Congress:

> Whereupon, Resolved, That the United States in Congress assembled, highly approve the pious and laudable undertaking of Mr. Aitken, as subservient to the interest of religion as well as an instance of the progress of arts in this country, and being satisfied from the above report, of his care and accuracy in the execution of the work, they recommend this edition of the Bible to the inhabitants of the United States, and hereby authorise him to publish this recommendation in the manner he shall think proper.[269]

Aitken accepted what he was given and printed Congress's recommendation on the front pages of his Bible.[270] But the congressional seal of approval apparently was not as valuable as he had hoped. Years later, he wrote to Washington complaining of his "exceedingly heavy" losses suffered because the market had become so "glutted . . . with Bibles that I was obliged to sell mine much below prime cost; and in the End, I actually Sunk above £3000 by the impression."[271]

As with Washington's Circular Letter, many have misrepresented the story of the Aitken Bible. In the distorted retelling, the Continental Congress "assumed all the rights and performed all the duties of a Bible society long before such an institution had an existence"[272] and helped publish the "Bible of the Revolution."[273] One the other hand, some who want to belittle the religious significance of the congressional action try to prove that Congress was really focused on mercantile concerns, specifically the creation of an American printing industry. They highlight the secular benefit of the resolution, particularly the phrase approving Aitken's Bible as "an instance of the progress of arts in this country."[274]

The reality is that even without serving as a "Bible society," the Continental Congress felt it was appropriate for a legislative body to import, review, and endorse the Bible. As the historian Derek Davis wrote, there were no contemporaneous objections to these activities "on the grounds that it violated some nascent notion of the separation of church and state."[275] Similarly, Congress felt no need to check the accuracy of Aitken's publication with a Catholic priest or a rabbi; the judgment of Congress's Protestant chaplains was sufficient.

At the time independence was won, government at both the state and congressional levels was expected to be intertwined, in varying degrees, with religion. Furthermore, the religion that government was to support was not a generic concept, encompassing all faiths. Even though South Carolina was the only state to proclaim officially that "the Christian Protestant religion shall be . . . the established religion of this State," there was a general consensus that Protestantism was the faith of the colonies. The near-unanimous reaction to the Quebec Act reveals that both individually and collectively, the colonies viewed themselves, in the words of the Address to the People of Great Britain, as "free, Protestant colonies."[276] The colonists did not see Catholics as part of a shared faith, instead proclaiming, in the words of the Continental Congress, their "dissimilarity of religion."[277]

Still, tremendous progress had been made from the days of executing Quakers and exiling Baptists. Discrimination surely persisted; other than Rhode Island, every state treated some of its residents as second-class citizens because of religion, whether by discriminating against non-Anglicans, non-Protestants, non-Christians, or Catholics. Nonetheless, most people of minority faiths were finally left free to practice their religion. Even if not necessarily welcomed, they were permitted to worship in peace.

In the language of its time, the country that won the Revolutionary War was a tolerant, Protestant nation.

CHAPTER 3

The Second American Revolution

THE PERIOD between the end of the Revolutionary War in 1783 and the framing of the Constitution in 1787 was a volatile time for the new nation. The Confederation Congress, still working under the Articles of Confederation, was largely ineffective in either uniting the disparate states into a common peacetime entity or shaping a national identity. The individual states were free to experiment, and Virginia, in 1786, launched what became in effect a second American Revolution. Just as the first Revolution brought a total break from both the king and the philosophical underpinnings of monarchy, this second revolution would lead to a new, fully American way of thinking about the relationship between government and religion.

The battle for the enactment of Thomas Jefferson's "Bill for Establishing Religious Freedom" began in 1776, when Virginia's House of Delegates created a Committee of Revisors to rewrite the entire set of the state's laws. Jefferson saw this as an opportunity to shake off the remnants of the colonial system and create a legal code "adapted to our republican form of government . . . with a single eye to reason, and the good of those for whose government it was framed."[1] It took several years for the committee, with Jefferson as the driving force, to finish their proposal for rewriting Virginia's laws. They finally presented their collection of 126 proposals in 1779.

On June 12, one of those proposals, the "Bill for Establishing Religious Freedom" was introduced into the House of Delegates.[2] It contained a long preamble, stating that "the opinions of men are not the object of civil government, nor under its jurisdiction." The law declared an absolute freedom of worship as well as a total ban on governmental attempts to either collect money for religious activities or reward those of a favored religion: "No man shall be compelled to frequent or support any religious worship, place, or ministry whatsoever, nor shall be enforced, restrained, molested, or burthened in his body or goods, nor shall otherwise suffer, on account of his religious opinions or belief; but that all men shall be free to profess, and by argument to maintain, their opinions in matters of religion, and that the same shall in no wise diminish, enlarge, or affect their civil capacities."[3]

The legislature voted to postpone the bill, effectively killing it.[4] Over the summer, petitions were sent to the legislature concerning Jefferson's proposal. While several supported the bill, many others were opposed. One petition from Essex, for example, announced that the signors, "being much alarmed at the appearance of a Bill entitled Religious Freedom, consider it very injurious to the Christian Religion." The petition urged the House to reject that bill and instead pass legislation permitting only a person "being a Protestant" and "professing the Christian Religion" to hold government office; forbidding "all Licentious and Itinerant Preachers [from the] collecting or Assembling of Negroes"; and creating a "general assessment for the support of Religious Worship."[5]

Momentum moved away from universal religious freedom and toward an active role for the government in promoting religion. On October 25, 1779, James Henry, a second cousin of Patrick Henry,[6] introduced a bill "for the encouragement of Religion and virtue."[7] The bill declared that the "Christian Religion" was to be "deemed and held to be the established Religion of this Commonwealth," with "all Denominations of Christians" entitled to equal civil privileges. To be considered a "Church of the Established Religion," a religious society had to agree to five articles of faith:

> First, That there is one Eternal God and a future State of Rewards and punishments.
> Secondly, That God is publickly to be Worshiped.
> Thirdly, That the Christian Religion is the true Religion.
> Fourthly, That the Holy Scriptures of the old and new Testament are of divine inspiration, and are the only rule of Faith.
> Fifthly, That it is the duty of every Man, when thereunto called by those who Govern, to bear witness to truth.

The fourth statement, that the old and new testaments were "the only rule of Faith," was apparently written to deny papal authority and exclude Catholics from the state's new establishment.[8]

For the "permanent encouragement" of "providing a sufficient number of ministers and teachers," the bill also created a "general assessment." Taxpayers could direct that their payment go to whatever "denomination of Christian he or she would choose to contribute." For those who did not so direct, for religious or other reasons, the tax would still be assessed and apportioned "between the several Religious Societies in the parish in which such person or persons shall reside." As the historian Thomas Curry noted, "The process of drawing up a general assessment bill demonstrated the narrowness of its proponents' views. Having championed religion as the bulwark of a stable society, they now revealed that by religion they meant Christianity."[9]

Despite the growing support for this bill, enough opposition arose that it was put aside. Thus, neither Jefferson's bill for religious freedom nor the general assessment survived the 1779 legislative sessions.

But one very significant law concerning religion was passed. The assessment to support the Anglican Church had been suspended since 1776, but the authorization for such a tax remained on the books. On November 18, George Mason presented a bill to officially delete the authorization. While Mason's proposal passed, the assembly removed his provocative preamble, which had declared the law's purpose: "To remove from the good People of this Commonwealth the Fear of being compelled to contribute to the Support or Maintenance of the former established Church, And that the Members of the said Church may no longer relye upon the Expectation of any Re-establishment thereof."[10] Even without the preamble, Mason's law codified the end of preferential tax support for the Anglican Church in Virginia.

The Anglican Church's fears about the ending of governmental support were well founded. Deprived of the revenue from what had been the largest single tax in Virginia,[11] Anglican ministers began leaving their parishes and became increasingly difficult to replace.[12] In 1776, Virginia's Anglican church had ninety-one ministers serving ninety-five parishes; by 1785, those numbers had dropped to just thirty-eight ministers for seventy-two parishes.[13]

There were renewed calls for a general assessment to support the ministry. On November 8, 1783, Anglicans from Lunenburg filed a petition with the assembly stating that since the end of governmental support, "we have with pain and regrett, seen the propagation of the Gospel die away in many parts of the country; and its diligent and faithful Ministers neglected."[14] Richard Henry Lee, in a 1784 letter to James Madison, stressed the difficulty of obtaining voluntary financial support for ministers and churches: "He must be a very inattentive observer in our Country, who does not see that avarice is accomplishing the destruction of religion, for want of a legal obligation to contribute something to its support."[15]

Another concern arose in Virginia as well. In the words of George Mason, "among us a depravity of manners and morals prevails, to the destruction of all confidence between man and man."[16] Many Virginians linked the perceived decline of morality to the lack of governmental financing for religion. In his letter to Madison, Lee had advocated a general assessment as necessary to support "our morals," since

"Refiners may weave as fine a web of reason as they please, but the experience of all times shews Religion to be the guardian of morals."[17]

Starting in November 1783, newspaper articles and petitions across the state lobbied for a general assessment.[18] By the following spring, it was clear that this effort had been effective. On May 15, 1784, Edmund Randolph wrote to Thomas Jefferson, informing him that the general assessment would be at the top of the agenda of the next session of the assembly.[19] Randolph added that the assessment "has Henry for its patron in private but whether he will hazard himself in public cannot be yet ascertained."

Patrick Henry did indeed take the lead in fighting for the assessment. On one level, his support of this cause is surprising, since he had a well-earned reputation as an opponent of the Anglican Church and a defender of the rights of religious dissenters. He had first obtained public notoriety in "The Parson's Cause" in 1763, by arguing against the claims of Anglican ministers. Traditionally, Anglican clergy had been paid with sixteen thousand pounds of tobacco each year. When drought reduced the tobacco crop, local vestrymen had substituted payment of two pence per pound of tobacco, greatly reducing the ministers' earnings.[20] One minister, the Reverend Maury, sued, and the court ruled that the substituted payment was illegal. The only issue that remained was the amount of damages to be awarded. The twenty-seven-year-old Henry was brought in to argue for the vestrymen.

It was Henry's argument before the court that first earned him the reputation as the greatest orator in America. With the law favoring the ministers, Henry delivered a scathing denunciation of the quality and morality of the Anglican clergy in Virginia:

> We have heard a great deal about the benevolence and holy zeal of our reverend clergy, but how is this manifested? Do they manifest their zeal in the cause of religion and humanity by practising the mild and benevolent precepts of the Gospel of Jesus? Do they feed

the hungry and clothe the naked? Oh, no, gentlemen! Instead of feeding the hungry and clothing the naked, these rapacious harpies would, were their powers equal to their will, snatch from the hearth of their honest parishioner his last hoe-cake, from the widow and her orphan children their last [milk] cow! the last bed, nay, the last blanket from the lying-in woman![21]

At the conclusion of Henry's address, the crowd in the courtroom erupted in cheers. The jury deliberated for five minutes and awarded Maury one penny.[22]

Henry also defended Baptists who were being harassed by the established order. Legend has it that in 1773, he not only obtained the release of a Baptist minister who had been jailed for his preaching, but also anonymously paid the hefty jail fees assessed against the minister so that he could go free.[23]

Patrick Henry did not see his advocacy of a general assessment to support the Christian religion as inconsistent with his earlier positions. He was, after all, seeking not to reestablish the Anglican Church but to help religion, or at least Christianity, in general. Dissenters would have their tax money used to support their own churches, not those of the Anglicans. Though Jefferson and Madison would disagree, many shared the view of the historian Steven Waldman that Henry's plan was "a broad-minded, tolerant, and pluralistic proposal."[24]

The assessment was not the only religious issue coming before the Virginia legislature. The Protestant Episcopal Church, which the Anglicans had adopted as their new name, filed a petition to have itself incorporated.[25] The request for incorporation was not in itself unreasonable, since it would enable the church to better control its own property and otherwise interact with the rest of society. Nonetheless, many saw it as the first step to reestablishing the Episcopal Church in Virginia. At that time there were no general incorporation laws, and individual entities wishing to incorporate needed to obtain specific approval from the legislature. Additionally, incorporation would have resulted in detailed statutory provisions regulating many of the specifics of church policy and practices. Thus, the Episcopal incorporation petition had the look, and perhaps the effect, of special pleading. A leading Presbyterian, John Blair Smith, wrote Madison, urging him to oppose the request on the grounds that the petition represented "an express attempt to draw the State into an illicit connexion & commerce with" the Episcopal Church.[26] By asking for the legislature "'to *Enable*' them to regulate all the spiritual concerns of that Church," Smith added, the Episcopalian petition invited "the Legislature . . . to consider itself as the head of that Party. . . . I am sorry that Christian Ministers should virtually declare their Church a mere political machine, which the State may regulate at pleasure."

In October 1784, as a new session of the Virginia Assembly began, Patrick Henry prepared to introduce both the incorporation and general assessment bills. Thomas Jefferson was out of the country, having joined Benjamin Franklin and John Adams as a minister to France. The leadership void among those opposed to Henry's bills was filled by James Madison. As Edmund Randolph had predicted to Jefferson, "This renders it probable, that our friend of Orange will step earlier into the heat of battle, than his modesty would otherwise permit."[27]

On November 11, 1784, Madison and Henry faced each other on the floor of the assembly as they debated the general assessment. As the future Virginia governor Beverley Randolph portrayed the conflict:

> The Generals on the opposite sides were Henry & Madison. The former advocated with his usual art, the establishment of the Christian Religion in exclusion of all other Denominations. By this I mean that Turks, Jews & Infidels were to contribute, to the support of a Religion whose truth they did not acknowledge. Madison displayed great Learning & Ingenuity, with all the Powers of a close reasoner; but he was unsuccessful in the Event, having a majority of 17 against him.[28]

But Madison had not lost the ultimate battle. The vote Randolph referred to was simply on Henry's resolution to draw up a general assessment bill on the principle that "the people of this Commonwealth, according to their respective abilities, ought to pay a moderate tax or contribution annually for the support of the Christian religion."[29] A committee was named to prepare this bill, and Henry was appointed its chairman.[30]

The prospects for the assessment grew even stronger on November 12 when the Presbyterians, the largest non-Episcopal denomination in Virginia, appeared to endorse the general assessment. A memorandum issued by the Presbytery of Hanover argued that because of religion's "happy influence upon the morality of its citizens, and its tendency to preserve the veneration of an oath, or an appeal to heaven, which is the cement of the social union," the legislature was entitled to pass laws for "the preserving of the public worship of the deity and the supporting of institutions for inculcating the great fundamental principles of all religion, without which society could not easily exist."[31] Should the legislature "exert this right of supporting religion in general by an assessment on all the people," the memorandum continued, "we would wish it to be done on the most liberal plan."

Madison would later write an angry letter to James Monroe, complaining that the Presbyterians "seem as ready to set up an establishm[en]t which is to take them in as they were to pull down that which shut them out. I do not know a more shameful contrast than might be formed between their Memorials on the latter & former occasion."[32]

With the general assessment on the verge of being enacted, Madison began a series of brilliant strategic political maneuvers that would not only halt the bill but lead to passage of Jefferson's Bill for Establishing Religious Freedom.

The first step was to neutralize Patrick Henry. "What we have to do," Jefferson wrote Madison, "is devoutly to pray for his death."[33] Madison's less drastic plan was to have the assembly elect Patrick Henry governor of Virginia.[34] While Madison's precise role in the election is not known, there must have been an interesting conversation when Madison, as a member of the three-person "courtesy committee," went to notify Henry of his election.[35] For Henry, one of the appeals of the governor's position was apparently that full-time life in Richmond would provide access "to more potential husbands for his marriageable daughters."[36] This part of the plan bore fruit: both of Henry's daughters were married within a year and a half of his election.[37]

While Henry's departure from the legislature may have been good for his family, Madison wrote archly that it was "a circumstance very inauspicious to his offspring," the general assessment bill.[38] On December 4, two days after it was introduced by Henry's ally Francis Corbin,[39] Madison wrote again to Monroe to say that the bill's "friends are much disheartened at the loss of Mr. Henry. Its fate is I think very uncertain."[40]

Madison's next tactic involved the bill to incorporate the Episcopal Church. On December 22, James Madison voted with Patrick Henry's allies in support of this bill, helping it pass by a margin of forty-seven to thirty-eight.[41] Madison had two motives for his vote to grant a special benefit to the former established church. First, as he wrote Jefferson, passage of the bill would mollify many Episcopalians who rightfully desired "some sort of incorporation for the purpose of holding & managing the property of the Church" and would divert their enthusiasm from the rest of the political agenda: "A negative of the bill too would have doubled the eagerness and the pretexts for a much greater evil, a General Assessment, which there is good ground to believe was parried by this partial gratification of its warmest votaries."[42]

Second, other religious groups, especially the Presbyterians, felt threatened by the incorporation of the Episcopal Church through special legislation. Earlier, the legislature had passed a resolution urging a more general incorporation law, applicable to "all societies of the Christian religion."[43] The more specific law focusing on the

Episcopalians conjured up images of the bygone days of establishment.[44] As Jefferson wrote to Madison, "I am glad the Episcopalians have again shewn their teeth and fangs. The dissenters had almost forgotten them."[45]

After the incorporation bill passed, the assembly began discussing the general assessment proposal. Acting on a proposal of the United Clergy of the Presbyterian Church, the bill was amended so that it not only funded Christian worship but was also "extended to those who profess the public worship of the Deity."[46] But, as Madison reported bitterly, "in a committee of the whole it was determined by a Majority of 7 or 8 that the word 'christian' should be exchanged for the word 'Religious.' On the report to the House the pathetic zeal of the late governor Harrison gained a like majority for reinstating discrimination."[47]

Some have argued that this discrimination against non-Christians was the only reason Madison opposed the general assessment and that he would have supported the bill if the legislature had maintained the version that funded all religions. One commentator wrote: "It is plausible that . . . Madison would have viewed the assessment scheme as nondiscriminatory and, thus, would have dropped his opposition to it."[48] Supreme Court Justice Clarence Thomas has written that he agrees that "Madison saw the principle of nonestablishment as barring governmental preferences for *particular* religious faiths."[49]

These assertions that framers such as Madison supported governmental aid to religion in general are unfounded. Some in the Virginia legislature, such as Richard Henry Lee, did favor such inclusive religious funding. As Lee wrote to Madison: "True freedom embraces the Mahomitan and the Gentoo as well as the Christian religion. And upon this liberal ground I hope our Assembly will conduct themselves."[50]

Madison himself never uttered such a statement. He never supported an "inclusive" funding bill and certainly never proposed it after Henry's bill was defeated. Moreover, as his notes for the arguments he presented on the assembly floor reveal, he opposed the general assessment bill on the overarching ground that "relig. [is] not within purview of Civil Authority." His notes for how he would answer assessment supporters who stressed the benefits that religion bestows on society show his opposition to all religious funding:

True question not—Is Rel: necesy.?
are Religs. Estabts. necessy. for Religion? no.[51]

After the assessment bill left the Committee of the Whole, it appeared to have the support of a majority of the legislature. Madison then resorted to a new tactic. On December 24, 1784, he persuaded the legislature to delay a final vote until the following November so that the opinion of the state's voters could be ascertained.[52] As he wrote in his old age, "The progress of the measure was arrested by urging that the respect due to the people required in so extraordinary a case an appeal to their deliberate will."[53] He then persuaded the legislature to publish handbills to distribute around the state. To allow his allies to know which legislators to target in the next election, these handbills contained not only the text of the bill but also the "names of the ayes and noes on the question" of delaying consideration.[54]

According to the handbill, the bill, entitled "A bill establishing a provision for teachers of the Christian religion," began by asserting that "the general diffusion of Christian knowledge hath a natural tendency to correct the morals of men, restrain their vices, and preserve the peace of society." Such diffusion, it continued, required learned teachers paid for by the legislature. The substance of the bill was milder than the 1779 proposal had been. Taxpayers could designate the "society of Christians" to which they wished to have their money allocated, but these "societies" no longer were required to embrace a five-point creed in order to qualify.[55] The revenue from those who did not designate a "Christian society" would no longer be divided among the eligible Christian groups, but distributed "under the direction of the General Assembly, for the encouragement of seminaries of learning."[56] Thus, the final version of the general assessment attempted to minimize both the government's involvement in religion and the specter of adherents of minority religions being forced to contribute to the religious worship of others.

Nonetheless, Madison was vehement in his opposition, and his attempt to rally statewide sentiment against the bill proved increasingly successful. On April 27, 1785, he reported to Jefferson that the general assessment had "produced some fermentation below the Mountains & a violent one beyond them. The contest at the next Session on this question will be a warm & precarious one."[57]

As Madison had hoped, the state assembly elections in spring 1785 favored the opponents of the general assessment. He wrote to James Monroe on April 28 to inform him that "in Culpeper Mr. Pendleton a worthy man & acceptable in his general character to the people was laid aside in consequence of his vote for the Bill, in favour of an Adversary to it."[58] A month later, he wrote again to say, "I have heard of several Counties where the late representatives have been laid aside for voting for the Bill, and not a single one where the reverse has happened."[59]

As opposition grew, the debate grew increasingly rancorous. In April, Edmund Pendleton wrote of "considerable clamours" against the bill.[60] It was reported that Carter H. Harrison, son of the former governor Benjamin Harrison, had, in the heat of argument, declared: "The greatest curse which heaven sent at any time into this Country, was sending Dissenters into it."[61] Madison was asked to confirm Harrison's impolitic statement, but declined to get involved, "wishing not to be made a Witness or Judge in any case where the characters of Gentlemen are concerned."[62]

In fact, Madison intended to stay relatively quiet during the legislative recess, but two brothers, George and Wilson Nicholas, convinced him that if people were silent about the general assessment, it "would be construed into an assent."[63] The brothers hoped to create a petition that they would then distribute broadly. George Nicholas asked Madison to draft it: "I know you are most capable of doing it properly."[64]

MADISON'S MEMORIAL AND REMONSTRANCE

On June 20, 1785, what has become known as Madison's "Memorial and Remonstrance" was completed.[65] Though drafted as a purely political document, it has rightfully been termed "one of the most eloquent statements on religious freedom in history."[66] Despite its forceful opposition to the religious assessment, it is neither hostile to religion nor atheistic. Its tone is that of a devout Christian speaking to his fellow congregants.

Madison began by terming the general assessment "a dangerous abuse of power." Asserting that it was "an unalienable right of individuals to exercise their religion solely as their own "conviction and conscience" may dictate, Madison declared that "Religion is wholly exempt from [the] cognizance" of civil society in general, and the legislature in particular.

In starkly religious terms, Madison argued that the right of religious freedom precedes and transcends the power of government: "Before any man can be considered as a member of Civil Society, he must be considered as a subject of the Governour of the Universe." Thus "every man who becomes a member of any particular Civil Society, do[es] it with a saving of his allegiance to the Universal Sovereign." Combining theories of religious obligation with personal autonomy, Madison stated, "It is the duty of every man to render to the Creator such homage and such only as he believes to be acceptable to him."

Madison also criticized the assessment bill for its explicit favoring of one faith over all others, declaring that it "violates that equality which ought to be the basis of every law": "Whilst we assert for ourselves a freedom to embrace, to profess and to observe the Religion which we believe to be of divine origin, we cannot deny an equal freedom to those whose minds have not yet yielded to the evidence which has convinced us." The phrase "the evidence which has convinced us" displays a fascinating perspective. It assumes that all who will be signing this petition share a common Christian religious orientation; they have all been "convinced" by the same biblical evidence.

Continuing in that voice, Madison pointed out the danger of narrow sectarian domination inherent in permitting the legislature to draw statutory lines favoring Christianity in general: "Who does not see that the same authority which can establish Christianity, in exclusion of all other Religions, may establish with the same ease any particular sect of Christians, in exclusion of all other Sects?"

Notice how Madison assumed that any tax to support religious teaching should be considered equivalent to the historic establishment of a state church. The size of the tax is irrelevant, he argued, if the principle permitting such governmental support is accepted, since "the same authority which can force a citizen to contribute three pence only of his property for the support of any one establishment, may force him to conform to any other establishment in all cases whatsoever."

Such establishments, he continued, harm both religion and the governments that support it. Rather than protecting the "purity and efficacy of Religion," Madison stated, establishments invariably lead to "pride and indolence in the Clergy, ignorance and servility in the laity, in both, superstition, bigotry and persecution." They also violate fundamental republican principles by permitting "Rulers who wished to subvert the public liberty" to utilize the "established Clergy [as] convenient auxiliaries." "In many instances," he wrote, religious establishments "have been seen upholding the thrones of political tyranny: in no instance have they been seen the guardians of the liberties of the people."

In late June, Madison sent his Memorial and Remonstrance to

George Nicholas, who began distributing it for signatures throughout the state.[67] Nicholas reported that it was very well received and that "one hundred and fifty of our most respectable freeholders signed it in a day."[68] Madison would later say: "It met with the approbation of the Baptists, the Presbyterians, the Quakers, and the few Roman Catholics, universally; of the Methodists in part; and even of not a few of the Sect formerly established by law."[69]

Virtually no one who signed the Memorial and Remonstrance was aware of who had written it. As Madison wrote to Edmund Randolph, "My choice is that my name may not be associated with it."[70]

Thus, when George Mason sent a copy to George Washington, Mason was appropriately discreet, saying it had been "confided to me by a particular Freind, whose Name I am not at Liberty to mention."[71] He told Washington that he had been "at the Charge of printing several Copys, to disperse in the different parts of the Country" and urged Washington to sign the petition: "If upon Consideration, You approve the Arguments, & the principles upon which they are founded, Your Signature will both give the Remonstrance weight, and do it Honour."[72]

Washington's brief response contains the seeds of one of the most important strands in America's development of a theory of religious liberty. After telling Mason that he intended to read "with attention" the Remonstrance as well as the final version of the general assessment bill, Washington revealed his own thinking on the volatile issue.[73] He began by saying that he did not object in principle to a religious tax as long as minority religions were provided appropriate exemptions: "Altho' no mans sentiments are more opposed to any kind of restraint upon religious principles than mine are; yet I must confess, that I am not amongst the number of those who are so much alarmed at the thoughts of making people pay towards the support of that which they profess, if of the denominations of Christians; or declare themselves Jews, Mahomitans or otherwise, & thereby obtain proper relief."[74]

This sentence has caused many scholars to assume that Washington "favored the bill"[75] and "supported the pro-assessment movement."[76]

But Washington was a far more nuanced thinker than he is generally considered. Despite his personal disagreement with Madison's philosophy on governmental support of religion (which he had not yet read), Washington told Mason that he did not believe the assessment bill was good for Virginia and that he hoped it would be defeated: "As the matter now stands, I wish an assessment had never been agitated—& as it has gone so far, that the Bill could die an easy death; because I think it will be productive of more quiet to the State, than by enacting it into a Law."[77] Given the strong opposition of a "respectable minority," Washington warned, passage of the bill would "rankle, & perhaps convulse the State."[78]

If Jefferson and Madison can be said to have had primarily philosophical objections to the assessment bill, Washington's objections might be described as political. His thoughts on the assessment bill reveal a deep awareness that an insensitive intermingling of government and religion can lead to serious, even destructive, political strife.

Madison, of course, was not unaware of such arguments. In his Memorial and Remonstrance, he lists as one of the arguments against the bill that it would "destroy that moderation and harmony which the forbearance of our laws to intermeddle with Religion has produced among its several sects." Making an appeal very similar to Washington's, he stated: "The very appearance of the Bill has transformed 'that Christian forbearance, love and charity' which of late mutually prevailed, into animosities and jealousies, which may not soon be appeased. What mischiefs may not be dreaded, should this enemy to the public quiet be armed with the force of a law?"[79]

Washington, who had labored so consistently during the Revolutionary War to ensure that religion would not cause "the smallest uneasiness & jealousy among the Troops," realized that the civilian population could not be subjected to similar dangers.[80] As the historian Paul Boller noted, "The agitation over the Virginia assessment plan seems to have convinced him, once and for all, of the impracticality of all proposals of this kind for state support of religion."[81]

In addition to the philosophical and political arguments against the general assessment bill, there existed a third, vitally important aspect to the opposition. In terms reminiscent of those used by Roger Williams, the Virginia Baptists enunciated deeply religious reasons for their opposition. In August, the Baptist General Committee wrote that the "Church of Christ is not of this world."[82] Therefore, "they cannot see on what defensible principles, the Sheriffs, County Courts and public Treasury are all to be employed in the management of money levied for the express purpose of supporting Teachers of the Christian Religion."

A petition from Prince George County similarly declared that the general assessment was "Contrary to the Spirit of the Gospel."[83] The petition noted that Christianity had thrived during its first three centuries without governmental support: "Certain it is, that The Blessed author of our Religion supported & maintained his Gospel in the world for Several hundred years, not only without the aid of civil power, but against all the powers of the Earth." Once governmental support for religion began, the church was "overrun with Error, Superstition and Immorality."

The Baptists' petitions garnered far more signatures than Madison's. By one estimate, nearly 5,000 people signed petitions asserting that the assessment violated the "Spirit of the Gospel," while a little more than 1,500 signed Madison's Memorial and Remonstrance.[84] It would be a gross mistake, however, to assume that the two approaches were at odds with one another. Even though we are conditioned today to assume that debates over the role of government and religion assume "a secular versus religious form," the history of the battle over the general assessment bill proves that need not be so.[85] There is nothing inconsistent or novel in religious people believing that governmental involvement harms religion.

In his Memorial and Remonstrance, Madison also made several religious arguments for opposing the tax. He argued, for example, that because the bill would cause non-Christians to avoid Virginia, it was "adverse to the diffusion of the light of Christianity," adding, "the first wish of those who enjoy this precious gift ought to be that it may be imparted to the whole race of mankind."[86]

It was not uncommon for philosophical and religious objections to appear together in other petitions opposing the general assessment. These positions were combined, for instance, in the petition written at a Presbyterian convention that met in Bethel, Virginia, on August 10, 1785.[87] This statement represented a significant change from the memorandum the Presbyterians had produced in November 1784, which had endorsed laws for "supporting of institutions for inculcating the great fundamental principles of all religion."[88] Madison attributed the change of attitude to resistance from rank-and-file parishioners and the strong reaction against the bill that incorporated the Episcopalian church: "The presbyterian clergy have at length espoused the side of the opposition, being moved either by a fear of their laity or a jealousy of the episcopalians. The mutual hatred of these sects has been much inflamed by the late act incorporating the latter. I am far from being sorry for it as a coalition between them could alone endanger our religious rights and a tendency to such an event had been suspected."[89]

The Presbyterians' Bethel petition echoed parts of Madison's Memorial and Remonstrance when it stated: "Religion is altogether personal, and the right of exercising it unalienable; and it is not, cannot, and ought not to be, resigned to the will of the society at large; and much less to the Legislature."[90] As the Baptists had done in their petition, the Presbyterians explained the religious underpinnings for their opposition to the assessment bill: "We are fully persuaded of the happy influences of Christianity upon the morals of men; but we have never known it, in the history of its progress, so effectual for this purpose, as when left to its native excellence and evidence to recommend it, under the all-directing providence of God, and free from the intrusive hand of the civil magistrate. Its Divine Author did not think it necessary to render it dependent on earthly governments."

The Baptist and Presbyterian petitions also shared a perspective that had been scarcely voiced previously by religious groups in America. Both recognized the common religious rights of non-Christians. The Prince George County petition stated that it would violate the principle enshrined in Virginia's Declaration of Rights that "all men by nature are born equally free" if those "who are not professors of the Christian Religion . . . shall be obliged to support the Christian Religion." The Presbyterians agreed, asserting that the assessment "unjustly subjects men who may be good citizens, but who have not embraced our common faith, to the hardship of supporting a system they have not as yet believed the truth of."

When the Virginia legislature reconvened on October 24, 1785, Madison saw that his strategy of delaying the vote and instigating opposition had been successful. He would later write to Jefferson: "The steps taken throughout the Country to defeat the Genl. Assessment, had produced all the effect that could have been wished. The table was loaded with petitions & remonstrances from all parts against the interposition of the Legislature in matters of Religion."[91]

There were some pro-assessment petitions, but petitions opposing the bill outnumbered those in support by almost four to one (seventy-nine to twenty),[92] and the almost 10,000 opposition signatures outweighed those of supporters by more than eight to one.[93] The assessment bill was brought before the assembly meeting as a committee of the whole and, after a few days of unrecorded debate, defeated.[94] In Madison's opinion, "the number of Copies & signatures prescribed displayed such an overwhelming opposition of the people, that the proposed plan of a genl assessmt was crushed under it."[95]

JEFFERSON'S BILL FOR RELIGIOUS FREEDOM

Madison took advantage of the new mood in the legislature to bring back Jefferson's bill for religious freedom. Several of the petitions against the assessment bill, most notably that of the Presbyterians, had in fact specifically recommended "adopting the bill in the revised law for establishing religious freedom."[96] On October 31, 1785, just days after the defeat of the assessment bill, Madison presented to the legislature the 118 bills from the *Report of the Revisors* that had not yet been enacted into law.[97] On December 14, the assembly began its consideration of number 82, the "bill for establishing religious freedom."[98]

There was general agreement on the substance of the bill, which banned governmental funding of religious worship or teaching and prohibited the government from penalizing or rewarding people because of their religious opinions or beliefs. The major battle over the next month would concern Jefferson's preamble.[99]

One especially illuminating dispute arose over the section of the preamble in which Jefferson wrote that "all attempts to influence by temporal punishments, or burthens, or by civil incapacitations, tend only to beget habits of hypocrisy and meanness, and are a departure from the plan of the holy author of our religion." According to Jefferson's *Autobiography*, an amendment was proposed to add the phrase "'Jesus Christ,' so that it should read 'a departure from the plan of Jesus Christ, the holy author of our religion.'"[100]

Even though this addition would not have altered the substance of the bill, Madison saw it as a threat to the principle of universal freedom of religion. If the legislature had spoken of "Jesus Christ, the holy author of our religion," Madison feared that this would "imply a restriction of the liberty defined in the Bill, to those professing his religion only."[101] He also noted that there was a religious argument against the amendment, namely, that a "better proof of reverence for that holy name wd be not to profane it by making it a topic of legisl.

Discussion." This argument proved especially effective in the legislature, he said, when it was "espoused by some members who were particularly distinguished by their reputed piety and Christian zeal."

The amendment was defeated, and Jefferson's reaction shows how he viewed the relationship between religious language and universal freedom. Although his preamble had contained such phrases as "Almighty God," "holy author of our religion," and "lord both of body and mind," he saw it as excluding no one. The omission of explicitly Christian language from the law, he wrote, proved that the legislature "meant to comprehend, within the mantle of its protection, the Jew and the Gentile, the Christian and Mahometan, the Hindoo, and Infidel of every denomination."[102]

Madison could not stop every legislative attempt to amend the preamble. After the bill passed the assembly, the senate insisted on removing some of Jefferson's more controversial language. For example, they disliked his statement that people's religious beliefs "follow involuntarily the evidence proposed to their minds" and that religion is able to extend "its influence on reason alone." These assertions were seen as disparaging those who believed in "the 'revealed' religion of Scripture."[103] Senators also objected to one of Jefferson's more stirring phrases, "the opinions of men are not the object of civil government," apparently because it sounded too absolute.

Madison's last strategic move was to accept the senate's amendments at the risk of angering his friend Jefferson, who complained bitterly when others edited his work. Madison explained to Jefferson that even though the changes "somewhat defaced the composition," he had "thought better to agree to than to run further risks, especially as it was getting late in the Session and the House growing thin."[104] His gamble paid off; the Virginia Statute for Establishing Religious Freedom became law on January 19, 1786.

The final version of the law's preamble, even in its edited form, stands as a major step in the development of American religious free-

dom. Its introductory phrase was shortened to the powerful statement "Whereas Almighty God hath created the mind free."[105] The
bill retained its assertion "that all attempts to influence [the mind] by
temporal punishments or burthens, or by civil incapacitations, tend
only to beget habits of hypocrisy and meanness, and are a departure
from the plan of the Holy author of our religion." It maintained Jefferson's statement "that to compel a man to furnish contributions of
money for the propagation of opinions which he disbelieves, is sinful
and tyrannical." Jefferson's preamble also argued, in contrast to George
Washington's private opinion, that for the government to force someone
to support a "teacher of his own religious persuasion" is unjust, since it
"is depriving him of the comfortable liberty of giving his contributions
to the particular pastor, whose morals he would make his pattern."

The Virginia Statute for Establishing Religious Freedom has been
praised as "an eloquent manifesto of the sanctity of the human mind
and spirit."[106] In a letter to Jefferson, Madison rejoiced in the statute's
enactment: "I flatter myself [that the enacting clauses] have in this
Country extinguished for ever the ambitious hope of making laws
for the human mind."[107]

Jefferson was equally enthusiastic and distributed the statute
throughout Europe, though the version he sent out was closer to his
original draft than the one actually enacted.[108] In August 1786, he
proudly wrote George Wythe, his former law teacher: "Our act for
freedom of religion is extremely applauded . . . it is inserted at full
length in several books now in the press; among others, in the new
Encyclopedie."[109]

BILLS 83–86

In recent years, critics have questioned whether the Virginia Statute for Establishing Religious Freedom should be viewed, as former
Supreme Court Justice Lewis Powell described it, as an "acknowledg-

ment of the principle of total separation of Church and State."[110] They contend, to the contrary, that "Jefferson's ultimate objective was less separation of church and state than the fullest possible expression of religious belief and opinion."[111]

The thrust of this argument is that the revision of Virginia laws put forward by Jefferson in 1779, which Madison introduced to the legislature in 1785, included four proposals dealing with religion in addition to the Bill for Establishing Religious Freedom (which was "Bill number 82"), and that "Jefferson's imprint on Bills No. 83–86 modifies conventional interpretations of Bill No. 82."[112]

Bill number 83, "A Bill for Saving the Property of the Church Heretofore by Law Established," simply preserved the Episcopal Church's control of the property it had acquired when it was the established church. While it dealt with church-related concerns, this proposal was focused on the narrow political issue of allocating property rights after disestablishment and does not relate to broader questions of the relationship between religion and government.

The other three bills require more extensive examination. Bill number 84, "A Bill for Punishing Disturbers of Religious Worship and Sabbath Breakers," has three parts.[113] The first prohibited the arrest of any minister "while such minister shall be publicly preaching or performing religious worship." The second part of Bill number 84 made it illegal to "disquiet or disturb any congregation assembled" in a house of worship. The final part of the bill makes it an offense for a person to work or "employ his apprentices, servants or slaves in labour" on a Sunday.

Bill number 85, "A Bill For Appointing Days Of Public Fasting And Thanksgiving," authorized the governor to call "days of public fasting and humiliation, or thanksgiving." The unusual part of the bill was that it included a fine for any "minister of the gospel" who failed to "attend and perform divine service and preach a sermon, or discourse, suited to the occasion . . . not having a reasonable excuse."

The last bill dealing with religion was Bill number 86, "A Bill Annulling Marriages Prohibited by the Levitical Law, and Appointing the Mode of Solemnizing Lawful Marriage."[114] The first part of the law declared as void "any marriage prohibited by the Levitical law."[115] The other major part recognized marriage licenses issued by a clerk of a court "as effectually as if the contract had been solemnized, and the espousals celebrated, in the manner prescribed by the ritual of any church."[116]

The legal historian Daniel L. Dreisbach has argued that to truly understand Jefferson's view on the intermingling of religion and government, we must consider all five bills as a whole. He concludes that Jefferson's "aim was to foster freedom of religious expression, and if that objective was best served through statutory cooperation between church and state, Jefferson appeared willing to endorse it."[117] Similarly, the political scientist Robert L. Cord has stated that the religious bills in the revisal show that Jefferson and Madison "subscribed to no tradition of absolute separation of Church and State, unless using state authority to punish 'Sabbath breakers' and proclaiming 'Thanksgiving days' do not violate that concept."[118]

But there is another way to understand these bills. First, they arose in a legislative context, not as part of a treatise on religious freedom. The original revisal was intended as a comprehensive rewriting of Virginia's law, which Jefferson hoped would be collectively adopted.[119] Given the need for approval by the assembly, it would not be surprising if he did not personally agree with every proposal as long as his legislative priorities were achieved.

Second, a careful reading of several of the bills reveals that Jefferson tried to include liberalizing provisions inside the religious laws. For example, the bill on "Levitical marriages" would have created, for the first time, a means for lawful marriages to be solemnized outside the religious context. The bill on "Sabbath breakers" specifically exempted slaves and other laborers from being forced to work on

Sunday, a prohibition lacking in the existing Sabbath law.[120] Jefferson, who a few years earlier had "rummaged over" calls for days of fasting and "cooked up a resolution" to motivate Virginians to support the patriots in Boston, was not beyond using religion to advance secular objectives.[121]

The use of religious words such as "Levitical" and "Sabbath" in these proposals is hardly proof of a Jeffersonian desire to link religion and government. As one commentator stated, "little significance should be attached to such nomenclature considering the ubiquity of religious discourse in the eighteenth century."[122] The Virginia marriage law then in effect prohibited marriages "if any person whatsoever shall hereafter marry within the levitical degrees prohibited by the laws of England."[123]

The most curious of Jefferson's proposals is that which would have penalized clergy who did not "perform divine service" on the thanksgiving and fasting days proclaimed by the governor. He never offered an explanation for this. One possible conjecture is that he added this provision in an attempt to appease the then governor of Virginia, none other than Patrick Henry. But this is merely a surmise. Jefferson's true motivation for including this provision will remain unknown. To say, as Robert Cord did, that the law proves that Jefferson's and Madison's view of the proper relationship between church and state included "using state authority to punish 'Sabbath breakers,'" vastly overstates the bill's significance. If Cord were correct that the bill reflected their perspectives, then one must also conclude that the Jeffersonian and Madisonian visions included the desirability of punishing clergy who did not follow the religious dictates of the governor—a position so absurd that no scholar, including Cord and Dreisbach, even suggests the possibility.

Nonetheless, it is a mistake for those who believe in a strict separation of church and state not to discuss these bills' possible significance. Dreisbach goes so far as to accuse Jeffersonian scholars of having chosen "either to ignore or suppress the fact that Jefferson may have held a more accommodating view of church-state relations than the strict separationist version of legal history would suggest."[124] While that may be a harsh assessment, it is true that most writers with such a view of Jefferson's opinion have not included the bills in their discussions. Those using history have an obligation to engage fully with the past, especially when it does not fit a simple, straightforward narrative.

The significance of Jefferson's Bills number 83–86 is ambiguous, but certainly not trivial. Dreisbach is undeniably correct that the bills show that Jefferson and Madison "did not consistently advocate absolute church-state separation throughout their public careers."[125] But as the historian Steven Green asserts, their opinions could have "evolved over time," and these bills could "indicate that notions of disestablishment, like ideas of church-state separation, were slowly developing, with immediate attention being given to the more egregious manifestations of religious establishments."[126]

The bills also show that Jefferson and Madison did not intend to cleanse the political dialogue of all religious references. The bills do not show where they thought the line of appropriateness should be drawn, but they do invite a discussion of when governmental involvement does and does not pose an unacceptable threat of the harms described in the Virginia Statute for Establishing Religious Freedom, and the Memorial and Remonstrance.

Finally, the bills remind us that when examining a long history involving complicated people confronting an issue of such complexity, we should not expect to emerge with a simple message. That does not mean we cannot draw important lessons from this intricate story. But a fundamental lesson is that the march toward religious liberty was not a simple choice of freedom versus tyranny, but a series of decisions, compromises, trials and errors.

Another important lesson to be drawn from the defeat of the

general assessment and enactment of the Virginia Statute for Establishing Religious Freedom is that the success cannot be attributed to a single source or perspective. Legislative victory required that Jefferson's and Madison's "liberal notions of religious freedom based upon Enlightenment principles" be combined with the "vociferous support of Virginia's growing population of evangelical dissenters (primarily Baptists and Presbyterians)."[127]

It is safe to say that the major proponents of both the philosophical and religious arguments would have agreed on certain principles. First, it is wrong to compel a person "to furnish contributions of money" for the support of religious institutions or the propagation of religious opinion regardless of whether the individual is an adherent of the religious views being supported. Second, any governmental support for religion is objectionable: the amount of financial support does not matter. As Madison wrote: "It is proper to take alarm at the first experiment on our liberties."[128]

Madison and his allies also would have agreed that a religious majority should never be permitted to "trespass on the rights of the minority." In the words of the Presbyterian petition, it is unjust to inflict hardship on those who "may be good citizens, but who have not embraced our common faith." More broadly, the government may neither harm nor favor people because of their religious beliefs: "Our civil rights have no dependence on our religious opinions, any more than our opinions in physics or geometry."

These principles would have been seen as components of Madison's broader proposition that "religion is wholly exempt from [the] cognizance" of legislative action. The outer contours of that proposition may have been unclear, but it would have been neither limited to these specifics nor extended to prohibit all mention of religion from political discussion. Further, there would have been enthusiastic agreement that a devoutly religious person could disagree with governmental assistance to religion on purely religious grounds. Many of those opposing Henry's bill did so out of a pious conviction that religious funding by government was "Contrary to the Spirit of the Gospel."[129]

We must recognize also what might be termed the political argument against the general assessment. Because it shaped him personally and because it influenced so much national policy, from the creation of the Constitution to the end of the founding period, George Washington's concern that a careless linkage between church and state can "rankle, & perhaps convulse" a political community became one of the most important factors in America's understanding of the proper relationship between government and religion.[130]

THE RELIGIOUS PROVISIONS OF
THE NORTHWEST ORDINANCE

The Confederation Congress, however, did not fully share Madison's and Washington's sensibilities, as shown by its last important piece of legislation, the Northwest Ordinance of 1787. Many scholars who wish to encourage contemporary governmental support of religion insist that through the Northwest Ordinance, Congress gave "its sanction of a benevolent promotion by the state of religious education."[131] Those who argue for greater separation of church and state contend that the ordinance "depicts the progression of separationist thought during the period away from the financial and symbolic support of religion."[132] In reality, the full history of the Northwest Ordinance reveals an unresolved battle in which neither side could claim total victory.

The Northwest Ordinance arose from the Confederation Congress's need to devise a plan for selling the approximately 160 million acres that would later become Ohio, Indiana, Illinois, Michigan, and Wisconsin. Congress faced two decisions: how to raise money by selling the land and how the territories created by those land sales would become states. Though the two concerns were obviously intertwined, Congress chose to deal with them separately.

In 1785, Congress began debate on a bill that would become "An Ordinance for ascertaining the Mode of disposing of Lands in the Western Territory."[133] In addition to detailing how lots would be sold, the bill also reserved some land in each future town for a variety of specific uses. The original proposal contained an explicit set-aside of land for religion: "There shall be reserved the central Section of every Township, for the maintenance of public Schools; and the Section immediately adjoining the same to the northward, for the support of religion. The profits arising therefrom in both instances, to be applied for ever according to the will of the majority of male residents of full age within the same."[134] Several legislators, led by William Ellery of Rhode Island and Melancton Smith of New York, objected to the government mandate supporting religion.[135] On April 23, they succeeded in having it deleted,[136] and the bill that was finally passed on May 20 reserved land only for education.[137]

James Madison, then in Virginia battling the general assessment, wrote James Monroe to express his relief at the removal of the religious provision:

> It gives me much pleasure to observe . . . that in the latter Congs. had expunged a clause contained in the first for setting apart a district of land in each Township, for supporting the Religion of the Majority of inhabitants. How a regulation, so unjust in itself, so foreign to the Authority of Congs. so hurtful to the sale of the public land, and smelling so strongly of an antiquated Bigotry, could have received the countenance of a Commtee is truly a matter of astonishment.[138]

Madison also suggested sardonically that Virginia might have benefited if the "unjust" religious provision had been retained. Freedom-loving Virginians who might have emigrated if the State enacted the odious general assessment bill would have stayed, since the national religious provision, "would have given a repellent quality to the new

Country, in the estimation of those whom our own encroachments on Religious Liberty would be calculated to banish to it."[139]

Two years later, the Ohio Company, a group of Revolutionary War veterans led by the Congregational minister Manasseh Cutler, prepared to purchase 1.5 million acres of land in what is now southeastern Ohio. The prospect of such a large purchase motivated Congress to reexamine the method for determining how the territories would gain statehood. As Congress was drafting the bill, the Reverend Cutler came to New York to meet with legislators and make several suggested changes to the proposed bill.[140] On July 11, 1787, largely through Cutler's intervention,[141] legislation was introduced that mandated support for religious institutions in the new territories: "Institutions for the promotion of religion and morality, schools and the means of education shall forever be encouraged."[142]

Two days later, without recorded debate, Congress passed the bill, which became known as the Northwest Ordinance, with one major change from the July 11 proposal.[143] The final Ordinance stated: "Religion, morality, and knowledge, being necessary to good government and the happiness of mankind, schools and the means of education shall forever be encouraged."[144]

This version confounds all who wish for a simple narrative of the development of America's vision of religion and government. The first part of the sentence ("Religion, morality, and knowledge, being necessary to good government and the happiness of mankind") places the congressional imprimatur on the principle that religion is necessary for government. Then the sentence suddenly shifts course. Unlike the wording in the July 11 proposal, the second half of the sentence ("schools and the means of education shall forever be encouraged") deliberately omits any mention of religion, declaring only that education in the broadest sense is to be encouraged.

The Northwest Ordinance is thus neither separatist nor accommodationist.[145] As the church historian Edwin S. Gaustad noted, "A single sentence in the Northwest Ordinance . . . summarizes the nature of a people divided on the question of what their government could or should do concerning religion in general or Christianity in particular."[146] It can be read as a governmental statement that religion is important for government but is not within the purview of governmental responsibility. As the Ohio Supreme Court stated in interpreting its own constitution, which contained language modeled after the Northwest Ordinance: "The declaration is not that government is essential to good religion, but that religion is essential to good government. . . . Religion is the parent, and not the offspring, of good government."[147]

The compromise did not satisfy the Reverend Cutler. On July 21, 1787, he sent Congress a proposal containing the language to be used in the formal land grant to be issued pursuant to the 1785 ordinance. This proposal included a provision that lots in each township be provided free of charge not only for schools but for religion as well: "Lot N 16 to be given perpetually by Congress to the maintenance of Schools & lot N 29 to the purposes of religion in the said townships."[148]

Congress, desperate to sell the land, acquiesced, and on July 23 voted that for the Ohio Company's land grant, lot number 16 would be given for educational purposes and "the lot N 29 in each township or fractional part of a township to be given perpetually for the purposes of religion."[149] This language appears in only one other land grant within the Northwest Territories, a 300,000-acre grant in southern Ohio to John Cleves Symmes,[150] who had insisted on the same terms as the Ohio Company.[151] No other grant reserved land "for the purpose of religion."[152]

The stories of the Northwest Ordinance and the Ohio Company land grant illustrate that the Confederation Congress, by the end of its tenure, had no clear position on the proper relationship between religion and government. Without question, it was comfortable with a far more active encouragement of religion than would be seen from any modern Congress. Not only the salutary phrasing of the Northwest Ordinance but also the placement of a requirement for religious support in two land grants demonstrates that the Confederation Congress did not practice a modern form of separation of church and state. At the same time, the legislators amended both the 1785 Land Ordinance and the 1787 Northwest Ordinance to remove a general requirement of supporting religion, and the overwhelming majority of land grants did not contain the religious requirement. These facts reveal a backing away from the symbiotic church-state relationship still practiced in most of the individual states.

All these actions predate the drafting of both the Constitution and the First Amendment and thus cannot provide direct evidence of the meaning of those documents. Unfortunately, advocates continue to misstate the history of the Northwest Ordinance and try to manufacture a link between the religious language in the ordinance and the actions of the federal government after the new Constitution went into effect.

The most noteworthy example of this line of reasoning was put forth by the late chief justice William Rehnquist. In 1985, contending that the Constitution permitted governments to provide "non-discriminatory aid to religion," Rehnquist attempted to connect events that occurred subsequent to the ratification of the Constitution with the Northwest Ordinance by declaring: "The actions of the First Congress, which *reenacted* the Northwest Ordinance for the governance of the Northwest Territory in 1789, confirm the view that Congress did not mean that the Government should be neutral between religion and irreligion."[153] He went on to explain:

> The House of Representatives took up the Northwest Ordinance on the same day as Madison introduced his proposed amendments which became the Bill of Rights; . . . it seems highly unlikely that the House of Representatives would simultaneously consider proposed amendments to the Constitution and enact an important piece of territorial legislation which conflicted with the intent of those proposals. The Northwest Ordinance, 1 Stat. 50, reenacted

the Northwest Ordinance of 1787 and provided that "[religion],
morality, and knowledge, being necessary to good government
and the happiness of mankind, schools and the means of education
shall forever be encouraged."[154]

Even accepting the problematic certainty with which he asserts
that the Confederation Congress intended the Northwest Ordinance
to embody a principle supporting "nondiscriminatory aid to religion,"
Rehnquist's subsequent retelling of history is misleading and inaccurate. His last sentence, "The Northwest Ordinance, 1 Stat. 50, reenacted the Northwest Ordinance of 1787 and provided that '[religion],
morality, and knowledge, being necessary to good government and
the happiness of mankind, schools and the means of education shall
forever be encouraged,'" contains three egregious errors, the correc-
tion of which refutes the very point he is trying to make.

First, the 1789 law, 1 Stat. 50, was not "the Northwest Ordinance."
Under the Constitution, Congress passes "acts," not "ordinances." But
if Rehnquist had called it the Northwest Act, it would have lost the
historical pedigree he was striving to establish.[155]

Second, Congress did not "reenact" the Northwest Ordinance
in 1789.[156] There was no attempt or need to "enact" the Northwest
Ordinance for a second time. All that the 1789 law did was recognize
that under the Constitution, executive functions would be performed
by the newly created position of president rather than Congress. In
order "to adapt the [Northwest Ordinance] to the present Constitution of the United States," as Congress stated in the preamble to the
1789 law, appointments that were originally to have been made by
"the United States in Congress assembled" were now to be made by
the "President of the United States." The 1789 law similarly required
that communications that were to have been sent to Congress were
now to be delivered to the president of the United States. There was
no discussion or "reenactment" of any of the substantive provisions
of the 1787 Northwest Ordinance.

A careful reading of the complete 1789 law reveals the final error, Rehnquist's assertion that the First Congress's 1789 law "provided" that "[religion], morality, and knowledge being necessary to good government."[157] The 1789 law did not even mention, let alone "provide," this iconic language. Whatever the ultimate significance of the language, it was entirely a creation of the earlier Confederation Congress. As we will see, Congress under the new Constitution did not avoid all mention of religion. One certainly does not need to attribute the complexities of the Northwest Ordinance to the 1789 Congress in order demonstrate its record of ambiguity under the new Constitution.

CHAPTER 4

"We Have Become a Nation":
Drafting the Constitution

AS THE Confederation Congress was debating the Northwest Ordinance, the Constitutional Convention was meeting to draft the Constitution. The decisions made in Philadelphia reflected a significantly different view of the relationship between religion and government from the ones being made in New York.

Many of the fifty-five delegates to the Constitutional Convention, including James Madison, Gouverneur Morris, John Dickinson, and Benjamin Franklin, were veterans of battles over the proper role of religion in state government. While the delegates were not hostile to religion, most were intent on creating a nation in which religion and government would be separated more than they had been in the past.

The Constitutional Convention's distinctive tone can be seen in an intriguing contrast with the Continental Congress. Whereas the First Continental Congress had voted to begin its meetings with a clergy-led prayer, the Constitutional Convention rejected Benjamin Franklin's suggestion for a similar daily evocation. On June 28, 1787, with the convention mired in unproductive discussions over whether small states should continue to have the same voting power as large states, Franklin urged the delegates to consider "humbly applying to the Father of Lights to illuminate our understanding."[1] Referring to the Continental Congress, he said: "In the beginning of the contest with Britain, when we were sensible of danger, we had daily prayers in this room for the divine protection! Our prayers, sir, were heard and they were graciously answered." Franklin suggested that the convention should similarly appeal for divine support: "I have lived, Sir, a long time. The longer I live, the more convincing proofs I see of this truth—that God governs in the affairs of men! And if a sparrow cannot fall to the ground without His notice, is it probable that an empire can not rise without his aid?" He then proposed: "Henceforth, prayers imploring the assistance of Heaven—and its blessing on our deliberations—be held in this Assembly every morning before we proceed to business; and that one or more of the Clergy of this city be requested to officiate in that service."

Roger Sherman of Connecticut seconded the motion, but it garnered little other support.[2] A legend has developed that Alexander Hamilton opposed it because "he did not see the necessity of calling in foreign aid."[3] According to Madison's notes, Hamilton expressed concern that beginning prayers at this late date, more than a month after deliberations had begun, would "lead the public to believe that the embarrassments and dissentions within the convention, had suggested this measure."[4] Hugh Williamson of North Carolina offered a more pragmatic criticism, stating that "the true cause of the omission could not be mistaken," namely, "the Convention had no funds."

Attempting to devise a mechanism to "explain" why they were belatedly beginning sessions with prayer, Edmund Randolph of Virginia proposed that a sermon be preached on the upcoming Fourth of July anniversary and then daily thereafter. Although Franklin seconded this motion, the session was adjourned without a vote, and the matter was never raised again.

Years later, Madison attributed the convention's disinclination to vote for daily prayers not only to "the lapse of time which had preceded" Franklin's motion but also to both "the Quaker usage, never discontinued in the State & the place where the Convention held its sittings," as well as "the discord of religious opinions within the Convention."⁵ Franklin's explanation was simpler. At the bottom of the paper on which he had written his remarks, he added a postscript: "The convention, except three or four persons, thought prayers unnecessary."⁶

A similar divergence of attitude between the Continental Congress and the Constitutional Convention concerned the appropriateness of acknowledging God in a foundational document. The Continental Congress had included in the Articles of Confederation: "Whereas it hath pleased the Great Governor of the World to incline the hearts of the legislatures we respectively represent in Congress, to approve of . . . said articles of confederation." The Constitution's preamble, by contrast, lacks any religious reference, indicating reliance on "We the people."

In this, the Constitution also differed from many state constitutions, which often employed religious language. Pennsylvania's, for example, began: "We, the representatives of the freemen of Pennsylvania, in general convention met, for the express purpose of framing such a government, confessing the goodness of the great Governor of the universe." Massachusetts's constitution declared: "We, therefore, the people of Massachusetts, acknowledging, with grateful hearts, the goodness of the great Legislator of the universe."

There was no recorded request during the convention to include a mention of God. During the subsequent debates over ratification, the omission received only occasional mention.⁷ Benjamin Rush of Pennsylvania wrote to John Adams: "Many pious people wish the name of the Supreme Being had been introduced somewhere in the new Constitution."⁸ He added his hope that "an acknowledgement may be made of his goodness or of his providence in the proposed amendments."

In Connecticut, a supporter of the Constitution criticized the phrasing of the Preamble and said that he would have preferred it to include an "explicit acknowledgment of the being of a God."⁹ The writer proposed: "We the people of the United States, in a firm belief of the being and perfections of the one living and true God, the creator and supreme Governor of the world, in His universal providence and the authority of His laws . . . and in order to form a more perfect union, etc."[10]

After ratification, the Preamble was often cited by clergy attempting to demonstrate, in the words of Timothy Dwight, president of Yale and a Congregationalist minister, "the sinful character of our nation."[11] In 1812, Dwight attributed "the irreligion, and the wickedness, of our land" to the fact that "we formed our Constitution without any acknowledgment of God; without any recognition of his mercies to us, as a people, of his government, or even of his existence . . . Thus we commenced our national existence under the present system, without God."[12]

In 1861, the Confederate states modeled their own Constitution on the U.S. Constitution, with a few key differences. In addition to barring any law from "impairing the right of property in negro slaves," the Confederate Constitution also modified the Preamble to read: "We, the people of the Confederate States, each State acting in its sovereign and independent character, in order to form a permanent federal government, establish justice, insure domestic tranquility, and secure the blessings of liberty to ourselves and our posterity invoking the favor and guidance of Almighty God do ordain and establish this Constitution for the Confederate States of America."[13]

In the North, there were also calls to amend the U.S. Constitution to modify the language of the Preamble, and the movement for such an amendment grew after the Civil War.[14] The most popular proposal would have altered the language to read: "We, the people of the United States, humbly acknowledging Almighty God as the source of all authority and power in civil government, the Lord Jesus Christ as the Ruler among the nations, his revealed will as the supreme law of the land, in order to constitute a Christian government, and in order to form a more perfect union."[15]

In 1874, at the "National convention to secure the religious amendment of the Constitution of the United States," Felix Bruno, the president
of the National Reform Association, argued that while "ours is a Christian
nation . . . the Constitution is unchristian."[16] Without an amendment,
he warned, the Constitution is "godless and repugnant to them all."

The nonreligious nature of the Preamble was an important symbol of the drafters' desire to create a new relationship between government and religion, different from that which existed in Europe or in
the various states. But far more important in implementing that vision
was the fact that, as Amos Singletary lamented at the Massachusetts
Convention, "there was no provision that men in power should have
any religion."[17] The provision Singletary was attacking, Article VI,
section 3, declared that "no religious Test shall ever be required as a
Qualification to any Office or public Trust under the United States."
This ban on religious tests for public office represented a "dramatic
departure from the prevailing practice in the states."[18]

The question of why the national constitution would contain a
ban on religious tests when such tests were common in the states
from which the delegates came has been the subject of much debate. Those who favor strict separation of church and state argue
that with the enactment of Article VI, "the advocates of a secular
state won" and furthered their goal of "a godless Constitution and a
godless politics."[19] Those who favor close ties between religion and
government view Article VI as actually favoring oaths; they contend
that its supporters "valued religious tests required under state laws,
and they feared a federal test might displace existing state test oaths
and religious establishments."[20] In their view, Article VI "had more
to do with federalism than with a radical secular agenda."[21]

Both of these positions are demonstrably wrong. The key to
understanding the significance of Article VI is to embrace the ambiguities that inevitably arise from decision making in a diverse group
of people embarked on a novel venture in a highly transitional time.

In divining the philosophy behind Article VI, we unfortunately cannot turn to the Constitutional Convention for guidance, since the provision, proposed by Charles Pinckney of South Carolina, apparently provoked little disagreement there. The only question raised was by Roger Sherman of Connecticut, who "thought it unnecessary, the prevailing liberality being a sufficient security agst. such tests."[22] And Sherman did not oppose Pinckney's proposal; Madison recorded that it passed "nem con," meaning without dissent.[23]

But Article VI faced substantial criticism during the ratification debate, and not a single person is recorded as arguing that it was needed in order to protect existing state religious oaths. This is powerful evidence that Article VI was not designed for that purpose. Generally, whenever specific provisions of the Constitution were meant to preserve state autonomy, supporters were sure to emphasize this.

For instance, the convention decided not to provide a uniform rule on who could vote for candidates for the House of Representatives, but to let voting vary by state, based on "the Qualifications requisite for Electors of the most numerous Branch of the State Legislature."[24] In defending this provision, Oliver Ellsworth of Connecticut stated that the right of suffrage was "strongly guarded by most of the State Constitutions. The people will not readily subscribe to the Natl. Constitution if it should subject them to be disfranchised. The States are the best Judges of the circumstances & temper of their own people."[25] When debating Article VI, no one made the analogous argument that "the States are the best Judges of the circumstances" for religious tests.

Some have argued that the decision to leave voting requirements to the individual states proves that the delegates to the convention were not motivated by a desire to protect religious freedom, and that "the rejection of religious tests did *not* stem from the delegates' condemnation of them as a matter of principle."[26] They point out that under the Constitution as drafted, some people, solely because of their religion, would be excluded from voting for national officers, "since the constitutional framers of 1787 knew that in some states—such as South Carolina—the requisite qualifications for suffrage included religious belief."[27]

The fact that local voting discrimination was allowed to continue does not indicate a lack of interest in protecting religious freedom on a national level. Madison himself explained why. Even though the convention imposed a common rule for who could serve as public officials under the Constitution, it could not do so for voting: "To have reduced the different qualifications [for voting] in the different States to one uniform rule, would probably have been as dissatisfactory to some of the States as it would have been difficult to the convention. . . . The qualifications of the elected, being less carefully and properly defined by the State constitutions, and being at the same time more susceptible of uniformity, have been very properly considered and regulated by the convention."[28]

When the convention did consider the qualifications for public officers under the Constitution, religious requirements were seen as an unfortunate relic of the past, which, though lingering in individual states, should be avoided in the new national system. Pinckney, who proposed Article VI,[29] did not view his proposal as a means to protect state religious tests, despite his home state's requirement that legislators be of "the Protestant religion."[30] In his words, a ban on religious requirements for office was necessary because it was what "the world will expect . . . in the establishment of a System founded on Republican Principles, and in an age so liberal and enlightened as the present."[31]

During the ratification process, many of the supporters of the Constitution defended Article VI by portraying the ban on religious oaths as essential protection against religious oppression. Samuel Spencer of North Carolina attacked religious tests as "the foundation of persecutions in all countries."[32] In Pennsylvania, Tench Coxe described such tests as a "trespass on the Majesty of Heaven."[33] In Massachusetts, Isaac Backus declared that "the imposing of religious tests hath been the greatest engine of tyranny in the world."[34]

The unanimity in favor of Article VI inside the Convention, though, should not be viewed as the result of a radical change in the general population's view of religion and government. As Gerard Bradley noted, there was not a "sudden and near universal explosion of Jeffersonian skepticism."[35]

Religious intolerance had not disappeared. During the ratification debates, one of the delegates who had been at the convention, Luther Martin of Maryland, attacked the provision before his state legislature. In an address entitled "The Genuine Information," Martin said sarcastically that while most delegates supported the ban, "there were some members so unfashionable as to think, that a belief of the existence of a Deity, and of a state of future rewards and punishments would be some security for the good conduct of our rulers, and that, in a Christian country, it would be at least decent to hold out some distinction between the professors of Christianity and downright infidelity or paganism."[36]

As in colonial days, most of those wishing that constitutional protections be limited to "Christianity" excluded Catholics from their purview. For example, Massachusetts's Amos Singletary, in his attack on Article VI, explained that "though he hoped to see Christians" in the new government, "yet by the Constitution, a Papist or an Infidel, were as eligible as they."[37] Throughout the ratification debate, opponents of this provision revealed which particular religions they found most alien by describing who they feared would be elected. For example, Thomas Lusk of Massachusetts said that he "shuddered at the idea, that Roman Catholicks, Papists, and Pagans might be introduced into office—and that Popery and the Inquisition may be established in America."[38] An essay by "A Watchman" in Massachusetts warned: "There is a door opened for the Jews, Turks, and Heathen to enter into publick office, and be seated at the head of the government of the

United States."³⁹ Others warned that Article VI "would admit deists, atheists, &c., into the general government."⁴⁰

One way supporters of Article VI responded to these concerns was to agree with the premise that non-Protestants should not be elected to public office, but to proclaim that such undesirables were not electable anyway. Samuel Spencer of North Carolina answered those who feared "that persons of bad principles, deists, atheists, &c., may come into this country; and there is nothing to restrain them from being eligible to offices," by asking "if it was reasonable to suppose that the people would choose men without regarding their characters."⁴¹

Yet some Anti-Federalists noted that while majority rule would prevent the election of undesirables in their own time, the Constitution was a document that was designed to last for all time. Thus, William Lancaster of North Carolina stated: "Let us remember that we form a government for millions not yet in existence. I have not the art of divination. In the course of four or five hundred years, I do not know how it will work. This is most certain, that Papists may occupy that chair, and Mahometans may take it."⁴²

Supporters of the Constitution had a ready answer: if these alien religious groups were somehow to be elected in the future, Article VI would prevent them from imposing their spiritual doctrine on the country. It was, says one modern commentator, "a constitutionalized Golden Rule with a Machiavellian spin to it: 'Constrain yourself as you would constrain others.'"⁴³ To those who argued that "if all religious tests should be excluded, the Congress would hereafter establish Popery or some other tyrannical way of worship," Isaac Backus responded by pointing to Article VI's salutary effects: "But it is most certain, that no such way of worship can be established, without any religious test."⁴⁴

The fact that many supporters of the Constitution viewed Article VI not as a means to protect the rights of minority religions but as one that would ensure that the majority religion would never be oppressed belies the notion that there existed "an affirmative desire on the part of most Americans to welcome Catholics, Jews, or, perhaps most unthinkable of all, atheists, into positions of leadership."[45] As one commentator noted, "The people were much more religiously chauvinistic and parochial than the Constitution offered in their name."[46]

Leaders of the fight for religious freedom were well aware of this paradox. In fact, James Madison worried that "the rights of conscience in particular, if submitted to public definition," would be much narrower than he wanted.[47]

Although the leaders in the battle for religious freedom did not represent the perspective of most of the citizenry, a revolution in thought was still occurring. Despite continuing religious intolerance, there was a growing sentiment that virtue was not the characteristic of a single religion and that, in America, people of different faiths could respect one another and work together. As Daniel Shute, a Congregationalist minister from Hingham, Massachusetts, said, "Far from limiting my charity and confidence to men of my own denomination in religion, I suppose, and I believe, sir, that there are worthy characters among men of every denomination—among the Quakers—the Baptists—the Church of England—the Papists—and even among those who have no other guide, in the way to virtue and heaven, than the dictates of natural religion."[48]

Supporters of Article VI invoked the image of virtuous adherents of other religions to argue that religious test oaths were not only oppressive but also counterproductive. An oath requirement would not limit immoral people, who would have no scruples about swearing an oath they did not believe; but "it would exclude from offices conscientious and truly religious people, though equally capable as others. . . . Conscientious persons would not take such an oath, and would be therefore excluded."[49]

Other supporters argued that it was hypocritical to fight for one's own right to worship according to the dictates of conscience while penalizing those of different faiths who did likewise. Federalists began to highlight the inconsistencies in their opponents' statements. During the Virginia Ratifying Convention, James Innes represented the growing belief that religious liberty was not truly protected unless granted to all. He mocked the opponents of the Constitution who simultaneously complained that Article VI permitted "Turks, Jews, Infidels, Christians, and all other sects . . . [to] be President, and command the fleet and army," while objecting that Congress "will ask me as a private citizen what is my opinion on religion, and punish me if it does not conform to theirs."[50] The assertions that "liberty of conscience is in danger" from the granting of freedom to others, he said, were "repugnant and incompatible objections."

The fear of an "infidel" president, incidentally, derived not only from the Article VI ban on religious test oaths, but also from another section of the Constitution that evinces a similar perspective on the relation of religion to government. In Article II, section 1, the president is required to give an oath of loyalty, and the exact language of the oath is precisely laid out: "I do solemnly swear (or affirm) that I will faithfully execute the Office of President of the United States, and will to the best of my Ability, preserve, protect and defend the Constitution of the United States."[51]

What is remarkable about this language is that "in contrast to the form of virtually every oath then current in the courts of law, the oath for president does not conclude with the familiar words, So Help Me God."[52] Not only was the phrase "so help me God" a customary part of the oaths used in England,[53] but it was also common in the states. The Massachusetts Constitution of 1780, for example, required the following oath: "I, A.B., do solemnly swear and affirm that I will faithfully and impartially discharge and perform all the duties incumbent on me as ———, according to the best of my abilities and understanding, agreeably to the rules and regulations of the constitution and the laws of the commonwealth: So help me, God."[54]

There was no discussion in the Constitutional Convention about the decision to omit "so help me God" from the presidential oath, but Anti-Federalists expressed their concern. The author "Agrippa," whose essays have been termed "the ablest anti-federal publications printed in Massachusetts,"[55] argued that "the framers of this new constitution did not even think it necessary that the president should believe that there is a God, although they require an oath of him."[56] John Sullivan of New Hampshire remarked that it was bad enough to lose the battle against the Article VI ban on test oaths, but "even if that was given up in all other cases, the President at least ought to be compelled to submit to it, for otherwise, says one, 'a Turk, Jew, Rom[an] Catholic, and what is worse than all, a Universal[ist], may be President of the United States.'"[57]

Despite the Article VI ban on religious oaths and the lack of religious reference in Article II, it is incorrect to view the document crafted in Philadelphia as representing a philosophy of "a godless Constitution and a godless politics."[58] First of all, the taking of an oath was understood to be a religious activity. Oliver Wolcott of Connecticut, for example, said that a religious test would be redundant since any oath, including those required by the Constitution, "is a direct appeal to that God who is the Avenger of Perjury," therefore "such an appeal to Him is a full acknowledgment of His being and providence."[59]

Even Madison saw the constitutional oaths as fundamentally religious. Edmund Pendleton had written to him suggesting that "since a belief of a Future State of Rewards & Punishments, can alone give consciensious Obligation to Observe an Oath, It would seem that [a religious] Test should be required or Oaths Abolished."[60] Madison answered that religious people would treat the oaths that were required as religious declarations. "Is not a religious test as far as it is necessary, or would operate, involved in the oath itself?" he asked.[61] "If the person swearing believes in the supreme Being who is invoked, and in the penal consequences of offending him, either in this or a future world or both, he will be under the same restraint from perjury as if he had previously subscribed a test requiring this belief. If the person in question be an unbeliever in these points and would notwithstanding take the oath, a previous test could have no effect."

On the assumption that oaths were inherently religious, the delegates at the convention provided the option of giving an "oath or affirmation." This phrase appears in sections describing Senators sitting to try an impeachment, the presidential oath, and the oath of loyalty to the Constitution that federal and state officials must take.[62] The option of "affirmation" was considered essential for religious denominations such as the Quakers whose interpretation of the Bible forbade the swearing of oaths.[63] These groups were willing to "affirm" that their statements were truthful, and in a rare display of universal respect for a minority religion, by 1789 every state had made some provision to permit those with religious scruples to substitute an affirmation for a sworn statement.[64] It was thus not surprising that the Constitutional Convention's decision to provide the "oath or affirmation" option was approved without debate. This language rightfully has been termed "one of the clearest illustrations of the Founders' affirmative accommodation of religious belief."[65]

There is no evidence that anyone at the convention suggested that the affirmation option was provided to benefit atheists or other nonbelievers. Nonetheless, the delegates chose not to follow the example of states that limited affirmations to adherents of specified religions. Maryland, for instance, provided that "the people called Quakers, those called Dunkers, and those called Menonists, holding it unlawful to take an oath on any occasion, ought to be allowed to make their solemn affirmation."[66] By permitting everyone to affirm in lieu of taking an oath, the delegates, intentionally or not, provided the broadest possible protection for liberty of conscience.

On the other hand, the framers did not avoid all religious connotation or say simply that federal and state officials "shall promise to support this Constitution." The "oath or affirmation" provisions reflect a conscious balancing. Religion was to be neither excluded nor required in the new national government.

RELIGIOUS LANGUAGE IN THE CONSTITUTION

There are two provisions of the Constitution that are said to demonstrate that the framers intended to support Christianity. Much has been made of the fact that the phrase "in the Year of our Lord," an unmistakable reference to Jesus Christ, appears in the so-called attestation clause at the end of the Constitution: "Done in Convention by the Unanimous Consent of the States present the Seventeenth Day of September *in the Year of our Lord* one thousand seven hundred and Eighty seven and of the Independance of the United States of America the Twelfth In witness whereof We have hereunto subscribed our Names."[67]

In the nineteenth century, Jasper Adams, an Episcopal minister, declared that this language constituted, "a distinct recognition of the authority of Christ, and of course, of his religion by the people of the United States."[68] More recently, the Heritage Foundation's *Guide to the Constitution* explained: "The language here is neither insignificant nor unintentional: these dates serve to place the document in the context of the religious traditions of Western civilization and, at the same time, to link it to the regime principles proclaimed in the Declaration of Independence, the Constitution having been written in the twelfth year after July 1776."[69]

If the delegates at the Constitutional Convention had discussed the phrase, the claim of religious significance might be credible. We might then have some evidence to set against the counterargument that "in the Year of our Lord" was a mere "formality that was a conventional mechanism for noting the date at the time the Constitution was written."[70] In reality, however, the phrase "in the Year of our Lord one thousand seven hundred and Eighty seven and of the Independance of the United States of America the Twelfth" has the dubious distinction of being the only part of the Constitution on which the delegates did not vote.

To understand the attestation clause, one must focus on the final days of the Constitutional Convention. On Saturday, September 15, the convention approved all seven articles of the Constitution and ordered that it be "engrossed,"[71] that is, copied neatly for presentation as a legal document. This work was performed by Jacob Shallus, an assistant clerk of the Pennsylvania State Assembly. On Monday, September 17, the final day of the convention, Shallus presented the delegates with "four elegant pages of parchment text."[72]

Some who seek religious import in the attestation clause erroneously claim that it is part of Article VII (which states in its entirety: "The ratification of the conventions of nine states shall be sufficient for the establishment of this Constitution between the states so ratifying the same.")[73] This even appears in a 2002 act of Congress, which refers to "the express religious reference 'Year of our Lord' in Article VII."[74] The attestation clause physically appears after Article VII and can in no way be considered part of it. By the time the attestation clause was added, all seven articles had been completed, voted upon, and engrossed on parchment.

As they prepared to sign the completed document, the delegates knew that ratification by the states would be made substantially more difficult if the convention was perceived as divided.[75] Benjamin Franklin wrote an address, read by James Wilson, urging unanimous approval of the Constitution. He urged each recalcitrant delegate to "doubt a little of his own Infallibility" and consider the dangers of certitude in either politics or religion:

> Most men indeed as well as most sects in Religion, think themselves in possession of all truth, and that whereever others differ from them it is so far error. Steele, a Protestant, in a Dedication tells the Pope that the only difference between our Churches in their opinions of the certainty of their doctrines is, the Church of Rome is infallible and the Church of England is never in the wrong. But

though many private persons think almost as highly of their own infallibility as of that of their sect, few express it so naturally as a certain French lady, who in a dispute with her sister, said "I don't know how it happens, Sister but I meet with no body but myself, that's always in the right—Il n'y a que moi qui a toujours raison."[76]

Unanimity, though, was not attainable. Several delegates, including George Mason, whose call for a Bill of Rights had been rejected, had already indicated that they would not sign the document. New York State was ineligible to vote, since only one member, Alexander Hamilton, of its three-member delegation was still attending the Convention.

To create the appearance of unanimity, Franklin proposed a devious locution.[77] Those individuals signing would not endorse the document itself, but only attest to the fact that the Constitution had been "Done in Convention by the *unanimous consent of the States present.*"[78] Since a majority of delegates of every state but New York supported the Constitution, and New York, with only one delegate in attendance, was not technically "present," the signers could truthfully declare there had been "unanimous consent" of "the states present." Though some "disliked the equivocal form of the signing," the delegates voted overwhelmingly to approve the motion.[79]

Franklin's motion, however, did not contain the phrase "in the Year of Our Lord." His exact motion for the attestation clause read: "Done in Convention, by the unanimous consent of the States present the 17th. of Sepr. &c—In Witness whereof we have hereunto subscribed our names."[80] Thus, the delegates voted for the language indicating unanimity, but they never voted on the phrase "in the Year of our Lord one thousand seven hundred and Eighty seven and of the Independence of the United States of America the Twelfth."

It is possible that the delegates signed the Constitution before the attestation clause was even added to it. They signed by state, and we know that Alexander Hamilton was the person who wrote the names of each state on the document.[81] Shallus, who was not a delegate, would not have been permitted in the room while the debates were being conducted and was "presumably . . . standing by outside the meeting room since he engrossed the adopted closing."[82]

Thus it appears that the decision to include the phrase "in the Year of our Lord," was made by Jacob Shallus, the amanuensis, not the delegates,[83] and he may even have written it after the signing was complete.[84] Regardless of when Shallus wrote those words, it is pointless to ascribe meaning to language the delegates did not draft and for which they did not vote.

There is, however, one provision that does reflect the drafters' awareness of the role Christianity played in their society. Article I, section 7, which details the amount of time allotted the president to decide whether to sign or veto a bill, provides: "If any Bill shall not be returned by the President within ten Days (Sundays excepted) after it shall have been presented to him, the Same shall be a Law, in like Manner as if he had signed it."[85]

The "Sunday excepted" language is obviously different from the ubiquitous state laws then in existence that banned work on "the Sabbath."[86] Nonetheless, the fact that the delegates viewed Sunday not to be a presidential workday is noteworthy.

The records do not indicate who proposed the "Sunday excepted" language. On August 6, 1787, the convention voted to give the President "seven days after it shall have been presented to him" to return a bill to Congress.[87] This was changed to its present form on August 15; Madison's records simply state that the delegates agreed that "'ten days (Sundays excepted)' instead of 'seven' were allowed the President for returning with his objections."[88]

Those who argue that the purpose of the "Sunday excepted" language was "not to endorse religious observance" contend that it was added to allow the president's obligation to consider the value of legislation with "due diligence and deliberation to coexist with the

eighteenth century's bans on Sunday labor and travel."[89] It is true that
the president and his advisors, were they in states with strict Sunday-
observance laws when a bill was passed, might find it difficult to meet
and deliberate on a Sunday. Nonetheless, such a narrow reading of
the provision overlooks the common legislative and governmental
practices of that time.

The convention itself employed the same "Sunday excepted"
phrase just three days after it was added to the draft of the Constitution. On August 18, the South Carolinian John Rutledge voiced his
concern over the length of the proceedings, and the convention approved his proposal that they meet six days a week: "Resolved, That
this Convention will meet punctually at 10 o'clock, every morning,
(Sundays excepted,) and sit till 4 o'clock in the afternoon."[90] The Continental Congress had used the same phrase when it decided to meet
more frequently: "Resolved, That for the more speedy and effectual
discharge of business, the following rules be invariably observed: That
Congress be opened every morning at 10 o'Clock, Sundays excepted."[91]

At the time the Constitution was drafted, the Christian view of
Sunday as the Sabbath day on which, at minimum, governmental
work would not be conducted, was generally accepted. The Constitution's "Sunday excepted" language permitted, without requiring, a
president to have ten full days to consider whether to approve legislation without sacrificing his likely day of rest. Even if the president
did work on Sundays, the phrase arguably provided the added benefit
of protecting Congress when it made its expected choice not to meet
on Sundays. Under the Constitution, if a president is unable to return
a bill to Congress because "Congress by their Adjournment prevent
its Return," the bill is killed, and unlike other vetoes, the president's
action is not subject to override by a two-thirds vote of each House.[92]
Thus, if the tenth day after a bill was sent to the president was a
Sunday, and Congress were to have adjourned for that day, their adjournment would "prevent" the president from returning the bill to

Congress. Under this interpretation, Congress would lose the opportunity to override, unless Sundays were specifically excluded.[93]

One should not read too much into the "Sunday excepted" language. Robert Baird, a nineteenth-century evangelical Presbyterian minister, argued that by excepting Sundays, the framers "were legislating not for Jews, Mohammedans, infidels, pagans, atheists, but for Christians. And, believing the Christian religion the only one calculated to sustain and perpetuate the government about to be formed, they adopted it as the basis of the infant republic. This nation had a religion, and it was the Christian religion."[94] Especially given that the delegates did not ban all governmental activity on Sundays, and in light of the other provisions of the Constitution already discussed, the "Sunday excepted" language is more properly seen as an acknowledgment of the dominant religious faith and a desire to permit those of that faith to exercise their religion. It reveals an intent "merely to recognize the right of the President in harmony with a prevailing custom to observe a weekly day of rest if he chose to do so and not to establish a Sabbath by law or in any way make its observance mandatory."[95]

For a document that is supposedly "silent on the subject of God and Christianity,"[96] the Constitution expresses some important thoughts on the relationship between religion and government, although these thoughts appear to point in different directions. The "Sunday excepted" and the "oath and affirmation" provisions demonstrate a governmental respect for religious practices and an awareness that the vast majority of American citizens were Christians. The "no religious test" clause, presidential oath, and Preamble reveal a counterimpulse, signifying that regardless of the individual religious beliefs of most citizens, the American government was not to be defined by even the broadest religious conception.

A complication in the attempt to strike this delicate and imprecise balance was the reality that the nation's population was far more religiously diverse than that of any delegate's own state. The framers knew they were drafting a charter to govern an "extended Country, embracing so great a diversity of interests."[97] Many of them understood that to govern and unite such a population would require a new and greater sensitivity to minority religions. For example, Oliver Ellsworth, a Connecticut delegate to the Constitutional Convention, wrote an essay (under the name "A Landowner") explaining why national religious tests would be impractical: "A test in favor of any one denomination of Christians would be to the last degree absurd in the United States. If it were in favor of either Congregationalists, Presbyterians, Episcopalians, Baptists, or Quakers, it would incapacitate more than three-fourths of the American citizens for any public office; and thus degrade them from the rank of freemen."[98]

Daniel Shute also used the size and diversity of the United States to argue against religious oaths: "In this great and extensive empire, there is and will be a great variety of sentiments in religion among its inhabitants. Upon the plan of a religious test, the question I think must be, who shall be excluded from national trusts? Whatever answer bigotry may suggest, the dictates of candour and equity, I conceive, will be none."[99]

Even in the midst of such diversity, one could find certain principles upon which most denominations would agree. Ellsworth conceded that it would not violate the religious precepts of most Americans to require "all persons appointed to office to declare, at the time of their admission, their belief in the being of a God and in the divine authority of the Scriptures."[100] But the framers did not seek this apparent common ground. One reason was that many of them understood that the drafting of the Constitution created the opportunity to consider what freedom of religion meant from a uniquely American perspective, a perspective that would differ from those in the individual states. According to the Baptist leader John Leland, the U.S. Constitution was founded on higher principles than those of many of the states: "The federal constitution certainly had the advantage of any of the state constitutions, in being made by the wisest men in the whole nation . . . and that constitution forbids Congress ever to establish any kind of religion, or require any religious test to qualify any officer in any department of federal government."[101] James Iredell declared that the Constitution proved that "it was the intention of those who formed this system to establish a general religious liberty in America."[102]

Under the aptly chosen pseudonym "An American Citizen," Tench Coxe explained how Article VI distinguished America from other nations:

> In Italy, Spain and Portugal, no protestant can hold a public trust. In England every Presbyterian, and other person not of their established church, is incapable of holding an office. No such impious deprivation of the rights of men can take place under the new Federal constitution. The convention has the honor of proposing the first public act, by which any nation has ever divested itself of a power, every exercise of which is a trespass on the Majesty of Heaven.[103]

A Pennsylvanian essayist who called himself "A Friend Of Society And Liberty" contended that the lack of religious discrimination "will lead to a sort of federal union among the various churches which it has pleased God to raise up in the world."[104] He proclaimed that when "the oppressed dissenters from the established churches of Britain, Ireland, Holland, Germany, France, Spain and Italy" learned of the Constitution, they would "at once cry out, America is 'the land of promise.'"

Many understood that this "promised land," united under its new Constitution, would have a fundamentally different view of religious minorities. Instead of merely tolerating those with different faiths, the new nation would embrace all religions.

This new mindset can be seen in two of the larger processionals that were held to celebrate the fact that once New Hampshire and Virginia had given their approval, the Constitution was officially ratified. In July 1788, Federalists hoped a large rally would encourage New York

State, where a difficult ratification battle was then occurring, to become the eleventh state to ratify. A giant processional was scheduled for July 22. Shortly before that date, the organizers agreed to a one-day delay "in order to give the Jews an opportunity to Join in the festivals, the 22nd being one of their holidays."[105] To reschedule a large public event out of respect for Jewish religious sensitivities would have been unthinkable a few years earlier. But now the concept of "American" was broad enough to include all, regardless of religious faith. Adrian Bancker, a New York Federalist who was a member of the First Reformed Dutch Church,[106] wrote, "I Observe the Grand procession is put of[f] to the 23d. I think it a great Compliment paid the Jews."[107]

An equally significant compliment had been "paid the Jews" a few weeks earlier at the Pennsylvania parade held on July 4, 1788. One of the highlights of the "grand, solemn, & pleasing spectacle," according to Joseph Grove John Bend, an assistant minister of the United Churches of Christ Church in Philadelphia, was the sight of seventeen clergymen marching together "who displayed a complete triumph over religious prejudices: The Jew joined the Christian; the Episcopalian the Presbyterian; & the Seceder the Roman Catholic, & all walked arm in arm, exhibiting a proof of brotherly affection, & testifying their approbation of the New Constitution."[108]

Benjamin Rush, a signer of the Declaration of Independence and leading Pennsylvanian Federalist, saw the interfaith processional as symbolic of the new American ethos: "The Rabbi of the Jews, locked in the arms of two ministers of the gospel, was a most delightful sight. There could not have been a more happy emblem contrived, of that section of the new constitution, which opens all its power and offices alike, not only to every sect of christians, but to worthy men of *every* religion."[109]

When the parade finished, seventeen thousand celebrants gathered on Bush Hill, where "a very large circular range of tables, covered with awnings, and plentifully spread with a cold collation, had been prepared the day before, by the committee of provisions."[110] In an extraordinary sign of respect, the committee of provisions set aside one table with kosher food, "a separate table for the Jews, who could not partake of the meals from the other tables; but they had a full supply of soused salmon, bread and crackers, almonds, raisins, etc."[111]

In Pennsylvania, where non-Christians were not permitted to serve in the state legislature, this seemingly small gesture communicated something revolutionary. Inclusion as an American was not to be determined by one's religion; differences in religion were to be celebrated, rather than punished; and under the new Constitution, religion would unite, not divide, the United States. As Benjamin Rush concluded his description of the Philadelphia processional, "'Tis done! We have become a nation."[112]

CHAPTER 5

Adding the First Amendment

T HE NATION had not finished drafting its constitutional charter. Led by James Madison, the first Congress corrected an ominous omission in the original Constitution and gave Anti-Federalists what many had said they wanted, a bill of rights.[1]

The first demand for a bill of rights had been raised at the very end of the Constitutional Convention. On September 12, 1787, as delegates were preparing to vote on the final language, George Mason announced that he wished the Constitution "had been prefaced with a Bill of Rights."[2] Suggesting that the delegates could copy language from the recently enacted state constitutions, Mason optimistically promised that "a bill might be prepared in a few hours." Other than Elbridge Gerry, Mason's last-minute proposal had no supporters and was voted down.[3]

The Constitution's opponents realized that the lack of a bill of rights provided them a potentially persuasive argument. Delaware ratified the Constitution quickly, on December 7, but opposition arose in the next state, Pennsylvania. Anti-Federalists deplored the lack of a bill of rights and criticized the absence of explicit protection for religious freedom. A letter to the *Philadelphia Freeman's Journal* exclaimed: "There is no declaration, that all men have a natural and unalienable right to worship Almighty God, according to the dictates of their own consciences and understanding; and that no man ought, or of right can be compelled to attend any religious worship, or erect or support any place of worship, or maintain any ministry, contrary to, or against his own free will and consent."[4]

James Wilson, who had been a delegate at the convention, answered that there was no need for a bill of rights. On October 6, 1787, he delivered a speech outside the Pennsylvania State House[5] that was reprinted throughout the nation and became, according to the historian Bernard Bailyn, "the single most influential and most frequently cited document in the entire ratification debate."[6] Wilson's central argument was that a bill of rights was unnecessary because the federal government would possess only the limited power explicitly given by the Constitution; it "would have been superfluous and absurd," he claimed, to have provided for "privileges, of which we are not divested." Throughout the ratification debate, the Federalists stressed the argument that Congress had only limited powers. As Madison would later declare, "There is not a shadow of right in the general government to intermeddle with religion."[7]

This line of argument did not reassure the Anti-Federalists. John Smilie, one of the leaders of the Pennsylvania Anti-Federalists, said that a declaration of rights was needed to establish "some criterion . . . by which it could be easily and constitutionally ascertained how far our governors may proceed, and by which it might appear when they transgress their jurisdiction." Later he argued that the unamended Constitution threatened religious freedom: "The Rights of Conscience are not secured.—Priestcraft useful to all tyrannical Govts.—Congress may establish any Religion."[8]

There are two interesting aspects to Smilie's argument. First, he linked the danger to "rights of conscience" with a congressional religious establishment. Second, since Pennsylvania had never established a state church, his opposition was not focused on any particular religion that Congress might establish, but on the very concept of established religion.

After the Pennsylvania convention voted to ratify the Constitution, by a vote of 46–23, twenty-one of the dissenting members signed
a document listing their objections and proposing amendments.
These were the first formal proposals to amend the newly drafted
Constitution. To protect freedom of religion, the dissenters offered
the following language: "The right of conscience shall be held inviolable; and neither the legislative, executive nor judicial powers of the
United States shall have authority to alter, abrogate, or infringe any
part of the constitution of the several states, which provide for the
preservation of liberty in matters of religion."[9]

The next three states to ratify, New Jersey on December 18, Georgia on January 2, 1788, and Connecticut on January 9, did so with
little disagreement. The New Jersey and Georgia conventions voted
unanimously, and Connecticut ratified by a 128–40 margin.

The first serious threat to ratification occurred in Massachusetts,
where Anti-Federalists demanded that the Constitution be amended
before they would agree to ratify it. The Federalists knew that this
would effectively destroy any chance of replacing the Articles of Confederation. As Madison wrote in *Federalist* 38, a second constitutional
convention would be irrevocably frustrated by "discord and ferment,"
and unable to reproduce the sense of compromise that had enabled
the Philadelphia convention to succeed.

Facing strong opposition, the Federalists in Massachusetts devised
a strategy to accommodate the desire for amendments. In exchange
for a vote on ratification, the Federalists would agree to attach a list
of proposed amendments to be considered when the new government
went into effect. The Massachusetts Federalist Nathaniel Gorham
wrote Madison that they would lose the vote "unless we can take of[f]
some of the opposition by amendments. I do not mean those to be
made the condition of the ratification—but recommendatory only."[10]
Despite this concession, when the Massachusetts convention voted
on February 6, the margin for ratification was the narrowest yet,

187–168.[11] The convention proposed nine amendments, including the right to a jury trial in civil cases. Massachusetts apparently did not consider the unamended Constitution a threat to its own religious establishment, since none of their proposed amendments concerned religion.[12]

At about this time, Madison was planning to leave New York City, where he was coauthoring *The Federalist* with Alexander Hamilton, in order to return to Virginia for that state's ratifying convention. Friends had written him that Anti-Federalists were gaining support in his home district of Orange County, and they advised him to return to campaign for a seat at the convention. Madison was warned that Patrick Henry, his primary adversary from the recent fight against the general assessment, had attracted the support of Madison's former allies, the Baptists, in opposing the Constitution.[13] On February 29, Edmund Randolph told Madison that "the baptist interest . . . [is] highly incensed by [Henry's] opinions and public speeches."[14] Joseph Spencer, a Virginia Baptist who had been imprisoned for illegal preaching in 1783,[15] also reported to Madison that Baptist preachers "are much alarm'd fearing Relegious liberty is not Sufficiently secur'd." He urged Madison to address their concerns directly by meeting personally with the most influential Baptist minister, John Leland: "As Mr. Leeland Lyes in your Way home from Fredricksburg to Orange [I] would advise you'l call on him & Spend a few Howers in his Company."[16]

John Leland, a Massachusetts native, had moved to Virginia in 1776, and in 1788 was seen as the most prominent Baptist leader in the state. He would eventually become a friend and ally of both Madison and Jefferson, and his visionary philosophy helped define the scope of the appropriate relationship between religion and government. He was the strongest American clerical voice since Roger Williams to advocate universal religious freedom. While Leland himself was devoutly religious, he was adamant that government had no role in favoring any religious doctrine. When government was "rightly formed," he said, "it embraces Pagans, Jews, Mahometans and Christians, within its fostering arms—prescribes no creed of faith for either of them—proscribes none of them for being heretics, promotes the man of talents and integrity, without inquiring after his religion—[and] impartially protects all of them."[17]

Leland spoke about other religions with genuine respect. In rebutting the argument John Adams had made while meeting with Baptists during the first Continental Congress, in which he defended the Massachusetts tax supporting Christian teaching on the grounds that it protected the "tender consciences" of those who sincerely believe that such governmental support was the best way to serve God,[18] Leland asked, "Had a Jew and a Turk been in the same convention, and founded a plea on tender conscience—the first, to abstain from hogs' flesh, and the last, to abstain from wine, would the gentleman have been so careful of hurting the soft feelings of the son of Isaac, and the son of Ishmael, that he would have abstained from pork and wine all his days?"[19]

Later in his career, Leland would continue his fight for religious acceptance by combating the wave of anti-Catholic hysteria that afflicted the United States in the 1830s. "No man," he declared, "who has the soul of an American, and the heart of affection for our democratic institutions, will either fear or wish to injure the papists."[20] Fundamental to his philosophy was the belief that the "rights of conscience and private judgment" were inalienable rights that no government could acquire and no individual could surrender: "Like sight, hearing, thinking and breathing, they are always attached to individuals."[21] Accordingly, he said, "religion is a matter entirely between God and individuals," and "civil rulers have nothing to do with religion in their official capacities."[22] Although he believed that religion and morality were essential for a good life, he asserted that, "a man has a civil right to believe that which is erroneous, and do that which is morally wrong."[23]

Leland also opposed religious test oaths as being both a violation of the rights of those who did not share the particular faith and a wrongful intrusion of the government into religion: "If a creed of faith, established by law, was ever so short, and ever so true; if I believed the whole of it with all my heart—should I subscribe to it before a magistrate, in order to get indulgence, preferment, or even protection—I should be guilty of a species of idolatry, by acknowledging a power, that the Head of the Church, Jesus Christ, has never appointed."[24]

Similarly, even though he would not pay a governmental tax to support religion, Leland believed it would violate his faith to ask for an exemption, "for, in so doing, I should confess that the legislature had authority to pamper one religious order in the state, and make all others pay obeisance to that sheaf."[25] His definition of an establishment of religion covered a wide range of governmental activities, including any form of governmental financial support for religion. He opposed the hiring of legislative chaplains, by which legislators "make the nation pay for their devotion," because "a legal compensation for religious services, is a species of religious establishment."[26]

Leland also viewed laws forbidding work on Sundays as equivalent to establishment: "As it is not the province of civil government to establish forms of religion, and force a maintenance for the preachers, so it does not belong to that power to establish fixed holy days for divine worship."[27] His opposition, he added, hardly reflected antagonism toward the Sabbath itself: "When I see men turn their backs upon public worship, and pursue their labor or recreation in preference to the service of God, either on Sunday or on any other day, my heart . . . vents itself in the words of Paul, 'I pray you in Christ's stead, be you reconciled to God.'"[28] Noting the effect Sunday Sabbath laws had on those of different faiths, Leland said: "The Jews among us, and those Christians who prefer the seventh day to the first, (though a very respectable body,) are a minority in these United States. If this day is clothed with a legal establishment to enforce its observance, it loses its Christian character and becomes a tyrant over conscience."[29]

Any such attempt by Christians to "regulate their religion by law," Leland felt, violated the Bible.[30] The apostles never spoke of governmental regulation of religion, he said, because "they understood better the will of their Master, who had said, 'my kingdom is not of this world.'"

All forms of religious establishment, Leland declared, also harmed the very religion they claimed to be trying to help. First, he said, "they are calculated to destroy those very virtues that religion is designed to build up; to encourage fraud and violence over the earth."[31] Second, the very combination of government and religion degraded religion: "The fondness of magistrates to foster Christianity, has done it more harm than all the persecutions ever did. Persecution, like a lion, tears the saints to death, but leaves Christianity pure: state establishment of religion, like a bear, hugs the saints, but corrupts Christianity, and reduces it to a level with state policy."[32]

Leland feared that the Constitution that came out of Philadelphia would not prevent such an evil from occurring on a national level. On March 7, 1788, he helped lead the Baptist General Committee of Virginia in its discussion of whether "the new Federal Constitution, which had now lately made its appearance in public, made sufficient provision for the secure enjoyment of religious liberty."[33] According to the report of that meeting, "it was agreed unanimously that, in the opinion of the General Committee, it did not."

When Joseph Spencer wrote to Madison urging him to meet with Leland, he was able to give Madison a unique insight into Leland's thoughts on the Constitution's defects. Leland had written a letter describing his major objections and had asked Spencer to deliver it to Thomas Barber, a strong Anti-Federalist who was running against Madison for a seat at the ratification convention. Spencer copied the document and enclosed it in his letter to Madison.

Leland's main objection was the lack of a bill of rights, especially the lack of specific protection for religious freedom: "What is dearest of all—Religious Liberty, is not Sufficiently Secured, No religious test is required as a Qualification to fill any office under the United States, but if a Majority of Congress with the president favor one System more then another, they may oblige all others *to pay to the Support* of their System as Much as they please."[34]

According to legend, Madison stopped on his trip back from New York City and spent an afternoon with Leland discussing the Constitution under the shade of an oak tree in Gum Spring, Virginia.[35] Whether they actually met by this tree, located in what is now known as Leland-Madison Park, is uncertain. Nonetheless, according to the historian Stuart Leibiger: "Madison followed Spencer's advice and met Leland, about March 22, somewhere between Fredericksburg and Orange. Exactly what transpired has been obfuscated by local myth, but it is clear that Madison overcame Leland's doubts about the Constitution and gained his support in the campaign."[36] Two strong pieces of evidence support Leibiger's conclusion. First, the vote, which had been leaning toward the Anti-Federalists, went overwhelmingly for Madison.[37] Second, one of those voting for Madison was Leland himself, who would later tell how he "gave [his] vote for a friend to its ratification, and have never repented it."[38]

By the time the Virginia Ratifying Convention convened on June 2, 1788, eight states had voted to approve the Constitution, one short of the nine necessary for official ratification. As they had in the 1785 battle over the general assessment, Patrick Henry and James Madison again led opposing sides in the ratification debates.

On June 6, Madison attempted to answer the Anti-Federalist concern that the lack of a bill of rights threatened religious freedom. Congress could not impose its will on religion, Madison said, because "this subject is, for the honor of America, perfectly free and unshackled: The Government has no jurisdiction over it."[39]

To answer Madison, Henry called upon an unlikely source, Thomas Jefferson. Madison knew that Jefferson was concerned that the Constitution did not have a bill of rights. The previous December, Jefferson had written to Madison from France, criticizing the Constitution for not "providing clearly and without the aid of sophisms for freedom of religion" and other fundamental rights.[40] Jefferson concluded by stating that "a Bill of Rights is what the people are entitled to against every government on earth, general or particular, and what no just government should refuse or rest on inferences."

Madison, of course, kept the letter secret, but another letter by Jefferson, this one written to a Richmond merchant, Alexander Donald, was passed to Henry. In this letter, Jefferson described his support for both the Constitution and for a bill of rights: "I wish with all my soul that the nine first Conventions may accept the new Constitution, because this will secure to us the good it contains, which I think great and important. But I equally wish that the four latest conventions, whichever they be, may refuse to accede to it till a declaration of rights be annexed."[41]

On June 12, Henry tried to use these words to prevent Virginia's ratification of the Constitution. Since New Hampshire was holding its ratification convention at the same time (and would ratify four days before Virginia), Henry argued that Jefferson would want Virginia to delay ratifying the Constitution. Mocking the Federalists, he said that Jefferson's amendments "go to that despised thing, called a bill of rights, and all the rights which are dear to human nature—trial by jury, the liberty of religion and the press, &."[42] He urged the delegates to follow the advice of the "illustrious citizen of Virginia, who is now in Paris," and "reject this Government, till it be amended."[43]

After several tense weeks of political infighting, Madison was able to craft a compromise similar to that which had worked in Massachusetts. Virginia's convention narrowly agreed to ratify the Constitution, by a vote of 89 to 79, with a recommendation that "subsequent amendments" be added to the document.[44] Among these was one directed at religious liberty,[45] modeled after Virginia's 1776 Declaration of Rights, with one significant difference. Both the 1776 Declaration and the proposed amendment began with the statement "That religion, or the duty which we owe to our Creator, and the manner of discharging it, can be directed only by reason and conviction, not by force or violence," and both said that all people were entitled "to the free exercise of religion, according to the dictates of conscience." The difference was that the 1776 Declaration ended with the phrase "it is the mutual duty of all to practice Christian forbearance, love, and charity toward each other." The 1788 proposal omitted this denominational language and instead ended by declaring that "no particular religious sect or society ought to be favored or established by law in preference to others."[46]

Although the ratification fight in Virginia had ended, Patrick Henry was determined to continue his battle with Madison. As Virginia was preparing to send its legislators to the first Congress, Henry, then governor, plotted to keep Madison out of the new federal government. First, he convinced the Virginia legislature not to appoint Madison to the U.S. Senate, declaring on the assembly floor that Madison's election "would terminate in producing rivulets of blood throughout the land."[47]

When Madison then decided to run for the House of Representatives, Henry drew the state's legislative map so that Madison's home county was placed in a district with counties that had sent Anti-Federalists to the ratification convention.[48] As Jefferson explained, Henry "so modelled the districts for representatives as to tack Orange to counties where himself has great influence that Madison may not be elected."[49] Henry also persuaded James Monroe, a friend of Madison's, to run against him.[50]

As an additional measure, Henry spearheaded a campaign to convince voters that Madison was opposed to amending the Constitution to add a bill of rights. Hardin Burnley, a Madison ally, wrote to him on December 16 to report that people were being told "that you are wholly opposed to any alteration in the Govt. having declared that you did not think that a single letter in it would admit of a change."[51]

Knowing that many of his supporters, especially among the Baptists, were insistent on the need for a bill of rights, Madison made what has been called "one of the most important campaign promises in American history."[52] In a series of letters, he admitted opposing amendments before ratification but declared that they were now appropriate. He wrote to the Baptist minister George Eve to tell him he believed "that the Constitution ought to be revised, and that the first Congress meeting under it, ought to prepare and recommend to the States for ratification, the most satisfactory provisions for all essential rights, particularly the rights of Conscience in the fullest latitude."[53]

This pledge proved critical in Madison's election campaign. On January 18, 1789, Eve attended a Saturday evening service at a church in Culpeper County.[54] Religious worship turned to political debate when Joel Early, an Anti-Federalist, began accusing Madison of having said that "the Constitution had no defects, and that it was the nearest to Perfection of any thing that Could be obtained."[55] According to another Madison supporter who attended the service, Benjamin Johnson, Eve "took a very Spirited and decided Part in your favour, he Spoke Long on the Subject, and reminded them of the many important Services which you had rendered their Society, in particular the Act for establishing Religious Liberty, also the bill for a general Assessment; which was averted by your Particular efforts; Mr. Eve urged that he thought they were under Obligations to you, and had much more reason to place their Confidence in you, than Mr. Monroe."[56]

With help from Eve, Leland, and others, Madison was able to defeat Monroe in the February 2 election.[57] Shortly afterward, Leland sent Madison a self-deprecating note: "I congratulate you in your Appointment, as a Representative to Congress; and if my Undertaking in the Cause conduced Nothing else towards it, it certainly gave Mr.

Madison one Vote." In return for his support, Leland said, "One Thing I shall expect; that if religious Liberty is anywise threatened, that I shall receive the earliest Intelligence."[58]

Despite his campaign pledge, Madison was not enthusiastic about adding a bill of rights to the Constitution. One of his major concerns, he wrote to Jefferson, was his fear that the country was not ready to provide complete protection for religious liberty: "There is great reason to fear that the most essential rights could not be obtained in the requisite latitude. I am sure that the rights of conscience in particular, if submitted to public definition, would be narrowed much more than they are likely ever to be by an assumed power."[59]

Madison also had little faith that any declaration of rights would be obeyed. He warned that bills of rights, which he termed mere "parchment barriers," could not withstand the will of "overbearing majorities." Recalling Virginia's battle over the general assessment, Madison remarked that "it is well known that a religious establishment wd. have taken place in that State if the legislative majority had found as they expected, a majority of the people in favor of the measure; and I am persuaded that if a majority of the people were now of one sect, the measure would still take place."[60]

Nonetheless, Madison explained to Jefferson, he respected those who wanted, for "the most honorable & patriotic motives," amendments that might provide "further guards to public liberty & individual rights." He added that he saw two benefits that might be derived from adding a bill of rights. First, the amendments would help educate the populace, since "political truths declared in that solemn manner acquire by degrees the character of fundamental maxims of free Government." Second, in instances where oppression occurred not from the desires of "the interested majorities of the people" but from the "usurped acts of the Government," a bill of rights would provide "a good ground for an appeal to the sense of the community."[61]

Jefferson tried to respond to Madison's doubts. First, he wrote, there was a third benefit to a bill of rights. Jefferson understood, well ahead of most people, that judicial review might be able to protect minority rights. As he told Madison: "You omit one which has great weight with me, the legal check which it puts into the hands of the judiciary."[62] In answer to Madison's concern that they would not be able to obtain the guarantees of rights "in the requisite latitude," Jefferson agreed, but also argued from necessity: "Half a loaf is better than no bread. If we cannot secure all our rights, let us secure what we can." The centuries-old battle over the meaning of the first amendment is in many ways a battle over how much of that loaf Madison was able to secure.

CRAFTING THE FIRST AMENDMENT

Regardless of his misgivings, by the time the new Congress convened, Madison was committed to adding a bill of rights. On June 8, stating, "I considered myself bound in honor and in duty,"[63] Madison fulfilled his campaign promise and introduced a bill of rights on the floor of the House of Representatives. His notes for that day's speech, stating, "Bill of Rights—useful—not essential,"[64] indicate his continued ambivalence over what he later described as "the nauseous project of amendments."[65] Still, he told the House, a bill of rights should be added to the Constitution out of respect for those who opposed ratification because of "the jealousy they have for their liberty."[66] Even more pressing, he said, was that a bill of rights might induce North Carolina and Rhode Island, which had not yet ratified the Constitution, "to throw themselves into the bosom of the Confederacy."

In detailing the benefits that would follow adoption of a bill of rights, Madison seems to have heeded Jefferson's explanation of the potential value of judicial protection. With a bill of rights in place, he declared, "independent tribunals of justice will consider themselves in a peculiar manner the guardians of those rights; they will be an impenetrable bulwark against every assumption of power in the legislative or executive; they will be naturally led to resist every encroachment upon rights expressly stipulated for in the constitution by the declaration of rights."[67]

Unconvinced of the need for amendments, many of his fellow Representatives complained that the time taken up with drafting would detract from more important items.[68] George Clymer of Pennsylvania suspected that the proposed amendments were meant to distract former opponents of the Constitution without providing the substantive change in the form of government that had really motivated their opposition. The Bill of Rights, Clymer wrote, was "merely a tub to the whale."[69]

Nonetheless, Madison persisted, and was able to persuade the House to debate his proposed amendments. He drew his list of nineteen amendments from the more than two hundred proposals put forward by state ratifying conventions.[70] In drafting the provisions dealing with religious freedom, Madison was able to consider the recommendations of his home state of Virginia as well as those of the three other states that had proposed amendments dealing with the Congress's power over religion: New Hampshire, New York, and North Carolina.[71] He went beyond them all in writing three amendments dealing with religion:

> That in article 1st, section 9, between clauses 3 and 4, be inserted these clauses, to wit: The civil rights of none shall be abridged on account of religious belief or worship, nor shall any national religion be established, nor shall the full and equal rights of conscience be in any manner, or on any pretext, infringed.
> . . .
> The right of the people to keep and bear arms shall not be infringed; a well armed and well regulated militia being the best security of a free country; but no person religiously scrupulous of bearing arms shall be compelled to render military service in person.
> . . .
> That in article 1st, section 10, between clauses 1 and 2, be inserted this clause, to wit:

> No state shall violate the equal rights of conscience, or the freedom of the press, or the trial by jury in criminal cases.[72]

This last provision, preventing states from violating basic rights such as liberty of conscience and freedom of the press, appears in none of the proposals from the state ratifying conventions. It represented Madison's attempt to convince Congress to agree to a proposal that was similar to one he had been unable to persuade the Constitutional Convention to adopt. Madison had argued in Philadelphia for a provision that would have permitted Congress "to negative all laws passed by the several States contravening in the opinion of the Nat: Legislature the articles of Union, or any treaties subsisting under the authority of the Union." This congressional veto over state laws, he had maintained, was "essential to the efficacy & security of the Genl. Govt."[73] The convention was not willing to grant Congress such power over the states, and his proposal was defeated. In disappointment, Madison would write to Jefferson of his fear that without this provision, the Constitution would "neither effectually answer its national object nor prevent the local mischiefs which every where excite disgusts agst the state governments."[74]

Now, Madison was trying again, this time telling the House that preventing oppression by the states was as important as preventing that by the national government. Calling this proposal "the most valuable amendment in the whole list," he declared: "If there was any reason to restrain the Government of the United States from infringing upon these essential rights, it was equally necessary that they should be secured against the State Governments."[75]

Although the House of Representatives voted to approve this provision, it was eliminated in the Senate. It would not be until 1940 that the Supreme Court, in interpreting the Reconstruction-era Fourteenth Amendment, ruled that the U.S. Constitution prohibited state interference with religious liberty.[76]

Madison's other religion amendments traveled a complicated,

largely secret path until they emerged in the final language of the current First Amendment. It is extremely frustrating to modern commentators wishing to divine the meaning of the amendment's Delphic phrasings that very little useful information can be gleaned from the legislative history. Only one day of substantive debate on the religion clauses in the House was recorded, and there is no record of the debate in either the Senate or the House-Senate conference that produced the final language.

Great attention has been focused on that one day of House debate, August 15, 1789.[77] Even discounting the fact that the only available report of it is "incomplete and sometimes inaccurate,"[78] remarkably little insight can be gained into the meaning of the language that was considered, and even less into that of the different language ultimately chosen more than a month later.

The debate centered on a modified version of Madison's original language. A House committee, which included Madison, had been appointed to review his proposals, and the committee had changed the first one to read: "No religion shall be established by law, nor shall the equal rights of conscience be infringed." There is no record of why his phrasing was altered.

At the debate of the committee's amendment, Peter Silvester of New York said that he "feared it might be thought to have a tendency to abolish religion altogether." It is not immediately obvious how such abolition would occur, but Benjamin Huntington, a Congregationalist from Connecticut, explained that "a support of ministers, or building of places of worship might be construed into a religious establishment." In such a case, he said, federal courts might refuse to enforce otherwise legal state obligations to support religious institutions.

Huntington did not concede that legally mandated payments, such as those in his home state, should be viewed as an "establishment" of religion; he merely said that they "might" be so understood. Madison, who had termed the Virginia general assessment plan an "establishment," did not argue the meaning of that term with Huntington. Instead, he proposed adding the word "national" so that the amendment read "no national religion shall be established," thus making it clear that only Congress was being restrained, not the states.

Elbridge Gerry pounced on the word "national." Recalling the debate over ratifying the Constitution, which he had opposed, he pointed out that during the ratification battle, the Federalists had insisted that they favored a federal government, which recognized the sovereignty of the individual states, rather than a national government, which would have "consolidated the Union."[79] Refusing to let go of an old grudge, Gerry said that since the Federalists had been in favor of ratification without amendments, while the Anti-Federalists had wanted amendments first, "Their names then ought not to have been distinguished by federalists and antifederalists, but rats and antirats."

Madison withdrew his suggestion of the word "national." Without further discussion, the House voted to replace the committee's language with that proposed by Samuel Livermore of New Hampshire: "Congress shall make no laws touching religion, or infringing the rights of conscience."[80] On August 20, the House again modified the language, accepting the proposal of Fisher Ames of Massachusetts that the amendment read, "Congress shall make no law establishing religion, or to prevent the free exercise thereof, or to infringe the rights of conscience."

This was the first version to include both the phrases "free exercise" and "rights of conscience." On a simple linguistic level, they point to two different aspects of religious worship.[81] "Exercise" refers to what a person does; "conscience" refers to a person's private beliefs. Thus, "conscience" involves one's belief system, while "exercise" connotes religious activity. This dichotomy was expressed in Virginia's 1776 Declaration of Rights, which proclaimed: "All men are equally entitled to the free exercise of religion, according to the dictates of conscience."

Arguably, therefore, the decision to add the phrase "free exercise" implied a decision to include protection for religious activity as well as mere belief. If so, it obviously would prohibit a law directly targeting an activity because of its religious nature, such as Maryland's 1704 law making it a crime for Catholics to "take upon themselves the Education . . . of Youth."[82] A harder question would be whether that protection would require exemptions from laws that were not directed at religion but that had the effect of restricting a particular group's religious activity.

This general issue was not discussed, but one aspect raised in the debate was whether to adopt the proposal to exempt those who were "religiously scrupulous" from being "compelled to bear arms." In the course of a relatively short discussion, a full range of opinions was expressed on the merits of permitting a religious exemption from military service.

Most supportive of the religious exemption was Elias Boudinot, a New Jersey Federalist who later became president of the American Bible Association. He viewed the exemption as a way of preventing religious oppression and of showing "the world that proper care is taken that the Government may not interfere with the religious sentiments of any person." Several speakers argued that only explicitly religious motivation should qualify persons for an exemption. They agreed with Boudinot's position on the desirability of preventing religious oppression, but wanted to create a clear line between those with religious objections and those who were either shirking their duties or had other nonreligious motives. Gerry urged that the exemption "be confined to persons belonging to a religious sect scrupulous of bearing arms." Thomas Scott of Pennsylvania added that the goal should be "to guard against those who are of no religion."

Some opposed any religious exemption. Egbert Benson of New York argued that the desire not to bear arms "may be a religious persuasion, but it is no natural right, and therefore ought to be left to the discretion of the Government."[83]

The House voted narrowly, 24–22, to approve Madison's proposal, but it was rejected by the Senate. Again, we do not know the basis for their decision to remove the religious exemption from the militia clause.

While the House's language concerning establishment and free exercise was not rejected by the Senate, it was not left untouched.[84] There is no record of the Senate debate, but we know that several proposals were considered before the Senate voted on September 9 to change the language to "Congress shall make no law establishing articles of faith or a mode of worship, or prohibiting the free exercise of religion." This version, which differed significantly from the House version, was then sent back to the House.[85]

To resolve the disagreement over this and many of the other amendments, the House and Senate set up a conference committee. For the religion clauses, the conference committee made two changes to the earlier House version, deleting the reference to the "rights of conscience," but adding the word "respecting," so that the amendment read: "Congress shall make no law respecting an establishment of religion, or prohibiting the free exercise thereof." This was the final language that both houses agreed upon. The complete final version of what became the First Amendment reads: "Congress shall make no law respecting an establishment of religion, or prohibiting the free exercise thereof; or abridging the freedom of speech, or of the press; or the right of the people peaccably to assemble, and to petition the government for a redress of grievances."[86]

One of the most remarkable aspects of the story of the Bill of Rights is the apparent lack of public interest in its ratification by the states. Unlike the vigorous newspaper wars over the ratification of the Constitution, there seems to have been practically no newspaper discussion of the amendments.[87]

With Vermont accepted as the fourteenth state on March 4, 1791, eleven states constituted the three-fourths needed for ratifications. Ten state legislatures quickly passed the ten amendments we know today as the Bill of Rights, with virtually no recorded debate regarding how any legislative body understood any amendment's meaning. Virginia was the eleventh state to ratify the amendments. Its ratification was delayed two years while Patrick Henry sought to introduce other amendments to alter the structure of the federal government. As Edmund Randolph wrote Madison, Henry was "pleased with some of the proposed amendments; but still asks for the great desideratum, the destruction of direct taxation."[88] After the amendments passed the Virginia Assembly, they were stalled in the state senate by a vote of 8–7. The eight senators issued a statement condemning them for not adequately protecting religion:

> Although it goes to restrain Congress from passing laws establishing any national religion, they might, notwithstanding, levy taxes to any amount, for the support of religion or its preachers; and any particular denomination of christians might be so favored and supported by the General Government, as to give it a decided advantage over others, and in process of time render it as powerful and dangerous as if it was established as the national religion of the country.[89]

While this statement seems to indicate that the eight senators interpreted the establishment clause to permit Congress to impose taxes to support particular, favored religious denominations, their critique was not taken seriously. One reason was that the senators, all Henry allies, had never fought to limit the role of government in religion and had supported both the funding of the Anglican Church and the general assessment.[90] Second, the critique was widely seen as a pretext for Henry's real goal of securing other amendments to alter the structure of the federal government. Edmund Randolph wrote to George Washington, predicting that the state senate would attempt to postpone the amendments, "for a majority is unfriendly to the government."[91] Madison, also writing to Washington, described the obstructionist tactics as "a latent hope of some contingent opportunity for prosecuting the war agst. the Genl. Government."[92] He added that the groups that had most favored amending the Constitution to protect religious freedom were strongly in support of the amendments: "One of the principal leaders of the Baptists lately sent me word that the amendments had entirely satisfied the disaffected of his Sect, and that it would appear in their subsequent conduct."

Ultimately, Henry lost his control over the state senate. On December 15, 1791, the Virginia Senate ratified all the amendments proposed by Congress. On March 1, 1792, Secretary of State Thomas Jefferson made the official announcement that the Bill of Rights was part of the Constitution.[93]

UNDERSTANDING THE FRAMERS' INTENT

The framers' understanding of the language of the religion clauses has been the subject of countless debates. While broad concepts can be identified readily, there is no consensus on why they chose the specific words they did. Although some commentators have tried to squeeze definitive meaning out of shards of debate or the history of its drafting, very few useful conclusions can actually be obtained.

Many scholars cite the drafting history to support their claim that the First Amendment bars all aid to religion, even that which is made available to "all religions evenhandedly."[94] According to this view, the "best evidence of the framers' intent" is that "the First Congress considered and rejected at least four drafts of the establishment clause that explicitly stated the 'no preference' view."[95] Justice David Souter wrote that the framers' intent for "the Establishment Clause's prohibition to encompass nonpreferential aid to religion" was confirmed by the fact that "unlike the earliest House drafts or the final Senate proposal, the prevailing language is not limited to laws respecting an establishment of 'a religion,' 'a national religion,' 'one religious sect,' or specific 'articles of faith.'" He supports this argument by noting:

"The Framers repeatedly considered and deliberately rejected such narrow language and instead extended their prohibition to state support for 'religion' in general."[96]

But because we do not know why the proposals were rejected, we cannot use the drafting history to determine whether nonpreferential aid to religion was meant to be banned by the First Amendment. Since a dozen proposals were considered and ultimately abandoned with no reason recorded for any decision, it is speculative at best to read substantive policy choices into select decisions. Souter's logic would permit the countervailing inference that because the House rejected Samuel Livermore's proposal barring Congress from making laws "touching religion," some federal laws that "touch" religion were meant to be permitted. The fact that a relatively clear proposal was rejected in favor of a more opaque one does not prove that a different meaning was intended. The framers' specific understanding of the amendment will have to be ascertained, to the extent it can be discovered at all, from sources other than its rejected alternatives.

There is, however, one perception that can be definitively refuted by the First Amendment's drafting history. A significant and highly respected group of scholars argue that the establishment clause was designed not to protect religious liberty but rather to protect existing state establishments. According to the legal scholar Akhil Amar, the establishment clause was written "as a pure federalism provision . . . The clause was utterly agnostic on the substantive issue of establishment; it simply mandated that the issue be decided state by state and that Congress keep its hands off, that Congress make no law 'respecting' the vexed question. In short, the original establishment clause was a home rule–local option provision mandating imperial neutrality."[97] Justice Clarence Thomas has written that "the Establishment Clause is best understood as a federalism provision—it protects state establishments from federal interference but does not protect any individual right."[98]

The idea that the main, or only, reason for the adoption of the establishment clause was to foreclose "the possibility that Congress could disestablish state churches" ignores the history that led to its drafting and ratification.[99] If the clause really had been designed to protect state establishments, one would expect it to have been proposed by the states with those establishments. Yet of the four states that proposed amendments barring a federal establishment, three were states that did not have an established church; of the five states with an establishment, only one made such a demand.

New York, North Carolina, and Virginia, all without established churches, proposed bans on a federal establishment.[100] Rhode Island, also without an established church, announced its support for such a ban during its 1790 ratification convention.[101] The motivation for these four states to try to prevent a federal establishment was the preservation of the religious freedom they had provided their citizens.

Similar sentiments were expressed in Maryland and Pennsylvania, neither of which had an established religion. In Maryland, Anti-Federalists asked their state convention to propose an amendment prohibiting Congress from establishing a religion, in order to preserve religious freedom: "That there be no national religion established by law; but that all persons be equally entitled to protection in their religious liberty."[102] In Pennsylvania, opponents of ratification wanted to prevent the federal government from overriding state laws concerning religion; their proposal was designed not to protect an establishment but to ensure that the federal government did not "alter, abrogate, or infringe any part of the constitution of the several states, which provide for the preservation of liberty in matters of religion."[103]

Thus, a demand to deny Congress the power to create a religious establishment emanated from six states without an established church to protect. Each of these states viewed the concept of an established religion, whether at the federal or state level, as a potential obstacle to religious liberty.

Of the states with established religions, only New Hampshire made a proposal limiting the federal government's power over religion.[104] None of the other states with established religions, Massachusetts, Connecticut, South Carolina, and Georgia, proposed amendments limiting the federal establishment of religion. This is particularly noteworthy, since both Massachusetts and South Carolina presented lists of proposed amendments covering the local concerns that they felt were potentially endangered by the new federal government.

One of South Carolina's five proposed amendments did, in fact, deal with religion, but it did not involve prevention of federal interference with state establishments. It would have inserted the word "other" between the words "no" and "religious" in the religious test clause of Article VI, so that federal and state officials would be bound by "Oath or Affirmation, to support this Constitution; but no *other* religious test shall ever be required."[105] This amendment represented an attempt to mandate that the oath of loyalty be seen as a religious exercise. But South Carolina, like most of the other states with a religious establishment, did not request an amendment to prevent Congress from controlling or eliminating the state's establishment.

The process of drafting the establishment clause further indicates that it was not designed for the limited task of protecting state establishments. Not a single person during any reported debate mentioned a need to prevent Congress from disestablishing his state's home church nor suggested that Congress might harm a state's establishment.[106]

Finally, the reaction to the First Amendment, once it was sent to the states, proves that it was not created primarily to protect state establishments. Rhode Island's 1790 convention to decide whether to ratify both the original Constitution and the Bill of Rights, briefly discussed the Constitution's limits on the power to establish religion. James Sheldon, a Baptist minister, complained that the establishment clause did not prevent other states from keeping their establishments. The Federalist Henry Marchant responded by saying that he too "wishes all men would agree not to establish any Religi[on]" but that it was "enough for us to keep it out of the Gen[eral] Gov[ernmen]t."[107] This statement reflects the understanding that the clause was seen as preventing Congress from imposing an established religion in states like Rhode Island, where no establishment had ever existed.

Even more telling is the fact that the three states that failed to ratify the Bill of Rights—Massachusetts, Connecticut, and Georgia—all had established religions. Massachusetts and Connecticut continued to impose a tax to support ministers and religious teaching; Georgia had enacted a law in 1785 providing for taxation to support a "Minister of the Gospel who shall on every sunday Publickly explain and Inculcate the great doctrines and precepts of the Christian Religion."[108] Not one of these states felt sufficiently threatened by the prospect of the federal government interfering with its internal regulation of religion to ratify the First Amendment.[109]

To prove how irrelevant the establishment clause was to those states with established religions, consider Governor John Hancock's speech to the Massachusetts legislature. In an address on January 19, 1790, Hancock urged the legislature to ratify the amendments and singled out three amendments that he deemed of particular value: "The seventh, eighth & ninth articles [i.e. the Fifth, Sixth, and Seventh Amendments] appear to me to be of great consequence," particularly those parts, he stressed, dealing with the "institutions of Grand and Petit juries."[110] But he said not a word about the need to protect his state establishment from federal interference.

In sum, the establishment clause was proposed almost entirely by states that did not have an established religion; fought for by James Madison, who strongly opposed any concept of establishment; debated without a single reference to the need to protect state establishments from Congress; supported with the strong approval of the Baptists, who were fighting state establishments; and ratified without the slightest sign of interest from most of the states with an establishment. The assertion that the framers enacted the establishment clause in order to protect state establishments is, at best, a rewriting of history to fit a contemporary constitutional vision.

The apathy of states with established religions toward the establishment clause can be traced to several factors. First, these States may not have believed that under the original Constitution, Congress possessed any regulatory power over religion. There would be no need for a protective amendment if, as James Iredell argued during the North Carolina ratification debate, the Constitution did not give "any power . . . to Congress in matters of religion."[111] This alone would have provided sufficient protection, Iredell stated, since if "any future Congress should pass an act concerning the religion of the country, it would be an act which they are not authorized to pass, by the Constitution, and which the people would not obey."

Additionally, these states may have felt that a ban on congressional actions "respecting the establishment of religion" was irrelevant to them because they did not believe that they had such an establishment. By the end of the Revolution, "'establishment' was a dirty word," even if people did not agree on its meaning.[112] James Madison, John Leland, and others considered all public funding of religious institutions to be an "establishment," but that was not the definition favored in states with such funding.[113] In 1803, Chief Justice Jedediah Smith of the New Hampshire Supreme Court ruled that his state's religious assessments were not an establishment, because "a religious establishment is where the State prescribes a formulary of faith and worship for the rule and government of all the subjects. Here the State [does] neither. . . . It is left to each town and parish not to prescribe rules of faith or doctrine for the members of the corporation but barely to elect a teacher of religion and morality for the society who is to be maintained at the expense of the whole."[114] If state leaders did not view their coerced taxation to fund particular denominations as an establishment, the establishment clause could not have been seen as protecting their state's practice.

Even if they conceded that their religious assessments did constitute an establishment, there is an additional reason those states may not have been troubled by the prospect of a federal establishment. For decades under British rule, the Congregationalist New England establishments had thrived, despite the existence of an extraordinarily strong established Anglican Church in England. Perhaps they assumed they could successfully ignore any federal establishment, as they had so completely ignored England's.

Since the states with established religions were not instrumental in the enactment of the establishment clause, the real issue is to determine the motivation of those states without established religions and of the groups that opposed establishments. While the Supreme Court has not fully explored the issue, the motivations of those who fought for the establishment clause explain why the Fourteenth Amendment, ratified in 1868, subjects states, in addition to Congress, to the restrictions of the establishment clause today. The Court has held that the due process clause of that amendment "incorporates," that is, applies to states and local governments, those provisions of the Bill of Rights whose guarantees are "implicit in the concept of ordered liberty."[115] In 1947, the Court held that the establishment clause was one of the provisions incorporated by the Fourteenth Amendment, but it did not explain how the clause was related to "ordered liberty."[116]

If the establishment clause had been solely designed to protect state establishments, it would not be protecting liberty and hence could not be incorporated.[117] But those who fought for the establishment clause considered the prevention of religious establishments to be an essential part of ordered liberty. They saw that protecting the right to exercise one's own religion was vital, but insufficient, for the preservation of religious freedom: religious establishments inevitably caused nonadherents to be considered lesser members of the body politic, and the benefits received by the established religion invariably came at their expense.

This evolving understanding was powerfully expressed by the Reverend William Tennent, a South Carolina Presbyterian minister, during his fight to disestablish the state's Anglican Church. On January 11, 1777, he told the state assembly, "All religious establishments are an infringement of religious liberty" because they "interfere with the rights of private judgment and conscience."[118] He said, "I am against all establishments in this State" because "every establishment must operate as a plan of injustice and oppression."

Tennent also opposed a proposal to give the Church of England the label of "established church," even if the taxation of other denominations was eliminated. The mere acknowledgment of one denomination as superior in the eyes of the state, he said, "operates as an abridgment of religious liberty."[119] Regardless of whether nonadherents could practice their own faith without penalty, Tennant concluded, they "must at least submit to this inferiority, or rather bear the reproach of the law as not being on a level with those that are Christians in its esteem."[120]

While the authorities in New England believed a society could have both an established religion and free exercise of religion, a growing number of others were reaching the opposite conclusion. They saw religious establishments, as the Virginian Presbyterians had argued in 1785, as synonymous with "oppression."[121] In his Memorial and Remonstrance, Madison stated that religious establishments have frequently "been seen upholding the thrones of political tyranny: in no instance have they been seen the guardians of the liberties of the people."[122] Under this viewpoint, religious establishments were incompatible with true freedom of religion.

Thus, it is incorrect to say that advocates of the establishment clause "did not adopt any substantive right or principle of religious freedom,"[123] or that "[under] the federal Establishment Clause, religious establishments were neither good nor bad—they were simply a matter left to the states."[124] Rather, the clause's strongest supporters viewed establishments as an affirmative evil to be limited to the largest extent possible.

The conclusion that the establishment clause protects religious liberty does not determine the scope of that protection. During the presidencies of George Washington, John Adams, Thomas Jefferson, and James Madison, a variety of approaches were used in an attempt to realize the provision's important, but uncertain, promise.

CHAPTER 6

Freedom of Religion in the New Nation

NEITHER THE Constitution nor the First Amendment created the American understanding of freedom of religion. That vision emerged from a shared national experience guided by the conduct of the government's early leaders. Washington, Adams, Jefferson, and Madison did not always act consistently, but their practices and examples led to the evolution of a collective wisdom that ultimately created the American ideal of religious liberty.[1]

The actions of George Washington regarding freedom of religion were especially important.[2] As the first president, he was acutely aware that his decisions and actions would define what would be considered appropriate in the future. As he wrote to Madison, "As the first of everything, in our situation will serve to establish a Precedent, it is devoutly wished on my part, that these precedents may be fixed on true principles."[3] Accordingly, Washington took great care in preparing for the address he was to deliver to Congress after his inauguration. He asked Madison to review a seventy-three-page draft written by his secretary David Humphreys. Madison, appalled to read what he later described as "so strange a production," proceeded to draft a completely new speech.[4]

While none of Humphrey's draft was retained, two passages touching on religion are worth noting.[5] First, Humphrey wanted Washington to use explicitly Christian language, referring to "the blessed Religion revealed in the word of God."[6] Although the final address contains much religious imagery, it includes nothing that is uniquely Christian.

Second, Humphrey's draft "included a short space for a prayer that was to be introduced after the first paragraph."[7] On the day of the inauguration, prayers were indeed offered, but they were not led by the president. Instead, they were conducted by the Senate chaplain, Samuel Provoost, during "divine services" held at Saint Paul's Church after the inaugural address.[8]

On the day of the inauguration, April 30, 1789, a formal procession with soldiers, dignitaries, and multiple carriages accompanied Washington to New York's City Hall, at Wall and Nassau Streets, where Congress met.[9] Fourteen clergymen, including Gershom Mendes Seixas, the rabbi of Congregation Shearith Israel, marched with the procession.[10] Washington entered the balcony where he was to take the oath of office through the Senate's second-story room.[11] With a large crowd in attendance, New York State's highest-ranking judge, Chancellor Robert R. Livingston, read the language prescribed by Article II of the Constitution: "I do solemnly swear that I will faithfully execute the Office of President of the United States, and will to the best of my Ability, preserve, protect and defend the Constitution of the United States." After Washington repeated the oath, Livingston declared, "Long live George Washington, President of the United States," and as Senator William Maclay wrote in his journal, the crowd "gave three cheers and repeated it on the President's bowing to them."[12]

Although many people believe that Washington added the phrase "so help me God" to the constitutional language,[13] it is unlikely that he did so.[14] Not a single contemporaneous account attributed the phrase to him. The first such attribution occurred in 1854, sixty-five years after the event, in a book by Rufus Griswold. Griswold was a New

York writer who said that he had recently heard it from Washington Irving, who was only six years old at the time of the inauguration.[15]

By contrast, none of the numerous eyewitness accounts from people who attended the inauguration reported that Washington used the phrase. The French consul, Comte de Moustier, wrote a detailed description of the events of the day for his superiors in Paris; he quoted Washington as repeating the constitutional oath without additional language.[16] Others reported that Washington devoutly kissed the Bible after the oath, but they made no mention of his adding words to the oath.[17]

Perhaps the most persuasive evidence that Washington did not say "so help me God" is the report of Ashbel Green, a Presbyterian minister who would become Senate chaplain in 1792. Years after attending the inauguration, Green wrote a letter to his son describing the events of the day. He said that Washington "took the oath prescribed by the constitution," but does not mention the use of any additional language.[18]

This is significant because at the time of his letter, the mid-1840s, Green had become the chief defender of Washington's personal religious convictions. In 1829, Thomas Jefferson's papers were published, and included the assertion that Gouverneur Morris "has often told me that Washington believed no more [in Christianity] than he himself did."[19] Green responded by writing a long essay for the *Christian Advocate,* citing numerous examples of Washington's piety.[20] In neither this essay nor his letter to his son did Green speak of the inaugural oath, though he did discuss Washington's inaugural address, which was given to Congress shortly after the oath was taken. When writing to his son, Green even used the inaugural address to highlight Washington's religious faith: "What a distinct and repeated recognition have we, in this address of President Washington, of the divine superintendence and influence in all human concerns, both public and private. Happy would it have been for our country, if all its chief magistrates had in this respect followed the example of the first."[21]

Indeed, the inaugural address, which was written with Madison's help, was replete with explicitly religious language. As the Reverend Forrest Church wrote, "Washington's first inaugural may lack explicit Christian reference, but with the exception of Lincoln's second, no subsequent inaugural address strikes a more religious tone."[22] Although Washington avoided using the word "God," the address opened with a direct religious "supplication": "[It] would be peculiarly improper to omit in this first official Act, my fervent supplications to that Almighty Being who rules over the Universe, who presides in the Councils of Nations, and whose providential aids can supply every human defect, that his benediction may consecrate to the liberties and happiness of the People of the United States."[23]

After this pious beginning, which he described as "tendering this homage to the Great Author of every public and private good," Washington described the role he believed divine intervention had played in the victory over the British: "No People can be bound to acknowledge and adore the invisible hand, which conducts the Affairs of men more than the People of the United States. Every step, by which they have advanced to the character of an independent nation, seems to have been distinguished by some token of providential agency."

Washington stated the peaceful creation of the government under the new Constitution required "some return of pious gratitude along with an humble anticipation of the future blessings which the past seems to presage." In closing, Washington returned to his religious theme: "I shall take my present leave; but not without resorting once more to the benign Parent of the human race, in humble supplication that . . . this divine blessing may be equally conspicuous in the enlarged views—the temperate consultations, and the wise measures on which the success of this Government must depend."[24]

Those wanting to prove that George Washington believed there was a place in governmental discourse for religion need look no further than the plain language of his inaugural address. For added support, one could turn to the religious language in his exchange of messages with both the House of Representatives and the Senate, also written with Madison's assistance. To the House, Washington wrote, "For all beyond, I rely on the wisdom and patriotism of those with whom I am to co-operate, and a continuance of the blessings of Heaven on our beloved Country."[25]

Washington was even more expansive in his address to the Senate:

> I now feel myself inexpressibly happy in a belief, that Heaven which has done so much for our infant Nation will not withdraw its Providential influence before our political felicity shall have been completed; and . . . supported by a firm trust in the great Arbiter of the Universe, aided by the collected wisdom of the Union, and imploring the Divine benediction on our joint exertions in the service of our Country, I readily engage with you in the arduous, but pleasing, task of attempting to make a Nation happy.[26]

Given this evidence of religious conviction, it is curious that so much emphasis has been placed on the uncertain story of Washington's oath. It is discomfiting to hear Justice Scalia treat a story of uncertain validity as historical fact. In an attempt to prove that religion has never been "strictly excluded from the public forum," Scalia asserted: "George Washington added to the form of Presidential oath prescribed by Art. II, § 1, cl. 7, of the Constitution, the concluding words 'so help me God.'"[27] Such an assertion weakens the largely accurate point he is trying to prove; if the factual predicate of his argument is doubtful, the persuasiveness of his reasoning is weakened.

Part of the appeal of the Washington oath story is that it permits advocates to quote Washington using the word "God." In most of his public addresses as president, Washington instead used such expressions as "Providence," "Heaven," "Director of Human Events," and the "Grand Architect."[28] Any argument based on Washington's use of religious language becomes more persuasive to modern ears if the more familiar word "God" can be attributed to him.

The oath story also permits partisans to link religious statements made by modern presidents with utterances made by Washington.

One commentator has written: "The hand of the past is palpable on every occasion of the taking of the presidential oath; every president has followed the lead of George Washington in adding the words 'so help me God' after the formal, prescribed constitutional oath."[29] This statement is entirely without factual foundation; neither John Adams, nor Thomas Jefferson, nor James Madison uttered the phrase. The first eyewitness documentation of any president saying "so help me God" is Chester Arthur, in 1881.[30] The power of history, however, would be considerably diminished if one were reduced to claiming that a tradition dates to Chester Arthur.

An American practice of including religious language in presidential speeches finds far better support in George Washington's thanksgiving proclamations. Most writers believe that the idea for the first thanksgiving proclamation came from Congress. As his biographer Frank Grizzard wrote, "At the urging of Congress, Washington proclaimed a national day of Thanksgiving."[31]

Although Congress did make such a request on September 28, 1789,[32] Washington had been considering issuing such a proclamation several weeks earlier. Sometime around September 8, he wrote to Madison, seeking advice on a variety of governmental matters. Among his questions was, "Should the sense of the Senate be taken on the propriety of sending public characters abroad—say, to England, Holland & Portugal—and of a day for thanksgiving."[33] There is no record of Madison's response, but Washington did wait for the formal congressional request before issuing his proclamation. Nonetheless, Washington's memo demonstrates that he needed no encouragement to issue a call for a national day of thanksgiving.

When the House of Representatives debated whether to call for the day of thanksgiving, Thomas Tucker of South Carolina opposed the proposal as an improper interference with religion. "Why," he asked, "should the President direct the people to do what, perhaps, they have no mind to do?"[34] He argued that the Constitution forbade

Congress from having any involvement with religion: "It is a business with which Congress have nothing to do; it is a religious matter, and, as such, is proscribed to us."[35]

Roger Sherman of Connecticut answered Tucker by citing the Bible, not the Constitution. He said that the practice of thanksgiving was "warranted by a number of precedents in holy writ: for instance, the solemn thanksgivings and rejoicings which took place in the time of Solomon, after the building of the temple, was a case in point. This example [was] worthy of Christian imitation on the present occasion."[36]

At the time, Congress was not limited by the First Amendment— the House voted to recommend a day of thanksgiving the same day Congress sent the Bill of Rights to the states for ratification— but the discussion reveals some interesting aspects of congressional thought on government and religion. First, while some, like Tucker, viewed a call for thanksgiving as an improper federal involvement with religion, this was a minority view. The majority simply saw it, as the resolution's House sponsor of the resolution, Elias Boudinot, put it, as "a measure both prudent and just."[37]

Another point to notice is Sherman's willingness to defend a legislative proposal on purely religious—in fact, strictly sectarian— grounds. To Sherman, it was permissible and desirable for the federal government to pursue an action because of its ties to Christianity.

When Washington issued his Thanksgiving Day proclamation on October 3, 1789, he did not favor similar denominational interests but continued his practice of employing inclusive religious language.[38] To appreciate this balance, we can compare his proclamation with one issued by the Continental Congress. Its 1777 proclamation begins with a religious directive to the people: "[It] is the indispensable Duty of all Men to adore the superintending Providence of Almighty God." Washington, by contrast, turned the focus away from individuals and toward the country as a distinct entity: "It is the duty of all Nations to acknowledge the providence of Almighty God."

The 1777 proclamation was explicitly Christian, urging "the good People . . . to join the penitent Confession of their manifold Sins . . . that it may please GOD through the Merits of Jesus Christ." Washington recommended that people be devoted "to the service of that great and glorious Being, who is the beneficent Author of all the good that was, that is, or that will be." Though unmistakably religious, Washington's proclamation displays an awareness of the diversity of religious belief across the nation and the need to respect religious freedom.

First, he called for thanks for "the civil and religious liberty with which we are blessed." Then, he made two separate appeals for national unity, urging that the people of the nation "all unite in rendering unto him our sincere and humble thanks" and "that we may then unite in most humbly offering our prayers and supplications to the great Lord and Ruler of Nations."[39]

The key to understanding Washington's view on religion and government is to appreciate that his continual quest as president was to use religion as a force for uniting the country. Just as he was concerned during the Revolutionary War with ensuring that religious differences did not raise "the smallest uneasiness & jealousy among the Troops," President Washington was determined not to permit religious differences to disrupt the new nation.[40] As Michael and Jana Novak noted, his goal was to find a way of communicating that "unites—rather than divides—a religiously pluralistic people."[41]

WASHINGTON'S LETTERS TO CONGREGATIONS AND CLERGIES

This commitment can be seen in a series of letters that Washington wrote to different religious leaders, revealing his fervent belief in religious liberty and inclusion. Shortly after his inauguration, several Baptist clergymen wrote to the new president, expressing their fear that the unamended Constitution permitted "religious oppression, should any one Society in the Union preponderate over all the rest."[42] Washington responded that he would never have supported ratification if he thought it could lead to religious tyranny: "If I could have entertained the slightest apprehension that the Constitution framed in the Convention, where I had the honor to preside, might possibly endanger the religious rights of any ecclesiastical Society, certainly I would never have placed my signature to it."[43] If such a risk were to develop, Washington added, he would work to "establish effectual barriers against the horrors of spiritual tyranny, and every species of religious persecution." He then announced his philosophy of religious freedom: "Every man, conducting himself as a good citizen, and being accountable to God alone for his religious opinions, ought to be protected in worshipping the Deity according to the dictates of his own conscience." Interestingly, he goes beyond simply announcing opposition to "every species" of religious tyranny and endorses a belief that all should be free to worship as they see fit. He adds, in the manner of Jefferson and Madison, a conviction that in matters of religious opinion, people are "accountable to God" only and not to civil government.

The one group whose religious opinions had troubled Washington during the Revolutionary War was the Quakers, whose "religious scruples" prevented them from joining the Continental Army. Washington had suspected many Quakers of disloyalty, and much of the country still treated them with hostility and suspicion after the war. At their annual meeting, held in October 1789, the Quakers sent Washington a letter, attempting to overcome lingering doubts about their loyalty to the country: "[As] we are a People whose Principles and Conduct have been misrepresented and traduced, we take the Liberty to assure thee, that we feel our Hearts affectionately drawn towards thee, and those in Authority over us."[44]

Washington, while defending their religious rights, showed that he still harbored some resentment over the Quakers' pacifism: "It is doing the People called Quakers no more than Justice to say, that (except their declining to share with others the burthen of the common defence) there is no Denomination among us who are more exemplary and useful Citizens."[45] Nonetheless, he declared that, as president, he was obligated to respect their religious rights and protect them from harm: "Government being, among other purposes, instituted to protect the Persons and Consciences of men from oppression, it certainly is the duty of Rulers, not only to abstain from it themselves, but according to their Stations, to prevent it in others."

He concluded his letter by acknowledging the need for the government to respect the right of individuals to live in accord with their religious faiths. Though not conceding that Quakers should be exempt from military obligations, he stated that "the Conscientious scruples of all men should be treated with great delicacy & tenderness."[46] Such sensitive treatment, he explained, meant that government should try not to penalize religiously motivated conduct: "The Laws may always be as extensively accommodated to [people's conscientious scruples], as a due regard to the Protection and essential Interests of the Nation may Justify, and permit."

Washington's public acceptance of Quakers' religious rights contributed to his goal of protecting them from oppression. According to the historian Paul Boller, Washington's letter "helped to dissolve the animosities toward the Society of Friends that still lingered from the Revolutionary period."[47]

Catholics also looked to Washington to help integrate them fully into American society. In a letter written by John Carroll, the priest who had accompanied Benjamin Franklin to Canada, representatives of the Roman Catholic clergy complained that they were still discriminated against in several states. "As the price of our blood spilt under your eyes," Carroll wrote, Catholics have "a well founded title to claim from her justice, the equal rights of citizenship." While they "pray for the preservation of them, where they have been granted,"

Carroll wrote, we "expect the full extension of them from the justice of those States, which still restrict them."

Washington did not respond with a federalism-based critique, arguing that states had the right to regulate religion within their borders. Instead, he declared his support for the Catholics' claim and expressed the hope that, over time, all the states would live up to the American ideal: "As mankind become more liberal, they will be more apt to allow, that all those who conduct themselves as worthy members of the Community are equally entitled to the protection of civil Government. I hope ever to see America among the foremost nations in examples of justice and liberality."[48] In a statement of deep religious and political significance, Washington articulated a position that was still rare in America: that Catholics should be considered part of the Christian community. He closed his letter by expressing his wish that "the members of your Society in America, animated alone by the pure spirit of Christianity, and still conducting themselves as the faithful subjects of our free Government, enjoy every temporal and spiritual felicity."

This letter, like Washington's other letters to religious groups, was written with the expectation that it would be shared with the larger population. Thus, when he declared that Catholics are animated "by the pure spirit of Christianity," he was "speaking, and perhaps with design, to the great non-Catholic population of the nation."[49] His message of religious acceptance was heard in England as well. In 1790, Carroll's letter and Washington's response were printed as a pamphlet in London, along with a preface chastising England for its discriminatory treatment of Catholics: "Is this not a lesson? Britons remain intolerant and inexorable to the claims of sound policy and of nature. . . . Where is the boasted liberty which suffers not a disposal of ourselves, but aims so effectually to shackle and annihilate the soul from God. Britons, view and blush!"[50]

Washington's willingness to transcend traditional religious bigotry is also evident in a series of letters he wrote to Jewish congregations. On May 6, 1790, Levi Sheftall, president of the Mikveh Israel synagogue in Savannah, Georgia, wrote to express gratitude for Washington's support of religious freedom: "Your unexampled liberality and extensive philanthropy have dispelled that cloud of bigotry and superstition which has long, as a veil, shaded religion."[51] Washington's response acknowledged that not every state had shown such "liberality" to Jews, and expressed the hope that all states would live up to this ideal: "Happily the people of the United States of America have, in many instances, exhibited examples worthy of imitation— The salutary influence of which will doubtless extend much farther, if gratefully enjoying those blessings of peace which (under favor of Heaven) have been obtained by fortitude in war, they shall conduct themselves with reverence to the Deity, and charity towards their fellow-creatures."[52]

The phrase "in many instances" denotes Washington's awareness of the lack of universal acceptance. Moreover, he chided those purportedly religious people who discriminate against Jews, saying that the "salutary influence" of religious inclusion would "extend much farther" if they would only "conduct themselves with reverence to the Deity." Just as he was willing to include Catholics in his definition of Christianity, Washington ended this letter by linking the religion of the Jews to that of the nation:

> May the same wonder-working Deity, who long since delivering the Hebrews from their Egyptian Oppressors planted them in the promised land—whose providential agency has lately been conspicuous in establishing these United States as an independent nation— still continue to water them with the dews of Heaven and to make the inhabitants of every denomination participate in the temporal and spiritual blessings of that people whose God is Jehovah.

Again, Washington displayed a commitment to inclusion that went far beyond the norms of the time. His invocation of "the same wonder-working Deity" to describe the Providence that oversaw both the Jewish exodus from Egypt and the American success in the Revolutionary War creates a theological link between Jews and the rest of the American population. This link is strengthened by his closing hope that people of "every denomination" can share in the "temporal and spiritual blessings" of the Jews.

A few months later, Washington wrote to a second Jewish congregation when he was visiting Newport, Rhode Island, describing his commitment to universal religious freedom.[53] He began by acknowledging the change in perception of the source of religious freedom, a change begun with the Virginia Declaration of Rights fourteen years earlier: "It is now no more that toleration is spoken of, as if it was by the indulgence of one class of people, that another enjoyed the exercise of their inherent natural rights."[54] He then offered his vision of the American guarantee of religious equality: "For happily the Government of the United States, which gives to bigotry no sanction, to persecution no assistance, requires only that they who live under its protection should demean themselves as good citizens, in giving it on all occasions their effectual support."[55]

Washington's focus on "the Government of the United States" reveals a critically important point: the Constitution provided a distinct national perspective on freedom of religion, one that was not restricted, as some have argued, to protecting "local approaches to religious liberty then extant in the states."[56] Unlike the Articles of Confederation, the Constitution helped form a country with a distinct national understanding of religious freedom that transcended that of the individual states. It was the "Government of the United States," that no longer sanctioned religious bigotry, regardless of the discrimination that still occurred under local jurisdictions.

In his closing, Washington reaffirmed his wish that America provide a sanctuary from religious oppression: "May the children of the Stock of Abraham, who dwell in this land, continue to merit and enjoy the good will of the other Inhabitants; while every one shall sit in safety under his own vine and fig tree, and there shall be none to make him afraid."

Yet many of those other inhabitants did not share Washington's view that "all possess alike liberty of conscience and immunities of citizenship."[57] Throughout his presidency, various clergymen tried to elicit statements from him indicating a preference for traditional Protestant Christianity. In every case, with considerable grace and subtlety, Washington refused.

On October 28, 1789, the Presbytery of the Eastward, consisting of ministers from Massachusetts and New Hampshire, wrote to Washington to complain that the Constitution lacked any Christian reference: "Among these we never considered the want of a religious test, that grand engine of persecution in every tyrant's hand: But we should not have been alone in rejoicing to have seen some Explicit acknowledgement of the only true God and Jesus Christ, whom he hath sent inserted some where in the Magna Charta of our country."[58] They added that they were nonetheless comforted by his presidency, since his "whole deportment bids all denominations confidently to expect to find in you the watchful guardian of their equal liberties— the steady Patron of genuine Christianity."

Washington defended the Constitution's absence of Christian language by stating that religion did not need governmental assistance: "You will permit me to observe that the path of true piety is so plain as to require but little political direction. To this consideration we ought to ascribe the absence of any regulation, respecting religion, from the Magna-Charta of our country."[59] He then drew a distinction between the religious and governmental spheres: "To the guidance of the ministers of the gospel this important object is, perhaps, more properly committed." He gently admonished the clergy that "it will be *your* care to instruct the ignorant, and to reclaim the devious—and, in the progress of morality and science, to which our government will give every furtherance, we may confidently expect the advancement of true religion, and the completion of our happiness."[60]

In defending the lack of religious acknowledgment in the Constitution, Washington avoided mentioning either "Christianity" or "Jesus" and stated that religion is for ministers, not the government. Moreover, the syntax of his last sentence indicates the limited role he saw for government in matters of religion. Government, he wrote, is not responsible for furthering the advancement of religion, but will give "every furtherance" to the "the progress of morality and science." It is through these secular pursuits that religion will be strengthened.

Washington was similarly circumspect when responding to the synod of the reformed Dutch Church in North America. On October 9, 1789, it wrote him to explain the unique value that they believed the "pure and undented religion of Christ" holds for America: "We are persuaded that good Christians will always be good citizens, and that where righteousness prevails among individuals the Nation will be great and happy. Thus while just government protects all in their religious rights, true religion affords to government its surest support."[61]

Washington's response is a fascinating exercise in studied ambiguity. While seeming to agree with the synod, he stressed the need to respect all Americans regardless of faith. First, he praised them for acting "the part of pious Christians and good citizens" by working "to preserve that harmony and good will towards men which must be the basis of every political establishment."[62] After placing "good will towards men" at the heart of the national system, he then carefully chose one phrase from the synod's letter to repeat: "I readily join with you that 'while just government protects all in their religious rights, true religion affords to government its surest support.'"

Many modern advocates of a closer connection between religion and government cut that last sentence in half and quote only the second part. For example, David Limbaugh, in his book *Persecution: How Liberals Are Waging War against Christianity,* in arguing that the framers believed that "Christian convictions . . . were foundational to American freedom," writes: "And Washington said, 'true religion affords to government its surest support.'"[63]

Such partial quotation obscures the point Washington was trying to make to the synod. By choosing that particular sentence to repeat, Washington was reminding the clergy of the importance of government in protecting "all" in their religious rights. Additionally, Washington was careful to make it appear possible, but not certain, that he was agreeing with the synod that "true religion" and the "pure and undented religion of Christ" were the same.

Still, the letter does reaffirm Washington's conviction that religion was of vital importance to the nation. As he wrote in another letter to "The Clergy of Different Denominations Residing In And Near The City Of Philadelphia," "Religion and Morality are the essential pillars of civil society."[64] The circumstances surrounding this letter also reveal Washington's refusal to be manipulated by those who wanted him to make a public endorsement of Christianity. During Washington's last week in office, Ashbel Green, the Senate chaplain, drafted a letter on behalf of himself and several local clergymen, telling Washington that they wanted "to acknowledge the countenance which you have uniformly given to his holy religion."[65] In the words of F. Forrester Church, this was a "curious misstatement of fact— Washington had never testified to a belief in the Christian gospel."[66]

At a meeting on March 3, 1797, his last full day as president, Washington responded to their message. While acknowledging the importance of religion and morality, Washington avoided any mention of Christianity and focused on his concept of religious inclusion. He told his audience that he viewed, "with unspeakable pleasure, that harmony and brotherly love which characterize the clergy of different denominations, . . . exhibiting to the world a new and interesting spectacle, at once the pride of our country and the surest basis of universal harmony."[67]

According to Thomas Jefferson, Green later told Benjamin Rush that the clergy had written to Washington "to force him at length to declare publickly, whether he was a Christian or not," but "the old fox was too cunning for them."[68] Green vehemently denied trying to "force" Washington to make such a declaration, but did admit that he had written the letter to give Washington "a full and fair opportunity" to publicly "recognise his Christian faith and character, as not to leave to the enemies of his Saviour, any plausible opening for their false surmises and suggestions."[69] Speaking of Washington's disinclination to take advantage of this opportunity, Green said that he "regretted this omission, and regrets it still."[70]

Washington was not always so careful in his public religious pronouncements. As Steven Waldman noted in his book *Founding Faith,* "Washington's faith-based rhetoric set a powerful and enduring precedent. . . . and sometimes in service of a very particular political cause."[71] After the suppression of the Whiskey Rebellion, a short-lived armed revolt in Pennsylvania, Washington's 1794 Annual Address to Congress, declared, "Let us unite, therefore, in imploring the Supreme Ruler of nations to spread his holy protection over these United States; to turn the machinations of the wicked to the confirming of our constitution."[72] The address, written by Alexander Hamilton, was directed at both the recent uprising and, implicitly, others then loudly opposing Washington's policies.[73]

It is probably not a coincidence that most of Washington's partisan use of religion occurred after he began turning to Alexander Hamilton for assistance with his writing. Hamilton was hardly averse to combining religion and politics. A revealing exchange between Edmund Randolph and Hamilton is written in the margin of Hamilton's draft of Washington's second thanksgiving proclamation. Randolph warned Hamilton, "This proclamation ought to savour as much as possible of religion; and not too much of having a political object."[74] Hamilton wrote an adjoining note dismissing Randolph's concern: "A proclamation by a government which is a national Act naturally embraces objects which are political. This is a mere benevolent sentiment in unison with public feeling."[75]

Washington accepted Hamilton's draft and, on January 1, 1795, issued the proclamation, calling for a "day of public thanksgiving and prayer" on February 19, three days before Washington's birthday.[76] In the address, he "recommend[ed] to all religious societies and denominations, and to all persons whomsoever," to "beseech the kind Author" of the nation's blessings "to diffuse and establish habits of sobriety, order, morality, and piety." During the week of February 19, churches combined their thanksgiving services with celebrations of Washington's birthday.[77] Churches were filled throughout the country, with many of the sermons urging public support for Washington while attacking his political opposition. One angry Jefferson ally, the New England pastor William Bentley, declared, "The Clergy are now the Tools of the Federalists, & Thanksgiving Sermons are in the order of the Day."[78]

Washington's Farewell Address was written in the same politically charged environment. When he was considering stepping down in 1792, at the close of his first term, he asked Madison to draft a "valedictory."[79] Four years later, having become alienated from both Madison and Jefferson because of bitter political differences over issues such as the National Bank and Jay's Treaty, Washington asked Hamilton to help revise Madison's draft. Hamilton rewrote the address and, on July 30, sent his new draft to Washington.[80] Unlike either Madison's drafts or Washington's notes, Hamilton's version contained specific references to religion and morality.[81] Washington accepted most of Hamilton's draft but made several significant editorial changes, including some to his section discussing religion. A comparison of Hamilton's language with Washington's demonstrates the difference in their views on the relationship between religion and government.

With minimal stylistic modifications from Hamilton's version,

Washington wrote: "Let us with caution indulge the supposition that morality can be maintained without religion. Whatever may be conceded to the influence of refined education on minds of peculiar structure, reason and experience both forbid us to expect that national morality can prevail in exclusion of religious principle."[82] In Hamilton's draft, however, the prediction of an end to "national morality" without religion was followed by a rhetorical question: "Does it not require the aid of a generally received and divinely authoritative Religion?" Washington deleted this line, thereby removing Hamilton's explicitly Christian allusion to "received . . . religion."

As president, Washington accomplished what many people today would consider an impossible task. On one hand, he was a leader, greatly underappreciated in modern times, in the battle for freedom of religion in America. In the words of Paul Boller, "Washington unquestionably deserves major credit, along with Jefferson and Madison, for establishing the ideals of religious liberty and freedom of conscience . . . for Protestants, Catholics, and Jews—and for Deists and freethinkers as well—firmly in the American tradition."[83] At the same time, he was able to speak in devout religious language without destroying the unity he was committed to creating. This success was due, at least in part, to what has been termed his "amazing ability" to speak the devotional language "of even rival religions": "To Presbyterians he spoke like a God-fearing Protestant, to Methodists he implied his support for revivals in religion, to Jews he invoked the Old Testament, and to American Catholics he wrote that they were 'animated alone by the pure spirit of Christianity.'"[84]

JOHN ADAMS AND THE
PLACE OF RELIGION IN GOVERNMENT

Washington's successor, John Adams, did not attempt to emulate this religiously inclusive style. In his inaugural address, Adams told his

listeners why the people should have confidence in his ensuing presidency. At the end of his extremely long list (which took three minutes
to read and is the longest sentence in any Presidential inaugural address),[85] Adams described his religious qualifications for the job: "a
veneration for the religion of a people who profess and call themselves
Christians, and a fixed resolution to consider a decent respect for Christianity among the best recommendations for the public service."[86]

While Washington never made such a public declaration, Adams
cited his own personal "veneration" of Christianity as a qualification
for serving as president. Moreover, Adams seemed to indicate that as
chief executive, he would consider "a deep respect for Christianity"
among the most important factors in deciding whom he would appoint for public service. His view of the appropriateness of a religious
litmus test for governmental hiring contrasts sharply with that of
Washington's letter to the Roman Catholics, declaring that the protection of civil government should be provided to "all those who conduct
themselves as worthy members of the Community."

Adams's willingness to combine the sacred with the political is
most evident in his two proclamations calling for days of "humiliation, fasting, and prayer." The first of these was issued during a time of
heightened tension with France. Alexander Hamilton, who was urging the nation to prepare for war, sent the following recommendation
to his ally in Adams's cabinet, Secretary of State Timothy Pickering:
"I would appoint a day of humiliation and prayer. In such a crisis this
appears to me proper in itself, and it will be politically useful to impress our nation that there is a serious state of things—to strengthen
religious ideas in a contest, which in its progress may require that
our people may consider themselves as the defenders of their country
against atheism, conquest, and anarchy."[87]

Adams, commenting on this letter, disdained Hamilton's depiction of the political utility of calling for such a day.[88] He denied that he
issued the fast-day proclamation because of Hamilton's intervention:

"I had determined on this measure long enough before Mr. Hamilton's letter was written." Adams also attempted to distinguish his own reasons for the proclamation from Hamilton's partisan cynicism: "I think there is nothing upon this earth more sublime and affecting than the idea of a great nation all on their knees at once before their God, acknowledging their faults and imploring his blessing and protection, when the prospect before them threatens great danger and calamity. It can scarcely fail to have a favorable effect on their morals in general, or to inspire them with warlike virtues in particular."[89]

In other words, Adams saw his proclamation as a fundamentally religious undertaking aimed at improving morals and "warlike virtues," in contrast to Hamilton's desire to gain political approval for a particular position. Thus, it is not surprising that Adams requested that the chaplains of Congress, the Reverends Bishop White and Ashbel Green, write his two fast-day proclamations.[90]

The first of these, issued March 23, 1798, was "more overtly Christian than Washington's" proclamations.[91] Unlike Washington, who considered it "the duty of all Nations" to acknowledge God, Adams placed this responsibility on each individual, declaring that it was "an indispensable duty which the people owe to Him."[92] Also unlike Washington, Adams employed explicitly Christian language in his recommendation that all citizens "offer their devout addresses to the Father of Mercies . . . beseeching Him at the same time, of His infinite grace, through the Redeemer of the World, freely to remit all our offenses, and to incline us by His Holy Spirit."

Even this language was not enough to prevent, according to Ashbel Green, the complaint that "the religious community of our country had made, namely, that the proclamation . . . lacked a decidedly Christian spirit." Accordingly, Green said, when Adams requested a second proclamation a year later, "I resolved to write one of an evangelical character."[93] The 1799 proclamation begins with a reference to the lessons of the "Volume of Inspiration" and exhorts the citizens of the nation to "call to mind our numerous offenses against the Most High God, confess them before Him with the sincerest penitence, implore His pardoning mercy, through the Great Mediator and Redeemer, for our past transgressions, and that through the grace of His Holy Spirit we may be disposed and enabled to yield a more suitable obedience to His righteous requisitions in time to come."[94] It concludes with the hope that God "would extend the blessings of knowledge, of true liberty, and of pure and undefiled religion throughout the world."

This time, the "religious community" was enthusiastic in praise. John Mitchell Mason, a Presbyterian minister, applauded Adams for displaying support "in one of his proclamations, to a number of the most precious truths of Revelation."[95]

Given that, "of the first four presidents, John Adams was the most overtly Christian from his bully pulpit,"[96] the language of the treaty he signed with Tripoli in 1797 to end pirate raids on American ships is particularly surprising. Article 11 of that agreement states:

> As the government of the United States of America is not in any sense founded on the Christian religion—as it has in itself no character of enmity against the laws, religion or tranquillity of Mussulmen—and as the said states never have entered into any war or act of hostility against any Mahometan nation, it is declared by the parties, that no pretext arising from religious opinions shall ever produce an interruption of the harmony existing between the two countries.[97]

At least one member of Adams's cabinet protested the language before the treaty was ratified. Secretary of War James McHenry wrote to Secretary of the Treasury Oliver Wolcott in 1800 to describe his protest against "this outrage upon the government and religion": "The Senate, my good friend, and I said so at the time, ought never to have ratified the treaty alluded to, with the declaration that 'the government of the United States, is not, in any sense, founded on the Christian religion.' What else is it founded on! This act always appeared to me like trampling upon the cross."[98]

Yet despite the efforts of many modern commentators, the treaty cannot be used as conclusive proof that "the fathers of the country did not establish a Christian nation."[99] Bill Press, in his book, *How the Republicans Stole Religion,* describes the treaty this way: "Ten years after the Constitutional Convention, as a new nation started flexing its foreign policy wings, the question 'Is the United States a Christian nation' actually came up. And the answer from the president and Congress was an emphatic *No!*"[100]

To treat this provision as the result of an in-depth debate over whether the country was founded as a Christian nation is to wrest it from its time and context. There was no public discussion of the article's significance at the time. For the United States, the issue was to prevent attacks on American ships. The obvious purpose of the provision was to demonstrate to Tripoli that America would not lead a religious crusade against the "Mahometan nation" and that peace would not be shattered by a difference of "religious opinions." There is no evidence that either George Washington, who was president when the treaty was negotiated, or John Adams, who signed it, suggested or cared about the language concerning the "Christian religion." We also do not know who is responsible for this language.[101] Significantly, when the treaty with Tripoli was renegotiated in 1805, the reference to "Christian religion" was removed, though the new treaty retained the statement declaring war would not result between the countries because of "Religious Opinions."[102]

Thus the 1797 Tripoli treaty hardly resolves the question of the religious nature of the American government. A second issue involving treaties presents the same interpretive dilemma.

The 1783 Treaty of Paris, which ended the Revolutionary War, contains the following preamble: "In the name of the most holy and undivided Trinity." Historically, very little import has been given to this opening. It has been noted that of the three Americans who negotiated the treaty, John Adams, Benjamin Franklin, and Thomas Jefferson, Adams was the only one who ever publicly or privately acknowledged a Trinitarian belief.[103]

There is no recorded discussion of this phrase, so it is not known whether the British inserted it or whether the Americans ignored it because they were far more concerned with obtaining a formal end to the war.[104] It is also possible that the phrase did not seem inappropriate to Americans at the time and that many in the Continental Congress welcomed its use. But if there is any significance to the appearance of this phrase in the Treaty of Paris, an interesting question emerges. Why does it disappear from every treaty ratified during the Washington, Adams, Jefferson, and Madison administrations? Numerous treaties were signed in the period, including two major agreements with Britain, the 1794 Jay Treaty and the 1814 Treaty of Ghent ending the War of 1812, yet none begin with "In the name of the most holy and undivided Trinity."[105] The disinclination to use this phrase could not have come from Britain, which continued to employ it in treaties well into the middle of the nineteenth century.[106] It is also noteworthy that after Madison left office, the reference to the Holy Trinity returned to American treaties, in an 1818 treaty with Sweden and Norway,[107] and again in one with Britain in 1822.[108]

It is not at all clear why the use of religious preambles ceased during the first four presidencies. Perhaps its absence from treaties can be seen as similar to the decision not to provide a religious Preamble to the Constitution, namely, as an indication that the American government was not to be defined in religious terms. Alternatively, it may just be an accident of history, reflecting which country was writing the actual treaty language.[109] The history of early American treaties can provide only a tantalizing but ultimately uninformative guide to the founders' view of the proper way to depict the religious nature of the national government.

Members of the founding generation themselves were divided over that depiction, and their differing views provided one of the central themes in the 1800 presidential election between Adams and Jefferson. In the view of one Adams supporter, John Mitchell Mason, "the approaching election of a president is to decide a question not merely of preference to an eminent individual, or particular views of policy, but, what is infinitely more, of national regard or disregard to the religion of Jesus Christ."[110] Jefferson was presented as both an anti-Christian and an atheist. As the *Gazette of the United States* famously framed the question: "Shall I continue in allegiance to GOD—AND A RELIGIOUS PRESIDENT; Or impiously declare for JEFFERSON—AND NO GOD!!!"[111]

In an influential pamphlet entitled *Serious Considerations on the Election of a President,* the Reverend William Linn, a New York Dutch Reformed minister and former chaplain of the House of Representatives, went beyond simply calling Jefferson an atheist and warned that his goal was "to see a government where the people have no religious opinions and forms of worship.[112] Linn attacked Jefferson for writing in his *Notes on the State of Virginia* that "it does me no injury for my neighbour to say there are twenty gods, or no god. It neither picks my pocket nor breaks my leg."[113] The irreligious, Linn responded, actually pose a grave threat to society: "But let my neighbour once persuade himself that there is no God, and he will soon pick my pocket, and break not only my leg but my neck."[114] Thus, Linn warned, should Jefferson be elected, the effect would be "to destroy religion, introduce immorality, and loosen all the bonds of society."[115]

John Mitchell Mason added his warning that Jefferson's election would lead to "wresting the bible from the hands of your children."[116] Refusing to vote for such a person because he was an "infidel," Mason said, did not "interfere with the rights of conscience," because the voter would merely be exercising "the right of a citizen and a Christian" to declare: "I cannot trust a man of such principles. . . . While he is an infidel, he shall never have my countenance."

According to the historian Frank Lambert, Mason and other clergymen were attempting to circumvent the Constitution's ban on religious tests by advocating "a voter-imposed religious test to be won in the arena of public opinion."[117] The election of 1800, Lambert wrote, gave "orthodox ministers . . . their best opportunity since 1787 to argue that a Christian nation must have Christian leaders."[118]

But in 1800, just as in 1787, they lost that argument. Jefferson's supporters used the Federalists' religious arguments to turn the election into a battle between those who wanted to return to the era of religious establishments versus those who supported religious freedom.[119] William Duane, a Republican newspaper editor, described the election as a choice between "an established church, a religious test, and an order of Priesthood" under Adams, and "religious liberty, the rights of conscience, no priesthood, truth and Jefferson."[120] Adams, Duane wrote, would continue to use "Priests and Judges incorporated with the Government for political purposes, and equally polluting the holy altars of religion, and the seats of Justice." Jefferson's election, by contrast, would lead to "good government without the aid of priestcraft, or religious politics."

The allegation of religious tyranny was effective not merely because of the sectarian appeals by Adams supporters but also because of lingering distaste over his fast-day proclamations. Rather than view the president's overt religious declarations as legitimate calls for piety, many religious groups considered them "Federalist plots to ensnare Republicans into praying for John Adams."[121]

Years later, Adams would tell his friend Benjamin Rush that the declarations were the reason he lost his bid for reelection: "The National Fast recommended by me turned me out of office."[122] According to Adams, the fear that he was supporting the Presbyterian Church as it "aimed at an Establishment as a National Church" both "allarmed and alienated Quakers, Anabaptists, Mennonists, Moravians, Swedenborgians, Methodists, Catholicks, protestant Episcopalians, Arians,

Socinians, Armenians, &c, &c, &c, Atheists and Deists might be added." The strong resistance to a sectarian president, Adams said, "is at the bottom of the unpopularity of national Fasts and Thanksgiving."[123] Too late to salvage his political career, Adams concluded: "Nothing is more dreaded than the National Government meddling with Religion."

This was not the lesson that Alexander Hamilton took from the 1800 election. When voting tallies showed that pro-Jefferson candidates had been elected to the New York state legislature, Hamilton suggested to Governor John Jay that he change the state's election law so that voters, rather than legislators, would select presidential electors. Recognizing that it was unseemly, at best, to alter electoral rules after the votes had been cast, Hamilton said that "the scruples of delicacy and propriety . . . ought not to hinder the taking of a legal and constitutional step to prevent an atheist in religion, and a fanatic in politics, from getting possession of the helm of state."[124] The religious appeal was unsuccessful; Jay wrote at the bottom of Hamilton's letter: "Proposing a measure for party purposes wh. I think it wd. not become me to adopt."[125]

Hamilton, though, was not bothered by the idea of using religion for party purposes. In April 1802, he wrote to James Bayard, a Delaware Federalist, to propose a plan for strengthening the Federalists by creating the "Christian Constitutional Society," whose two stated goals would be "the support of the Christian religion" and "the support of the Constitution of the United States."[126] Hamilton hoped that this group would form small "societies" throughout the nation that would be responsible for writing newspaper articles and pamphlets, working to "promote the election of fit men," and running "institutions of a charitable and useful nature in the management of Federalists."

What makes Hamilton's plan appear particularly cynical is that he wrote to Bayard that the Christian Constitutional Society was needed because the Federalists had lost the last election by failing to appeal to the emotions of the electorate. "Nothing is more fallacious," he explained, "than to expect to produce any valuable or permanent results in political projects by relying merely on the reason of men. Men are rather reasoning than reasonable animals, for the most part governed by the impulse of passion." The religious society would aid in "the competition for the passions of the people" and help the Federalists "contrive to take hold of, and carry along with us some strong feelings of the mind."[127]

Bayard politely rejected Hamilton's scheme. The plan, he said, was "marked with great ingenuity," but the creation of an "association, organized into clubs, on the part of the federalists, would revive a thousand jealousies and suspicions which now begin to slumber."[128]

Hamilton's Christian Constitutional Society was never created, but it seems fair to conclude, in the words of his biographer Ron Chernow, that "Hamilton was not honoring religion but exploiting it for political ends."[129] A decade later, John Adams compared Hamilton's use of religion with that of Jefferson and Madison. With bitter sarcasm, Adams reported: "The pious and virtuous Hamilton, in 1790, began to teach our Nation Christianity, and to commission his followers to cry down Jefferson and Madison as Atheists in league with the French Nation, who were all Atheists."[130]

Interestingly, Adams had grown far more sympathetic to Jefferson and Madison for the religious attacks they had withstood, and to see the unfairness of treating those opposed to established religions as if they were opposed to religion. He said of the fight for religious freedom in Virginia: "They abolished the whole establishment. This was enough to procure them the characters of Atheists all over the World. I mean among the fanatical Advocates for Establishments, and these have been almost universally the fashionable Advocates, till very lately all over the Christian World."[131]

JEFFERSON AND THE WALL OF SEPARATION

Ironically, Jefferson not only refrained from attempting to eradicate religious principles from the minds of the people, but also consciously employed religious language throughout his presidency. He avoided John Adams's Christian imagery, but certainly did not restrict himself to purely secular language.

In his first inaugural address, on March 4, 1801, Jefferson described the country as one united by religion. Americans, he said, were "enlightened by a benign religion, professed indeed and practised in various forms, yet all of them inculcating honesty, truth, temperance, gratitude and the love of man, acknowledging and adoring an overruling providence, which by all its dispensations proves that it delights in the happiness of man here, and his greater happiness hereafter."[132] This sentence represents an attempt to acknowledge the variety of religious practices while stressing an underlying commonality of belief. Stressing that the United States had "banished from our land that religious intolerance under which mankind so long bled and suffered," Jefferson also expressed his concerns for protecting minority interests. He termed it a "sacred principle, that though the will of the majority is in all cases to prevail, that will, to be rightful, must be reasonable; that the minority possess their equal rights, which equal laws must protect, and to violate would be oppression." He ended his inaugural with a nondenominational religious plea similar in tone to that spoken by Washington: "May that infinite power, which rules the destinies of the universe, lead our councils to what is best, and give them a favorable issue for your peace and prosperity."

Jefferson's speeches throughout his presidency would use similar religious language. In his second message to Congress, he declared that "our just attentions are first drawn to those pleasing circumstances which mark the goodness of that Being from whose favor they flow and the large measure of thankfulness we owe for His bounty."[133] In his 1805 message to Congress, he noted there had been an outbreak of yellow fever, but that "Providence in His goodness gave it an early termination on this occasion and lessened the number of victims which have usually fallen before it."[134] At the same time, Jefferson strove to avoid what he termed the "loathsome combination of church and state."[135] Unlike both his predecessors, he did not issue a thanksgiving- or fast-day proclamation.

His attempt to explain his view of the proper relationship between religion and government led to his famous letter to the Danbury Baptists, containing perhaps the most influential metaphor in American history:

> Believing with you that religion is a matter which lies solely between Man & his God, that he owes account to none other for his faith or his worship, that the legitimate powers of government reach actions only, & not opinions, I contemplate with sovereign reverence that act of the whole American people which declared that their legislature should "make no law respecting an establishment of religion, or prohibiting the free exercise thereof," thus *building a wall of separation between Church & State.* Adhering to this expression of the supreme will of the nation in behalf of the rights of conscience, I shall see with sincere satisfaction the progress of those sentiments which tend to restore to man all his natural rights, convinced he has no natural right in opposition to his social duties.[136]

While this letter was first quoted by the Supreme Court in an 1878 decision that upheld a federal ban on polygamy,[137] the "wall of separation" entered the constitutional lexicon in 1947 when the Court used it to explain the meaning of the establishment clause. "In the words of Jefferson," the Court ruled, "the clause against establishment of religion by law was intended to erect 'a wall of separation between church and State.'"[138] This image became a powerful symbol for those who wanted to minimize or eliminate governmental involvement with religious institutions and ceremonies, especially when the Court built on the metaphor by declaring that the wall "must be kept high and impregnable."[139]

Those favoring greater governmental support for religion have strongly attacked the Court for relying on the Danbury letter. In 1985, then–associate justice Rehnquist complained that "the Establishment Clause has been expressly freighted with Jefferson's misleading metaphor for nearly 40 years."[140] Explaining why its use should be "frankly and explicitly abandoned,"[141] Rehnquist wrote:

> Thomas Jefferson was of course in France at the time the constitutional Amendments known as the Bill of Rights were passed by Congress and ratified by the States. His letter to the Danbury Baptist Association was a short note of courtesy, written 14 years after the Amendments were passed by Congress. He would seem to any detached observer as a less than ideal source of contemporary history as to the meaning of the Religion Clauses of the First Amendment.[142]

The attempt to marginalize Jefferson's authority by referring to his being in France when the First Amendment was ratified can be readily dismissed. Jefferson was a leading theorist in creating the American theory of freedom of religion. It was in his Virginia Statute for Religious Freedom, according to Madison, "where religious liberty . . . is unfolded and defined, in its precise extent."[143] Jefferson's letters to Madison helped inform the latter's understanding of both the need for the Bill of Rights and how such amendments would be considered by the courts.[144] And Jefferson's very election to the presidency was in many ways an early referendum on the constitutional relationship between government and religion.

Jefferson's views are not the exclusive source of the founders' understanding of freedom of religion, but they are an essential element in the creation of that understanding. To appreciate the lessons that can be derived from his Danbury letter, we must consider the context in which it was written.

The letter was a response to an 1801 letter from a committee of

Connecticut Baptists protesting their state's religious establishment.[145] They wrote that in Connecticut, "Religion is considered as the first object of Legislation; & therefore what religious privileges we enjoy (as a minor part of the State) we enjoy as favors granted, and not as inalienable rights." Referring to the requirement that Baptists obtain government certificates to avoid paying religious taxes, the letter added that "these favors we receive at the expence of such degrading acknowledgements . . . are inconsistent with the rights of fre[e]men."

The committee did not ask Jefferson to intervene directly in state affairs. In fact, it acknowledged "that the national government cannot destroy the Laws of each State." Nonetheless, the committee expressed the hope that "the sentiments of our beloved President . . . will shine & prevail through all these States and all the world till Hierarchy and tyranny be destroyed from the Earth."[146]

Jefferson knew that his reply would be widely circulated; he wrote to his attorney general, Levi Lincoln, that he saw his response as an opportunity "of sowing useful truths & principles among the people, which might germinate and become rooted among their political tenets."[147] The letter protesting the continuing establishment in Connecticut would provide him the opportunity to present "a condemnation of the alliance between church and state, under the authority of the Constitution." But he thought it might also "furnish . . . an occasion too, which I have long wished to find, of saying why I do not proclaim fastings & thanksgivings, as my predecessors did."[148]

He sent a draft response to Attorney General Lincoln, asking whether his explanation for not offering thanksgiving proclamations would have political repercussions. Jefferson expected that his reasoning would "give great offence to the New England clergy: but the advocate for religious freedom is to expect neither peace nor forgiveness from them." He was more concerned with whether it would have an "ill effect" among the rest of the people of New England. He told Lincoln: "You understand the temper of those in the North, and can weaken it, therefore, to their stomachs; it is at present seasoned to the Southern taste only."

The language of Jefferson's draft was more emphatic than his final letter, referring to a "wall of *eternal* separation between Church & State."[149] He then gave his "Southern" explanation for not issuing thanksgiving proclamations on Constitutional grounds: "Congress thus inhibited from acts respecting religion, and the Executive authorised only to execute their acts, I have refrained from prescribing even those occasional performances of devotion, practiced indeed by the Executive of another nation as the legal head of its church, but subject here, as religious exercises only to the voluntary regulations and discipline of each respective sect."[150]

Here, Jefferson was essentially saying that the call for a day of thanksgiving was the practice of the king of England as head of the Church of England. Lincoln cautioned him that it would be impolitic to include this description, because New England had "always been in the habit of observing fasts and thanksgivings in performance of proclamations from their respective Executives."[151] More importantly, Lincoln noted, not only Jefferson's political opponents but also the "Republicans of those States generally have a respect for it." Accordingly, Jefferson was urged to rewrite his letter so it would be, "incapable of [being] construed into an implied censure of the usages of any of the States."[152]

Jefferson followed Lincoln's political advice and removed all references to thanksgiving proclamations. Probably for similar reasons, he deleted the word "eternal" from the phrase "wall of eternal separation between Church & State." What remained was an expression of kinship with the Connecticut Baptists.

With slight rephrasing, he reiterated their belief that government had no role in the regulation of religion and that because religion was "a matter which lies solely between Man & his God, . . . the legitimate powers of government reach actions only, & not opinions." He then crafted a careful compromise between his desire for religious freedom and his belief in the principles of federalism, which reserved those issues for the states. First, he quoted the First Amendment and described it as "building a wall of separation between Church & State." He, then, without referring specifically to Connecticut, expressed the hope that following the example of the "supreme will of the nation in behalf of the rights of conscience," the states would soon exhibit "the progress of those sentiments which tend to restore to man all his natural rights."[153]

The attention Jefferson gave to drafting his response to the Danbury Baptists illustrates that Justice Rehnquist was incorrect in dismissing it as a "short note of courtesy."[154] Others have tried to discount its importance by asserting that the editing process reveals it to have been composed as "a political letter, not as a dispassionate theoretical pronouncement on the relations between government and religion."[155] This contention overlooks the very problem that Jefferson was addressing: once church and state are entangled, as they were in Connecticut, any discussion of religion is necessarily political.

A third way some have tried to minimize the significance of Jefferson's letter is to note that he had issued a call for a day of thanksgiving when he was governor of Virginia in 1779, and had subsequently employed religious language in many of his public addresses. Thus, the argument goes, Jefferson's "wall" was "a statement delineating the legitimate jurisdictions of the federal and state governments on matters pertaining to religion. . . . [which] had less to do with the separation between church and all civil government than with the separation between the federal and state governments."[156]

Jefferson's call for a day of thanksgiving in 1779 does not reveal him to be a secret supporter of such proclamations. In the middle of the Revolutionary War, the Continental Congress, stating that God "hath prospered our arms and . . . been a shield to our troops in the hour of danger," called on each state governor to "appoint Thursday the 9th of December next, to be a day of publick and solemn Thanksgiving to Almighty God."[157] The fact that Governor Jefferson followed the call of the wartime Continental Congress hardly indicates that he believed such proclamations were appropriate.

The argument that Jefferson was primarily focused on issues of federalism ignores his lifelong commitment to religious liberty and undervalues the significance of his statement in his letter to Lincoln describing himself as an "advocate for religious freedom." The letter to the Danbury Baptists was a deliberate attempt to support a religious minority without implying an overreaching power of the federal government.

The idea that Jefferson was not espousing a view of religious freedom but rather of states' rights also ignores the fact that, to the framers, freedom was protected both by specific declarations of individual liberty and by the constitutional structure of government. Thus, in answering the Reverend Samuel Miller, a Presbyterian minister who had requested that Jefferson call a day of thanksgiving, Jefferson offered two distinct reasons why the federal government was prohibited from "intermeddling with religious institutions, their doctrines, discipline, or exercises."[158] According to Jefferson, "This results not only from the provision that no law shall be made respecting the establishment, or free exercise, of religion, but from that also which reserves to the states the powers not delegated to the U.S."

Jefferson then explained that even a president's mere recommendation of a day of thanksgiving carried an implicit threat. At minimum, he said, it would lead to "some degree of proscription perhaps in public opinion." Because "Fasting & prayer are religious exercises" and "every religious society has a right to determine for itself the times for these exercises, & the objects proper for them," the right to call for days of fasting and prayer "can never be safer than in their own hands, where the constitution has deposited it." When speaking of the right of states, as opposed to the federal government, to call for such days, Jefferson was adroitly ambiguous: "It must then rest with the states, as far as it can be in any human authority." Precisely how far it could rest with human authority, he left to the reverend to decide.[159]

Jefferson was similarly circumspect when discussing presidential calls for thanksgiving in his second inaugural address. Albert Gallatin, his secretary of the treasury, reviewed a preliminary draft and warned Jefferson that simply stating that acts of fasting and prayer "ought not to be prescribed or controlled by the general government" could prove politically damaging: "It implies censure not only on predecessors, but on the State governors, city mayors, &c., who, though they have no more authority under the States than the President under the general government for that object, have nevertheless issued proclamations of that kind."[160] This is the same problem Lincoln had raised with the Danbury letter. Any attempt by Jefferson to justify his not issuing calls for days of fast or thanksgiving risked being construed as an attack on the same practices when performed by the states.

James Madison, ever the political pragmatist, suggested that Jefferson explicitly state that these religious practices were permissible if conducted by the states. Madison's language would have declared that "religious exercises, could therefore be neither controuled nor prescribed" by the federal government and "have accordingly been left as the Constitution found them, under the direction and discipline acknowledged within the several States."[161] Jefferson amended Madison's language to limit its approval of state religious practices. In the version he delivered on March 4, 1805, Jefferson said that because the free exercise of religion was "independent of the powers of the General Government," he had "undertaken on no occasion to prescribe the religious exercises suited to it."[162]

Instead of following Madison's suggested phrasing, indicating that the Constitution had left religion "under the direction and discipline *acknowledged within the several States*" Jefferson stated that he had left religious exercises "as the Constitution found them, under the direction and discipline of *state or church authorities acknowledged by the several reli-*

gious societies."[163] His added language stressed that "church authorities" should also be directing religious exercises. More significantly, the final phrase indicated that the right of states to direct religious exercises was limited to situations in which the religious responsibilities of the state authorities were "acknowledged by the several religious societies." In other words, the state would have no power over the religious observances of those who did not acknowledge its religious authority.

This is not a powerful endorsement of either religious liberty or states' rights. It also is not an expression of a philosophical position. Instead, the second inaugural represented Jefferson the politician trying to justify his controversial reluctance to call for a day of thanksgiving while creating the fewest repercussions from those who supported such calls.

Jefferson's desire to avoid political controversy in his second inaugural also led him to mask his "indignations" about the views of the Federalists and their religious allies by attacking the religion and customs of Native Americans instead. In the notes he prepared when writing this address, Jefferson expressed the desire to respond to the Federalists' "barbarism, bigotry & despotism."[164] But to avoid "direct warfare on them," he decided to express his thoughts as though they "directly applied to the Indians only, but admits by inference a more general extension." Accordingly, in discussing the "obstacles" faced by those trying to "enlighten" the "aboriginal inhabitants," Jefferson's address stressed their "habits of their bodies, prejudices of their minds, ignorance, pride, and the influence of interested and crafty individuals among them who feel themselves something in the present order of things and fear to become nothing in any other." In language intended to apply to his political opponents as well, Jefferson added that Native Americans "have their antiphilosophists who find an interest in keeping things in their present state, who dread reformation, and exert all their faculties to maintain the ascendancy of habit over the duty of improving our reason and obeying its mandates."

Jefferson's indirect and imprecise defenses of his refusal to issue thanksgiving proclamations while president do not prove that he did not believe in the "wall between Church and State." But they do reveal a politician willing to locate useful crevices in his wall.

A more noteworthy example occurred two days after Jefferson wrote his letter to the Danbury Baptists, when he attended Sabbath services in the Capitol to hear a sermon preached by his friend and ally John Leland. Leland had come to Washington to deliver a gift to Jefferson, a wheel of cheese more than six feet in diameter and weighing 1,235 pounds. This "mammoth cheese" had been made by the Baptists of the town of Cheshire, Massachusetts, as a tribute to Jefferson: "The greatest Cheese in America—for the greatest Man in America."[165] Leland, who, like Jefferson, was willing to combine religion with political messages, presented a letter with the cheese, declaring the town's belief "that the Supreme Ruler of the Universe, who raises up men to achieve great events, has raised up a Jefferson at this critical day to defend Republicanism, and to baffle the arts of aristocracy."[166] Notwithstanding other issues, it is safe to say that the founding generation did not observe a strict wall between church and politics.

The fullest description of Leland's service in the Capitol came from Manasseh Cutler, the Congregationalist minister who had insisted on including religion clauses in the Ohio Company's land grant. Cutler, who had been elected to the House of Representatives, was an ardent Federalist, and his disdain for Leland resulted from a combination of political partisanship and religious intolerance. Cutler described Leland as "a poor, ignorant, illiterate, clownish preacher" whose sermon was "bawled with stunning voice, horrid tone, frightful grimaces and extravagant gestures."[167] What especially irked Cutler was the topic of the sermon: "And behold a greater than Solomon is here" (Matthew 12:42). According to Cutler, "The design of the preacher was principally to apply the allusion, not to the person intended in the text, but to *hint* who was then present."

Why was Jefferson there at all, attending a religious service in the Capitol? After all, "religious services in government buildings were and are a gap in the wall of separation."[168] Some commentators, wishing to show that Jefferson endorsed active governmental support for religion,[169] have argued that his "attendance at church services in the House was, then, his way of offering symbolic support for religious faith and for its beneficent role in republican government."[170]

What is misleading about such a claim is that it ignores the reality of life in the new capital city. When Congress first moved into the Capitol in 1800, Washington had very few other buildings. Only two structures were available for religious services. The Christ Church, Washington Parish, was a converted tobacco barn where Jefferson occasionally attended services; the Catholic chapel was described as "a little frame building."[171] According to a study by the Society of Architectural Historians, the Christ Episcopal Church, erected in 1807, is the "earliest structure in the city built to serve an ecclesiastical purpose."[172]

Thus religious services were held in the Capitol for the obvious reason that there was no church large and proper enough for both houses of Congress to attend on a regular basis. Jefferson's attendance at Leland's service in 1802 is hardly proof of his views on issues of church and state. But even after more buildings, including larger churches, were constructed, Congress continued to hold religious services in the Capitol,[173] and President Jefferson continued to attend services there.[174] Perhaps he could have stayed away on the principle that religious services did not belong on governmental property, but such a move would have been perceived as an affront to a coequal branch. During his presidency, Jefferson consciously avoided confrontations on particular religious issues. In the case of religious services in the Capitol, especially since the tradition of religious services on governmental property began as a matter of necessity, his acquiescence in the continuation of this tradition tells us little about whether he thought such a practice should be permitted to begin except in case of an initial building shortage. But it also reveals that Jefferson did not treat the "wall" as "high and impregnable."

An even more glaring contradiction for those who view Jefferson as a "strict separationist"[175] was the treaty he ratified with the Kaskaskia tribe in 1803. This treaty guaranteed that federal money would be used for explicitly religious purposes. In exchange for tribal land amounting to nearly half of the current state of Illinois,[176] the treaty allotted various grants of money and provided that since the "greater part of the said tribe have been baptised and received into the Catholic church to which they are much attached, the United States will give annually for seven years one hundred dollars towards the support of a priest of that religion."[177] In addition to paying for a Catholic priest, the U.S. government also promised to "give the sum of three hundred dollars to assist the said tribe in the erection of a church."

Robert Cord, a leading opponent of strict separation, has argued that this treaty provides strong evidence that the framers, including Jefferson, sought to guarantee only that "one religion, religious sect or religious tradition [would not] be placed in a legally preferred position."[178] According to Cord, the framers supported "state collaboration" with religion and the "nonpreferential or nondiscriminatory use of religious institutions by government."

The simple reason that the Kaskaskia treaty does not prove Cord's point is that payment for a Catholic priest cannot be termed "nonpreferential or nondiscriminatory." If the treaty is seen as representing any philosophy of the relationship between government and religion, that philosophy would be that government can favor one specific denomination, and none other.[179] No one could seriously contend that Thomas Jefferson ever endorsed such a view. Still, it would be wrong to ignore the treaty, as so many others have done, when considering Jefferson's understanding of church-state relations. We need an explanation for his signing a treaty favoring one religious denomination, an action that, if duplicated by a modern president, would surely raise cries that it violated both the principles and the letter of the First Amendment.

The most important factor for deriving meaning from the Kaskaskia treaty is that it involved Native Americans, a group whose religious beliefs and practices were almost universally deemed unworthy of respect. As the legal philosopher Martha Nussbaum has noted: "It was easy for many of the founders to assume that Native religion was hardly religion at all."[180] From the time of the first charter in Virginia in 1606, the teaching of Christianity was seen as a way to bring the "Savages, living in those parts, to human Civility."[181] In 1646, the General Court in Massachusetts "prohibited Indians from performing worship to false gods."[182] In general, Native American religions were seen as nothing "more than pagan ignorance at best, and nefarious devil worship at worst."[183]

In contrast to their attitude toward other traditional religious minorities, the framers, including Jefferson, saw little need to respect Native Americans' religious choices. As Jefferson wrote to John Jay, "the last step of the process" for a "plan of civilizing the Indians" should be instruction from "religious missionaries."[184] In another letter, Jefferson described the steps for "civilizing these people."[185] He said, "Habits of industry, easy subsistence, attachment to property, are necessary to prepare their minds for the first elements of science, and afterwards for moral and religious instruction."

Jefferson's ratification of the Kaskaskia treaty thus reveals far more about his restricted view of Native American religion than about his opinion on how government should interact with religion. Nonetheless, his secretary of state, James Madison, recognized the potential difficulty in separating these two considerations.

Jefferson sent Madison a draft of his third annual message to Congress, in which he would announce the details of the Kaskaskia treaty (along with news about the recently concluded Louisiana Purchase). Madison's major editorial suggestion was to delete references to the religious aspects of the treaty: "May it not be as well to omit the detail of the stipulated considerations, and particularly that of the Roman Catholic Pastor. The jealousy of some may see in it a principle, not according with the exemption of Religion from Civil power."[186] Not mentioning the religious funding would preserve the "exemption of Religion from Civil power," Madison somewhat cynically observed, since "in the Indian Treaty it will be less noticed than in a President's speech." Jefferson followed this advice and in the address simply stated that money would be given to the tribe for "implements of agriculture, and other articles of their choice."[187]

PRESIDENT MADISON AND
THE ESTABLISHMENT CLAUSE

When Madison became president, he too was forced by political realities to temper the implementation of his philosophy on the proper relationship between government and religion. Yet his balancing differed notably from Jefferson's. Madison was much more aggressive in proclaiming the separation of church and state, even while using similar religious language in official proclamations. For example, he ended his first inaugural address, in 1809, with a devout entreaty to "the guardianship and guidance of that Almighty Being whose power regulates the destiny of nations, whose blessings have been so conspicuously dispensed to this rising Republic, and to whom we are bound to address our devout gratitude for the past, as well as our fervent supplications and best hopes for the future."[188] Earlier in the address, however, he announced as one of his guiding principles his commitment "to avoid the slightest interference with the rights of conscience, or the functions of religion so wisely exempted from civil jurisdiction."

Some points quickly become obvious. Madison understood the constitutional limits of governmental involvement in religion as more

than simply concerns about federalism; his reference to "civil jurisdiction" demonstrates that he viewed the Constitution as embodying
the principle he enunciated in his Memorial and Remonstrance, that
religion must be "exempt from the authority of the Society at large."[189]
Additionally, he did not see the use of nonsectarian religious language
in official speeches as exceeding those limits. Madison's conception
of the separation of church and state did not require the cleansing of
all religious language from public dialogue.

He was more uncomfortable with official proclamations recommending public days of thanksgiving and fasts. Unlike Jefferson,
Madison felt compelled to issue such recommendations throughout
his presidency, though later in life he was far more explicit about his
objections to them.

The impetus for Madison's proclamations was the necessity of
rallying the country around the War of 1812, which faced strong opposition. The vote for the official declaration of war, 79–49 in the House
of Representatives and 19–13 in the Senate, was the "closest vote on
any declaration of war in American history."[190] In addition, many
people began demanding a national day to pray for success in the war
effort. On June 4, 1812, the same day that the House of Representatives approved its declaration of war, Benjamin Rush wrote to John
Adams, complaining that Madison was not following the example of
the Continental Congress in appealing "to the God of armies and nations for support."[191] Rush asked Adams, "Are we not the only nation
in the world, France excepted, whether Christian, Mohammedan,
pagan, or savage, that has ever dared to go to war without imploring
supernatural aid, either by prayers, or sacrifices, or auspices, or liba-
tions of some kind?"

Less than a month later, in response to a specific request by both
houses of Congress, Madison issued the first of his four religious proclamations. His July 9 proclamation was a call for "a day of public humiliation and prayer."[192] Among the activities he proposed were "ren-

dering the Sovereign of the Universe and the Benefactor of Mankind the public homage due to His holy attributes" and "acknowledging the transgressions which might justly provoke the manifestations of His divine displeasure."

After he left office, Madison explained to a friend that when he issued a religious proclamation, he was "always careful to make the Proclamations absolutely indiscriminate, and merely recommendatory; or rather mere designations of a day, on which all who thought proper might unite in consecrating it to religious purposes, according to their own faith & forms."[193] For example, Madison opened his second proclamation by "recommending to all who shall be piously disposed" to unite "in addressing at one and the same time their vows and adorations to the Great Parent and Sovereign of the Universe," who had blessed the United States with the "sacred rights of conscience."[194] He then provided a theological defense of his position that government should never attempt to impose religious observation on its citizenry. "If the public homage of a people can ever be worthy [of] the favorable regard of the Holy and Omniscient Being to whom it is addressed," he said, "it must be that in which those who join in it are guided only by their free choice, by the impulse of their hearts and the dictates of their consciences." The total lack of governmental coercion, Madison continued, "must be interesting to all Christian nations as proving that religion, that gift of Heaven for the good of man, freed from all coercive edicts, from that unhallowed connection with the powers of this world which corrupts religion into an instrument or an usurper of the policy of the state, and making no appeal but to reason, to the heart, and to the conscience, can spread its benign influence everywhere."

Some commentators have incorrectly read the beginning of this part of his address as if Madison had "alluded to America as a 'Christian nation.'"[195] This is a misconstruing of the quotation, which, after all, does not say that the American experience will prove interesting to "*other* Christian nations." Instead, it is addressed to the European community, particularly his wartime enemy, Great Britain, which continued the practice of established churches and religious discrimination.

Madison closed his discussion with further religious reasoning, saying that the lack of governmental coercion would "attract to the divine altar those freewill offerings of humble supplication, thanksgiving, and praise which alone can be acceptable to Him whom no hypocrisy can deceive and no forced sacrifices propitiate."[196]

Even with such a commitment to "freewill offerings," Madison never accepted that such proclamations, including his own, were appropriate. In his "Detatched Memoranda," a collection of private papers written after he left office in 1817,[197] Madison explained his opposition to religious proclamations, which "imply a religious agency, making no part of the trust delegated to political rulers."[198] Calling these proclamations "advisory," he wrote, did not ameliorate the problem, since "an advisory Govt is a contradiction in terms." In a clear refutation of those who argue that America was founded as a "Christian nation," Madison warned that these proclamations "nourish the erroneous idea of a national religion."[199] Even were everyone of the same creed, Madison said, "reason and the principles of the Xn religion" require that any attempt to unite in an act of religion "ought to be effected thro' the intervention of their religious not of their political representatives."[200] In a country with multiple religions, he warned, the proclamations had the tendency to "narrow the recommendation to the standard of the predominant sect." If not carefully guarded against, this tendency "naturally terminates in a conformity to the creed of the majority and a single sect, if amounting to a majority."[201] Finally, he noted that religious proclamations are often written to advance a political agenda, "to the scandal of religion, as well as the increase of party animosities." Overlooking his own proclamations, which were written to serve political needs at a time of war, Madison singled out Washington's second proclamation, written "just after the suppression of the Insurrection in [Pennsylvania] and at a time when the public mind was divided on several topics."[202]

While Madison's analysis of thanksgiving proclamations was not made public until long after he died, he did take advantage of two veto messages to explain his understanding of the establishment clause.

His first veto was of a bill "incorporating the Protestant Episcopal Church" in the District of Columbia.[203] Since general incorporation laws were not yet utilized, this bill was limited to the Episcopal Church. Madison voiced two objections.

First, he said, the act violated the establishment clause because it "exceeds the rightful authority to which governments are limited, by the essential distinction between civil and religious functions."[204] In particular, he objected to the manner in which the bill "establishes by law, sundry rules and proceedings relative purely to the organization and polity of the church incorporated." Unlike an earlier church-incorporation law signed by Jefferson,[205] this law detailed procedures for internal church policies, such as requiring that church decisions be "decided by a majority of the votes; and the said ministers shall in no case have a negative on the proceedings."[206] For Madison, if government were that closely entwined with church operations, it would violate the constitutionally mandated "distinction between civil and religious functions."

Madison's other reason for vetoing the incorporation bill is far more provocative. He objected to a provision authorizing the church to provide for the "support of the poor"[207] because such authorization might serve as "a precedent for giving to religious societies, as such, a legal agency in carrying into effect a public and civil duty."[208] While this could be read as indicating that Madison would disapprove of all "faith-based initiatives" in which religious groups participate with other nonprofit organizations in providing social services, that interpretation would reach far beyond the provisions of the law being vetoed. Based on the fact that a single church was being authorized, the veto message can better be read as indicating that Madison did not want the government to transfer legal authority for performing public duties either to one denomination or to a coalition limited to religious organizations.

The second bill Madison vetoed would have granted specific plots of land to four private individuals as well as "five acres of land, including Salem Meeting-house, in the Mississippi Territory, for the use of the Baptist Church."[209] The Baptist church had requested the land because, after erecting the church building, it discovered that the structure was on federal property.[210] Unable to obtain clear title to the property, the church petitioned Congress.

Madison's veto message declared that this grant would violate the establishment clause by setting a "precedent for the appropriation of funds of the United States for the use and support of religious societies." Afterward, two Baptist churches in North Carolina wrote to Madison, commending him for his veto of a law that was "not Consistent with the Spiritual interest of Religion."[211] Further, they agreed that the continued granting of property to religious organizations would "inevitably give to Religious Societies an undue weight and Corrupt influence in public affairs at large and diminish Religious enlargement impairing our civil and Religious liberties."

Madison's response saluted the Baptist churches for continuing to support the separation of religion and government "in a case favoring the interest of your brethren as in other cases."[212] He then reiterated that he "regarded the practical distinction between Religion and Civil Government as essential to the purity of both and as guaranteed by the Constitution of the United States."

It is unmistakable that Madison understood the establishment clause as providing for far more than merely a protection of states' rights. Since the Salem church, like the Episcopal church involved in the first veto, was located on property subject to federal jurisdiction, Madison's concerns could not have involved protecting the ability of states to regulate property. Instead, both vetoes reveal that Madison viewed the First Amendment as a substantive limit on federal power, preventing, at minimum, the government from appropriating property or money "for the use and support of religious societies," regulating the internal affairs of religious organizations, or transferring governmental power and responsibility to religious organizations.

Congress appears to have accepted Madison's analysis. An attempt to overturn his veto of the incorporation bill was defeated overwhelmingly in the House of Representatives, with only 29 voting to override and 71 voting to sustain the veto.[213] The veto of the Baptist Church Property Act was also sustained in the House, with 33 voting in favor of the bill and 55 opposing it.[214] Not only were Madison's vetoes upheld, but a substantial majority of House members voted in support of his views as well.

Although there was no extensive debate on the property veto, a few House members protested Madison's reasoning in vetoing the incorporation bill. Representative Timothy Pitkin of Connecticut said that he viewed the First Amendment more narrowly, as intended only "to prevent the establishment of a National Church, such as the Church of England—a refusal to subscribe to the tenets of which was to exclude a citizen from office, &c."[215] This was consistent with the position held by many New Englanders at the time, namely, that even a system of religious taxes that favored a particular denomination did not constitute an establishment as long as the state did not prescribe "a formulary of faith and worship for the rule and government of all the subjects."[216]

Laban Wheaton of Massachusetts agreed with Pitkin that the veto should be overturned. The Constitution, according to Wheaton, did not distinguish between "a bill for regulating the funds of a religious society" and the houses of Congress "electing, paying or contracting with their Chaplains."[217] Thus, Wheaton argued, if the incorporation bill violated the establishment clause, "both branches of the Legislature, since the commencement of the government, had been guilty of such infringement."

Since the House voted by a more than two-to-one margin to uphold the veto, one could argue that Congress rejected Pitkin's and Wheaton's constitutional interpretation. Certainly, during the founding period, Congress generally did not enact laws indicating the same type of sectarian preferences that the New England states favored. Nonetheless, as Representative Wheaton correctly pointed out, Congress was on occasion willing to engage in conduct that blurred the distinction between civil and religious functions. The legislative chaplaincies that he mentioned are perhaps the clearest example of congressional action with a purely religious motive.

CONGRESSIONAL CHAPLAINS AND SUNDAY MAIL

On April 7, 1789, the second day of its existence, the U.S. Senate voted to create a committee to meet with the House of Representatives to decide two issues it considered fundamental to legislative operations: how the two bodies would conduct conference committees and how they would appoint chaplains.[218] Two days later, the House of Representatives appointed a five-person committee, including James Madison, to meet with the Senate committee.[219] In less than a week, the committees reported back to their respective houses, proposing rules for conference committees and "that two Chaplains, of different denominations, be appointed to Congress, for the present session, the Senate to appoint one, and give notice thereof to the House of Representatives, who shall, thereupon, appoint the other; which Chaplains shall commence their services in the Houses that appoint them, but shall interchange weekly."[220]

This proposal, which was adopted by both houses, shows an attempt to deal with America's religious diversity. Not only would different denominations be represented, but the weekly rotation meant also that services in neither house would be dominated by a single denomination.

On April 25, 1789, the Senate appointed as chaplain Samuel Provoost, an Episcopal minister who had served previously as chaplain to the Confederation Congress.[221] William Linn, a Presbyterian minister, was selected by the House of Representatives a few days later.[222] Apparently, neither chaplain was paid until September 22, when Congress passed and President Washington signed an omnibus bill providing "compensation to the members of the Senate and House of Representatives of the United States, and to the officers of both Houses," including $500 a year for each chaplain.[223]

In upholding the constitutionality of Nebraska's practice of paying a chaplain to open legislative sessions with prayer, Chief Justice Warren Burger stated that James Madison and the others who wrote the Bill of Rights "did not view paid legislative chaplains and opening prayers as a violation" of the establishment clause.[224] Others have gone further, arguing that Madison's failure to object to the funding of legislative chaplains proves he did not believe in a strict separation of church and state.[225]

Madison's actions as a legislator are far too ambiguous to warrant such conclusions. Neither the committee that created the chaplaincy, which also dealt with rules for conference committees, nor the vote on funding chaplains, which also funded legislators and their staffs, was solely focused on the chaplains.[226] There is no record of what, if anything, Madison proposed in the committee or what he said about funding at the time.

After he left public office, Madison wrote that he considered the payment of governmental funds for legislative chaplains a "deviation" from the principle of "immunity of Religion from civil jurisdiction."[227] Noting that, in his view, the First Amendment "forbids everything like an establishment of a national religion," Madison said it was unconstitutional to provide for religious worship "approved by the majority, and conducted by Ministers of religion paid by the entire nation."[228] It would have been better evidence of the legislators' piety, he said, "if the members had contributed for the purpose, a pittance from their own pockets."[229]

Recognizing that Congress was unlikely to end legislative chaplaincies, Madison said they should be viewed not as reflecting constitutional norms, but as insignificant violations: "As the precedent is not likely to be rescinded," he wrote, "the best that can now be done, may be to apply to the Constn. the maxim of the law, *de minimis non curat* [the law does not concern itself with trifles]."[230]

Even though Madison appears to have considered payment for legislative chaplains inconsistent with the constitutional guarantee of freedom of religion, the rest of Congress did not. Some have tried to dismiss the import of Congress's actions by saying that "most congressmen in the First Congress gave little thought to the issue of the possible inconsistency of chaplaincies with the First Amendment and therefore somewhat casually allowed tradition (the established practice of chaplaincies) to rule over principle (the possibility of 'establishment' problems)."[231]

This analysis fails to consider the degree to which many members of Congress valued the religious significance of beginning legislative sessions with prayer and considered it to be an important part of their responsibilities.[232] For example, Elias Boudinot, who joined Madison on the House committee that authorized legislative chaplains, had long supported the practice. In 1775, he had made a similar proposal to the First Provincial Congress of New Jersey. Stating that the Provincial Congress needed to "depend on the all powerfull Influence of the Spirit of God, whose divine aid and assistance it becomes us as a Christian People most devoutly to implore," Boudinot moved that "some Minister of the Gospel be requested to attend this Congress every morning . . . during the Sessions in order to open the Meeting with Prayer humbly supplicating Almighty God to preside over and direct our Councills for the Accomplishment of Peace."[233]

Like sentiments can be seen in the early Congresses' approach to military chaplains. The first authorization for an army chaplain was in 1791.[234] In 1806, Congress passed, and President Jefferson signed, an "Act for establishing Rules and Articles for the government of the Armies of the United States," which included the admonition that it was "earnestly recommended to all officers and soldiers, diligently to attend divine service."[235]

Congress also provided tax exemptions that favored religious organizations. For example, it imposed a tax on "household furniture" in 1815, but specifically exempted items belonging to "any charitable, religious or literary institution."[236]

But congressional actions, like those of presidents, did not always display a consistent view of the proper relationship between government and religion. While Jefferson and Madison both occasionally acted in ways that suggested a desire for a greater connection between church and state than one might expect, the early Congresses sometimes acted more like strict separatists.

The most notable example of congressional acts separating church and state was the requirement that mail be delivered on Sundays. In 1810, Congress passed a law requiring postmasters to keep their offices open "on every day on which a mail, or bag, or other packet, or parcel of letters shall arrive" and to deliver mail "on every day of the week."[237] Religious objections to Sunday mail delivery quickly arose. James P. Wilson, the minister of Philadelphia's First Presbyterian Church, wrote to Congress, urging the termination of Sunday mail delivery because of its "tendency to justify every species of breach of the laws made for the strict observance of the first day of the week, as set apart by the command of God for his more immediate service."[238]

Once the War of 1812 began, Sunday mail delivery was defended as a military measure, with the House Committee on the Post Office and Post Roads "deeming it of great national importance, particularly in time of war, that no delay should attend the transportation of the mail."[239] Cyrus King of Massachusetts tried to limit the authorization of Sunday mail delivery to apply only "during the present war," but his proposal was rejected.[240] Instead, the House of Representatives approved a resolution declaring it "inexpedient" to change the mail delivery schedule.[241]

Many of those opposed to ending Sunday mail delivery were motivated by their understanding of the establishment clause as well as by a concern for military defense. In January 1815, several House members, including Representative John Rhea, chair of the Committee on the Post Office and Post Roads, argued that those who advocated changing the existing law were trying to "blend the affairs of church and state."[242]

After the war ended, Congress continued to require Sunday mail delivery. Several years later, when Congress received a new set of petitions calling for an end to the practice, Senator Richard M. Johnson of Kentucky issued a response that was endorsed by a vote of the entire Senate. Noting that different religions observed the Sabbath on different days, Johnson said: "It is not the legitimate Province of the legislature to determine what religion is true, or what false. Our government is a civil, and not a religious, institution."[243] Instead of exempting Sunday, he concluded, Congress should "adhere strictly to the spirit of the Constitution, which regards the general government in no other light than that of a civil institution, wholly destitute of religious authority."

John Leland, then seventy-six years old, agreed with Johnson and wrote a strong attack on those seeking, in his words, to have Congress "assume an ecclesiastico-political power" and decide which day of the week should be the nation's day of rest.[244] "The only way to prevent religion from being an engine of cruelty," he concluded, "is to exclude religious opinions from the civil code."[245] While Congress often did not often follow Leland's advice on the separation of religion and government, it did for the Sunday mail controversy. Sunday mail deliveries continued until 1912.[246]

JEFFERSON'S WALL AND MADISON'S LINE

No simple metaphor can describe how the founding generation understood freedom of religion, and the "Jeffersonian wall" has proved incapable of capturing the complexities of this inquiry. The "wall" metaphor implies a solidity and certainty that is frequently impossible to obtain. As Sidney Mead, a historian of religion, noted, the "reference to a 'wall' conjures up the image of something quite tangible and solid, which was built once for all in the beginning."[247] Mead added that the word implies "a clearly defined and impregnable barrier."

The problem, however, rests not with Jefferson's allusion but with modern interpreters. Most significantly, Jefferson's wall of separation was meant to exist between "Church & State"—not "Religion & State" or "God & State." His assertion was that the government should neither interfere with, nor aim to support, particular religious institutions or denominations. The letter was written to demonstrate sympathy with the Connecticut Baptists, who were fighting their state's discriminatory religious taxation system.

While the history of the founding period demonstrates widespread agreement that the national government should not provide such sectarian support, that is only part of the inquiry. Jefferson's solid wall does not answer the more difficult question of nonsectarian, generic religious references by government (such as his own use of religious language in his inaugural addresses).

A useful metaphor for these different concerns can be found in a letter James Madison wrote a few years before his death. In 1833, the

Reverend Jasper Adams sent Madison a copy of a sermon declaring that "the people of the United States have retained the Christian religion as the foundation of their civil, legal, and political institutions [and] have consented to tolerate all other religions."[248] Madison's response was a strong but respectful refutation of Adams's argument.

He began by framing the issue in a manner many will find surprising. The "simple question to be decided," he argued, was whether "a support of the best & purest religion, the Xn religion itself, ought, not so far at least as pecuniary means are involved, to be provided for by the Govt rather than be left to the voluntary provisions of those who profess it."[249] This description of Christianity as "the best & purest religion" is unusual for Madison; it constitutes one of the few statements he is known to have made in which he openly aligned himself with a particular faith. His answer to his own "simple question" was far more predictable. The American experience proves that no such support is needed, said Madison, since the end of legal support of religion had resulted in "greater purity & industry of the Pastors and in the greater devotion of their flocks."

Madison desired more than just the end of financial support for religion. To prevent either religion or government from corrupting or usurping the role of the other, Madison told Adams, there should be "an entire abstinence of the Govt from interference in any way whatever, beyond the necessity of preserving public order, & protecting each sect agst trespasses on its legal rights by others." Even with such an explicit directive, he recognized the difficulty of adhering to such a principle in practice. "I must admit," he said, "that it may not be easy, in every possible case, to trace the line of separation between the rights of religion and the Civil authority with such distinctness as to avoid collisions & doubts on unessential points."

There is a subtle but important distinction between Jefferson's reference to "Church & State" and Madison's use of "religion and Civil authority."[250] Most fundamentally, "church" and "religion" are not synonymous. A church is part of a sectarian religious denomination, representing both a particular faith as well as the institution supporting it. By contrast, religion includes all expressions of a connection to a divine power or presence. As both Jefferson and Madison understood, the relation of government to denominational institutions was different from its relation to the general concept of religion.

To prevent the evils of the classic establishments, Jefferson's wall accurately describes the rigid barrier against governmental alignment with particular religious institutions. When evaluating governmental involvement with generic "religion," as opposed to a sectarian "church," Madison's "line of separation" is more apt.[251] Both metaphors acknowledge the importance of separating church and state or, in Madison's words, religion and civil authority. But Madison's line of separation does not connote two realms that can be kept totally distinct from each other and whose boundaries can be easily demarcated. Madison's line retains a flexibility that a wall does not; it permits George Washington's thanksgiving proclamations on one side, while discouraging the sectarian addresses of John Adams.[252] Finally, Madison's concept of line drawing implies a sense of humility, since he admits that "it may not be easy, in every possible case, to trace the line of separation."

Putting Madison's "line" in place of Jefferson's "wall" would not result in a reunification of church and state. Madison himself noted that in drawing the line, it would be difficult to avoid "collisions & doubts on *unessential* points." But for the essential principles of separation of religion and government—those that were created, fought for, and preserved by the founding generation—the line should be indelible.[253]

CHAPTER 7

Original Wisdom

F OR SO-CALLED originalists, those to whom "the discoverable meaning of the Constitution at the time of its initial adoption [is] authoritative for purposes of constitutional interpretation in the present,"[1] the framers' understanding of freedom of religion will answer many contemporary questions involving the relationship between government and religion. Originalists such as former judge Robert Bork rely on the "original understanding" of a provision, which is derived from a determination of what "the public of that time would have understood the words to mean."[2] Others use history not to resolve specific issues but to determine the "general and abstract principles" embodied in the First Amendment.[3] A third group, considered "non-originalists," treat "the original meaning as the starting point for any interpretive inquiry," but consider such other factors as recent history, morality, and other policy concerns in evaluating the meaning of the Constitution's religion clauses.[4]

Regardless of the approach to constitutional interpretation, creating an accurate picture of what freedom of religion meant at the time of the framing is essential. What individuals do with that information will vary, but our constitutional dialogue will improve if we can create a more accurate and less partisan understanding of this formative period. Unfortunately, the historical record reveals that there is no simple definitive statement of the "original understanding" of the religion clauses. Nonetheless, an honest review of that history will reveal much "original wisdom," which it would be shortsighted to ignore.

The first difficulty in trying to construct an accurate interpretation of the framers' understanding is that the concept of religious freedom was undergoing an intellectual revolution throughout the period. As the historian Bernard Bailyn has written, the successful rebellion against England "destroyed the traditional sources of public authority [and] called forth the full range of advanced ideas. Long-settled attitudes were jolted and loosened."[5] Bailyn noted that after the military revolution was completed, "what had happened was seen to have been good and proper, steps in the right direction. The glass was half full, not half empty; and to complete the work of fate and nature, further thought must be taken, theories tested, ideas applied."

The drafting of the First Amendment, in 1789, occurred at "a stage in the movement" of America's understanding of religious freedom, not at the movement's culmination.[6] Because opinions and practices were constantly changing, any attempt to describe a general understanding of religious liberty during this period of intellectual upheaval will of necessity be both imprecise and incomplete.

Further complicating the task of describing the framer's vision for freedom of religion is the lack of any unified understanding of most important issues during the framing period. As a leading historian of religion, Thomas Curry, noted, the majority of Americans did not have "clearly defined positions" on the proper relationship between religion and government.[7] With few exceptions, he adds, "they passed to subsequent generations the task of working out the consequences of the principle that the state had no competence in religious matters in a society wherein customs, mores, laws, and religion intertwined and wherein the majority equated religion with Protestantism."[8]

The most irresponsible way to describe the framers' views is to ignore the statements and actions that contradict one's preformed expectations or current agenda. Such a technique appears on countless websites, ranging from those that advocate a "Christian country" to those that argue for a "secular nation." A similar charge can be leveled against the Supreme Court's 1947 decision in *Everson v. Board of Education,* which declared that discrimination against Baptists, as well as religious taxation, served to "shock the freedom-loving colonials into a feeling of abhorrence."[9] To describe the "freedom-loving colonials," especially the Congregationalists of New England, as being opposed to discriminatory taxation, or to describe the colonists as unified on the appropriateness of religious regulation, is to contradict the period's history.

A more honest, though still flawed approach to dealing with the framers' divergent views is to try to identify a narrow meaning that would not have been objectionable to any of the competing viewpoints of the time. In *Church, State, and Original Intent* (2010), Donald Drakeman argues that the fact that people with divergent views supported the First Amendment "demonstrates that it cannot reasonably be seen as encompassing a philosophy about church and state that can somehow be applied to modern issues."[10] Drakeman concludes that the establishment clause was not meant to enunciate a principle of "secularism, separation, disestablishment, or anything else. It was the answer to a very specific question: Would the new national government countenance a move by the larger Protestant denominations to join together and form a national church? The answer was no."[11]

The proof that no greater meaning is to be found in this constitutional provision, according to Drakeman, is that "if the establishment clause was seen by its contemporaries as attempting to settle, once and for all, highly controversial church-state questions, there would have been a much less desultory debate in the Congress, followed by an outpouring of contentious commentary."[12]

The argument that the lack of in-depth discussion proves that the establishment clause—or the entire Bill of Rights—had only a limited meaning incorrectly imposes a modern understanding of constitution-alism on the framing generation. It overlooks the fact that the very concept of a constitution was changing in that era. As the historian Jack Rakove has explained, at the end of the eighteenth century, there was a substantial "transformation in the ways in which Americans thought about the legal authority of 'bills' or 'declarations' of rights."[13]

Originally, bills of rights were viewed as "general statements of declaratory principles." They were not expected to be directly enforce-able by courts, but were seen largely as affirmations of existing rights. Not only were broad statements of principles the norm, but the nature of constitution writing also would have precluded any attempt to describe completely the full contour of an issue such as freedom of religion. As Rakove asks, how can one "possibly encapsulate a con-cept as complicated as a right within the concise mode of expression favored by the framers of the Constitution?"[14]

A major transformational change in thinking about the purpose and structure of a bill of rights occurred with the advent of judicial review. While the possibility of courts striking down legislation as violative of constitutional norms preceded *Marbury v. Madison*—the 1803 case that firmly established the principle of judicial review in the United States the subsequent active involvement of judges in determining the meaning of constitutional provisions altered the way those provisions were considered.[15] For example, when the Equal Rights Amendment was proposed in 1972, it was met with the sort of "outpouring of contentious commentary" that Drakeman imagined.[16] Supporters energetically described how they thought courts would in-terpret the ERA and what would be the precise judicial consequences of the particular words of the amendment.[17] Those who wrote the First Amendment did not have this sort of debate because, unable to foresee how the Constitution would be used in a system of judicial re-view, they did not attempt to create a precise formulation of important concepts. They would have seen no need to reconcile their different interpretations of the word "establishment" when crafting a terse summary of a general concept.

That does not mean that the Constitution was to be merely a "parchment barrier." There was a nascent appreciation, which Jefferson had conveyed to Madison, that courts would enforce a bill of rights and that an important consequence of stating rights was "the legal check which it puts into the hands of the judiciary."[18] Not until much later, however, did Americans understand what that check would be and how it would be exercised. As the historian Gordon Wood has noted, no one at the time of the framing "could have foreseen just how significant judicial review of possible violations of the Bill of Rights would become in the last half of the twentieth century."[19]

To interpret the First Amendment based on how the framers expected it to be enforced, therefore, is historically anachronistic. It is simply inapposite to read the religion clauses, as Drakeman proposes, as if they were the conscious product of an explicit legislative compromise in which the New England members of Congress had announced their refusal to go along unless specifically selected narrow language was chosen.

The framers expected that the real meaning of the ill-defined language of the First Amendment would be derived from the practices of those charged with fulfilling its promise. In *Federalist 37*, Madison, with a notably religious allusion, discussed the "unavoidable inaccuracy" of language: "When the Almighty himself condescends to address mankind in their own language, his meaning, luminous as it must be, is rendered dim and doubtful by the cloudy medium through which it is communicated." Thus, Madison said, constitutional provisions, like any new laws, "though penned with the greatest technical skill, and passed on the fullest and most mature deliberation, are considered as more or less obscure and equivocal, until their meaning be liquidated and ascertained by a series of particular discussions and adjudications."

Only after reviewing the "discussions and adjudications" of the presidential administrations of Washington, Adams, Jefferson, and Madison, along with those of the first several Congresses, can we begin to ascertain how the framing generation understood the meaning of freedom of religion under the new Constitution. The philosophy and actions of the new federal government during the framing period not only were motivated by the principles that defined this American view of religious liberty, but also helped shape them.

The concurrent actions at the state level, by contrast, are of relatively little value in determining the American vision of freedom of religion. This vision was not derived from a simple composite of the individual states' beliefs and actions; it was a revolutionary creation designed for and by the new national government.

In 1789, John Carroll, the Catholic priest who had accompanied Benjamin Franklin to Quebec, described the paradox of trying to "preserve inviolate for ever, in our new empire, the great principle of religious freedom" while "the constitutions of some of the States continue still to intrench on the sacred rights of conscience."[20] Carroll added: "If bigotry and narrow prejudice have prevented hitherto the cure of these evils, be it the duty of every lover of peace and justice to extend them no further."

The new empire's understanding of religious freedom transcended the "bigotry and narrow prejudice" that still infected the states. Indeed, one of the hallmarks of the national view of religious freedom was a greater respect for minority religious beliefs than was displayed in most of the states. In part, this was a phenomenon foreshadowed by the observation in James Madison's *Federalist* 10 essay that in individual states, with their relatively small populations, it was easier for "a majority [to] be found of the same party" and to "concert and execute their plans of oppression." The national government, with a much larger population, would "extend the sphere, and . . . take in a greater variety of parties and interests." This, Madison predicted, would "make

it less probable that a majority of the whole will have a common motive to invade the rights of other citizens."[21]

A statistical analysis conducted by Roger Finke and Rodney Stark
for their book *The Churching of America, 1776–2005* reveals the extent of
that variety. In the United States as a whole, compared to the individual states, larger denominations were far less prominent and smaller
denominations were far more numerous. For example, the largest
denomination in Massachusetts in 1776, the Congregationalists, made
up more than 71 percent of all the state's religious congregations.
Southern states were not as dominated by a single group, with Episcopalian congregations, at 35 percent, the greatest number in Virginia,
and Presbyterians, at 28.5 percent, the largest in North Carolina. But
no state matched the diversity of the entire United States, in which
the largest denomination, Congregationalists, comprised barely more
than 20 percent of all congregations.

Another way to measure religious diversity is to count the
significant-sized denominations then in existence. Eight different
denominations, Congregationalists, Presbyterians, Baptists, Episcopalians, Quakers, the German Reformed, Lutherans, and the Dutch
Reformed, each accounted for at least 3 percent of all the nation's
congregations. Most individual states contained only four to six such
denominations, New York being the sole state with eight of that size.[22]

A third way to evaluate diversity is to calculate how many people
belonged to small religious groups. If we define "small" denominations
as those containing less than 3 percent of the congregations in a particular area, we see that small denominations were, in the aggregate,
a much more significant political factor on the national level. In the
United States, small denominations, including Methodists, Catholics,
Moravians, Separatists and Independents, Dunkers, Mennonites,
Huguenots, Sandemanians, and Jews, constituted 13.6 percent of all
denominations. Small denominations totaled between just 4 and 6
percent in each individual state. It is not surprising, therefore, to find

more deference paid to the interests and sensitivities of religious minorities at the national than at the state level, and far more pressure on the local level to assist the most powerful denominations.[23]

Even at the state level, however, momentum was building against the establishment of religion. Between 1776 and 1788, three states, North Carolina, New York, and Virginia, ended their religious establishments. Along with Delaware, New Jersey, Pennsylvania, and Rhode Island, that meant that seven states were without such establishments. During that same time, however, Massachusetts reaffirmed its state establishment; South Carolina created a new formal religious establishment; and Georgia, Maryland, New Hampshire, and Vermont reconfirmed the right to impose religious taxes.[24] The last state establishment, in Massachusetts, did not end until 1833.

Today, some commentators question how supporters of the establishment clause could have believed it would enhance religious liberty, since it did not affect existing state establishments.[25] To answer this question, we must recognize the drastic change that has occurred since the eighteenth century in the relative roles of federal constitutional provisions compared to their state counterparts in the protection of individual rights.

Today, the U.S. Constitution sets a "floor" for individual rights, a level of protection that states can increase but cannot reduce.[26] A state can always provide greater protection for religious activity than the Constitution requires.[27] A state cannot, however, diminish the rights granted by the federal Constitution. Florida was not permitted to penalize a religious group for the crime of engaging in "ritual sacrifices of animals" because "laws that suppress religious belief or practice" violate "the Nation's essential commitment to religious freedom."[28] If the Supreme Court were to permit a state to continue such discriminatory actions, it would mean that such actions did not violate the First Amendment as applied to the states by the Fourteenth Amendment.

By contrast, when the First Amendment was drafted and ratified, federal courts had no power to strike down state laws that violated freedom of religion. States could decide what rights to give their citizens. Massachusetts and Connecticut were free to provide their citizens with less than full religious freedom, and Virginia and Pennsylvania could opt to provide more religious freedom by choosing not to have an established religion. Any national religious establishment created by Congress would have diminished the unrestrained religious liberty those states had created. Their citizens would no longer have enjoyed the expansive freedom that their states desired. The Constitution, with its antiestablishment clause, ensured that states would be free, if they so chose, to create a jurisdiction with as much religious freedom as possible. The framers' Constitution created a ceiling, rather than a floor, for individual rights. The First Amendment was designed to prevent the federal government from creating an establishment that thereby would have *reduced* the amount of religious liberty enjoyed by much of the local citizenry.

That explains why Baptists and others were so supportive of the First Amendment, and why Massachusetts and Connecticut, the states with the strongest establishments, did not care enough to ratify it. Opponents of establishments understood the religion clauses as providing space for those states that chose to maximize religious liberty. The states with established religions may not have shared the negative view of establishments, but since their establishments were not being affected, they had little interest in the protections of the First Amendment.

But even though the federal constitutional mandates of religious freedom did not apply to the states directly, those provisions influenced the evolution of religious liberty at the state level. As one author noted, "Federal constitutional reform spurred state constitutional reform."[29] South Carolina held a convention in 1790 that, according to Judge Joseph Brevard, who wrote the first major compilation of South Carolina law, "established a constitution for the government of the state, conformably to the principles of the constitution of the United States."[30] Meeting just a month after the state ratified the federal Bill of Rights, the delegates voted to end South Carolina's establishment of the "Christian Protestant religion." In place of the 1778 Constitution's protection of religious freedom for "all denominations of Christian Protestants," the 1790 Constitution provided that "the free exercise and enjoyment of religious profession and worship, without discrimination or preference, shall forever hereafter be allowed within this State to all mankind."[31] The state removed not only the requirement that governmental officials be "of the Protestant religion" but also the phrase "so help me God" from the oath for government officials.[32]

David Ramsey, who has been called "the first historian of the post-Revolutionary South,"[33] exalted that "the whole of this system distinguishing between toleration and establishment—between christian protestants and others, was abolished by the constitution of 1790; and religion was placed where it ought to be in a state of perfect freedom."[34] According to Ramsey, South Carolina's 1790 convention was called to "model the constitution of the state in conformity to that of the United States [and] formed a constitution adapted to the new order of things."[35]

Many other states also conformed their constitutions' religious provisions to the federal model. As the historian Derek Davis noted, "The federal test ban . . . contributed to a growing and widespread, 'public perception that religious test oaths had no place in republican governments.'"[36] In 1792, Delaware actually copied the language from Article VI. Its 1776 requirement that officeholders "profess faith in God the Father, and in Jesus Christ His only Son, and in the Holy Ghost"[37] was replaced by the declaration that "no religious test shall be required as a qualification to any office, or public trust, under this State."[38] Other state constitutions, including those in Georgia (1789), Indiana (1816), Illinois (1818), Maine (1819), and Missouri (1820), added provisions to their constitutions that explicitly barred religious tests.[39]

Not all states were willing to emulate the federal ban on test oaths. In 1790, Pennsylvania deleted its requirement that representatives "acknowledge the Scriptures of the Old and New Testament to be given by Divine inspiration," but replaced it with a requirement that they acknowledge "the being of a God."[40] Displaying an imperfect understanding of the federal example, Tennessee, in its first constitution, drafted in 1796, copied Article VI, declaring that "no religious test shall ever be required as a qualification to any office or public trust under this State," but added the contradictory provision barring from public office "anyone who denies the being of God."[41]

Some states simply were not willing to embrace the "new order" and end ancient prejudices. But even in those states, the U.S. Constitution was cited as an ideal by those fighting for religious freedom. Maryland, for instance, kept its requirement limiting office holding to Christians. In 1819, when a state assembly committee proposed what was termed the "Jew Bill," granting Jews the right to hold public office, it argued that Maryland should emulate the federal government:

> It is the interest, and it ought to be the wish, of every religious sect among us to see all political distinctions for ever abolished. Under the constitution of the United States, the most perfect freedom is allowed in this respect; and it is surely inconsistent, it is surely strange, that a Jew who may hold a seat in congress, who may even be raised to the highest and most honorable station in the universe, the chief magistrate of a free people, cannot hold any office of profit or trust under the constitution of Maryland.[42]

The "Jew Bill" finally passed in 1826, and Jews were permitted to serve in the legislature. Nonetheless, Maryland government officials were required to declare a "belief in the existence of God" until this provision was ruled unconstitutional by the U.S. Supreme Court in 1961.[43]

Not surprisingly, Massachusetts was particularly slow to join the trend toward full religious equality. At its 1820 Constitutional Convention, the eighty-five-year-old John Adams proposed altering the Massachusetts Constitution "so that instead of 'every denomination of

Christians,'" it should read, "'all men, of all religions, demeaning themselves peaceably, and as good subjects of the Commonwealth, shall be equally under the protection of the law.'"[44] His proposal was defeated. The convention did, however, agree to remove the requirement that officeholders declare that they "believe the Christian religion and have a firm persuasion of its truth."[45] It was not until 1833, the year the state establishment was officially ended, that the Massachusetts Constitution was finally changed to provide protection for "all religious sects and denominations, demeaning themselves peaceably."[46]

Adams, like most other national leaders of the framing period, felt that the states often detracted from the image of religious freedom that they envisioned for the national government. Two years before Adams attempted to expand Massachusetts's protection beyond Christians, he wrote to a New York rabbi, Mordecai Manuel Noah, expressing his recognition that the states did not yet uniformly provide full religious equality. "I wish your nation may be admitted to all the privileges of citizens in every country of the world," Adams wrote. "This country has done much. *I wish it may do more;* and annul every narrow idea in religion, government, and commerce."[47]

Adams knew that the states, with their "narrow ideas" of religion, lagged behind the national government's vision of religious freedom. This view is reminiscent of George Washington's response to the Catholics' complaint about the "States, which still restrict" the "equal rights of citizenship." The situation in the states would improve, Washington told them, "as mankind become more liberal."[48]

A THEORY OF RELIGIOUS FREEDOM

Washington and Adams, followed by Jefferson and Madison, had the opportunity to define an American ideal of religious liberty free from the historic constraints of the preexisting states.[49] Their vision was shaped by the words of the Constitution and the First Amendment, and their actions helped shape the meaning of those words. To reconstruct their theory of freedom of religion requires identifying a set of principles that provide a "good fit" with the history of the founding period.[50] These principles must explain most, even if not all, of the actions that were taken as well as reflect the philosophy that was expressed. The set of principles must also be coherent enough that they "are consistent with each other, and any potential conflicts among them [can] be resolved in a consistent and principled manner."[51]

The quality of the ultimate fit between the principles deduced and the historical practices from which they are derived will inevitably be imperfect because the members of the framing generation did not always act consistently with their own principles. Consider Madison's recommendation that President Jefferson not mention the funding of a Catholic priest or the erection of a church for the Kaskaskia tribe in a speech to Congress because "in the Indian Treaty it will be less noticed than in a President's speech."[52] Rather than revealing their true view of separation of church and state, the incident seems to show that they were real-world politicians who sometimes needed to compromise their principles.[53]

On the other hand, some commentators have been too willing to disregard practices such as the use of religious language by Jefferson and Madison in their inaugural addresses as mere political expediency. These practices are dismissed as instances where the actions of Jefferson and Madison "diverged from principle" or, as Justice David Souter succinctly put it, "Homer nodded."[54] In reality, the framers' principles were sophisticated enough to include religious acknowledgments along with the view that "the functions of religion [are] so wisely exempted from civil jurisdiction."[55]

As seen in the 1785 battle over the general assessment in Virginia, there were three distinct, though related strands of thought that contributed to the American concept of freedom of religion, none of which were hostile or opposed to religion. Supporters of religious freedom were motivated by religious, philosophical, and political concerns. While these were not considered mutually exclusive, and often were combined in speeches and petitions, it is useful to also think of them separately, since each provides separate insights into the principles underlying religious liberty in America. The religious argument, as epitomized by John Leland, contended that the biblical admonition "my kingdom is not of this world" meant that "religion, in all its parts, is distinct from civil government."[56] Jefferson and Madison represent the philosophical argument. According to Madison, "religion is essentially distinct from civil Government, and exempt from its cognizance; [and] a connection between them is injurious to both."[57] For Jefferson, the fight to prevent religious establishments was based on his "eternal hostility against every form of tyranny over the mind of man."[58] The third strand was best exemplified by George Washington, who strove to ensure that the combination of religion and government would not "rankle, & perhaps convulse the State."[59] By the time he became president, Washington was greatly concerned with the tendency of religious disputes to divide a nation. As he wrote to a friend in Ireland: "Religious controversies are always productive of more acrimony and irreconcilable hatreds than those which spring from any other cause."[60]

The legal philosopher Martha Nussbaum has objected to relying on a concern with "civil peace" when determining the meaning of the Constitution's religion clauses, saying that it permits the retention of discriminatory religious practices.[61] According to Nussbaum, the desire to avoid social conflict can serve as the basis for "favoring majority beliefs and making a virtue of convenience."[62] In other words, if civil peace is considered threatened only when the majority or a sizable minority feels threatened, the perverse effect would be to diminish the protections for the smallest religious minorities. This concern can be addressed by noting that Washington's interest was not merely to avoid conflict but to unify the country. Thus, he believed that each individual had to be treated as an equal member of society and that "every man, conducting himself as a good citizen . . . ought to be protected in worshipping the Deity according to the dictates of his own conscience."[63]

The key question for the framing generation, therefore, was this: if religion is to be a force for good without being divisive or oppressive, what is the role of government? The early national leaders strove to devise, in admittedly different ways, a balance in which government was able to express support for religion while keeping the religious and governmental spheres distinct, and without threatening national unity.

In creating this balance, the most important tenet of the framing generation was that religion can be a force both for magnificent good and for unspeakable evil. John Adams captured this duality in a letter he wrote to Thomas Jefferson in 1817: "Twenty times, in the course of my late reading, have I been on the point of breaking out, 'this would be the best of all possible worlds, if there was no religion in it!!!' But in this exclamation, I should have been as fanatical as Bryant [Adams's former parish priest] or Cleverly [his former schoolmaster]. Without religion, this world would be something not fit to be mentioned in polite company—I mean hell."[64]

George Washington often expressed the view that religion was necessary for creating virtuous leaders and citizenry. In 1797, he wrote: "Religion and Morality are the essential pillars of civil society."[65] This theme was repeated in his Farewell Address, in which he declared that "reason and experience both forbid us to expect that national morality can prevail in exclusion of religious principle."[66] Such respect for religion is not contradicted by an awareness that religion has also been the cause of oppression and tyranny. As Thomas Jefferson wrote in 1776 in preparation for debates on his bill for religious freedom, in the name of religion, "Millns. burnt—tortd.—find.—imprisd. yet men *differ*."[67]

In a republic where the people ruled, the framers recognized that combining religion and government posed the additional danger that religion would be misused for political gain. Most national leaders during the framing rejected any attempt to create, in John Leland's phrase, "an ecclesiastico-political power."[68] Alexander Hamilton was a dishonorable exception, as seen both in his cynical plan to create the Christian Constitutional Society to help Federalists in "the competition for the passions of the people,"[69] and in his advice that a fast-day proclamation would be "politically useful to impress our nation that there is a serious state of things."[70] Such manipulation, according to Madison, resulted in "the scandal of religion, as well as the increase of party animosities."[71]

Jefferson's victory over Adams in 1800 can be interpreted as a rejection of the politicization of religion, at least on the national level. When Adams's supporters tried to frame the campaign as a choice between "god—and a religious president" and "Jefferson—and no god!!!"[72] Jefferson's allies were able to recast the alternatives as between an "established church, a religious test, and an order of Priesthood," on the one hand, and "Religious liberty, the rights of conscience, no priesthood, truth and Jefferson" on the other.[73] Jefferson's election, according to Abraham Bishop, a Connecticut Republican, helped destroy "that kind of religion which is made a foot-ball or stalking horse, and which operates only to dishonor God and ruin man."[74]

That election can also be seen as a rejection of the view that America was a "Christian nation." The voters refused to heed the call of ministers who had urged their followers to vote for Adams because "a Christian nation must have Christian leaders."[75] Adams lost not because voters opposed "God and a religious president," but because they rejected the concept of an "established church, a religious test, and an order of Priesthood."

Nonetheless, a majority of Americans today believe that the country is a "Christian nation"[76] and that its founders "treated America as a Christian nation."[77] That categorization, however, was broadly and strongly rejected by the framers.

The phrase "Christian nation" means far more than the simple demographic fact that an overwhelming majority of the nation's citizens were Christian during the framing period and that a significant majority are Christian today. Just as the phrase "white nation," while demographically accurate, implies that nonwhites are not quite legitimate citizens, "Christian nation" carries a similar message for non-Christians.[78]

On May 9, 1789, shortly after Washington took the oath of office, the *Gazette of the United States* published an article urging that non-Protestants be barred from office, asserting that "the Protestant Religion is the important bulwark of our Constitution."[79] John Carroll responded with an impassioned letter, calling the assertion an attempt "to revive an odious system of religious intolerance."[80] According to Carroll, to attribute America's freedom or Constitution to the Protestant faith was "ridiculous," since the country's opponents in the battle for freedom were also Protestants. "The bitterest enemies of our national prosperity," he wrote, "possess the same religion as prevails generally in the United States." As an explanation of America's greatness, he concluded, "religion is out of the question." Carroll did not try to include Catholicism within the national religion, nor did he assert that there existed some generic national religion. Instead, he declared that "the establishment of the American empire was not the work of this or that religion, but arose from a generous exertion of all her citizens to redress their wrongs, to assert their rights, and lay its foundation on the soundest principles of justice and equal liberty."

John Leland also rejected the attempts to describe America in religious terms, basing his objections largely on religious grounds. "The notion of a Christian commonwealth," he wrote, "should be exploded forever" because it violates biblical commands: "A national church takes in the whole nation, and no more; whereas, the Gospel Church, takes in no nation, but those who fear God, and work righteousness in every nation."[81] That a majority of a nation's people shared a religion was irrelevant, according to Leland, because even "if all the souls in a government were saints of God, should they be formed into a society by law, that society could not be a Gospel Church, but a creature of state."[82] Finally, he warned of the "shocking monster of *Christian nation*" that would be created if the different Christian denominations in the country were all to "unite to form a *Christian Phalanx*, to be established by Congress as the religion of the United States. . . . [The] glory of America will depart—the blood and treasure expended in the revolution will all be lost—and the asylum for the distressed turned to a prison and an inquisition."[83]

Even though Carroll's and Leland's views were not yet generally adopted on the state level, they embodied the philosophy and actions of the new federal government. Failure to accept this critical distinction led to Justice Daniel Brewer's infamous 1892 Supreme Court decision in *Church of the Holy Trinity v. United States,* in which he declared that the United States "is a Christian nation."[84]

To establish that his proposition was "historically true," Justice Brewer devoted several pages to describing the explicit religious references in various colonial charters.[85] He then stated: "Coming nearer to the present time, the Declaration of Independence recognizes the presence of the Divine in human affairs."[86] Brewer then stopped discussing the federal government and wrote: "If we examine the constitutions of the various States we find in them a constant recognition of religious obligations."[87] He concluded his historical review by discussing court cases declaring that Christianity was part of the common-law system for the states of Pennsylvania and New York. Other than quoting the First Amendment and the constitutional provision giving the President ten days, "Sundays excepted," to decide whether to sign or veto legislation, Brewer made no mention of any aspect of the federal government during the framing period. The entire body of "historical" evidence that Brewer cited to support his conclusion that "this is a Christian nation" focused on practices at the state or local level.[88]

The reason Brewer ignored the actions of the federal government during the framing period is that the words and actions of the national leaders refute his conclusion. Most obviously, not once during their presidencies did Washington, Adams, Jefferson, or Madison ever state or imply that either the nation or the national government was a "Christian nation."

George Washington was frequently urged to express his support for a religious interpretation of the national government, and each time he refused. When the Presbytery of the Eastward called Washington "the steady Patron of genuine Christianity,"[89] he reminded them that it was actually to "the guidance of the ministers of the gospel this important object is, perhaps, more properly committed."[90] Similarly, when the Senate chaplain Ashbel Green wrote to him "to acknowledge the countenance which you have uniformly given to his holy religion,"[91] Washington responded by referring to all of the religious leaders in the country. He praised "that harmony and brotherly love, which characterize the clergy of different denominations," which, he added, was "the surest basis of universal harmony."[92]

Washington, of course, knew that religious discrimination continued within the states and that many still provided financial and other support for favored denominations. But as he wrote to the Swedenborgian New Jerusalem Church of Baltimore, the national government was different: "In the Enlightened Age and in this Land of equal Liberty it is our boast, that a man's religious tenets will not forfeit the protection of the Laws, nor deprive him of the right of attaining and holding the highest Offices that are known in the United States."[93]

Not only was the United States not a "Christian" nation during the founding period, it also was not a "Judeo-Christian" one.[94] The term "Judeo-Christian" did not exist at that time; it first appeared in print in 1899 and was not used to describe America until after the end of World War II.[95] There is, not surprisingly, no record of any of the framers asserting that the shared ideologies of Christianity and Judaism lay at the core of the American system. Moreover, use of the term "Judeo-Christian," especially by those involved in the modern debate over the proper role of government and religion, tends to have the feel of a corporate hostile takeover. Without appreciating the irony, the House of Representatives, in its 2007 resolution "Recognizing the importance of Christmas and the Christian faith," justified its proclamation by declaring, "Whereas the United States, being founded as a constitutional republic in the traditions of western civilization, finds much in its history that points observers back to its Judeo-Christian roots."[96]

The framers, while not denying that most of the population consisted of religious people,[97] also did not characterize the country as a "religious nation." To have done so would have risked encouraging what Madison termed the "erroneous idea of a national religion."[98] The persistence of this "erroneous idea" would not have surprised him. He thought it had been "improperly adopted by so many nations which have embraced Christianity, [that it] is too apt to lurk in the bosoms even of Americans, who in general are aware of the distinction between religious & political societies."[99]

Maintaining this distinction, at least at the national level, was considered a matter of fundamental importance during the founding period. The administrations of Washington, Jefferson, and Madison, and even to a large extent that of Adams, reflected the principle enunciated by Madison in explaining his 1811 veto of a grant of land to a Baptist church. They all regarded "the practical distinction between Religion and Civil Government as essential to the purity of both and as guaranteed by the Constitution of the United States."[100] As Washington explained, it was the responsibility of the clergy "to instruct the ignorant, and to reclaim the devious," while government was responsible for furthering "the progress of morality and science."[101] With such a division of labor, Washington concluded, the country might "expect the advancement of true religion."

This distinction was never understood to cleanse all religious references from political speech. Despite what many "strict separatists" believe, the framers were not afraid of religion in the public arena. As presidents, both Madison and Jefferson, like Washington before them, employed sincere religious language in their inaugurals. Madison gave his pious supplication to "the guardianship and guidance of that Almighty Being whose power regulates the destiny of nations."[102] Jefferson, in his second inaugural, went further, even requesting that his fellow citizens pray for him: "I shall need, too, the favor of that Being in whose hands we are, who led our forefathers, as Israel of old, from their native land. . . . And to whose goodness I ask you to join with me in supplications, that he will so enlighten the minds of your servants, guide their councils, and prosper their measures."[103]

The framers recognized the important distinction between governmental action and governmental speech. The federal government was considered virtually prohibited from regulating or funding religious activities. But genuine, devout governmental religious speech was to be permitted, within carefully delimited bounds.

According to the historian of religion Thomas Curry, it was widely accepted during the framing period that the government "had no power to prohibit the free exercise of peaceable religion."[104] By the time the Constitution was ratified, even the state governments had stopped prohibiting or penalizing the practices of minority religions that did not result in the disruption of "peace & good order."[105]

Some found universal religious acceptance difficult to countenance. Justice Joseph Story, in his monumental *Commentaries on the Constitution of the United States* (1833), argued that the framing generation was interested only in protecting and furthering Christianity:

> Probably at the time of the adoption of the constitution, and of the amendment to it, now under consideration, the general, if not the universal, sentiment in America was, that Christianity ought to receive encouragement from the state, so far as was not incompatible with the private rights of conscience, and the freedom of religious worship. An attempt to level all religions, and to make it a matter

of state policy to hold all in utter indifference, would have created universal disapprobation, if not universal indignation.[106]

To support the framers' supposed disinclination "to level all religions," Story cites just one source: the House debate on the First Amendment, in which the word "Christianity" is never mentioned and there is no discussion of other religions.[107] At least concerning his views of the First Amendment, Story's *Commentaries* have accurately been called "propagandistic" and designed to serve "the purpose for which Story wrote them—expositing the Constitution from a conservative, New England perspective."[108]

Story's personal antipathy to non-Christian religions can be seen in a decision he wrote for the U.S. Supreme Court in an 1844 case, *Vidal v. Philadelphia*.[109] The case involved a question of purely state law: whether a provision in a will violated Pennsylvania law. The will had provided money for a college on the condition that "no ecclesiastic, missionary, or minister of any sect whatsoever, shall ever hold or exercise any station or duty whatever in the said college."[110] Pennsylvania courts had previously held that "Christianity, general Christianity, is, and always has been, a part of the common law of Pennsylvania."[111] Story held that the will did not violate Pennsylvania common law because it did not display any antagonism to Christianity. He then added that the case might be different were the college to be established "for the propagation of Judaism, or Deism, or any *other form of infidelity*."[112] Such a disreputable motive, he added, "is not to be presumed to exist in a Christian country."[113]

In his *Commentaries*, Story transposed his own hostility to other religions into the thoughts of those who wrote the First Amendment. Again citing no source other than the House debates, he declared: "The real object of the amendment was, not to countenance, much less to *advance Mahometanism, or Judaism, or infidelity*, by prostrating Christianity; but to exclude all rivalry among Christian sects, and to prevent any national ecclesiastical establishment."[114] Justice Sandra Day O'Connor quoted this passage and remarked that "Justice Story probably reflected the thinking of the framing generation."[115] Actually, Story was reflecting only the "central tenet of New England conservative ideology —that states should 'foster and encourage the Christian religion generally, as a matter of sound policy as well as of revealed truth.'"[116]

A far more accurate summary of the thinking of the framing generation, at least those charged with implementing the new Constitution, can be found in the writings of St. George Tucker, the second law professor at the College of William and Mary. Thirty years before Story published his *Commentaries,* Tucker produced an annotated edition of *Blackstone's Commentaries* that became "the standard work on American law for a generation."[117] Tucker's annotation, "the first systematic effort by any figure in American law to describe the contours of the new system created by the amended Constitution,"[118] explained how the United States, especially its Constitution and Bill of Rights, improved upon the English common-law system.[119]

To Tucker, the American guarantee of religious freedom applied universally: "Not only all Christians, but all men of all religions, ought to be considered by a state as equally entitled to its protection, as far as they demean themselves honestly and peaceably."[120] The U.S. Constitution "guaranteed to the citizens of the United States" that "every honest and peaceable man, whatever is his faith, be protected there; and find an effectual defence against the attacks of bigotry and intolerance. In the United States, may religion flourish!"[121]

Tucker also believed that religion should be permitted to flourish without the assistance of government. Statesmen should help religion by setting a good personal example, he said, but "they cannot, as public men, give it any other assistance." And there was a stronger reason than this for government to leave religion alone: "All, besides, that has been called a public leading in religion, has done it an essential injury, and produced some of the worst consequences."[122]

There are many reasons to consider Tucker's description more accurate than Story's. Not only was Tucker's book published much closer to the drafting of the First Amendment, but his analysis also "drew heavily on the learned jurist's own William and Mary law lectures, which were composed almost contemporaneously with the framing and adoption of the . . . Amendment."[123] Tucker also had access to private information about the drafting of the First Amendment, since his "closest friend, John Page, and his brother Thomas Tucker, served in the first House; they and others kept him informed, by correspondence, of its events."[124] Most importantly, Tucker's analysis is a far better description of how the federal government treated religious issues during the founding period. Rather than denigrate "Mahometanism, or Judaism, or infidelity," the national government followed Washington's assertion that "the Government of the United States, which gives to bigotry no sanction, to persecution no assistance, requires only that they who live under its protection should demean themselves as good citizens, in giving it on all occasions their effectual support."[125]

The commitment to equal treatment led to a confirmation of another principle, first established during the 1785 fight over the Virginia general assessment, that tax money should not be used to support religious enterprises.[126] As proclaimed in Virginia's Statute for Religious Freedom, "to compel a man to furnish contributions of money for the propagation of opinions which he disbelieves, is sinful and tyrannical." While the New England states continued to allocate public money to favored religions, such spending was falling out of favor at even the local level. By the time Madison left the White House in 1817, only Connecticut, New Hampshire, and Massachusetts still funded religion, and within two years, both Connecticut and New Hampshire had ended the practice. Moreover, many people recognized that governmental religious funding violated the principles of the U.S. Constitution. While the First Amendment did not yet apply to the states, it was cited as an ideal; Isaac Backus, in his ongoing battle against New England's religious assessments, wrote that the First Amendment was "part of the constitution of our general government, and yet . . . Massachusetts and Connecticut act contrary to it to this day."[127]

This understanding of the First Amendment was confirmed in Madison's 1811 veto of a bill granting land to a Baptist church, in which he explained that "the appropriation of funds of the United States for the use . . . of religious societies [was] contrary to the article of the Constitution which declares that 'Congress shall make no law respecting a religious establishment.'"[128] Madison's veto was not merely upheld, but endorsed in the House of Representatives by a strong majority, 55–33.[129]

Some commentators have argued that Madison's concern was limited to appropriations favoring one religious group over another. According to this view, the First Amendment permits the government to confer "special aid or benefits upon religion in general, as long as the aid or benefits are given without preference to any religious denominations."[130] In his book *Church-State Relationships in America,* Gerard Bradley concluded that "a rigorous historical inquiry into the adoption of the Establishment Clause has shown that it prohibits sect preferences in the government's dealings with religion," but that "the framers intended nondiscriminatory aid to religion."[131]

This so-called non-preferentialist view of the First Amendment is inconsistent with the primary lesson from the framing period; as John Leland wrote, when government is "rightly formed . . . it embraces Pagans, Jews, Mahometans and Christians, within its fostering arms . . . [and] impartially protects all of them."[132] Indeed, for this time period, there is no evidence that nondiscriminatory religious aid was ever given at the national level. Bradley's book, for example, does not cite a single instance of the early national government providing such aid. As Douglas Laycock noted, the framing generation "did not substitute nonpreferential taxes for preferential taxes; they rejected all taxes. They did not substitute small taxes for large taxes; three pence was as bad as any larger sum. The principle was what mattered. With respect to money, religion was to be wholly voluntary. Churches either would support themselves or they would not, but the government would neither help nor interfere."[133] Meanwhile, at the state level, nondiscriminatory aid to religion was attempted only a few times. These attempts were rejected as equivalents of state establishments.[134]

The first such attempt occurred in Georgia, in 1785, the same year that Virginia rejected Patrick Henry's call for a general assessment. On February 21, 1785, the Georgia legislature approved a law entitled "For the regular establishment and support of the public duties of Religion," under which money would be appropriated from the general treasury, "for the support of religion within [each] County."[135] The choice of minister was not to be made by the state. Instead, any "Subscription of not less than thirty heads of Families" would be empowered to choose its own minister, and the amount of money allotted would be based on the "the valuation of the property of such Subscribers." The only limitation for receiving public funds was that the minister "shall on every sunday Publickly explain and Inculcate the great doctrines and precepts of the Christian Religion."

The act met immediate opposition and appears to have been repealed without having been put into effect.[136] The objections to this general assessment were based not on its exclusion of non-Christians but rather on the premise that government should not be providing any financial support for religion. The state Baptist Association filed a remonstrance opposing the general assessment as an improper use of governmental authority, declaring "that civil and religious government ought not to be blended together."[137] All government funding was to be opposed, the Baptist Association argued, because, "when religion is turned into a policy and made subservient to private interests, it will ever bring tyranny along with it, and should, therefore, be opposed in its first appearances." The remonstrance warned that once an assessment to aid religion in general was permitted, it would lead to a return to sectarian partiality; the general assessment was "a stepping stone to the establishment of a particular denomination in preference and at the expense of the rest."

When Connecticut passed a similar "nondiscriminatory" funding law in 1816, entitled "An Act for the Support of Religion and Literature," it too was attacked as providing "a precedence to future legislation" that would "advance the temporal interest of *one* favorite sect at the expense of every other."[138] Connecticut's bill distributed money that had been returned to the state as reimbursement for payments made during the War of 1812. It divided the money among the major denominations according to their percentages of the population in order to ensure that "no preferences have been given to one denomination of Christians over another."[139]

The bill, enacted in the waning days of Connecticut's Standing Order, as its Congregationalist establishment was termed, was seen as a desperate attempt to offer money "to make voters . . . support an expiring faction."[140] While some minority religions in the state complained about their percentages,[141] "the important argument was that money allotted by the state for religious purposes was then as always, a form of unity between church and state which was intrinsically unscriptual and potentially tyrannical."[142] The Methodist Society in Burlington issued a resolution attacking the bill because the government "has no authority to take that money which the good people have paid for the defense of the country and appropriate it to the above use."[143] The First and Second Baptist Churches of Groton passed a resolution saying: "It is unjust to apply the monies of those who pretend to no religion and were paid by them for other purposes to the support of religion they do not believe in when it is known to be contrary to their desire."[144]

The lesson from the framing period is that nonpreferential funding of religion is functionally equivalent to the religious funding that benefits a particular sect. In both cases, the government was viewed as being improperly intertwined with religion. Additionally, even when funding was labeled "nonpreferential," it was seen as tending to further the interests of a particular favored religion. Certainly, on the federal level, the government was considered barred from applying public monies directly to support religion, on either a sectarian or a nondiscriminatory basis.

While even "neutral" religious spending was understood to be prohibited, the framing generation did not reach a clear consensus concerning the right of religious minorities to obtain exceptions from the requirements of religiously neutral laws. While "most of the colonies and states . . . exempted religious objectors from military conscription and from oath requirements,"[145] an exemption from military service for those "religiously scrupulous of bearing arms" was deleted from the proposal that became the Second Amendment.[146]

The Supreme Court has ruled that religious individuals have no constitutional right to be exempted from "neutral laws." In the 1990 case *Employment Division v. Smith,* the Court held that even if a person's ability to engage in religious conduct is prohibited as "the incidental effect of a generally applicable and otherwise valid provision, the First Amendment has not been offended."[147] In a separate concurring opinion, Justice O'Connor argued that the First Amendment's guarantee of religious liberty should require "the government to justify any substantial burden on religiously motivated conduct by a compelling state interest and by means narrowly tailored to achieve that interest."[148] According to Justice Scalia, who wrote the *Smith* decision, this so-called compelling interest test was inappropriate because of the country's enormous variety of religions and their widely divergent practices: "We cannot afford the luxury of deeming presumptively invalid, as applied to the religious objector, every regulation of conduct that does not protect an interest of the highest order."[149]

Despite Scalia's problematic use of the word "luxury," his reasoning may well be closer to that of the framing generation. There is little evidence that exemptions from general laws were systematically granted except when to do so would have threatened public interests of "the highest order."[150] But the Court in *Smith* was presented with a false dichotomy, the choice of a "compelling interest test," a relatively recent invention first used in the 1950s[151] or no restriction at all. The framers did not formulate their analysis in such a binary manner.

Thomas Jefferson seemed to limit his protection to "liberty of conscience" and permitted governmental regulation that affected religious conduct. In his Virginia Statute for Religious Freedom, Jefferson wrote that it "is time enough for the rightful purposes of civil government for its officers to interfere when principles break out into overt acts against peace and good order."

James Madison appears to have been more protective of religious conduct. In his 1776 proposal for the Virginia Declaration of Rights, Madison wrote that the free exercise of religion should be protected against governmental interference "unless the preservation of equal liberty and the existence of the State are manifestly endangered."[152] He later wrote that an individual's religious practice should be protected "in every case where it does not trespass on private rights or the public peace."[153]

Perhaps the difference of opinion between Jefferson and Madison, and the split on the Supreme Court, could best be reconciled by reference to President Washington's message to the Quakers. Unlike the Court in its *Smith* ruling, Washington did not believe that government should be free to ignore the importance of religious practice to the devout: "I assure you very explicitly that in my opinion the Consciencious scruples of all men should be treated with great delicacy & tenderness."[154] But Washington did not articulate a "compelling interest" test either. He expressed his "wish and desire that the Laws may always be as extensively accommodated to them as a due regard to the Protection and essential Interests of the Nation may Justify, and permit."[155]

Washington's sentiments do not fit into the legal dichotomy presented by the Court in *Smith*. The concept that a government should treat the requirements of minority religions with "great delicacy & tenderness" avoids the extremes of both the majority and the dissent and instead suggests that the civil powers should at least consider whether an individual's religious needs reasonably can be accommodated without sacrificing the goals of a particular governmental action.[156]

In a 1997 case, Catholic high school students in a Texas town were barred from wearing rosaries as necklaces because their school considered them to be "gang-related apparel" after a local gang, the "United Homies," started wearing them as an identifying symbol.[157] Similarly, the army court-martialed a Jewish military officer for wearing a yarmulke,[158] and the Newark city police department fired a Muslim police officer who refused to shave his beard.[159] Following Washington's guidance, the governmental officials in each instance should have treated the religious requirements as deserving of great respect and ascertained whether some reasonable alternative to the bans would have protected the legitimate governmental interests.[160]

But that does not mean that every religious request must trump governmental interests. Consider the case of a church in the small town of Lenox, Massachusetts, that wanted to construct a parish center that would house a 150-person social hall, despite the fact that the size of the center violated numerous local zoning laws.[161] While the desire to avoid traffic congestion may not rise to a "compelling interest," a town should be able to limit the size of all buildings, including religious ones, in the name of preserving its quality of life.

While Washington described a subtle balance for dealing with religious exemptions from general laws, he set a clearer example for including religious references in governmental pronouncements.[162] Starting from his first inaugural address, in which he stated that it would be "peculiarly improper to omit in this first official Act, my fervent supplications to that Almighty Being who rules over the Universe," Washington helped shape an American understanding of religious freedom that incorporated the use of inclusive religious language by government officials.[163]

John Adams's sectarian proclamations violated the Washingtonian model. Adams often used denominational language, imploring in his 1799 thanksgiving proclamation that "through the grace of His Holy Spirit we may be disposed and enabled to yield a more suitable obedience to His righteous requisitions in time to come."[164] Years later, Adams, the only one of the first four presidents to use explicitly Christian language in his speeches and the only one defeated in his bid for reelection, would understand how his sectarian proclamations came to be viewed as a "dreaded" instance of "the National Government meddling with Religion."[165]

In many of their private writings, both Jefferson and Madison expressed discomfort at any governmental encouragement of private religious practice. Jefferson found even a mere recommendation for a day of fasting and prayer inappropriate, since it would "indirectly assume to the U.S. an authority over religious exercises which the Constitution has directly precluded them from."[166] Madison, in retirement, similarly wrote that religious proclamations "imply a religious agency, making no part of the trust delegated to political rulers."[167] Nonetheless, Madison not only used religious language in his inaugural addresses but also repeatedly acceded to requests for religious proclamations during the War of 1812. And while Jefferson as president did not issue religious proclamations, he frequently used devout language in his public speeches.

To some extent, Jefferson's and Madison's willingness to use religious language shows that they did not find all use of such language to violate the separation of religion and government. But the demands of the public also reveal that during their lifetimes, much of the population did not share the full Jeffersonian and Madisonian vision. In an 1818 letter to Rabbi Mordecai Noah, Jefferson wrote that public opinion prevented the eradication of anti-Semitism, because "although we are free by the law, we are not so in practice; public opinion erects itself into an inquisition, and exercises its office with as much fanaticism as fans the flames of an *auto de fe* [literally, "act of faith," a reference to the burning of heretics at the stake]."[168] A few years later, Jefferson described the difficulty of changing community sentiment: "If the freedom of religion, guaranteed to us by law in theory, can ever rise in practice under the overbearing inquisition of public opinion, truth will prevail over fanaticism."[169]

A nineteenth-century English author, Frances Trollope (novelist Anthony Trollope's mother), shared Jefferson's view of American public opinion. Her time in the United States, she wrote, "has shown me that a religious tyranny may be exerted very effectually without the aid of the government, in a way much more oppressive than the paying of tithes."[170] She added: "The whole people appear to be divided into an almost endless variety of religious factions, and I was told, that to be well received in society, it was necessary to declare yourself as belonging to some one of these."

But public opinion need not be so harmful. The history of the founding period shows that the public favored Washington's inclusive religious language over Adams's sectarian proclamations. A review of President Washington's religious references reveals his extraordinary ability to use devout language in a manner fully consistent with his commitment that religion be used to unite a diverse country.

We would do well, nonetheless, to heed a warning given by Madison in his Detached Memoranda. The practice of issuing religious proclamations, he said, "if not strictly guarded naturally terminates in a conformity to the creed of the majority and of a single sect, if amounting to majority."[171] This tendency is evident in Justice Scalia's defense of the posting of the Ten Commandments inside Kentucky courthouses. According to Scalia, "Publicly honoring the Ten Commandments is . . . indistinguishable, insofar as discriminating against other religions is concerned, from publicly honoring God."[172] This was so, Scalia wrote, because "the three most popular religions in the United States, Christianity, Judaism, and Islam—which combined account for 97.7% of all believers—are monotheistic," and because "all of them, moreover (Islam included), believe that the Ten Commandments were given by God to Moses, and are divine prescriptions for a virtuous life." He concluded that since honoring both the Ten Commandments and God "are recognized across such a broad and diverse range of the population—from Christians to Muslims—they cannot be reasonably understood as a government endorsement of a particular religious viewpoint."

There are numerous difficulties with this analysis, starting with the assumption that "97.7% of all believers . . . believe that the Ten Commandments were given by God to Moses, and are divine prescriptions for a virtuous life." First, Justice Scalia's equating of the number of Christians, Jews, and Muslims with the number of people who believe in the divinity of the Ten Commandments relies on the untenable presumption that every person who is a member of a religion believes in all of its tenets.[173] Second, by using as his statistical base the number of "all believers" rather than "all citizens," he deliberately ignores the sensibilities and interests of a sizable portion of the population.[174] In fact, the same census report that Scalia relied upon indicates that more than 14 percent of American adults regarded themselves as having "no religion."[175]

More important, perhaps, is that Justice Scalia's arithmetical analysis was rejected by George Washington. During Washington's presidency, the percentage of Protestants in the country was at least as high as the 97.7 percent figure for Christians, Jews, and Muslims on which Scalia relied. According to one estimate, in 1776, Protestants made up 98.1 percent of all congregations in the nation, with Catholics at 1.7 percent and Jews at 0.2 percent.[176] If Washington had shared Scalia's reasoning, he would have used strictly Protestant language in his proclamation; or, to be safe, he could have used Christian terminology in keeping with the beliefs of 99.8 percent of the population. But he did not; rather, he deliberately chose nondenominational language.

His goal was that "the national government, which, by the favour of Divine Providence, was formed by the common councils, and peaceably established with the common consent of the people, *will prove a blessing to every denomination of them.*"[177]

Unlike Justice Scalia, Washington was not content to use denominational speech merely because it "was recognized across . . . a broad and diverse range of the population." His vision for the nation was far more inclusive. "The bosom of America is open," he wrote, "to receive the oppressed and persecuted of all nations and religions; whom we shall welcome to a participation of all our rights and privileges, if by decency and propriety of conduct, they appear to merit the enjoyment."[178]

Nonetheless, it would be a mistake to treat the religious language used by Washington, Jefferson, and Madison as empty formality. Their words were carefully chosen to be devout as well as inclusive. Those in the framing generation were not trying to establish a "civil religion." This term originated with French philosopher Jean-Jacques Rousseau[179] and was first applied to the United States by Robert Bellah.[180] While "civil religion" is an ill-defined term, it generally has been thought to be "a distinctive form of religion."[181] According to Bellah, "American civil religion has its own prophets and its own martyrs, its own sacred events and sacred places, its own solemn rituals and symbols."[182] As one commentator wrote:

> American civil religion, following the forms and structures of Judeo-Christianity in general, and Protestantism in particular, finds expression in myths of origin and eschatology, of first and last things (the Revolution, the Boston Tea Party, the Great Society, the American Century); a pantheon of heroes, saints and martyrs (the Founding Fathers, the fallen Lincoln, the Unknown Soldier); sacred places (the Lincoln Memorial, Plymouth Rock); a liturgical calendar of consecration and remembrance (the Fourth of July, Memorial Day, Thanksgiving); sacred texts (the Declaration of Independence, Lincoln's Second Inaugural Address); and an all-embracing worldview (the American Way of Life, the Four Freedoms).[183]

However accurate or inaccurate this concept, as the historian Derek Davis noted, "prior to the Civil War, civil religion was still in formation and not a readily recognizable form of American religion."[184] This fact, Davis concluded, "effectively eliminates . . . the need to consider civil religion as an element of the framers' 'original intent' respecting the desired relationship between religion and the federal government."[185]

Certainly, the framers never evinced a desire to construct a public religion that was distinct from traditional religions. They were trying to create a spiritual public vocabulary that could be appreciated by the full range of individuals in a diverse population. Those from orthodox religions could hear this language not merely as consistent with their prayers but as part of them. They could recite the official religious language along with that of their own faith and not feel as if they had left their religion behind.

But the framers' language was expansive enough to permit those who belonged to minority religions, along with those outside the mainstream of religious belief, to join in the experience of a conscientious communion with the rest of their nation. Some will always decline this invitation, and that is their right. But the framers' language was designed to communicate to all, including the Deistic, agnostic, and atheistic, that they were valued members of the political community.

As Justice Scalia points out, any public reference to "God" has the potential of offending someone and of "contradicting the beliefs of some people that there are many gods, or that God or the gods pay no attention to human affairs."[186] Citing Washington's thanksgiving proclamation, Scalia reasoned: "With respect to public acknowledgment of religious belief, it is entirely clear from our Nation's historical practices that the Establishment Clause permits this disregard of polytheists and believers in unconcerned deities, just as it permits the disregard of devout atheists."[187]

Scalia's cavalier assumption that the framing generation's use of religious language demonstrates a "disregard" of such people is contradicted by the history of the Virginia Statute for Religious Freedom. Jefferson's original draft declared that "Almighty God hath created the mind free" and that governmental penalties for religious beliefs "are a departure from the plan of the holy author of our religion." A proposal to change the sentence to read "a departure from the plan of Jesus Christ, the holy author of our religion"[188] was rejected by the legislature. Both Madison and Jefferson perceived a fundamental difference between the original language and the proposed amendment: the original language was universal, but the amendment was exclusionary. Madison believed that the phrase "Jesus Christ, the holy author of our religion" would "imply a restriction of the liberty defined in the Bill, to those professing his religion only."[189] Jefferson wrote that the legislature's decision to omit that phrase from the final statute demonstrated an intent "to comprehend, within the mantle of its protection, the Jew and the Gentile, the Christian and Mahometan, the Hindoo, and infidel of every denomination."[190]

Thus, to Jefferson, phrases like "Almighty God" and "holy author of our religion" encompassed the belief systems of both the polytheistic Hindu[191] and the "unbeliever" infidel.[192] His view of the inclusiveness of this language is consistent with his belief that religion could be divided into "the moral branch of religion, which is the same in all religions; while in that branch which consists of dogmas, all differ, all have a different set."[193] The Ten Commandments, or any other text directly derived from a particular denomination, would not convey the same universality.

Thus the key to the framing generation's religious language was the use of terminology that expressed reverential concepts without implying that those not of a favored faith were second-class citizens. The national leaders of this time strove to avoid any action that, in the words of Madison's Memorial and Remonstrance, "degrades from the equal rank of Citizens all those whose opinions in Religion do not bend to those of the Legislative authority."[194]

To describe the framing generation's consensus, we must modify a famous tenet of Justice O'Connor. In explaining why governmental "endorsement" of religion violates the establishment clause, O'Connor stated: "Endorsement sends a message to nonadherents that they are outsiders, not full members of the political community, and an accompanying message to adherents that they are insiders, favored members of the political community."[195] The framers were indeed committed to ensuring that citizens, regardless of their religious beliefs, were "full members of the political community." But their public addresses indicate that they did not see every acknowledgment of religion as communicating second-class citizenship to nonadherents. The nondenominational religious language that appeared in Washington's thanksgiving proclamation, Jefferson's Statute for Religious Freedom, and Madison's inaugural address was considered neither divisive nor insulting. To paraphrase Justice O'Connor, the framing generation considered it violative of the American understanding of freedom of religion only if the government were to endorse religion *in such a way* that it sends a message to nonadherents that they are outsiders, not full members of the political community, and an accompanying message to adherents that they are insiders, favored members of the political community.

Knowing when an endorsement of religion sends such messages is not easy. When politicians and governmental officials talk about religion, they should be mindful of the careful balance represented by our public religion yet still feel free to acknowledge their own religious beliefs. Thus, it was not inappropriate for presidential candidate George W. Bush to respond to a question in a 1999 debate about which political philosopher had the greatest influence on his life by saying "Jesus."[196] There is nothing inherently wrong with political figures describing their personal religious beliefs. What is problematic is when politicians do not make clear that their personal religion must not be confused with "the erroneous idea of a national religion," or that those with differing beliefs are not somehow different or lesser citizens. Thus, the troubling parts of Bush's discussion were his subsequent remarks in which he refused to recognize that his religion might not be universal: "When you turn your heart and your life over to Christ, when you accept Christ as the savior, it changes your heart," Bush said, "It changes your life. And that's what happened to me."[197]

On the other hand, religious people and organizations should not be disadvantaged in the political arena either. In 2008, opponents of Proposition 8, which outlawed gay marriage in California, released a vicious anti-Mormon advertisement in which two Mormons break into a lesbian couple's home to steal their wedding rings and rip up their marriage license, as a voice-over declares: "Fact: members of the Mormon Church have given over $20 million to pass proposition 8."[198] To attack political opponents on the basis of their religion, rather than their political position, threatens to bring about the same type of societal division that Washington was trying to avoid.

Moreover, the appropriateness of religious speech by political and governmental leaders depends on its context. What is acceptable in a legislative chamber may not belong in a courthouse. Similarly, what is appropriate for a presidential address to the nation may be improper for a teacher in a public-school classroom.

We can only speculate as to what the framers would think about teacher-led prayer in public schools. The concept of universal public education was foreign to their generation; it did not begin to become a feature of American life until the mid-1820s.[199] But we do know that the framers were deeply concerned with any governmental action that infringed upon an individual's liberty of conscience or that coerced religious practices. As Thomas Jefferson wrote: "No provision in our Constitution ought to be dearer to man than that which protects the rights of conscience against the enterprises of the civil authority. It has not left the religion of its citizens under the power of its public functionaries."[200]

Although our children's religion is not under the power of public functionaries, their education certainly is. Unfortunately, the role of religion in America's founding period has been largely absent from much of the public school curriculum. As one writer noted, "America's religious heritage has often gone uncovered in public schools. . . . Religious studies has become a 'black hole' in American public education."[201] In the words of Stephen Prothero, a professor of religion at Boston University, "High school textbooks . . . [follow] Emily Post's dictum not to discuss religion in polite company."[202]

There are many reasons that America's religious history should be taught in public schools. The first is simply that failing to do so results in an inaccurate and incomplete understanding of history itself. One report, supported by groups as diverse as the Americans United for the Separation of Church and State and the Christian Legal Society, concluded: "Omission of facts about religion can give students the false impression that the religious life of humankind is insignificant or unimportant."[203] The report also pointed out that "study about religion is . . . important if students are to value religious liberty."[204]

The history that should be taught must be complete, including the good and the bad and the complicated balances created by the framing generation. Students must learn that religion has provided both the inspiration for good and the excuse for discrimination; that during the American Revolution, piety coexisted with virulent anti-Catholic hatred; that the religious speech of the framers did not contradict their commitment to liberty of conscience; and that they strove to create a nation in which religion united everyone, regardless of their beliefs.

Teaching about religion presents its own dangers. Some may take improper advantage and attempt the religious indoctrination of their captive audience. Others may try to ensure that their own denomination receives top billing. Still others may feel uncomfortable with any mention of religion in the public school setting. We as a society are not accustomed to talking about religion and government in a nonpartisan way. The framing period, while far from Edenic, was a time during which our national leaders were forced to discuss these matters. From those discussions, they were able to create an American vision of religious freedom that is equally capable of crossing today's rigid political and religious divides.

The nation's dialogue would substantially improve if we understood the limitations of our false dichotomies. We must recognize that one may be deeply religious, like John Leland, and still believe that a close tie between church and state degrades all religion and threatens the freedom of those not belonging to the majority denominations. We must understand that one may care deeply about religious liberty, like George Washington, and still believe that public acknowledgment of religion does not threaten the rights of others.

There is no perfect compromise on the question of how government and religion should interact. Religion is an issue of such personal force that it is unrealistic to demand universal mutual respect from adherents of vastly different creeds. But by learning the lessons of those who helped create the American understanding of freedom of religion, we can begin to move closer to a more perfect union.

ABBREVIATIONS

Adams Corr.	Lyman Henry Butterfield, Wendell D. Garrett, and Marjorie E. Sprague, eds., *Adams Family Correspondence* [1761–88], vols. 1 and 2 (Cambridge, Mass.: Belknap Press of Harvard University Press, 1963)
Adams Diary	Lyman Henry Butterfield, Leonard C. Farber, and Wendell D. Garrett, eds., *Diary and Autobiography of John Adams* [1755–1804], 4 vols. (Cambridge, Mass.: Belknap Press of Harvard University Press, 1961)
AFC	Jon L. Wakelyn, ed., *America's Founding Charters: Primary Documents of Colonial and Revolutionary Era Governance,* 3 vols. (Westport, Conn.: Greenwood, 2006)
AKC	Henry Wilder Foote, *Annals of King's Chapel from the Puritan Age of New England to the Present Day,* 2 vols. (Boston, Mass.: Little, Brown, 1882, 1896)
Annals	Joseph Gales et al., eds., *The Debates and Proceedings in the Congress of the United States* [1789–1824], 42 vols. (Washington, D.C., 1834–56)
ASP	William Addison Blakely, comp., *American State Papers Bearing on Sunday Legislation* (Washington, D.C.: Religious Liberty Association, 1911)
CMPP	James D. Richardson, ed., *A Compilation of the Messages and Papers of the Presidents,* 10 vols. (Washington, D.C.: Government Printing Office, 1905)
CWBF	John Bigelow, ed., *The Complete Works of Benjamin Franklin* (New York: Putnam's Sons, 1888)

DHCUSA   Bureau of Rolls and Library, *Documentary History of the Constitution of the United States of America,* 5 vols. (Washington, D.C.: Department of State, 1905)

DHFFE   Gordon DenBoer, ed., *The Documentary History of the First Federal Elections, 1788–1790,* vol. 2 (Madison: University of Wisconsin Press, 1984)

DHRA   Edwin S. Gaustad and Mark A. Noll, eds., *A Documentary History of Religion in America: To 1877* (Grand Rapids, Mich.: Eerdmans, 2003)

DHRC   Merrill Jensen, John P. Kaminski, and Gaspare J. Saladino, eds., *The Documentary History of the Ratification of the Constitution,* 23 vols. (Madison: Wisconsin Historical Society Press, 1976–2009)

DHSNY   E. B. O'Callaghan, ed., *The Documentary History of the State of New-York* (Albany, N.Y.: Weed, Parsons, 1850)

DHSRL   Charles Fenton James, ed., *Documentary History of the Struggle for Religious Liberty in Virginia* (Lynchburg, Va.: Bell, 1900)

DPC   *The Debates and Proceedings of the Congress of the United States,* vol. 22 (11th Cong., 3rd Sess.) (Washington, D.C.: Gales and Seaton, 1853)

Elliot's *Debates*   Jonathan Elliot, *The Debates in the Several State Conventions on the Adoption of the Federal Constitution,* 2nd ed., 5 vols. (Washington, D.C.: Taylor and Maury, 1836)

Farrand   Max Farrand, *The Records of the Federal Convention of 1787,* 3 vols. (New Haven, Conn.: Yale University Press, 1911)

Ford's *Pamphlets*   Paul Leicester Ford, ed., *Pamphlets on the Constitution of the United States, Published during Its Discussion by the People, 1787–1788* (Brooklyn, N.Y., 1888; reprint, New York: Da Capo, 2000)

FSC   Francis Newton Thorpe, ed., *The Federal and State Constitutions, Colonial Charters, and Other Organic Laws of the States, Territories, and Colonies* (Washington, D.C.: Government Printing Office, 1909)

Hening   William Waller Hening, ed., *The Statutes at Large; Being a Collection of All the Laws of Virginia, from the First Session of the Legislature in the Year 1619* (New York: Bartow, 1823)

JCC	*Journals of the Continental Congress, 1774–1789,* 34 vols. (Washington, D.C.: Government Printing Office, 1904–37)
JHDV	Virginia General Assembly, *Journal of the House of Delegates of the State of Virginia* (Richmond, Va.: White, 1828)
LDC	Paul H. Smith et al., eds., *Letters of Delegates to Congress, 1774–1789,* 25 vols. (Washington, D.C.: Library of Congress, 1976–2000)
LMCC	Edmund C. Burnett, ed., *Letters of Members of the Continental Congress,* 7 vols. (Washington, D.C.: Carnegie Institution, 1921–36)
LWJM	James Madison, *Letters and Other Writings of James Madison,* vol. 3 (Philadelphia: Lippincott, 1865)
OFL	Alexander Biddle, ed., *Old Family Letters* (Philadelphia: Lippincott, 1892)
PAH	Harold C. Syrett and Jacob E. Cooke, eds., *Papers of Alexander Hamilton* (New York: Columbia University Press, 1961)
PGW: Confederation	W. W. Abbot, ed., *The Papers of George Washington: Confederation Series* [1784–87], 6 vols. (Charlottesville: University of Virginia Press, 1992–97)
PGW: Diaries	Donald Jackson and Dorothy Twohig, eds., *The Diaries of George Washington* [1748–99], 6 vols. (Charlottesville: University of Virginia Press, 1976–79)
PGW: Presidential	W. W. Abbot, Dorothy Twohig, Jack D. Warren, Mark A. Mastromarino, Robert F. Haggard, Christine Sternberg Patrick, John C. Pinheiro, David R. Hoth, and Carol S. Ebel, eds., *The Papers of George Washington: Presidential Series* [1788–97], 16 vols. to date (Charlottesville: University of Virginia Press, 1987–)
PGW: Retirement	W. W. Abbot and Edward G. Lengel, eds., *The Papers of George Washington: Retirement Series* [1797–99], 4 vols. (Charlottesville: University of Virginia Press, 1998–99)
PGW: War	Philander D. Chase, Frank E. Grizzard, Jr., Edward G. Lengel, David R. Hoth, and William M. Ferrano, eds., *The Papers of George Washington: Revolutionary War Series* [1775–83], 20 vols. (Charlottesville: University of Virginia Press, 1985–2010)
PJM: Congressional	William T. Hutchinson, Robert A. Rutland, Charles F.

	Hobson et al., eds., *The Papers of James Madison: Congressional Series* [1751–1801], 17 vols. (Chicago: University of Chicago Press, 1962–77; Charlottesville: University of Virginia Press, 1977–91)
PJM: Presidential	J. C. A. Stagg, series ed., *The Papers of James Madison: Presidential Series* [1809–17], 6 vols. to date (Charlottesville: University of Virginia Press, 1984–)
PJM: Retirement	J. C. A. Stagg, series ed., *The Papers of James Madison: Retirement Series* [1817–36], 1 vol. to date (Charlottesville: University of Virginia Press, 2009–)
Poore	Benjamin Perley Poore, ed., *The Federal and State Constitutions, Colonial Charters, and Other Organic Laws of the United States*, 2 vols. (Washington, D.C.: Government Printing Office, 1877)
PTJ	Julian Boyd, Charles T. Cullen, John Catanzariti et al., eds., *The Papers of Thomas Jefferson*, 36 vols. to date (Princeton, N.J.: Princeton University Press, 1950–)
PTJ: Retirement	J. Jefferson Looney, series ed., *The Papers of Thomas Jefferson: Retirement Series*, 7 vols. to date (Princeton, N.J.: Princeton University Press, 2004–)
TGA	Richard L. Bushman, ed., *The Great Awakening: Documents on the Revival of Religion, 1740–1745* (Chapel Hill: University of North Carolina Press, 1989)
WBF	Albert Henry Smyth, ed., *The Writings of Benjamin Franklin* (New York: Macmillan, 1906)
WGW	Jared Sparks, ed., *The Writings of George Washington*, 12 vols. (Boston: American Stationers' Company, 1837)
WJA	*The Works of John Adams* (Boston, Mass.: Little, Brown, 1854)
WJL	John Leland, *The Writings of John Leland* (New York: Wood, 1845)
WJM	Gaillard Hunt, ed., *The Writings of James Madison* (New York: Putnam's Sons, 1900), and Gaillard Hunt, ed., *The Writings of James Madison, 1819–1836* (New York: Knickerbocker, 1910)
WTJ	Paul Leicester Ford, ed., *The Writings of Thomas Jefferson*, 10 vols. (New York: Putnam's Sons, 1892–99)
WTJ (Wash.)	Henry A. Washington, ed., *The Writings of Thomas Jefferson*, 9 vols. (Washington, D.C.: Taylor and Maury, 1853–54)

NOTES

INTRODUCTION

1. The term "great seal" came from England, which had both a "great seal," which was used for official royal decrees, and a smaller seal, called the "privy seal," which was used by the king's chamber for the king's private business; see Low and Pulling, *Dictionary of English History,* 927; U.S. Department of State, *Great Seal of the United States,* 1–4. Even though there is no lesser seal, the United States seal is usually referred to as the "Great Seal."

2. *JCC* 5:517–18, July 4, 1776. For the most complete history of the Great Seal, see Patterson and Dougall, *Eagle and Shield.*

3. John Adams to Abigail Adams, Aug. 14, 1776, *Adams Corr.* 2:95–97. John Adams described Du Simitière as "a Painter by Profession whose Designs are very ingenious, and his Drawings well executed."

4. Ibid. Adams's proposal was derived from an engraving by Simon Gribelin, which was based on a 1712 drawing by Paolo de Matteis.

5. *JCC* 5:689–91, Aug. 20, 1776. Franklin had originally written that Moses was to be clothed "in the Dress of High Priest," but he crossed out that phrase.

6. John Adams to Abigail Adams, Aug. 14, 1776, *Adams Corr.* 2:96.

7. *JCC* 5:690, Aug. 20, 1776.

8. Ibid. The version printed in the *Journal of the Continental Congress,* taken from James Lovell's notes, uses the word "Pillow" instead of "Pillar," but the word "pillar" appears both in Jefferson's notes and in the translation of Exodus 13:21 printed in the 1769 version of the King James Bible published by Oxford; see http://www.kingjamesbiblonline.org/Exodus-13-21. The committee's report also placed Franklin's motto, "Rebellion to Tyrants is Obedience to God," on the reverse side.

9. *JCC,* 5:691, Aug. 20, 1776. The committee's proposal was brought back to Congress in 1777, and it was again rejected (*JCC* 7:58–59, Jan. 23, 1777).

10. A second committee had been appointed in 1780, consisting of James Lovell of Massachusetts, John Morin Scott of New York, and William Churchill Houston of New Jersey (*JCC* 16:287, Mar. 25, 1780). Their proposal was rejected (*JCC* 17:434, May 17, 1780). A third committee, consisting of Arthur Middleton and John Rutledge of South Carolina, and Elias Boudinot of New Jersey, was appointed in 1782. This information is not in the

Congressional Journal, but is found in Charles Thomson's "Committee Book" (Patterson and Dougall, *Eagle and Shield*, 44). The third committee's proposal was rejected as well.

11. Thomson worked with a consultant, the Philadelphia lawyer William Barton, whose uncle was David Rittenhouse, an astronomer and mathematician who would be the future first director of the U.S. Mint (Patterson and Dougall, *Eagle and Shield*, 49).

12. Patterson and Dougall, *Eagle and Shield*, 88–89. Patterson and Dougall also give as an example *"Da facilem cursum, atque audacibus annue coeptis"* ("Give [me] an easy course, and favor [my] daring undertakings"). See generally Virgil, *Works of Virgil*, 486.

13. Hunt, *Seal of the United States*, 20–21; U.S. Department of State, *Great Seal of the United States*, 4. Instead of *"Annuit Coeptis,"* Barton had proposed *"Deo favente,"* which translates as "God favoring" or "with God's favor" (Patterson and Dougall, *Eagle and Shield*, 69).

14. *JCC* 22: 339, June 20, 1782.

15. Ibid.

16. This is the translation provided by the State Department (U.S. Department of State, *Great Seal of the United States*, 4). The phrase has also been translated as "a new order of centuries" (Patterson and Dougall, *Eagle and Shield*, 90).

17. See generally Witte, "First Amendment Religion Clauses," 490–91.

18. Some accommodationists believe that government support for religion is permissible if it favors no particular religion; see, e.g., Lynch v. Donnelly, 465 U.S. 668, 673 (1984) (Burger, C.J.), stating that the First Amendment does not "require complete separation of church and state; it affirmatively mandates accommodation, not merely tolerance, of all religions, and forbids hostility toward any." Others believe that government can support a "Judeo-Christian" faith; see, e.g., Van Orden v. Perry, 545 U.S. 677, 692 (Scalia, J., concurring), arguing "that there is nothing unconstitutional in a State's favoring religion generally, honoring God through public prayer and acknowledgement or, in a nonproselytizing manner, venerating the Ten Commandments." Still others, though it is probably a stretch to call them accommodationists, believe that the Constitution permits government to advance the concept of America as a "Christian nation"; see, e.g., Barton, *Original Intent*.

19. The omission of Jefferson's proposal for the Great Seal from most of Jefferson's biographies became apparent from my research. I confirmed this impression by conducting several searches in Google Books. I examined books published after 1950 and used two different searches. To find biographies of Jefferson that discussed religion at all, I used "'Virginia Statute for Religious Freedom' and intitle:Jefferson." To find biographies that mentioned the details of Jefferson's Great Seal proposal, I used, "'the children of Israel' and intitle:Jefferson," on May 15, 2011, and reviewed the use of the phrase in each book. Of the more than 200 Jefferson biographies, only 12 described his Great Seal proposal.

20. Feiler, *America's Prophet*, 67.

21. Hutson, *Religion and the Founding*, 51.

22. Barton, *Original Intent*, 90.

23. Hercules was the son of Zeus and a mortal woman, Alcmena. See Miles, *Classical Mythology in English Literature*, 39.

24. Libertas, the goddess of liberty, and Astria, the goddess of Justice, were "lesser deities"; see, e.g., T. Nichols, *Religions of the World*, 27.

25. See, e.g., Patterson and Dougall, *Eagle and Shield*, 7, noting that Franklin "turned to simple illustrative or allegorical material rather than to the formal hereditary badges and devices of European royalty and nobility."

26. D. Davis, *Religion and the Continental Congress*, 143; Davis notes also that the reverse side of the Great Seal "has more obvious religious implications" (144).

27. Ibid., 144.

28. See and Howard, "Jefferson's Art Gallery," 583–600, and *Oil Paintings at Montpellier* (n.d., box 3, Papers of Notable Virginia Families, MS 2988, University of Virginia Library, Charlottesville).

29. My approach is similar to that offered in Dworkin, *Taking Rights Seriously*, 340. I will consider the events of the time and attempt to create a theory of freedom of religion that provides a "good fit" with the events of that time. Unlike Dworkin, who was attempting to create a theory that is better "from the standpoint of political morality" (*Law's Empire*, 256), I will try to create a theory that is closest to the framers' political philosophy.

30. Collingwood, *Religion and Philosophy*, 74.

31. Pólya, *Mathematics and Plausible Reasoning*, 8.

32. See, e.g., Reynolds v. United States, 98 U.S. 145, 164 (1878), stating that Thomas Jefferson's letter to the Danbury Baptist Association urging "a wall of separation between church and State" may be "accepted almost as an authoritative declaration of the scope and effect," of the First Amendment; and Lee v. Weisman, 505 U.S. 577, 603 (1992) (Blackmun, J., concurring), stating at note 3: "The discussion in *Everson* [*v. Board of Education of Ewing*, 330 U.S. 1 (1947)] reflected the Madisonian concern that secular and religious authorities must not interfere with each other's respective spheres of choice and influence."

33. Dreisbach, Hall, and Morrison, *Forgotten Founders*, xiv–xv (emphasis in original).

34. Ragosta, "Jefferson's Statute for Religious Freedom."

35. See, e.g., Muñoz, "Religion and the Common Good," 1 (Washington "was no less dedicated to securing religious freedom than his second and third presidential successors"); and Ross and Smith, *Under God*, xix ("Certainly, the views of the Father of the Country, George Washington, should be taken into consideration").

36. George Washington to James Madison, May 5, 1789, *PGW: Presidential* 2:216–17.

37. George Washington to George Mason, Oct. 3, 1785, *PGW: Confederation* 3:293.

38. See generally Boorstin, "Mythologizing of George Washington," 337–355; Longmore, *Invention of George Washington*.

39. Ross and Smith, *Under God*, xx. Ross and Smith do add that Washington's encouragement of religion was "typically non-denominational and tolerant of religious minorities" (xviii).

40. George Washington to the Presbytery of the Eastward, Nov. 2, 1789, *PGW: Presidential* 4:274.

41. Isaac Backus, a Massachusetts Baptist, was another important figure in the fight for religious freedom, but he was not as willing as Leland to extend such freedom to all faiths. Backus, for example, supported the provision in the 1780 Massachusetts Constitution that limited religious freedom to "every denomination of Christians"; see Isaac Backus, "Article of Dec. 2, 1779, Boston Independent Chronicle," reprinted in *Diary of Isaac Backus* (app. 3, 25).

42. John Leland, "Events in the Life of John Leland: Written by Himself" (1834), *WJL*, 39.

43. Ibid.

44. John Leland, "Speech Delivered in the House of Representatives of Massachusetts, on the Subject of Religious Freedom" (1811), *WJL*, 358.

45. Benjamin Franklin to Ezra Stiles, Mar. 9, 1790, in Stiles, *Literary Diary*, 3:387.

46. A large number of books have tried to ascertain the framers' personal religious beliefs. For a small sample, see D. Holmes, *Faiths of the Founding Fathers*; Lillback, *Washington's Sacred Fire*; Mapp, *Faiths of Our Fathers*; and Sanford, *Religious Life of Jefferson*.

47. George Washington to the Hebrew Congregation in Newport, Rhode Island, Aug. 18, 1790, *PGW: Presidential* 6:284 (emphasis added).

48. This is the title of a book by the historian Bernard Bailyn; see Bailyn, *To Begin the World Anew: The Genius and Ambiguities of the American Founders*. It is based on a phrase from Thomas Paine's *Common Sense:* "We have it in our power to begin the world over again" (Paine, *Common Sense*, 120).

49. J. Underwood, *Constitution of South Carolina*, 42–43.

50. Ramsay, *History of South-Carolina*, 2:139.

51. George Washington to Benedict Arnold, Sept. 14, 1775, *PGW: War* 1:455.

52. Jefferson, *Autobiography*, 71.

53. S. Green, "A 'Spacious Conception,'" 477.

54. Pew Forum on Religion and Public Life, *U.S. Religious Landscape Survey*, 5.

55. According to the Pew Forum's 2008 Landscape Survey (12), the following are the percentages for each American denomination: 26.3 percent Evangelical (including the following churches "in the evangelical tradition": Baptist, Methodist, Pentecostal, Holiness, Adventist, Lutheran, Presbyterian, Anglican/Episcopal, Restorationist, Congregationalist, Reformed, and Anabaptist); 23.9 percent Catholic; 18.1 percent mainstream Protestant (including the following churches in the "mainline tradition": Baptist, Methodist, Lutheran, Presbyterian, Anglican/Episcopal, Restorationist, Congregationalist, Reformed, Anabaptist, and Friends); 6.9 percent historically black churches (including Baptist, Methodist, nondenominational, and Pentecostal churches); 1.7 percent Mormon; 1.7 percent Jewish; and 0.6 percent Muslim. Those who are Buddhist, Hindu, Jehovah's Witness, other Christian, Orthodox, Wiccan, Native American, or pagan, or adherents of any other world religion, make up about 3.9 percent of the population. "Unaffiliated," including atheists, agnostics, and those reporting no religion, totals 16.1 percent.

CHAPTER 1. BEFORE THE BEGINNING

1. Fielding, *Tom Jones*, 133. The religious historian Sidney Mead coined the phrase "Parson Thwackum syndrome" to describe those who insist that their narrow sectarian group is the only true representative of the broader religious community (Mead, *Old Religion in the New World*, 65).

2. "The First Charter of Virginia," Apr. 10, 1606, in Eliot, ed., *American Historical Documents*, 52.

3. Cobb, *Religious Liberty in America*, 80 (emphasis added). See also Anderson, *History of the Church of England*, 1:205.

4. "Second Charter of Virginia," signed May 23, 1609, in Preston, *Documents of American History*, 20.

5. American Historical Association, *Annual Report for the Year 1899*, 1:311.

6. Act I, March 1629–30, Hening, 1:149.

7. Act LXIII, March 1642–43, Hening, 1: 277.

8. See Law of Virginia General Assembly, Mar. 2, 1643, in *DHRA*, 58.

9. Linder, *Reformation Era*, 66. See also Waldman, *Founding Faith*, 6–7, quoting one Puritan as saying, "They are nothing else but reliques of Popery, and remnants of Baal."

10. The Pilgrims had previously left England for Holland, and it was from Holland that they sailed to Plymouth (Curry, *First Freedoms*, 3).

11. See ibid.: "For most of the years of its existence as an individual colony, until its

merger with Massachusetts in 1690, Plymouth sheltered in the lee of its famous neighbor. The Pilgrims, however, although they unquestionably shared the beliefs and opinions of their fellow Puritans, tended to temper their religious zeal with a moderation born partly of poverty and partly of loose organization."

12. "The Great Patent of New England," 1620, in *Compact, Charter and Laws of New Plymouth,* 1.

13. Winthrop, "Modell of Christian Charity," 45, 47.

14. Hutchinson, *Collection of Original Papers,* 57.

15. "Fundamental Orders of Connecticut," in Poore 1:249. There is some confusion over whether to date the Fundamental Orders from 1638 or 1639. The latter is based on the modern Gregorian calendar; the former is the year based on the calendar then in use. For consistency in the narrative, I will use the modern Gregorian calendar in the text.

16. See D. Hall, *Antinomian Controversy,* 348, 388; Winship, *Times and Trials of Hutchinson,* 1, 114. Though charged with being a heretic, she was banished for having testified that she had received divine revelations, and excommunicated for lying to the tribunal.

17. The story was told in Clarke, "Ill Newes from New-England," 27, and J. Holmes, *American Family of Obadiah Holmes,* 18–30.

18. Clarke, "Ill Newes from New-England, 32.

19. J. Holmes, *American Family of Obadiah Holmes,* 22, 25.

20. Curry, *First Freedoms,* 21.

21. G. Ellis, *Puritan Age,* 439.

22. Ibid.

23. Ibid., 448.

24. Sewel, *History of the Quakers,* 199.

25. G. Ellis, *Puritan Age,* 461, 470.

26. Cotton, "The Answer of Mr. John Cotton, of Boston, in New England," reprinted in Underhill, *Bloudy Tenent of Persecution,* 20.

27. Ibid., 60.

28. Ward, "Simple Cobler of Aggawam," 9–10.

29. Roger Williams, "Mr. Cotton's Letter Examined and Answered," reprinted in Underhill, *Bloudy Tenent of Persecution,* 435.

30. Ibid., 213 and 2. Roger Williams became a Baptist in March 1639 (xxvi), but left that denomination within a year (J. Davis, *Moral Theology of Roger Williams,* 166).

31. Emphasis added.

32. Charter of Rhode Island and Providence Plantations (1663), FSC 6:3212–13.

33. Curry, *First Freedoms,* 91.

34. T. Hall, "Williams and Religious Liberty," 489. Some scholars have argued that Williams's writings continued to be read in England, if not America. Martha Nussbaum, for example, contends that Locke "probably knew" of Williams's work (*Liberty of Conscience,* 67).

35. There is some mystery about how this provision became part of the Rhode Island code in 1716, with some believing that it was not actually approved by the legislature; see Bates, *Rhode Island and the Union,* 30. Nonetheless, the statute was reaffirmed by the assembly in 1730, 1745, and 1767 (Conley and Flanders, *Rhode Island State Constitution,* 60).

36. Penn, "Great Case of Liberty of Conscience" (1670), 131, 134.

37. Curry, *First Freedoms,* 75.

38. "Laws of Pennsylvania," no. 35, in Hazard, *Register of Pennsylvania,* 359.

39. Ibid., nos. 34 and 37.

40. "Act to Ascertain the Number of Members of Assembly and to Regulate the Election," printed in Mitchell, *Statutes of Pennsylvania*, 2:219.

41. Curry, *First Freedoms*, 75.

42. Sanford, *Religious Life of Jefferson*, 10.

43. Locke, *Letter Concerning Toleration* (1689), 11.

44. Ibid., 63.

45. There were numerous alterations to the Fundamental Constitution, but the final version of Apr. 11, 1698, kept most of the original's major provisions. See J. Underwood, "Religious Freedom in South Carolina," 124.

46. Fundamental Constitutions of the Carolinas, Mar. 1, 1669, secs. 109, 97, 95, 101, in *AFC* 1:232, 231.

47. Brinsfield, *Religion and Politics in South Carolina*, 8.

48. Fundamental Constitutions of the Carolinas, Mar. 1, 1669, sec. 96, *AFC* 1:231.

49. "Instructions to George Burrington, Dec. 14, 1730, No. 74," in Saunders, *Colonial Records of North Carolina* 3:110.

50. "Instructions for Governor Francis Nicholson, August 30, 1720, No. 82," *AFC* 1:433; see also Knight, *Education in North Carolina*, 77.

51. Connor, *History of North Carolina*, 1:199.

52. J. Underwood, "Religious Freedom in South Carolina," 143, 142.

53. Brinsfield, *Religion and Politics in South Carolina*, 47.

54. Browne, *Archives of Maryland*, 1:244–47.

55. Ibid., 8:362; see also Curry, *First Freedoms*, 52–53.

56. O'Gorman, *Roman Catholic Church in the United States*, 234–35.

57. Oct. 3, 1704, Browne, *Archives of Maryland*, 26:340.

58. Ibid., 26:341.

59. McKinley, *Suffrage in the Thirteen Colonies*, 75.

60. See Channing, *History of the United States*, 1:474.

61. O'Callaghan and Fernow, *Colonial History of New York*, 14:402–3.

62. K. Jackson and D. Dunbar, *Empire City*, 33.

63. S. Jackson, *Encyclopedia of Religious Knowledge*, 9:429–30.

64. Curry, *First Freedoms*, 64–65.

65. Fletcher quoted in Colonel Lewis Morris to the Society for the Propagation of the Gospel, Feb. 20, 1711, *DHSNY* 3:245.

66. "An Act for Settling a Ministry & Raising a Maintenance for them in the City of New York County of Richmond Westchester and Queens County," in *Colonial Laws of New York* 1:328.

67. Ibid., 1:329.

68. Hawkins, *Missions of the Church of England*, 18–20.

69. Colonel Lewis Morris to the Society for the Propagation of the Gospel, Feb. 20, 1711, *DHSNY* 3:246.

70. Cobb, *Religious Liberty in America*, 345.

71. The Reverend John Bartow to the Society for the Propagation of the Gospel, Dec. 1, 1707, *DHSNY* 3:211.

72. The actual court decision has not survived, but the ruling was noted, with sadness, in a letter from the Reverend John Poyer to the Society for the Propagation of the Gospel, dated June 16, 1731, in which he stated that the Jamaica Church, of which "we had the possession 25 years is taken from us by a trial at law" (*DHSNY* 3:310). Twenty years later, the issue arose again, this time over the question of whether King's College, now Columbia

University, should be Anglican controlled; see generally Beneke, *Beyond Toleration,* 100. That dispute ended ambiguously. Anglicans retained nominal control of the university, but "each of the city's Protestant denominations was granted a seat on the board of governors and, although Sunday church observance was mandatory, students were free to attend their own houses of worship" (102).

73. Levy, *Establishment Clause,* 16.

74. See J. Nichols, "Religious Liberty in the Thirteenth Colony," 1711–14.

75. See D. Holmes, *Faiths of the Founding Fathers,* 34; Beneke, *Beyond Toleration,* 102.

76. D. Holmes, *Faiths of the Founding Fathers,* 16; Curry, *First Freedoms,* 73.

77. Henry Caner to the Archbishop of Canterbury, Aug. 16, 1763, in Perry, *American Colonial Church,* 3:504.

78. *AKC* 1:464, quoting "an appeal made to the Archbishop of Canterbury."

79. Bishop of London to Mr. Price, Jan. 28, 1734–35, *AKC* 1:465.

80. "An Act to Exempt Persons commonly called Quakers, within this Province, from being taxed for and towards the Support of Ministers" was passed in December 1731 (*AKC* 1:443).

81. Mr. Checkley to the Lord Bishop of London, 1728, *AKC* 1:451–52.

82. See Draft Memorial of Christ Church and King's Chappel, Feb. 7, 1731–32, *AKC* 1:452.

83. Matthias Plant, missionary at Newbury, to secretary of the Society for the Propagation of the Gospel in Foreign Parts, Sept. 7, 1726, in Perry, *American Colonial Church* 3:204.

84. William Dummer, Jr., to Mr. Plant, Dec. 12, 1726, *AKC* 1:448.

85. Currier, *"Ould Newbury,"* 386.

86. Matthias Plant to secretary of the Society for Propagation of the Gospel in Foreign Parts, July 23, 1742, in Currier, *"Ould Newbury,"* 386.

87. G. Jackson, "America's First Mass Media," 410.

88. C. C. Goen has argued that the New Lights should be considered as divided between two groups: "radical New Lights," who "went all out for itinerary and lay preaching, emotional manifestations as evidence of the Spirit's presence, dramatic conversion and extreme censoriousness toward those who were deemed unconverted, and enthusiastic impulses as the rule of judgment and action"; and "conservative New Lights," who "had recognized the hand of God in the revival and had participated wholeheartedly in it, seeking at the same time to restrain the excesses which were the targets of so much Old Light criticism" (*Revivalism and Separatism in New England,* 34–35).

89. Compare Alan Heimert, who believes that the Great Awakening formed a large part of the intellectual and political background of the Revolution (*Religion and the American Mind*) with Allen Guelzo, who argued that the Great Awakening was not particularly "revolutionary" ("God's Designs," 163).

90. Guelzo, "God's Designs," 163.

91. Waldman, *Founding Faith,* 27–28. Other prominent Great Awakening ministers included Gilbert Tennent and Jonathan Edwards.

92. See Billingsley, *Life of George Whitefield,* 377.

93. See Gillies and Whitefield, *Memoirs of Rev. George Whitefield,* 25–26, 163.

94. Franklin, *Autobiography,* 118–19.

95. According to Walter Isaacson, "During 1739–41 more than half the books that Franklin printed were by or about Whitefield" (*Benjamin Franklin,* 600).

96. Franklin, *Autobiography,* 117–18.

97. Ibid., 116.

98. Seymour, *Life and Character of George Whitefield*, 308.

99. Franklin, *Autobiography*, 116.

100. Ibid., 129.

101. Hoyt, *Life of Thomas Bradbury Chandler*, 9.

102. Stout and Onuf, "Davenport and the Great Awakening," 573.

103. Joseph Talcott to Colonel Samuel Lynde, Sept. 4, 1741, in Talcott, *Talcott Papers*, 372–73.

104. "Ecclesiastical Law of May 1742," in Trumbull, *History of Connecticut*, 2:162–65.

105. Sprague, *Annals of the American Pulpit*, 83.

106. Stout and Onuf, "Davenport and the Great Awakening," 556.

107. "Religious Excess at New London," *Boston Weekly Post-Boy*, Mar. 28, 1743, in Bushman, *Great Awakening*, 51–53.

108. Kidd, *Great Awakening*, 153.

109. "Religious Excess at New London," *Boston Weekly Post-Boy*, Mar. 28, 1743, in Bushman, *Great Awakening*, 51–53. An English traveler reported that he was told it was fortunate the bonfire had not been set, because "had fire been put to the pile, [Davenport] would have been obliged to strut about bare-arsed" (diary entry of Dr. Alexander Hamilton, in Williams, *America's Religions*, 147).

110. "Disestablishment in New England," 156. See also Bainton, *Reformation of the Sixteenth Century*, 99.

111. Backus, *History of New England*, 2:141.

112. Benedict, *Baptist Denomination in America*, 420.

113. Hawks, *Episcopal Church in Virginia*, 121.

114. James, *Religious Liberty in Virginia*, 29.

115. Cobb, *Religious Liberty in America*, 113.

116. James Madison to William Bradford, Jan. 24, 1774, *PJM: Congressional* 1:106.

117. Looking back later in life, Madison, describing himself in the third person, would write that, *"Not-withstanding the enthusiasm which contributed to render them [the Baptists] obnoxious to sober opinion* as well as to the laws then in force, against Preachers dissenting from the Established Religion, he spared no exertion to save them from imprisonment & to promote their release from it" (Adair, "Madison's Autobiography," 199 [emphasis added]). Thus, Madison was not immune from religious prejudice, yet was still firmly opposed to all persecution based on religious ideology.

118. Cross, *Anglican Episcopate*, 35–36.

119. Chandler, *Appeal in Behalf of the Church of England*, 87.

120. Van Tyne, *Causes of the War of Independence*, 349.

121. Cross, *Anglican Episcopate*, 182.

122. "The American Whig," Mar. 14, 1768, in *DHRA*, 217.

123. William Livingston to Samuel Cooper, Mar. 26, 1768, in Sedgwick, *Life of William Livingston*, 137.

124. Nybakken, *Centinel*, 19.

125. This was "Centinel Number VIII," published on May 12, 1768; see Nybakken, *Centinel*, 19. See also Frost, *Perfect Freedom*, 56; Hooker, "Dickinson on Church and State," 97.

126. "Centinel Number VIII," in Nybakken, *Centinel*, 128.

127. While most of the heated opposition to the American episcopate came from New England and the mid-Atlantic region, there was significant southern opposition as well. For example, on July 12, 1771, the Virginia House of Burgesses passed a resolution condemning "the pernicious Project of a few mistaken Clergymen for introducing an American Bishop:

a Measure by which much Disturbance, great Anxiety, and Apprehension would certainly take place among his Majesty's faithful American Subjects" (Cross, *Anglican Episcopate*, 235). Similarly, on Oct. 20, 1765, the Reverend Charles Martyn of South Carolina wrote to the Bishop of London that the southern clergy were "totally averse" to an American bishop (Sweet, *Religion in Colonial America*, 70).

128. "His Majesty's Most Gracious Speech to Both Houses of Parliament, on Friday, October 27, 1775."

129. Middlekauff, *Glorious Cause*, 236-38.

130. Fenton, "Birth of a Protestant Nation," 29. While Quebec was technically a province at this time, the words "Quebec" and "Canada" were virtually interchangeable designations for the northern colony (51n1).

131. Crosskey and Jeffrey, *Politics and the Constitution*, 3:45.

132. The Quebec Act, sec. 5, in Kennedy, *Canadian Constitution*, 134.

133. Maier, *From Resistance to Revolution*, 238 (quoting "Vox Vociferantis in Eremo," from *Essex Gazette*, in *Boston Gazette*, Aug. 15, 1774).

134. Cogliano, *No King, No Popery*, 47 (quoting the *Boston Gazette* on Aug. 22, 1774). Other colonial newspapers focused on the threat to liberty posed by the king's assumption of the power to appoint the provincial legislature; see Langston, "'Tyrant and Oppressor!'"

CHAPTER 2. A TOLERANT, PROTESTANT NATION

1. Middlekauff, *Glorious Cause*, 239.

2. Jefferson, "Autobiography," *WTJ* 1:6.

3. "Resolution of the House of Burgesses Designating a Day of Fasting and Prayer," May 24, 1774, *PTJ* 1:105.

4. Middlekauff, *Glorious Cause*, 239.

5. Jefferson, "Autobiography," *WTJ* 1:7.

6. Nelson, *Blessed Company*, 178.

7. Jefferson, "Autobiography," *WTJ* 1:7.

8. Diary of George Washington, *PGW: Diaries* 3:254.

9. Georgia was concerned by "an uprising of Creek Indians on the northern frontier, [and] decided against sending delegates, lest it be deprived of British arms" (Middlekauff, *Glorious Cause*, 240).

10. According to John Adams, Thomas Cushing of Massachusetts made the initial motion that daily sessions open with prayer; see John Adams to Abigail Adams, Sept. 16, 1774, *Adams Corr.* 1:156. Another delegate, Abraham Clark from New Jersey, also claims to have made the motion; see Abraham Clark to James Caldwell, Aug. 2, 1776, *LDC* 4:605. See generally D. Davis, *Religion and the Continental Congress*, 73-74.

11. James Duane's Notes of Debates, Sept. 6, 1774, *LDC* 1:31.

12. Ibid.

13. John Adams to Abigail Adams, Sept. 16, 1774, *Adams Corr.* 1:156.

14. Ibid.

15. Diary of Samuel Ward, Sept. 9, 1774, *LDC* 1:55.

16. John Adams to Abigail Adams, Sept. 16, 1774, *Adams Corr.* 1:156. See also Freeman, *George Washington*, 3:375.

17. John Adams to Abigail Adams, Sept. 16, 1774, *Adams Corr.* 1:156.

18. Meacham, *American Gospel*, 65-66.

19. John Adams to Abigail Adams, Sept. 16, 1774, *Adams Corr.* 1:156.

20. *Book of Common Prayer,* 18.

21. "Appendix: Duché's First Prayer in Congress," Charles Thomson, *LDC* 25:551.

22. Silas Deane to Elizabeth Deane, Sept. 7, 1774, *LDC* 1:34.

23. Recorded in *Adams Diary* 2:131.

24. John Adams to Abigail Adams, Sept. 16, 1774, *Adams Corr.* 1:156.

25. See, e.g., McClellan, *Liberty, Order, and Justice,* 171.

26. *JCC* 1:67, Oct. 14, 1774.

27. *JCC* 1:67–70, Oct. 14, 1774.

28. *JCC* 1:66–67, Oct. 14, 1774.

29. *JCC* 1:72, Oct. 12, 1774.

30. Ibid.

31. Backus, "Article of Dec. 2, 1779," in *Diary of Isaac Backus,* App. 3:25.

32. "Entry in the Diary of Isaac Backus, Sept. 7, 1774," in Backus, *History of New England,* 2:200.

33. Petition of the Association of twenty Baptist churches meeting at Medfield, Sept. 14, 1744, in Backus, *History of New England,* 2:200.

34. See *Adams Diary* 3:311.

35. Stiles, *Literary Diary of Ezra Stiles,* 472.

36. *Adams Diary* 3:311.There were several other delegates present at the meeting, including Hopkins and Ward, James Kinzie of New Jersey, and Joseph Galloway and Thomas Miflin of Pennsylvania; see Hovey, *Life of Isaac Backus,* 204.

37. Backus, *History of New England,* 2:201.

38. *Adams Diary* 3:311.

39. Stiles, *Literary Diary of Ezra Stiles,* 472–74.

40. Backus, *History of New England,* 2:202.

41. Hovey, *Life of Isaac Backus,* 211.

42. Stiles, *Literary Diary of Ezra Stiles,* 474.

43. Backus, "A Plea Before the Massachusetts Legislature" (1774), in *DHRA,* 225–26.

44. *Adams Diary* 3:312.

45. Backus, *History of New England,* 2:202.

46. *Adams Diary* 3:312.

47. Ibid.

48. Isaac Backus, "Article of Dec. 2, 1779," in *Diary of Isaac Backus,* App. 3:25.

49. Stiles, *Literary Diary of Ezra Stiles,* 474.

50. *Adams Diary* 3:312.

51. Ibid.

52. Backus, *History of New England,* 2:204.

53. The nonimportation pledge was to become effective on Dec. 1, 1774, if the Intolerable Acts were still in place.

54. *JCC* 1:89–101, Oct. 21, 1774. The letter also said that when a people are opposing their ruler, "duty to Almighty God, the creator of all, requires that a true and impartial judgment be formed of the measures leading to such opposition; and of the causes by which it has been provoked."

55. *JCC* 1:100, Oct. 21, 1774.

56. See *JCC* 1:82–90, Oct. 21, 1774.

57. *JCC* 1:83, 88, Oct. 21, 1774.

58. *JCC* 1:88, Oct. 21, 1774.

59. *JCC* 1:117, Oct. 26, 1774.

60. *JCC* 1:103, Oct. 26, 1774.

61. *JCC* 1:111, Oct. 26, 1774. The address also stated that the Quebec Act had not actually benefited the Catholics of the region: "And what is offered to you by the late Act of Parliament in their place? Liberty of conscience in your religion? No. God gave it to you; and the temporal powers with which you have been and are connected, firmly stipulated for your enjoyment of it. If laws, divine and human, could secure it against the despotic caprices of wicked men, it was secured before" (ibid.).

62. *JCC* 1:112, Oct. 26, 1774.

63. Zubly, "Sermon on American Affairs" (1775), 128.

64. Furman, "Address Concerning the American War for Independence."

65. *Pa. Journal*, Nov. 9, 1774, in Griffin, *Catholics and the American Revolution*, 22.

66. *Pa. Journal*, Nov. 23, 1774, in ibid.

67. While there is some uncertainty about Hamilton's actual date of birth, his biographer Ron Chernow believes the most likely date is Jan. 11, 1755 (*Alexander Hamilton*, 17).

68. *PAH* 23:45.

69. See Irvin, *Samuel Adams*, 127.

70. *Address of Massachusetts to Mohawk Indians*, March 1775, in S. Adams, *Writings of Samuel Adams*, 3:213.

71. Ibid. (emphasis in original).

72. According to the historian Robert Ferguson: "At a time when the largest colonial newspapers and most important pamphlets had circulations under 2,000, *Common Sense* reached between 120,000 and 150,000 copies in its first year alone. It was the first American best-seller. Hundreds of thousands of Americans, perhaps a fifth of the adult population in all, either read *Common Sense* or had it read to them during the course of the Revolution" (Ferguson, "Commonalities of Common Sense," 465).

73. Paine, *Common Sense*, 56.

74. R. Smith, *Civic Ideals*, 75. The reason the Protestant references may be considered a bit "disingenuous" is that Paine "was a deist who belonged to no church" (Duncan, *Citizens or Papists?* 36).

75. Paine, *Common Sense*, 66.

76. Duncan, *Citizens or Papists?* 36.

77. Paine, *Common Sense*, 64.

78. Ibid., 56.

79. J. Ellis, *His Excellency*, 85.

80. George Washington to Benedict Arnold, Sept. 14, 1775, *PGW: War* 1:456. In his letter to the "Inhabitants of Canada," which he wrote for Arnold to give to the Canadians, Washington added a note of religious tolerance, declaring that "the Cause of America, and of Liberty, is the Cause of every virtuous American Citizen; whatever may be his Religion or his Descent, the United Colonies know no Distinction but such as Slavery, Corruption and arbitrary Dominion may create" (Address to the Inhabitants of Canada, Sept. 14, 1775, *PGW: War* 1:462).

81. Boller, "Washington and Religious Liberty," 491.

82. Young, *Soul of the Revolution*, 149; see also Barrington, *Other Side of the Frontier*, 11.

83. For an example of a private letter that addresses the Quebec Act but does not display religious hostility, see George Washington to Bryan Fairfax, Aug. 24, 1774, *PGW: Colonial* 10:154–56; see also Boller, "Washington and Religious Liberty," 491, stating that

Washington "criticized the Quebec Act, but at no time did he join Alexander Hamilton and other patriot leaders in charging that its purpose was to establish 'Popery' in the colonies."

84. Congress had written the "Inhabitants of Canada" a second letter on May 29, 1775, asserting "the fate of the protestant and catholic colonies to be strongly linked together" (*JCC* 2:68).

85. See *JCC* 4:151–52, Feb. 15, 1776. In Philadelphia, Franklin "donated to the building fund of each and every church built" (Isaacson, "Franklin and Other Founders," in *American Sketches*, 27), including the Congregation Mikve Israel's synagogue; see Rosenbach, *Dedication of the New Synagogue*, 12–13.

86. *JCC* 4:215–17, Mar. 20, 1776.

87. Mayer, "Introductory Memoir," 24.

88. Ibid., 33.

89. Franklin, *Works of Benjamin Franklin*, 1:581.

90. Sparks, *Life of Gouverneur Morris*, 1:47–49.

91. Kirschke, *Gouverneur Morris*, 334.

92. "Plan of Accommodation with Great Britain," resolution adopted by the New York Provincial Congress, June 24, 1775, in *ASP*, 81; see also Sparks, *Life of Gouverneur Morris*, 48.

93. New York Delegates to New York Provincial Congress, July 6, 1775, *LDC* 1:596.

94. *JCC* 5:530, July 9, 1776.

95. *JCC* 6:886–87, Oct. 17, 1776.

96. Duché explained that despite his opposition to the Declaration of Independence, he took the position before he had a chance to really consider its implications: "Surprised and distressed, as I was, by an event I was not prepared to expect; obliged to give an immediate attendance, without the opportunity of consulting my friends, I easily accepted the appointment" (Duché to George Washington, Oct. 8, 1777, in Sparks, ed., *Correspondence of the Revolution*, 1:450).

97. Ibid., 448–51.

98. This "Protestant Carroll" was a reference to a different Charles Carroll, a Protestant lawyer who was a member of the Maryland Assembly; see Griffin, *Catholics and the American Revolution*, 19, 352.

99. John Adams to Abigail Adams, Oct. 25, 1777, *Adams Corr.* 2:359.

100. D. Davis, *Religion and the Continental Congress*, 76.

101. *JCC* 12:1110, Nov. 7, 1778.

102. *JCC* 12:1139, Nov. 17, 1778.

103. See D. Davis, *Religion and the Continental Congress*, 84–88. The fast days were usually in the spring, while the days for thanksgiving were in the autumn.

104. *JCC* 9:854–55, Nov. 1, 1777.

105. D. Davis, *Religion and the Continental Congress*, 86.

106. John Adams to James Warren, July 23 1775, *LDC* 1:650.

107. *JCC* 5:431, June 11, 1776.

108. John Adams to Timothy Pickering, Aug. 22, 1822, in *LMCC* 1:515. A similar story appears in Adams's autobiography.

109. Julian Boyd leaned to the view that the phrase was Jefferson's (*Declaration of Independence*, 22), while Carl Becker and John Fitzpatrick see it as Franklin's addition (Becker, *Declaration of Independence*, 142n1; Fitzpatrick, *Spirit of the Revolution*, 12).

110. Jefferson, Notes of Proceedings in the Continental Congress, *PTJ* 1:314–15.

111. John Adams to Timothy Pickering, Aug. 22, 1822, in *LMCC* 1:516.

112. See *JCC* 5:504, July 1, 1776.

113. See Boyd, *Declaration of Independence*, 17; see also Becker, *Declaration of Independence*, 139.

114. Isaacson, *American Sketches*, 29. See also Waldman, *Founding Faith*, 88–89: "This was the language of the Enlightenment theology that grew up in the eighteenth century as a result not only of philosophical innovations—John Locke, David Hume, and others—but also, more important, of scientific innovations." Whether Jefferson himself was a "Deist" is a matter of some dispute. Compare Gould, "Religious Opinions of Jefferson," 191–208 ("Jefferson was not a deist. He . . . was a decided Unitarian"), with Malone, *Jefferson and His Time*, 3:381 ("Actually, he was a deist, not an atheist").

115. Emphasis added. The word "inalienable" in Jefferson's draft was changed to "unalienable" in the final draft, but it is believed that this was of no great significance. Some suspect that it might well have been a printer's error that was never authorized by Congress. See Lucas, "Justifying America," 124n50; see also D. Davis, *Religion and the Continental Congress*, 265n29.

116. Mapp, *Faiths of Our Fathers*, 7.

117. Dwight, *Theology*, 2:9.

118. Many literary historians believe that the work of Congress as the nation's "Founding Editors" improved the overall quality of the Declaration; see Abrams, "America's Founding Editors," 12.

119. Leonard, *Life of Charles Carroll*, 130. Jefferson was particularly displeased with Congress's removal of his paragraph condemning King George for "enslaving the inhabitants of Africa"; see Thomas Jefferson, Notes of Proceedings in the Continental Congress, *PTJ* 1:314–15.

120. Thomas Jefferson to James Madison, Aug. 30, 1823, in *LMCC* 1:516.

121. Thomas Jefferson to Robert Walsh, Dec. 4, 1818, in *WTJ* 10:120. Franklin then proceeded to tell Jefferson the story of a hatter who intended to post a sign by his store reading "'John Thompson, *Hatter, makes* and *sells hats* for ready money,' with a figure of a hat subjoined." He showed the sign to his friends for comments. One found it redundant to say that a "hatter" makes "hats"; another thought it was obvious that he was selling the hats and not giving them away. The result of this editing process, Franklin concluded, was that "the inscription was reduced ultimately to 'John Thompson' with the figure of a hat subjoined."

122. Maier, *American Scripture*, 148.

123. D. Davis, *Religion and the Continental Congress*, 102.

124. A. Green, "Jefferson's Papers," 81.

125. Ibid., 82.

126. Bellah, *Beyond Belief*, 174.

127. D. Holmes, *Faiths of the Founding Fathers*, 47.

128. Waldman, *Founding Faith*, 89.

129. Novak, *On Two Wings*, 17. In 1915, a Louisiana court used the language of the Declaration of Independence to make the following point: "There have been differences in expressions of opinion as to whether this is a Christian land or not, in a strictly limited sense; but there is not, and there has not been, a question as to its being a godly land, or that we are a religious people" (Herold v. Parish Board of School Directors, 68 So. 116, 119 [LA, 1915]).

130. *JCC* 5:431, June 11, 1776. The original motion to prepare the Articles of Confederation was made by Richard Henry Lee on June 7 (*JCC* 5:425–26n2).

131. The editors of the *Letters of Delegates to Congress* concluded that "Dickinson obviously played the dominant role in creating the Articles" (*LDC* 4:251).

132. Rakove, *Beginnings of National Politics*, 152.

133. Ibid., 153–54.

134. Maryland's insistence that Virginia cede most of its western lands to Congress delayed final ratification of the Articles of Confederation until 1781; see Rakove, *Revolutionaries*, 311.

135. *JCC* 4:358, May 15, 1776.

136. *JCC* 4:342, May 10, 1776.

137. Vermont, which New York still claimed as within its borders, adopted a constitution during this time as well.

138. Nevins, *American States*, 127. Both New Hampshire and South Carolina created constitutions earlier than Virginia, but both of these were viewed as interim documents (126).

139. For an excellent treatment of the growth of religious freedom in Virginia, see Buckley, *Church and State in Virginia*; see also Isaac, *Transformation of Virginia*.

140. *DHSRL*, 34.

141. See Isaac, *Transformation of Virginia*, 201–2; Eckenrode, *Church and State in Virginia*, 40. The English Toleration Acts of 1689 granted a general freedom of worship to dissenting Protestants (*DHSRL*, 41–47).

142. See Eckenrode, *Church and State in Virginia*, 42.

143. *DHSRL*, 51.

144. Ibid., 52.

145. Ibid., 53.

146. Ibid.

147. Buckley, *Church and State in Virginia*, 17.

148. In 1827, James Madison wrote Mason's son: "I retain however a perfect impression that . . . [George Mason] was the author of the Declaration as originally drawn" (Madison to George Mason, Jr., Dec. 29, 1827, *WJM* 9:293–94).

149. Paine, *Rights of Man*, 78.

150. *PJM: Congressional* 1:177. This comment was found in notes Madison wrote around 1827. In his autobiography, written in the 1830s, Madison wrote that the change in language "declared the freedom of conscience to be a *natural and absolute* right" (Adair, "Madison's Autobiography," 199). In his papers, Madison had underlined the phrase "natural and absolute" (199n13).

151. *PJM: Congressional* 1:177.

152. Conway, *Omitted Chapters of History*, 30.

153. *PJM: Congressional* 1:177.

154. Virginia Bill of Rights, sec. 16, in Poore 2:1909.

155. O'Malley, *"Dictates of Conscience,"* 5.

156. Eckenrode, *Church and State in Virginia*, 45.

157. Buckley, *Church and State in Virginia*, 36; Isaac, *Transformation of Virginia*, 280–81.

158. Jefferson, "Autobiography," *WTJ* 1:39.

159. "Memorial of the Presbytery of Hanover," in Church, *Separation of Church and State*, 43.

160. *PTJ* 1:530.

161. Hening, 9:164.

162. Buckley, *Church and State in Virginia*, 62.

163. Hening, 9:164.

164. Ragosta, *Wellspring of Liberty*, 109.

165. See ibid., 113.

166. Constitution of New Jersey, July 2, 1776, arts. 18 and 19, in Poore 2:1310.

167. Constitution of Delaware, Sept. 10, 1776, art. 22, in Poore 1:276.

168. See Waldman, *Founding Faith,* 25. By 1776, the Quakers had lost political control of Pennsylvania. An influx of immigrants, combined with popular anger toward the governing Quakers' refusal to authorize military action to protect the citizenry, led to a different, and less religiously tolerant, political leadership.

169. C. Marshall, *Diary of Christopher Marshall,* 1:90.

170. Stephen Smith, "Prelude to Article VI," 1–25.

171. Ibid.

172. Hallahan, *Day the American Revolution Began,* 153.

173. Stephen Smith, "Prelude to Article VI," 1–25.

174. Ibid.

175. Ibid.

176. Benjamin Franklin to Joseph Priestley, Aug. 21, 1784, in Smyth, *Writings of Franklin,* 9:266.

177. See ibid.

178. Constitution of Pennsylvania, Sept. 28, 1776, sec. 10, in Poore 2:1540.

179. Ibid., 1542.

180. Constitution of Maryland, Nov. 11, 1776, arts. 33 and 35, in Poore 1:817.

181. See Constitution of North Carolina, Dec. 18, 1776, art. 32, in Poore 2:1409: "That no person, who shall deny . . . the truth of the Protestant religion . . . shall be capable of holding any office, or place of trust or profit, in the civil department, within this State." See also Constitution of Georgia, Feb. 5, 1777, art. 6, in Poore 1:379: "The representatives shall . . . be of the Protestant religion, and of the age of twenty-one years"; Constitution of South Carolina, Mar. 19, 1778, art. 3, in Poore 2:1621 ("A governor, a lieutenant-governor, . . . and a privy council, all of the Protestant religion"), and arts. 12 and 13, in Poore 2:1622–23 (no person shall be eligible to sit in the Senate or House of Representatives unless "he be of the Protestant religion.").

182. Among the five creedal requirements was the belief "that the holy scriptures of the Old and New Testaments are of divine inspiration, and are the rule of faith and practice" (Constitution of South Carolina, Mar. 19, 1778, art. 38, in Poore 2:1620).

183. Harking back to the decades-long battle over whether the Anglican church had been established in lower New York, the new constitution would not concede there had been an establishment, referring instead to statutes "as may be construed to establish or maintain any particular denomination of Christians" (Constitution of New York, Apr. 20, 1777, art. 35, in Poore 2:1328).

184. Committee of Safety and Council of Safety of the State of New York, *Journals of the Provincial Congress* 1:844. See also Hamburger, "Right of Religious Exemption," 925.

185. John Adams to Edmund Jenings, June 7, 1780, *PJA* 9:388.

186. Edmund Quincy, *Life of Josiah Quincy,* 379.

187. John Adams to William D. Williamson, Feb. 25, 1812, in *Proceedings of the Massachusetts Historical Society,* 300.

188. Lippy, "1780 Massachusetts Constitution," 536.

189. Constitution of Massachusetts, Mar. 2, 1780, in Poore 1:956.

190. Chapter 6, Massachusetts Constitution. Benjamin Franklin said that he regretted that Massachusetts had not "kept quite clear" of religious test oaths (Benjamin Franklin to Richard Price, Oct. 9, 1780, *CWBF* 7:139–40). Franklin explained in a somewhat patronizing manner that more could not be expected of Massachusetts, because "if we consider

what the people were one hundred years ago, we must allow they have gone great lengths in liberality of sentiment on religious subjects; and we may hope for greater degrees of perfection, when their constitution, some years hence, shall be revised."

191. Sam Adams, in a letter written to accompany the draft constitution when it was sent to the various state towns for ratification, explained why Catholics were excluded: "We have nevertheless found ourselves obliged, by a solemn test, to provide for the exclusion of those from offices who will not disclaim those principles of spiritual jurisdiction which Roman Catholics *in some countries* have held, and which are subversive of a free government established by the people" (Wells, *Life of Samuel Adams*, 3:96 [emphasis in original]).

192. "Iraeneus," *Chronicle*, Feb. 10, 1780, quoted in Morison, "Adoption of the Constitution of Massachusetts," 379–80.

193. McLoughlin, *New England Dissent*, 1:614. Samuel Eliot Morison, writing in 1917, concluded that "the Congregational churches were favored rather than established in Massachusetts" (*Constitution of Massachusetts*, 24n1).

194. In 1807, Adams wrote the following story: A "German clergyman" asked him whether the state had established the Presbyterian religion in the 1780 constitution. Adams replied that the constitution "obliges no man to pay to the support of any particular sect. Every man is at liberty to apply his taxes to the support of his own church and minister." According to Adams, the minister, after noting that taxes were obligatory for building churches and supporting ministers, declared, "'Well, that is an establishment of Christianity.' This was said with an arch and smiling countenance, which I understood very well to mean: I am very glad they have established Christianity, but I must not acknowledge it, because my people have been taught to believe that any establishment in Pennsylvania will be an establishment of Scotch Presbyterianism" (John Adams to Mercy Warren, Aug. 8, 1807, in "Correspondence between Adams and Warren," 435).

195. Oakes v. Hill, 27 Mass. 333, 345 (1831).

196. Morison, "Adoption of the Constitution of Massachusetts," 368–81.

197. Curry, *First Freedoms*, 164.

198. Laycock, "'Nonpreferential' Aid to Religion," 900. However, according to Leonard Levy, "Baptist, Quaker, Episcopalian, Methodist, Unitarian, and even Universalist churches received public tax support under the establishment of 1780, as well as Congregational churches" (*Establishment Clause*, 31).

199. Laycock, "'Nonpreferential' Aid to Religion," 900–901.

200. The law presumed that every citizen belonged to the oldest religious society in his town or precinct, unless he or she expressly joined another (*Oakes*, 27 Mass. 333).

201. Nevins, *American States*, 422.

202. Backus, *History of New England*, 2:470.

203. Backus, *Diary of Isaac Backus*, 1612.

204. Backus, "Article of Dec. 2, 1779," in *Diary of Isaac Backus*, App. 3:25.

205. McLoughlin, *New England Dissent*, 1:605.

206. See Bancroft, *History of the United States*, 6:155.

207. Clune, "Joseph Hawley's Criticism," 54.

208. Ibid., 41.

209. Ibid., 50. The words in parentheses were presumed to be the actual words used by Hawley, but the editor was not certain, since small parts of the original manuscript had been damaged (49n23).

210. A. Holmes, "Repeal of the Clause," 243–44.

211. Waldman, *Founding Faith*, xiv.

212. Boller, *Washington and Religion*, 128.

213. George Washington to John Hancock, June 8, 1777, *PGW: War* 9:645.

214. Boller, *Washington and Religion*, 124, quoting Fitzpatrick, *George Washington Himself,* 18. A famous example of Washington's lack of religious bigotry is his 1784 letter requesting the hiring of a carpenter and a bricklayer: "If they are good workmen, they may be of Assia, Africa, or Europe. They may be Mahometans, Jews, or Christians of any Sect—or they may be Atheists" (Washington to Tench Tilghman, Mar. 24, 1784, *PGW: Confederation* 1:232).

215. George Washington to Benedict Arnold, Sept. 14, 1775, *PGW: War* 1:455–56.

216. General Orders, Nov. 5, 1775, *PGW: War* 2:300.

217. See Boller, *Washington and Religion*, 126.

218. Haltigan, *Irish in the American Revolution,* 348.

219. Boller, "Washington and Religious Liberty," 493.

220. J. Murray, *Life of John Murray*, 215.

221. Nathanael Greene to Catharine Greene, Sept. 10, 1775, *Papers of Nathanael Greene,* 13:116. In this letter, Nathanael Greene told his wife, "I am now going to dine with his Excellency General Washington, and Mr Murray with me."

222. General Orders, Sept. 17, 1775, *PGW: War* 2:1.

223. Authority to Collect Clothing, Nov. 1, 1777, *PGW: War* 12:76.

224. Washington to Brigadier General John Lacey, Jr., Mar. 20, 1778, *PGW: War* 14:238.

225. See, e.g., Boller, "Washington and Religious Liberty," 495: "Yet on two occasions during this period he reacted with courtesy and consideration in personal encounters with the Quakers."

226. Washington to Thomas Wharton, Jr., Apr. 6, 1778, *PGW: War* 14:416.

227. D. Davis, *Religion and the Continental Congress,* 80.

228. Boller, *Washington and Religion*, 56.

229. General Orders, Nov. 30, 1777, *PGW: War* 12:444.

230. After Orders, May 5, 1778, *PGW: War* 15:38–39.

231. General Orders, June 30, 1778, *PGW: War* 15:590; General Orders, Oct. 20, 1781, George Washington Papers (Library of Congress).

232. General Orders, May 16, 1776, *PGW: War* 4:310.

233. General Orders, July 4, 1775, *PGW: War* 1:54.

234. General Orders, May 2, 1778, *PGW: War* 15:13.

235. General Orders, Aug. 3, 1776, *PGW: War* 5:551.

236. See Boller, *Washington and Religion*, 56.

237. General Orders, July 9, 1776, *PGW: War* 5:245.

238. General Orders, July 2, 1776, *PGW: War* 5:180.

239. See General Orders, Nov. 30, 1777, *PGW: War* 12:444.

240. General Orders, July 9, 1776, *PGW: War* 5:245.

241. General Orders, May 2, 1778, *PGW: War* 15:13.

242. *Circular to the States,* June 8, 1783, *WGW* 26:485.

243. Freeman, *George Washington,* 5:446.

244. George Washington to Alexander Hamilton, Mar. 31, 1783, in Bancroft, *History of the United States,* 6:76.

245. F. Steiner, *Religious Beliefs of Our Presidents,* 20–21. It is unclear when this rewriting of the Circular Letter first appeared, but a 1921 book termed it a "recent discovery" (Hoskins, *Washington's Diaries,* 99).

246. Houghton, *Revolutionary War Road Trip,* 31.

247. "A Message to Young People," *Friend* 19 (February 1922), 40.

248. See, e.g., 149 Cong. Rec. S2549 (Feb. 24, 2003); 148 Cong. Rec. S979 (Feb. 25, 2002); 146 Cong. Rec. S649 (Feb. 22, 2000); 144 Cong. Rec. S797 (Feb. 23, 1998); 142 Cong. Rec. S1305 (Feb. 26, 1996).

249. 155 Cong. Rec. H4558 (Apr. 21, 2009) (remarks of Rep. Bachmann).

250. Novak and Novak, *Washington's God,* 256n13.

251. This is how it was labeled in the Library of Congress exhibition *Religion and the Founding of the American Republic.* The description is available online at http://www.loc .gov/exhibits/religion/rel06.html. The curator of the exhibit, James H. Hutson, tried to simultaneously distance himself from the appellation by adding, "Some have called this concluding paragraph 'Washington's Prayer.'"

252. Novak and Novak, *Washington's God,* 97.

253. S. Johnson, *Dictionary of the English Language.* Shakespeare commonly used "pray" in its nonreligious sense. For instance, in *Much Ado About Nothing,* act 5, scene 1, Leonato says: "I pray thee, cease thy counsel, / Which falls into mine ears as profitless / As water in a sieve: give not me counsel; / Nor let no comforter delight mine ear."

254. George Washington to Samuel Chase, Dec. 3, 1785, *PGW: Confederation* 3:428–29.

255. George Washington to Henry Laurens, May 12, 1778, *PGW: War* 15:108. Likewise, when Jefferson resigned as secretary of state, Washington wrote him, "Let a conviction of my most earnest prayers for your happiness accompany you in your retirement" (Washington to Jefferson, Jan. 1, 1794, *PGW: Presidential* 15:1).

256. See generally Lengel, *Inventing George Washington.*

257. Boller, *Washington and Religion,* 71.

258. M. Hills, "First American Bible," 3. See also Metzger and Coogan, *Oxford Companion to the Bible,* 618.

259. D. Davis, *Religion and the Continental Congress,* 144–45.

260. *LDC* 7:311.

261. *JCC* 8:536, July 7, 1777.

262. Letter of Congress to Henry Miller, July 7, 1777, *LDC* 7:311.

263. *JCC* 8:734, Sept. 11, 1777.

264. Ibid., 734–35.

265. D. Davis, *Religion and the Continental Congress,* 148.

266. M. Hills, "First American Bible," 3.

267. Ibid., 4.

268. *JCC* 23:573, Sept. 12, 1782.

269. Ibid.

270. D. Davis, *Religion and the Continental Congress,* 148.

271. Robert Aitken to George Washington, June 9, 1790, *PGW: Presidential* 5:494.

272. Strickland, *American Bible Society,* 20–21.

273. Federer, *America's God and Country,* 149. The phrase "Bible of the Revolution," apparently originated in 1930, when Robert Dearden was attempting to increase sales of his reprint of the Aitken Bible (Dearden, *Bible of the Revolution*).

274. Rodda, *Liars for Jesus,* 1:13–15.

275. D. Davis, *Religion and the Continental Congress,* 149.

276. *JCC* 1:82–90, Oct. 21, 1774.

277. "Declaration and Resolves," *JCC* 1:72, Oct. 14, 1774.

CHAPTER 3. THE SECOND AMERICAN REVOLUTION

1. Thomas Jefferson, *"Autobiography,"* WTJ 1:42.

2. Before the report of their work could be formally presented, the House of Delegates elected Jefferson as governor, starting June 2, 1779. John Harvie, a lifelong friend of Jefferson, introduced the religion bill. The formal report containing all the bills was presented on June 18, 1779, but several bills were considered before the report was filed. Some bills that were deemed priorities, such as establishing a board of war and a board of trade, were passed in May.

3. *PTJ* 2:545.

4. *PTJ* 2:547.

5. Eckenrode, *Church and State in Virginia,* 57.

6. Clement, *History of Pittsylvania County,* 153.

7. Eckenrode, *Church and State in Virginia,* 58.

8. W. Miller, *First Liberty,* 20.

9. Curry, *First Freedoms,* 139.

10. Ragosta, *Wellspring of Liberty,* 67.

11. See Ragosta, "Jefferson's Statute for Religious Freedom," 8.

12. Eckenrode, *Church and State in Virginia,* 65.

13. *PJM: Congressional Series* 8:313 (editor's note).

14. Eckenrode, *Church and State in Virginia,* 72.

15. Richard Henry Lee to James Madison, Nov. 26, 1784, *PJM: Congressional* 8:149.

16. George Mason to Patrick Henry, May 6, 1783 in Rowland, *Life of George Mason* 2:44.

17. Richard Henry Lee to James Madison, Nov. 26, 1784, *PJM: Congressional* 8:150.

18. See Ragosta, *Wellspring of Liberty,* 117.

19. Edmund Randolph to Thomas Jefferson, May 15, 1784, *PTJ* 7:260.

20. The Virginia House of Burgesses had passed a law permitting payment in money instead of tobacco for several taxes, including the vestry tax, but the law was disallowed by the king. The House of Burgesses opted to enforce the void law anyway (Coleman, *History of the American Church,* 43).

21. Henry, *Patrick Henry,* 1:41.

22. See ibid., 42.

23. See, e.g., Morgan, *True Patrick Henry,* 125–26.

24. Waldman, *Founding Faith,* 115.

25. Eckenrode, *Church and State in Virginia,* 78.

26. John Blair Smith to James Madison, June 21 1784, *PJM: Congressional* 8:81.

27. Edmund Randolph to Thomas Jefferson, May 15, 1784, *PTJ* 7:260.

28. Eckenrode, *Church and State in Virginia,* 85.

29. Ibid., 86.

30. Ibid., 88.

31. T. Johnson, *Virginia Presbyterianism,* 103.

32. James Madison to James Monroe, Apr. 12, 1785, *PJM: Congressional* 8:261.

33. Thomas Jefferson to James Madison, Dec. 8, 1784, *PTJ* 7:558. Jefferson's suggestion came in a letter that dealt with both the general assessment and the attempt to rewrite the Virginia constitution, and was not specifically referring to the general assessment.

34. See, e.g., Brant, *Madison the Nationalist,* 345–46; W. Miller, *First Liberty,* 33.

35. Nov. 20, 1784, *JHDV* 32. See also James Madison to James Monroe, Nov. 14, 1784, *PJM: Congressional* 8:137n4.

36. Buckley, *Church and State in Virginia,* 101.

37. Ragosta, *Wellspring of Liberty,* 123.

38. James Madison to James Monroe, Nov. 27, 1784, *PJM: Congressional* 8:158.

39. Dec. 2, 1784, *JHDV* 51.

40. James Madison to James Monroe, Dec. 4, 1784, *PJM: Congressional* 8:175.

41. Dec. 22, 1784, *JHDV* 79.

42. James Madison to Thomas Jefferson, Jan. 9, 1785, *PJM: Congressional* 8:228–29.

43. Nov. 17, 1784, *JHDV* 27.

44. According to John A. Ragosta, the incorporation bill drove, "a wedge between Presbyterians—now vociferously opposed to this incorporation act—and Episcopalians" (*Wellspring of Liberty,* 123).

45. Thomas Jefferson to James Madison, Dec. 8, 1784, *PTJ* 7:558.

46. Nov. 12, 1784, *JHDV* 21.

47. James Madison to Thomas Jefferson, Jan. 9, 1785, *PJM: Congressional* 8:229.

48. Dreisbach, "Jefferson and Bills Number 82–86," 167; see also Cord, *Separation of Church and State,* 20–23.

49. Rosenberger v. Rector and Visitors of the University of Virginia, 515 U.S. 819, 856 (1995) (Thomas, J., concurring) (emphasis in original).

50. Richard Henry Lee to James Madison, Nov. 26, 1784, *PJM: Congressional* 8:149–150.

51. Madison's Notes for Debates on the General Assessment Bill, *PJM: Congressional* 8:197. In these notes, Madison also wrote, "Experience shews Relig: corrupted by Estabt."

52. Dec. 24, 1784, *JHDV* 82.

53. See Madison, "Detached Memoranda," in Fleet, "Madison's Detached Memoranda," 555.

54. Dec. 24, 1784, *JHDV* 82.

55. In a strained attempt at religious sensitivity, the bill gave Quakers and Mennonites more freedom as to how the money should be spent than the other denominations. The bill required other denominations to appropriate the money for the "provision for a Minister or Teacher of the Gospel of their denomination, or the providing places of divine worship, and to none other use whatsoever," while Quakers and Mennonites were permitted to place the money "in their general fund, to be disposed of in a manner which they shall think best calculated to promote their particular mode of worship."

56. See *Rosenberger,* 515 U.S. at 853n1 (Thomas, J., concurring).

57. James Madison to Thomas Jefferson, Apr. 27, 1785, *PJM: Congressional* 8:268.

58. James Madison to James Monroe, Apr. 28, 1785, *PJM: Congressional* 8:272.

59. James Madison to James Monroe, May 29, 1785, *PJM: Congressional* 8:286.

60. Edmund Pendelton to Richard Henry Lee, Apr. 18, 1785, in Lee, *Memoir,* 1:198.

61. John Blair Smith to James Madison, May [ca. 16], 1785, *PJM: Congressional* 8:282.

62. James Madison to John Blair Smith, May 27, 1785, *PJM: Congressional* 8:286.

63. George Nicholas to James Madison, Apr. 22, 1785, *PJM: Congressional* 8:264.

64. Ibid.

65. "A Memorial and Remonstrance," June 20, 1785, *PJM: Congressional* 8:300.

66. Ragosta, *Wellspring of Liberty,* 131.

67. See George Nicholas to James Madison, July 7, 1785, *PJM: Congressional* 8:316.

68. Ibid.

69. Fleet, "Madison's Detached Memoranda," 555–56.

70. James Madison to Edmund Randolph, July 26, 1785, *PJM: Congressional* 8:328.

71. George Mason to George Washington, Oct. 2, 1785, *PGW: Confederation* 3:290.

72. Ibid.

73. See George Washington to George Mason, Oct. 3, 1785, *PGW: Confederation* 3:292.

74. Ibid., 292–93.

75. Antieau, Downey, and Roberts, *Freedom from Federal Establishment,* 66–67.

76. Dreisbach, "Jefferson and Bills Number 82–86," 165.

77. George Washington to George Mason, Oct. 3, 1785, *PGW: Confederation* 3:293.

78. Ibid.

79. James Madison, "A Memorial and Remonstrance," June 20, 1785, *PJM: Congressional* 8:300.

80. George Washington to John Hancock, June 8, 1777, *PGW: War* 9:644.

81. Boller, *Washington and Religion,* 122.

82. Eckenrode, *Church and State in Virginia,* 107.

83. "Prince George County Petition," Nov. 28, 1785, in Curry, *Farewell to Christendom,* 123–24.

84. Ragosta, "Jefferson's Statute for Religious Freedom," 12.

85. See Wolfe and Katznelson, *Religion and Democracy,* 424.

86. "A Memorial and Remonstrance," June 20, 1785, *PJM: Congressional* 8:303.

87. "Memorial of Convention at Bethel, August, 1785," *DHSRL,* 236–40.

88. T. Johnson, *Virginia Presbyterianism,* 103.

89. James Madison to Thomas Jefferson, Aug. 20, 1785, *PJM: Congressional* 8:345.

90. "Memorial of Convention at Bethel, August, 1785," *DHSRL,* 237.

91. James Madison to Thomas Jefferson, Jan. 22, 1786, *PJM: Congressional* 8:473.

92. Ragosta, *Wellspring of Liberty,* 131. This count reflects petitions received after Nov. 11, 1784, when the General Assembly passed the resolution in favor of the assessment.

93. See Eckenrode, *Church and State in Virginia,* 112.

94. See Ragosta, *Wellspring of Liberty,* 164; Eckenrode, *Church and State in Virginia,* 113.

95. Fleet, "Madison's Detached Memoranda," 556.

96. "Memorial of Convention at Bethel, August, 1785," *DHSRL,* 240.

97. Dreisbach, "Jefferson and Bills Number 82–86," 183.

98. Eckenrode, *Church and State in Virginia,* 113.

99. An early proposal to replace the entire preamble with language from the 1776 Declaration of Rights was defeated by a 66–38 vote (Ragosta, *Wellspring of Liberty,* 133). See also James Madison to Thomas Jefferson, Jan. 22, 1786, *PJM: Congressional* 8:473–74, where Madison reported, "The bill was carried thro' the H of Delegates, without alteration. The Senate objected to the preamble, and sent down a proposed substitution of the 16th. art: of the Declaration of Rights. The H. of D. disagreed."

100. Jefferson, "Autobiography," *WTJ* 1:45.

101. Fleet, "Madison's Detached Memoranda," 556.

102. Jefferson, "Autobiography," *WTJ* 1:45.

103. Ragosta, *Wellspring of Liberty,* 134.

104. James Madison to Thomas Jefferson, Jan. 22, 1786, *PJM: Congressional* 8:474.

105. "An Act for establishing Religions Freedom, Passed the 26th of December 1785," in Virginia General Assembly, *Collection of All Such Acts,* 29.

106. Peterson, *Jefferson and the New Nation,* 134.

107. James Madison to Thomas Jefferson, Jan. 22, 1786, *PJM: Congressional* 8:474.

108. Ragosta, "Jefferson's Statute for Religious Freedom," 7.

109. Thomas Jefferson to George Wythe, Aug. 13, 1786, *PTJ* 10:244.

110. Committee for Public Education and Religious Liberty v. Nyquist, 413 U.S. 756, 772 (1973).

111. Dreisbach, "Jefferson and Bills Number 82–86," 184.

112. Ibid., 209. This argument is also made in Cord, *Separation of Church and State*, 221–22.

113. *PTJ* 2:555. Other than the Bill for Religious Freedom (no. 82), this was the only one of the five religious bills to be enacted into law. See Dreisbach, "Jefferson and Bills Number 82–86," 189, 193 (nos. 85 and 83 never enacted); 200 (no. 86 passed a second reading, but never acted upon); 192n187 (no. 84 enacted).

114. *PTJ* 2:556.

115. The bill also would have declared void "a marriage between a person of free condition and a slave, or between a white person and a negro, or between a white person and a mulatto" (*PTJ* 2:557).

116. *PTJ* 2:558.

117. Dreisbach, "Jefferson and Bills Number 82–86," 211.

118. Cord, *Separation of Church and State*, 221–22.

119. See Dreisbach, "Jefferson and Bills Number 82–86," 163.

120. The 1705 law exempted from Sabbath laws "those working as, is necessary for the sustenance of man or beast," ASP, 34–35.

121. Jefferson, *"Autobiography," WTJ* 1:6–7.

122. S. Green, *Second Disestablishment*, 42.

123. "An Act for the effectual suppression of Vice; and restraint and punishment of blasphemous, wicked and dissolute Persons. And for preventing incestuous marriages and copulations," in Hening 4:245.

124. Dreisbach, "Jefferson and Bills Number 82–86," 203.

125. See ibid., 196.

126. S. Green, *Second Disestablishment*, 42.

127. Ragosta, "Jefferson's Statute for Religious Freedom," 8.

128. "A Memorial and Remonstrance," *PJM: Congressional* 8:300.

129. "Prince George County Petition, November 28, 1785," in Curry, *Farewell to Christendom*, 123–24.

130. George Washington to George Mason, Oct. 3, 1785, *PGW: Confederation* 3:293.

131. Rice, *Supreme Court and Public Prayer*, 31.

132. S. Green, "'Spacious Conception,'" 478.

133. *JCC* 28:375.

134. *JCC* 28:293, Apr. 23, 1785.

135. *PJM: Congressional* 8:287n5.

136. *JCC* 28:293, Apr. 23, 1785.

137. *JCC* 28:378, May 20, 1785.

138. James Madison to James Monroe, May 29, 1785, *PJM: Congressional* 8:286. Interestingly, Monroe voted to retain the religious language (*JCC* 28:295). Sadly, there is no record of Monroe and Madison discussing his vote.

139. James Madison to James Monroe, May 29, 1785, *PJM: Congressional* 8:286.

140. Barrett, *Ordinance of 1787*, 71–72.

141. Withington, "Cutler and the Ordinance of 1787," 502.

142. *JCC* 32:318, July 11, 1787.

143. The official name of the law is "An Ordinance for the Government of the Territory of the United States North-West of the River Ohio" (*JCC* 32:334, July 13, 1787).

144. *JCC* 32:340.

145. See Peters, "Religion and the Northwest Ordinance," 743.

146. Edwin S. Gaustad, quoted in Boston, *Why the Religious Right Is Wrong,* 81.

147. Board of Education v. Minor, 23 Ohio St. 211, 248–49 (1872). The Ohio Constitution provided that "religion, morality, and knowledge . . . being essential to good government, it shall be the duty of the general assembly to pass suitable laws to protect every religious denomination in the peaceable enjoyment of its own mode of public worship, and to encourage schools and the means of instruction." In 1872, the Ohio Court held that the state did not have the responsibility, or right, to encourage religion. The Court also stated, "Religion, morality, and knowledge are essential to government, in the sense that they have the instrumentalities for producing and perfecting a good form of government. On the other hand, no government is at all adapted for producing, perfecting, or propagating a good religion" (*Minor,* 23 Ohio St. at 248–49).

148. Hulber, *Proceedings of the Ohio Company,* lxv.

149. *JCC* 33:400. On July 26, when Cutler wrote back to Congress to demand additional changes to the July 23 grant, he alluded to his early demand: "We suppose this measure has been adopted in consequence of proposals made by us" (*JCC* 33:427). As an indication of Cutler's influence, his letter contained a threat that he would pull out of the deal if Congress did not comply with his new demands. It quickly voted to agree with his requests.

150. W. Peters, *Ohio Lands and Their Subdivision,* 361–62.

151. In his petition to Congress, Symmes had specified he wanted "a contract to be made with him for a certain tract of western territory on similar terms with that made with Sergeant Cutler" (*JCC* 33:512, Sept. 21, 1787).

152. Donaldson *Public Domain,* 209.

153. Wallace v. Jaffree, 472 U.S. 38, 100 (1985) (Rehnquist, J., dissenting) (emphasis added). In 1985, Rehnquist was still an associate justice. He was elevated to the position of chief justice in 1986.

154. Ibid.

155. The formal name of the 1789 law was "An act to provide for the Government of the Territory Northwest of the river Ohio."

156. Rehnquist is not the only person who mistakenly refers to the 1789 act as "reenacting" the Northwest Ordinance. See, e.g., Antieau, Downey, and Roberts, *Freedom from Federal Establishment,* 188: "The same First Congress that proposed the First Amendment to the Constitution readopted the Northwest Ordinance of 1787 with its memorable language that 'Religion, morality, and knowledge, being necessary to good government and the happiness of mankind, schools and the means of education shall forever be encouraged.'"

157. The complete text of the 1789 law, 1 Cong. Ch. 8; 1 Stat. 50, is:

"An act to provide for the Government of the Territory Northwest of the river Ohio.

"Preamble.

"Whereas, in order that the ordinance of the United States in Congress assembled, for the government of the territory north-west of the river Ohio may continue to have full effect, it is requisite that certain provisions should be made, so as to adapt the same to the present Constitution of the United States:

"SECTION 1. Be it enacted by the Senate and House of Representatives of the United States of America in Congress assembled, That in all cases in which by the said ordinance any information is to be given, or communication made by the governor of the said territory to the United States in Congress assembled, or to any of their officers, it shall be the duty of the said governor to give such information, and to make such communication to the President of the United States; and the President shall nominate, and by and with advice and consent of the Senate, shall appoint all officers which, by the said ordinance, were to have been appointed by the United States in Congress assembled; and all officers, so appointed, shall be commissioned by him; and in all cases where the United States in Congress assembled, might, by the said ordinance, revoke any commission, or remove from any office, the President is hereby declared to have the same powers of revocation and removal.

"Sec. 2. And be it further enacted, That in case of the death, removal, resignation, or necessary absence of the governor of the said territory, the secretary thereof shall be, and he is hereby authorized and required to execute all the powers, and perform all the duties of the governor, during the vacancy occasioned by the removal, resignation, or necessary absence of the said governor."

CHAPTER 4. "WE HAVE BECOME A NATION"

1. June 28, 1787, Farrand 1:451.

2. Vile, *Constitutional Convention,* 593.

3. The story probably first appeared in 1825, in a letter from William Steele to his son, Jonathan D. Steele, purporting to be an anecdote told to the father by Jonathan Dayton, a delegate from New Jersey (Farrand 3:472).

4. June 28, 1787, Farrand 1:452.

5. James Madison to Thomas S. Grimke, Jan. 6, 1834, Farrand 3:531.

6. Franklin, *Life and Writings of Franklin,* 1:389.

7. Although their complaints were not recorded in the official report of the Massachusetts ratification debates, "some delegates objected to the lack of any reference to God in the Constitution" (Maier, *Ratification,* 170).

8. Benjamin Rush to John Adams, June 15, 1789, Butterfield, *Letters of Benjamin Rush,* 1:516–17.

9. William Williams to the Printer American Mercury, Feb. 11, 1788, *DHRC* 3:589.

10. Ibid.

11. Dwight, *Discourse in Two Parts,* 46. In an 1800 sermon, "The Voice of Warning to Christians," John Mitchell Mason declared: "The federal Constitution makes no acknowledgement of that God who gave us our national existence, and saved us from anarchy and internal war. This neglect has excited in many of its best friends, more alarm than all other difficulties" (in Sandoz, *Political Sermons,* 2:1453).

12. Dwight, *Discourse in Two Parts,* 46.

13. Richardson, *Messages and Papers of the Confederacy,* 37.

14. In 1864, the National Reform Association was formed to advocate for changing the preamble (Fredrickson, "Coming of the Lord," 122).

15. National Reform Association, *Proceedings of the Convention,* vii.

16. Ibid., 33.

17. Massachusetts Convention Debates, Jan. 19, 1788, *DHRC* 6:1254–55.

18. McConnell, "Free Exercise of Religion," 1474. Article VI has also been termed "a bold and significant departure from the prevailing practices in . . . most of the states" (Dreisbach, "Christian Commonwealth," 951).

19. Kramnick and Moore, *Godless Constitution,* 22.

20. Dreisbach, "Christian Commonwealth," 951.

21. Dreisbach, review of *The Godless Constitution*, 646. See also Botein, "Religious Dimensions," 321–22, asserting that there was a general acquiescence in the Constitution's lack of religious acknowledgment because the citizenry did not expect "the new federal government [to become] a true nation-state, on the European model, for which some traditional religious identity might have been desirable."

22. Aug. 30, 1787, Farrand 2:468. Gouverneur Morris and Charles Cotesworth Pinckney (the cousin of the Charles Pinckney who proposed motion) then spoke in favor of the proposal, but their comments were not reported.

23. Ibid.

24. Art. I, sec. 2.

25. Aug. 7, 1787, Farrand 2:201.

26. Bradley, "No Religious Test Clause," 689.

27. Dreisbach, *A Godless Constitution?* See also Bradley, "No Religious Test Clause," 693, stating that the "reticence" to intervene in voting requirements indicated the limited nature of "the Framers' intentions: Congress should not regulate the 'subject of religion.'"

28. James Madison, *Federalist 52*.

29. Aug. 30, 1787, Farrand 2:468. His actual language was "no religious test shall ever be required as a qualification to any office or public trust under the authority of the U. States." Pinckney had first proposed similar language on Aug. 20: "No religious test or qualification shall ever be annexed to any oath of office under the authority of the United States" (Farrand 2:342).

30. Art. 13, South Carolina Constitution (1778), Poore 2:1623.

31. Charles Pinckney, "Observations on the Plan of Government Submitted to the Federal Convention, in Philadelphia," Farrand 3:122. This statement is in notes he prepared to deliver on May 28, 1787. It is unclear when the statement was actually delivered on the floor of the convention.

32. Samuel Spencer, North Carolina Ratifying Convention, Elliot's *Debates* 2:200.

33. Tench Coxe, *An American Citizen IV*, Oct. 21, 1787, in Ford's *Pamphlets*, 146.

34. Convention Debates, Feb. 4, 1788, DHRC 6:1422.

35. Bradley, "No Religious Test Clause," 691.

36. Luther Martin, "Genuine Information," DHRC 16:89.

37. Massachusetts Convention Debates, Jan. 19, 1788, DHRC 6:1255.

38. Ibid., Feb. 4, 1788, DHRC 6:1421.

39. *Worcester Magazine*, Feb. 7, 1788, DHRC 5:880–81.

40. Charles Jarvis, Debate in Massachusetts Ratifying Convention, Jan. 30, 1788, DHRC 6:1375. See also Instructions from the town of Townshend, Massachusetts, Dec. 31, 1787: "Nor can we on any consideration agree to a Constitution which will admit into governt. Atheists Deists Papists or abettors of any false religion; tho we would not Exclude any Denomination of Protestants who hold the fundamentals of our religion" (DHRC 5:1057).

41. Elliot's *Debates* 4:200.

42. Elliot's *Debates* 4:215.

43. "Originalist Analysis of the Test Clause," 1658, quoting Bradley, "No Religious Test," 703.

44. Backus, "Newspaper Report of the Massachusetts Ratification Convention," Feb. 4, 1788, Elliot's *Debates* 2:148–49.

45. Levinson, *Wrestling with Diversity*, 197.

46. Bradley, "No Religious Test Clause," 702.

47. James Madison to Thomas Jefferson, Oct. 17, 1788, DHCUSA 5:87.

48. Elliot's *Debates* 2:132.

49. Samuel Spencer, North Carolina Ratifying Convention, Elliot's *Debates* 4:200.

50. James Innes, Virginia Ratification Convention Proceedings, June 25, 1788, *DHRC* 10:1523.

51. Article II, sec. 1.

52. Pfander, "So Help Me God," 550. See also Cloud, "One Nation, Under God," 315: "The only oath prescribed in the Constitution, that of the office of the President of the United States set forth in Article II, conspicuously omits the words, 'So help me God,' which at that time were prevalent in virtually every oath administered in the courts of law and in virtually every state constitution."

53. According to James E. Pfander, "virtually all" of the common English prescribed oaths concluded "with the phrase, 'so help you God,' or 'as God you help, and by the contents of this book'—a reference to the Bible" ("So Help Me God," 551n4).

54. Chapter 6, Constitution of Massachusetts, Mar. 2, 1780, in Poore 1:956.

55. Ford, *Essays on the Constitution,* 51.

56. "Agrippa XVIII," *Massachusetts Gazette,* Feb. 5 1788, *DHRC* 5:868.

57. John Sullivan to Jeremiah Belknap, Feb. 26, 1788, in *Collections of the Massachusetts Historical Society,* 6th ser., 4 (1895): 394.

58. Kramnick and Moore, *Godless Constitution,* 22.

59. Oliver Wolcott's Speech at the Connecticut Ratification Convention, Jan. 9, 1788, *Elliot's* Debates 2:202.

60. Edmund Pendleton to James Madison, Oct. 8, 1787, *DHRC* 10:1774.

61. James Madison to Edmund Pendleton, Oct. 28, 1787, *PJM: Congressional* 10:223.

62. Article I, sec. 3; Article II, sec. 1; Article VI. The phrase also appears in the Fourth Amendment, which became part of the Constitution in 1791.

63. The passage that was cited for this prohibition was Matthew 5:33–37: "But I say unto you, swear not at all; neither by heaven; for it is God's throne: Nor by the earth; for it is his footstool: neither by Jerusalem; for it is the city of the great King. Neither shalt thou swear by thy head, because thou canst not make one hair white or black. But let your communication be, Yea, yea; Nay, nay; for whatsoever is more than these cometh of evil"; see McConnell, "Free Exercise of Religion," 1467.

64. For example, the Maryland Constitution provided "that the people called Quakers, those called Dunkers, and those called Menonists, holding it unlawful to take an oath on any occasion, ought to be allowed to make their solemn affirmation" (Maryland Constitution of 1776, Declaration of Rights, art. 36, *FSC* 3:1690).

65. Adams and Emmerich, "Heritage of Religious Liberty," 1630.

66. Maryland Constitution of 1776, Declaration of Rights, art. 36, *FSC* 3:1690.

67. Emphasis added. The peculiar capitalization and spelling of "Independance" is how the clause appears on the engrossed copy of the Constitution that was physically signed by the delegates. The clause can be seen in the photograph available at the National Archives Website, http://www.archives.gov/exhibits/charters/constitution_zoom_1.html.

68. Dreisbach, *Religion and Politics in the Early Republic,* 63.

69. Spalding, "Attestation Clause," 302. According to Daniel L. Dreisbach, "It cannot be denied, therefore, that the date denotes that Christ was, perhaps subconsciously, a reference point for the architects of an ambitious new order" ("Christian Commonwealth," 967).

70. R. Steiner, "One Nation Indivisible," 968.

71. Sept. 15, 1787, Farrand 2:633.

72. Beeman, *Plain, Honest Men,* 357–58.

73. Article VII was approved by the convention on Sept. 12 (Farrand 2:305).

74. Act of November 13, 2002 Pub. L. No. 107–293, sec. 1(16). This act was written in support of keeping the phrase "under God" in the Pledge of Allegiance.

75. Hamilton worried that "a few characters of consequence, by opposing or even refusing to sign the Constitution, might do infinite mischief by kindling the latent sparks which lurk under an enthusiasm in favor of the Convention which may soon subside" (Farrand 2:645).

76. Farrand 2:642.

77. Madison wrote that "this ambiguous form had been drawn up" by Gouverneur Morris "in order to gain the dissenting members, and put into the hands of Docr. Franklin that it might have the better chance of success" (Farrand 2:643).

78. Emphasis added.

79. Farrand 2:647n.

80. Farrand 2:643. Franklin sent copies of his address to several friends. In his version of the address, his motion reads, "Then the Motion was made for adding the last Formula, viz Done in Convention by the unanimous Consent &c—which was agreed to and added—accordingly" (DHRC 13:215). In no version is the phrase "in the Year of Our Lord" attributed to Franklin.

81. PAH 4:274.

82. Rapport, "Printing the Constitution," 75.

83. See also Dreisbach, "Christian Commonwealth," 967, saying that "the specific words chosen in 1787 may have been merely a scrivener's touch."

84. Whether Shallus wrote the clause "before or after the delegates signed is not clear" (Rapport, "Printing the Constitution," 75).

85. Art. I, sec. 7.

86. See, e.g., Thomas Jefferson's proposal titled "A Bill for Punishing Disturbers of Religious Worship and Sabbath Breakers," PTJ 2:555.

87. Farrand 2:181.

88. Farrand 2:302.

89. Randall, "Sundays Excepted," 518.

90. Saturday, Aug. 18, 1787, Elliot's Debates 1:248.

91. Dec. 7, 1776, JCC 6:1010.

92. Art. I, sec. 7.

93. In 1938, the Supreme Court ruled that adjournments of less than three days would be viewed as "a recess . . . not an adjournment by the Congress," which would permit a pocket veto (Wright v. United States, 302 U.S. 583, 592 [1938]).

94. Baird, Religion in America, 261, quoted in Dreisbach, "Christian Commonwealth," 977. Similarly, Justice David Brewer included the "Sundays excepted" language as part of his facts that he said proved that the United States "is a Christian nation" (Church of the Holy Trinity v. United States, 143 U.S. 457, 470–71 [1892]).

95. Blakely and Colcord, Papers Bearing on Sunday Legislation, 763n1.

96. Dreisbach, "Christian Commonwealth," 997.

97. George Mason in Rowland, Life of George Mason, 2:151.

98. "A Landholder VII," Connecticut Courant, Dec. 17, 1787, DHRC 3:499.

99. Convention Debates, Jan. 31, 1788 (A.M.), DHRC 6:1376.

100. "A Landholder VII," Connecticut Courant, Dec. 17, 1787, DHRC 3:499.

101. Leland, "The Rights of Conscience Inalienable," WJL, 191.

102. Elliot's Debates 4:193.

103. Tench Coxe, *An American Citizen IV*, Oct. 21, 1787, in Ford's *Pamphlets*, 146.

104. A Friend of Society And Liberty, July 23, 1788, *DHRC* 18:281.

105. Peter Collin to Nicholas Low, July 16, 1788, *DHRC* 21:1595. The "holiday" was the Jewish fast day of "Tzom Tammuz." (The date was calculated using a "perpetual Jewish calendar" located at http://www.jewishpeople.com/cgi-bin/jewish-cal.cgi?month=7&year=1788.)

106. Hastings, *Ecclesiastical Records*, 3727.

107. Adrian Bancker to Evert Bancker, July 20, 1788, *DHRC* 21:1327.

108. Joseph Grove John Bend to Abraham Beach, July 9, 1788, in G. Hills, *History of the Church in Burlington*, 715.

109. Rush, "Observations on the Fourth of July Procession in Philadelphia," *Pennsylvania Mercury*, July 15, 1788, *DHRC* 18:265.

110. Hopkinson *Miscellaneous Essays*, 401.

111. "Federal Parade of 1788." The description is from Naphtali Phillips to James McAllister, Jr., New York, Oct. 24, 1868, written when Phillips was ninety-five years old. According to Joan Nathan (*Jewish Cooking in America*, 134), soused salmon, a dish in which salmon was seasoned with spices, boiled in vinegar, and served cold, was a typical Jewish preparation in the colonies (quoting a recipe from Esther Levy, *The Jewish Cookery Book* [1871]).

112. Rush, "Observations on the Fourth of July Procession in Philadelphia," *Pennsylvania Mercury*, July 15, 1788, *DHRC* 18:266.

CHAPTER 5. ADDING THE FIRST AMENDMENT

1. For some Anti-Federalists, the call for a bill of rights was really a pretext hiding their objection to the increased power of the central government: "Despite the attention paid to a bill of rights, only the Virginia and North Carolina conventions had formally asked that one be added to the Constitution; however, every state that recommended amendments demanded [a limit to Congress's ability to impose a] direct tax" (Maier, *Ratification*, 444).

2. Sept. 12, 1787, Farrand 2:587–88.

3. The vote was 10 states no, 0 yes, 1 absent, Sept. 12, 1787, Farrand 2:588.

4. "Centinel II," *Philadelphia Freeman's Journal*, Oct. 24, 1787, *DHRC* 13:466. Most likely, "Centinel" was Samuel Bryan of Philadelphia.

5. The full text of Wilson's speech can be found in Ford's *Pamphlets*, 157.

6. Bailyn, *Debate on the Constitution*, 1:1142. Pauline Maier has termed Wilson's speech a "landmark in the ratification debate" (*Ratification*, 80).

7. Virginia Ratifying Convention, General Defense of the Constitution, June 12, 1788, *PJM: Congressional* 11:130–31.

8. Convention Debates, P.M., Notes of the Debate in the Pennsylvania Convention Taken by James Wilson, Dec. 12, 1787, *DHRC* 2:592.

9. *DHRC* 2:623. The dissenters stated, "The rights of conscience may be violated, as there is no exemption of those persons who are conscientiously scrupulous of bearing arms" (*DHRC* 2:638). This seems to imply that the "rights of conscience" requires religious exemptions from military service.

10. Nathaniel Gorham to James Madison, Jan. 27, 1788, *PJM: Congressional* 10:436.

11. *DHRC* 16:64.

12. *DHRC* 16:67–69.

13. On Jan. 30, Madison's father had written, "The Baptists are now generally opposed" to the Constitution (James Madison, Sr., to James Madison, Jan. 30, 1788, *PJM: Congressional* 10:446).

14. Edmund Randolph to James Madison, Feb. 29, 1788, *PJM: Congressional* 10:542.

15. W. Scott, *Orange County, Virginia,* 50.

16. Joseph Spencer to James Madison, Feb. 28, 1788, *PJM: Congressional* 10:541. It is possible that there were two people named "Joseph Spencer." According to the editors of the James Madison Papers, there was a second Joseph Spencer who had been a captain in the Revolutionary Army (542n5). Considering the author of the letter's familiarity with the local Baptist situation, as well as the fact that he was trusted by John Leland to transmit Leland's objections to the Constitution (see Joseph Spencer to James Madison, Feb. 28, 1788, *DHRC* 8:424–25), it seems likely that the author was the same person as the formerly imprisoned Baptist minister.

17. Leland, "The Government of Christ: A Christocracy" (1804), *WJL,* 476.

18. Leland referred to Adams as "a gentleman, at the head of his party" in Massachusetts (Leland, "An Elective Judiciary" [1805], *WJL,* 295). This incident is described in Chapter 2.

19. Leland, "Elective Judiciary," *WJL,* 295.

20. Leland, "Free Thoughts on Times and Things" (1836), *WJL,* 671.

21. Leland, "Short Essays on Government" (1820), *WJL,* 474.

22. Leland, "The Virginia Chronicle" (1790), *WJL,* 117–18.

23. Leland, "Short Essays on Government," *WJL,* 476.

24. Leland, "Virginia Chronicle," *WJL,* 106n.

25. Leland, "The Rights of Conscience Inalienable, and Therefore, Religious Opinions Not Cognizable by Law" (1791), *WJL,* 190.

26. Leland, "Elective Judiciary," *WJL,* 293.

27. Leland, "Virginia Chronicle," *WJL,* 119.

28. Leland, "On Sabbatical Laws" (1815), *WJL,* 444.

29. Leland, "Leland Again" (1828), *WJL,* 539.

30. Leland, "Government of Christ," *WJL,* 297.

31. Leland, "Virginia Chronicle," *WJL,* 118.

32. Leland, "Government of Christ," *WJL,* 278.

33. Semple, *Baptists in Virginia,* 102.

34. "Revd. John Leeland's Objections to the Federal Constitution Sent to Col. Thos. Barber by his Request," *DHRC* 8:426 (emphasis in original). I have corrected a few of the misspellings in the original document for ease of reading.

35. M. Marshall, "Episode in Madison's Career," 340.

36. Leibiger, *Founding Friendship,* 92.

37. There were four candidates, and voters could choose two. The top two candidates—Madison with 202 votes, and James Gordon, Jr., with 187—were supporters of the Constitution. The Anti-Federalist candidates, Thomas Barbour and Charles Porter, received just 56 and 34 votes respectively (*PJM: Congressional* 11:2n2).

38. Leland, Address Delivered at Dalton, Massachusetts, Jan. 8, 1831, *WJL,* 605.

39. June 6, 1788, *DHRC* 9:994.

40. Thomas Jefferson to James Madison, Dec. 20, 1787, *PTJ* 12:440.

41. Thomas Jefferson to Alexander Donald, Feb. 7, 1788, *PTJ* 12:571.

42. June 12, 1788, Elliot's *Debates* 4:314–15.

43. June 9, 1787, *DHRC* 9:1051–52.

44. Virginia Convention, June 27, 1788, *DHRC* 10:1558.

45. Ibid., 1553.

46. Though North Carolina adjourned its Constitutional Convention on Aug. 1, 1788, without ratifying the Constitution, its convention did recommend numerous amendments, including a religion provision identical to Virginia's proposal (Elliot's *Debates* 4:242–46, 248–49). North Carolina finally ratified the Constitution on Nov. 21, 1789, after the Bill of Rights had been sent to the states for approval.

47. Henry Lee to James Madison, Nov. 19, 1788, *PJM: Congressional* 11:356.

48. See Labunski, *Madison and the Bill of Rights,* 148; for an excellent discussion of the election, see 147–77.

49. Thomas Jefferson to William Short, Feb. 9, 1789, *PTJ* 14:529.

50. Monroe had been a moderate Anti-Federalist during the debate over the ratification of the Constitution; see Dodd, *American Statesmen,* 121; Cunningham, *Jefferson and Monroe,* 10; Vile, *James Madison,* 161.

51. Hardin Burnley to James Madison, Dec. 16, 1788, *PJM: Congressional* 11:398–99. Another friend, George Nicholas, told Madison that Henry was telling voters that Madison was "now opposed to all amendments" (Nicholas to Madison, Jan. 2, 1789, *PJM: Congressional* 11:406).

52. Waldman, *Founding Faith,* 143.

53. James Madison to George Eve, Jan. 2, 1789, *PJM: Congressional* 11:405. Madison made a similar pledge in his letter to Thomas Mann Randolph of Jan. 13, 1789, *PJM: Congressional* 11:415.

54. Scarberry, "Leland and Madison," 794.

55. Benjamin Johnson to James Madison, Jan. 19, 1789, *PJM: Congressional* 11:423–24.

56. Ibid., 424.

57. For a convincing analysis of Leland's likely role in the election, see Scarberry, "Leland and Madison," 789–92.

58. John Leland to James Madison, Feb. [ca. 15,] 1789, *DHFFE* 2:347.

59. James Madison to Thomas Jefferson, Oct. 17, 1788, *PJM: Congressional* 11:297.

60. Ibid., 11:298.

61. Ibid., 11:299.

62. Thomas Jefferson to James Madison, Mar. 15, 1789, *PTJ* 14:659.

63. *Annals* 1:441.

64. "Notes for Speech in Congress," June 8, 1789, *PJM: Congressional* 12:193.

65. James Madison to Richard Peters, Aug. 19, 1789, *PJM: Congressional* 12:346–47.

66. "Amendments to the Constitution," June 8, 1789, *PJM: Congressional* 12:198.

67. Ibid.

68. William Loughton Smith of South Carolina complained about the "inexpediency of taking up the subject at the present moment . . . while matters of the greatest importance and of immediate consequence were lying unfinished" (*Gazette of the United States,* June 10, 1789, in Bickford, Bowling, and Veit, *Debates in the House,* 11:805).

69. George Clymer to Richard Peters, June 8, 1789, in Crosskey and Jeffrey, *Politics and the Constitution,* 1:688.

70. "Madison at the First Session of the First Federal Congress," Apr. 8–Sept. 29, 1789, *PJM: Congressional* 12:58.

71. New Hampshire's was the shortest of the religious freedom proposals: "Congress shall make no laws touching religion, or to infringe the rights of conscience." New York's proposal was similar to Virginia's, declaring, "That the people have an equal, natural, and

unalienable right freely and peaceably to exercise their religion, according to the dictates of conscience; and that no religious sect or society ought to be favored or established by law in preference to others." North Carolina, which had not yet ratified the original Constitution, copied Virginia's language. It is probable that Madison would also have looked at proposed amendments written by Anti-Federalists in both Pennsylvania and Maryland, even though the proposals had not been formally recommended by those states' ratifying conventions. Anti-Federalists in Pennsylvania had proposed: "The right of conscience shall be held inviolable, and neither the legislative, executive nor judicial powers of the United States shall have authority to alter, abrogate, or infringe any part of the constitution of the several states, which provide for the preservation of liberty in matters of religion" ("The Address and Reasons of Dissent of the Minority of the Convention of the State of Pennsylvania to their Constituents," DRC 2:623). Maryland's had proposed: "That there be no national religion established by law; but that all persons be equally entitled to protection in their religious liberty" ("A Fragment of Facts, Disclosing the Conduct of the Maryland Convention, on the Adoption of the Federal Constitution," in Elliot's Debates 2:547, 553).

72. "Amendments to the Constitution," June 8, 1789, PJM: Congressional 12:201.

73. July 17, 1787, Farrand 2:27–28.

74. James Madison to Thomas Jefferson, Sept. 6, 1787, PJM: Congressional 10:163–64.

75. Aug. 17, 1789, PJM 12:344.

76. Cantwell v. Connecticut, 310 U.S. 296, 303 (1940).

77. The House debate can be found in Debates and Proceedings in the Congress of the United States, 757–59; quotations from the debates in the next several paragraphs all come from this source.

78. According to Douglas Laycock, "No verbatim record exists, the reporter's notes are incomplete and sometimes inaccurate, and the notes fill slightly less than two columns in the Annals of Congress" ("'Nonpreferential' Aid to Religion," 885).

79. See Madison, Federalist 39.

80. This was the same language that Livermore's home state of New Hampshire had used in its proposed amendments.

81. See generally McConnell, "Free Exercise of Religion," 1489.

82. "Act to Prevent the Growth of Popery" (1704), in Scharf, History of Maryland, 1:369.

83. Somewhat similarly, James Jackson of Georgia said that exempting some people from the militia would be unfair, since "one part would have to defend the other in case of invasion." As a compromise, he would have permitted an exemption, but conditioned the exemption upon the payment of some "equivalent" amount.

84. The version passed by the House and sent to the Senate was a slight variation of the Ames proposal. It read: "Congress shall make no law establishing religion, or prohibiting the free exercise thereof, nor shall the rights of conscience be infringed."

85. One proposal was first rejected by the Senate, then passed: "Congress shall make no law establishing one Religious Sect or Society in preference to others, nor shall the rights of conscience be infringed." Another proposal, which was rejected, read: "Congress shall not make any law, infringing the rights of conscience, or establishing any Religious Sect or Society." On Sept. 3, the Senate approved a proposal to change the language to "Congress shall make no law establishing any particular denomination of religion in preference to another, or prohibiting the free exercise thereof, nor shall the rights of conscience be infringed." The Senate proposals can be found in De Pauw, Documentary History of the First Congress, 1:151 (Senate Journal).

86. The "First Amendment" was not the first on the list sent to the states. The first

two proposed amendments, dealing with the size of House districts and congressional salaries, were not approved, so what had been the third amendment became the first (Elliot's *Debates* 1:338). In 1992, the congressional pay proposal was revived and approved by a sufficient number of states to become the Twenty-Seventh Amendment.

87. See, e.g., Levy, *Establishment Clause*, 189, 259, quoting Sol Bloom, *History of the Formation of the Union under the Constitution* (1941), 316: "The finished amendments were not the subject of any special newspaper comment, and there is little comment in the available correspondence."

88. Edmund Randolph to James Madison, Aug. 18, 1789, *PJM: Congressional* 12:345.

89. See Levy, *Establishment Clause*, 107.

90. Esbeck, "Uses and Abuses of Textualism," 79.

91. Edmund Randolph to George Washington, Dec. 6, 1789, *PGW: Presidential* 4:374.

92. James Madison to George Washington, Nov. 20, 1789, *PJM* 12:453. Later, Madison wrote to Washington predicting that the Virginia Senate's opposition "will do no injury to the Genl. Government. On the contrary it will have the effect with many of turning their distrust towards their own Legislature. The miscarriage of the [First Amendment] particularly, will have this effect" (Madison to Washington, Jan. 5, 1790, Madison, *Letters and Other Writings*, 1:501).

93. Jefferson's announcement was strangely anticlimactic: "I have the honor to send you herein enclosed, two copies duly authenticated, of an Act concerning certain fisheries of the United States, and for the regulation and government of the fishermen employed therein; also of an Act to establish the post office and post roads within the United States; also the ratification by three fourths of the Legislatures of the Several States, of certain articles in addition and amendment of the Constitution of the United States, proposed by Congress to the said Legislatures" (Schwartz, *Great Rights of Mankind*, 186–87).

94. Laycock, "'Nonpreferential' Aid to Religion," 877.

95. Ibid., 880.

96. Lee v. Weisman, 505 U.S. 577, 614–15 (1992) (Souter, J., concurring).

97. Amar, *The Bill of Rights*, 246; see also Steven Smith, *Foreordained Failure*, 30.

98. Elk Grove Unified School District v. Newdow, 542 U.S. 1, 50 (2004) (Thomas, J., concurring).

99. Paulsen, "Religion, Equality, and the Constitution," 321.

100. New York had proposed: "That the people have an equal, natural, and unalienable right freely and peaceably to exercise their religion, according to the dictates of conscience; and that no religious sect or society ought to be favored or established by law in preference to others" (Elliot's *Debates* 1:328). Virginia's convention had proposed two religion-related amendments: "Nineteenth, That any person religiously scrupulous of bearing arms ought to be exempted upon payment of an equivalent to employ another to bear arms in his stead," and "Twentieth, That religion or the duty which we owe to our Creator, and the manner of discharging it can be directed only by reason and conviction, not by force or violence, and therefore all men have an equal, natural and unalienable right to the free exercise of religion according to the dictates of conscience, and that no particular religious sect or society ought to be favored or established by Law in preference to others" (Virginia Ratifying Convention, Proposed Amendments June 27, 1788, Elliot's *Debates* 3:659). North Carolina proposed the same language as Virginia's "twentieth" amendment (Elliot's *Debates* 2:244).

101. Rhode Island's statement, which occurred after the Bill of Rights had been sent to the states, copied the language of Virginia's proposed amendments concerning religion (Elliot's *Debates* 1:334).

102. "A Fragment of Facts, Disclosing the Conduct of the Maryland Convention, on the Adoption of the Federal Constitution," Elliot's *Debates* 2:547, 553.

103. The Address and Reasons of Dissent of the Minority of the Convention of the State of Pennsylvania to their Constituents, *DRC* 2:623. A Pennsylvania Anti-Federalist named John Smilie expressed concerns that the unamended Constitution threatened religious freedom: "The Rights of Conscience are not secured.—Priestcraft useful to all tyrannical Govts.—Congress may establish any Religion" (Convention Debates, P.M., Notes of the Debate in the Pennsylvania Convention Taken by James Wilson, Dec. 12, 1787, *DHRC* 2:592).

104. New Hampshire's proposal: "Congress shall make no laws touching religion, or to infringe the rights of conscience" (Elliott's *Debates* 1:326).

105. *DHRC* 9:779. South Carolina's Thomas Tudor Tucker proposed this change twice in the House of Representatives, but it was rejected both times (Aug. 18, 1789, and Aug. 22, 1789, *Annals* 1:790, 807). It was also raised and rejected in the Senate (*Senate Journal* 1:72 [Sept. 7, 1789]).

106. Benjamin Huntington of Connecticut did suggest that federal courts might refuse to enforce a legal obligation to fund a church, but the establishment clause language— "Congress shall make no law respecting an establishment of religion"—obviously was not designed to address that concern.

107. Antieau, Downey, and Roberts, *Freedom from Federal Establishment*, 153–54.

108. "An Act For the regular establishment and support of the public duties of Religion," Feb. 21, 1785, in *Colonial Records of Georgia*, 395–98. The act also provided for different denominations to be funded in the same county if twenty families desired to create "separate and distinct congregations." Even though it appears that the tax was never actually imposed, (see, e.g., White, *Abraham Baldwin*, 90), the fact remains that Georgia, at the time when it was considering ratification of the Bill of Rights, reserved to itself the power to impose a religious tax.

109. According to Carl Esbeck, Georgia chose not to ratify on the grounds that it was too soon to know whether amendments were needed. Connecticut's failure to ratify was based on the fear of local Federalists that approving amendments would show that the Anti-Federalists had been correct in arguing that the Constitution was flawed. Though both the House and the Senate in Massachusetts provisionally approved the Bill of Rights, a special committee blocked them in order to encourage Congress to consider the amendments Massachusetts had proposed in 1788 ("Uses and Abuses of Textualism," 80). All three states ratified the Bill of Rights in 1939, the 150th anniversary of the Bill of Rights' submission to the states.

110. Quoted in Myers, *Massachusetts and the First Ten Amendments*, 10.

111. James Iredell, North Carolina Ratifying Convention, Elliott's *Debates* 4:194.

112. Feldman, *Divided by God*, 41–42.

113. Ibid., 41: "The dominant majority answered that the so-called New England Way could not be considered an established church, because it made provision for opting out of the system by exemption"; see also Curry, *First Freedoms*, 174–75: "Officially, the state [i.e., Massachusetts] maintained no establishment, and neither did defenders of the ecclesiastical system describe it as such."

114. Muzzy v. Wilkins, 1 N.H. (1 Smith) (1803), printed in *Decisions of the Superior and Supreme Courts*, 12–13.

115. Palko v. Connecticut, 302 U.S. 319, 324–25 (1937).

116. Everson v. Board of Education, 330 U.S. 1 (1947).

117. For example, Justice Thomas has written: "The Establishment Clause is best under-

stood as a federalism provision—it protects state establishments from federal interference but does not protect any individual right. These two features independently make incorporation of the Clause difficult to understand" (*Newdow,* 542 U.S. 1 [Thomas, J., concurring]). See also "Incorporation of the Establishment Clause," 1708: "Because the establishment Clause is animated by the principle of federalism, its incorporation against the states . . . is logically impossible."

118. "Mr. Tennent's Speech on the Dissenting Petition, Delivered in the House of Assembly, Charles-Town, January 11, 1777," reprinted in Jones, "Writings of William Tennent," 197.

119. Ibid., 202.

120. Like Isaac Backus, Tennent did not include non-Protestants in his vision of religious equality. He believed: "The state may give countenance to religion by defending and protecting all denominations of Christians who are inoffensive and useful" ("Mr. Tennent's Speech on the Dissenting Petition," 197). He declared his approval of the eventual state establishment of "the Christian Protestant religion": "Not one sect of Christians in preference to all others but Christianity itself is the established religion of the state" (203).

121. H. Adams, *Jefferson and the University of Virginia,* 229–30.

122. "A Memorial and Remonstrance," June 20, 1785, *PJM: Congressional* 8:303.

123. Steven Smith, *Foreordained Failure,* 17.

124. Lash, "Adoption of the Establishment Clause," 1091–92.

CHAPTER 6. FREEDOM OF RELIGION IN THE NEW NATION

1. See, e.g., Waldman, *Founding Faith,* 158: "Washington, Adams, Jefferson, and Madison struggled to interpret the Constitution and act accordingly . . . And what did they do when they had the chance to sort this out once and for all? They disagreed."

2. According to Gary Wills, Washington was seen as a "law giver," not "in the autocratic sense . . . [but] as a wise man of the law" (*Cincinnatus,* 107).

3. George Washington to James Madison, May 5, 1789, *PGW: Presidential* 2:216–17.

4. James Madison to Jared Sparks, May 30, 1827, *PJM: Retirement* 11:446n1.

5. H. Adams, *Life and Writings of Sparks,* 2:211.

6. Jared Sparks, the original editor of the *Writings of George Washington,* destroyed the version of Humphrey's draft that Washington had copied by hand. Sparks cut the seventy-three pages into small pieces and gave them to people who wanted something with Washington's handwriting. The twentieth-century editors of the Papers of George Washington were able to reassemble small portions of the original, one of which read: "The blessed Religion revealed in the word of God will remain an eternal and awful monument to prove that the best Institutions may be abused by human depravity; and that they may even, in some instances be made subservient to the vilest of purposes" ("Undelivered First Inaugural Address: Fragments," *PGW: Presidential* 2:166).

7. H. Adams, *Life and Writings of Sparks,* 2:211.

8. *PGW: Presidential* 2:52–58. Senator Richard Henry Lee had proposed that the services be held when Congress was planning the activities of Inauguration Day (Church, *So Help Me God,* 448).

9. *PGW: Presidential* 2:152–58.

10. Norwood and Pollack, *Encyclopedia of American Jewish History,* 1:21. Technically, Seixas was a "hazzan," a congregational leader, but not a rabbi, since he had not been trained

and certified by a senior rabbi. See "Gershom Mendes Seixas, 1745–1816," *The Jewish Virtual Library*, http://www.jewishvirtuallibrary.org/jsource/biography/Seixas.html. Nonetheless, he performed all of the functions of a rabbi.

11. Byrd, *The Senate*, 19.

12. Maclay, *Journal of William Maclay*, 9.

13. Church, *So Help Me God*, 18.

14. Edward Lengel, the editor in chief of the *Papers of George Washington*, concluded that "any attempt to prove that Washington added the words 'so help me God' requires mental gymnastics of the sort that would do credit to the finest artist of the flying trapeze" (Lengel, *Inventing George Washington*, 105).

15. Griswold, *Republican Court*, 141–42. Washington Irving included the story three years later in his 1857 book *Life of George Washington*, 4:549, but did not say that he heard it directly.

16. *DHFFC* 15:404–5. Eliza Susan Morton Quincy, who attended the inauguration at the age of fifteen, wrote an account in 1821, similarly saying that "Chancellor Livingston read the oath according to the form prescribed by the Constitution; and Washington repeated it" (Eliza Quincy, *Memoir*, 52).

17. *DHFFC* 15:404–5. There was also a letter published in the *Gazette of the United States*, May 13, 1789, saying that Washington "kissed the sacred volume"; see http://raglinen.com/2010/08/27/griswolds-only-eyewitness-account-of-george-washingtons-1789-inauguration/.

18. Ashbel Green to Jacob Green, Sept. 10, 1842, in A. Green and J. Jones, *Life of Ashbel Green*, 167–68.

19. Jefferson's Anas, *WTJ* 1:284.

20. A. Green, "Jefferson's Papers." His argument concluded with his observation: "General Washington's creed and system of action, in relation to morals and religion, were the very antipodes to those of all such men as Mr. J. and Governeur Morris."

21. A. Green and J. Jones, *Life of Ashbel Green*, 171.

22. Church, *So Help Me God*, 41.

23. *CMPP* 1:44.

24. Ibid., 1:46.

25. Reply to the House of Representatives, May 8, 1789, *PGW: Presidential* 2:232.

26. Reply to the Senate, May 18, 1789, *PGW: Presidential* 2:324.

27. McCreary County v. ACLU, 545 U.S. 844, 886 (2005) (Scalia, J., dissenting).

28. Grizzard, *Ways of Providence*, 4.

29. Blomquist, "Presidential Oath," 1, 34.

30. According to Beth Hahn, the historical editor for the U.S. Senate Historical Office, "The first eyewitness documentation of a president saying 'So help me God' is an account of Chester Arthur's Sept. 22, 1881, inauguration in the *New York Times*" (Grossman, "No Proof Washington Said 'So Help Me God'").

31. Grizzard, *George Washington*, 385.

32. Journal of the Senate, Sept. 26, 1789, 90, and Sept. 28, 1789, 92.

33. George Washington to James Madison, Sept. 8, 1789, *PJM: Congressional* 12:390.

34. Sept. 25, 1789, *Annals* 1:949–50.

35. Ibid. Tucker also said: "If a day of thanksgiving must take place, let it be done by the authority of the several States; they know best what reason their constituents have to be pleased with the establishment of this constitution."

36. Ibid.

37. Sept. 25, 1789, *Annals* 1:950.

38. According to Paul Boller, "This first national thanksgiving proclamation under the Constitution had been written by William Jackson, one of Washington's secretaries, and approved by Washington with only one minor revision" (*Washington and Religion*, 62).

39. The positive response to Washington's inclusive message can be seen in the sermon given by the New York rabbi Gershom Mendes Seixas in which he declared that since Jews were "situated under the best of Constitutions," it was their duty "to contribute, as much as lays within our power, to the support of that government which is founded upon the strict principles of equal liberty and justice" (Seixas, *Religious Discourse*, 16).

40. George Washington to John Hancock, June 8, 1777, *WGW* 5:419.

41. Novak and Novak, *Washington's God*, 14.

42. United Baptist Churches of Virginia to George Washington, May 1789, *PGW: Presidential* 2:425n1.

43. George Washington to the United Baptist Churches of Virginia, May 1789, *PGW: Presidential* 2:424.

44. "The Answer of the President of the United States to the Address of the Religious Society Called Quakers," October 1789, *PGW: Presidential* 4:267n1.

45. Ibid., 265–66.

46. In his letter, Washington spelled "Conscientious" as "Consciencious."

47. Boller, *Washington and Religion*, 146.

48. George Washington's Letter to Roman Catholics in America, March 1790, *PGW: Presidential* 5:299–300.

49. Guilday, *Life and Times of John Carroll*, 364.

50. John Peter Coghlan, "Preface to the London Edition of An Address from the Roman Catholics of America to George Washington Esq President of the United States," in Guilday, *Life and Times of John Carroll*, 367.

51. Mikveh Israel Congregation to George Washington, May 6, 1790, *PGW: Presidential* 5:449.

52. George Washington to the Savannah, Ga., Hebrew Congregation, May 1790, *PGW: Presidential* 5:448–49.

53. He was accompanied by Thomas Jefferson on this journey, and some people have suggested that Jefferson helped write his letter to the Hebrew Congregation in Newport (*PTJ* 19:609–10).

54. George Washington to the Hebrew Congregation in Newport Rhode Island, Aug. 18, 1790, *PGW: Presidential* 6:284–85.

55. The famous phrase "to bigotry gives no sanction, to persecution no assistance" was in the letter written by the Newport congregation (*PGW: Presidential* 6:284–85). It was not uncommon for Washington to repeat phrases he agreed with when responding to letters, embellishing them with his own additional language.

56. Schragger, "Role of the Local," 1825.

57. Washington to the Hebrew Congregation in Newport.

58. The Presbytery of the Eastward to George Washington, Oct. 28, 1789, *PGW: Presidential* 4:275.

59. George Washington to the Presbytery of the Eastward, Nov. 2, 1789, *PGW: Presidential* 4:274.

60. Ibid. (emphasis added).

61. The Synod of the reformed Dutch Church in North America to George Washington, Oct. 9, 1789, *PGW: Presidential* 4:265n1.

62. George Washington to The Synod of the reformed Dutch Church in North America, October 1789, *PGW: Presidential* 2:264.

63. Limbaugh, *Persecution,* 320.

64. George Washington to The Clergy of Different Denominations Residing In And Near The City Of Philadelphia, Mar. 3, 1797, *WGW* 12:245.

65. A. Green, "Jefferson's Papers," 305.

66. Church, *So Help Me God,* 107.

67. George Washington to The Clergy of Different Denominations Residing In And Near The City Of Philadelphia, Mar. 3, 1797, *WGW* 12:245.

68. "Notes on a Conversation with Benjamin Rush," *PTJ* 31:352. In his retelling, Jefferson incorrectly refers to Ashbel Green as "Asa Green."

69. A. Green, "Jefferson's Papers," 309. Jefferson's version was basically supported by a letter from Green's nephew, Arthur Bradford, which was quoted in B. F. Underwood, "Was Washington a Christian?": "He [Green] explained more at length the plan laid by the clergy of Philadelphia at the close of Washington's administration as President to get his views of religion for the sake of the good influence they supposed they would have in counteracting the Infidelity of Paine and the rest of the Revolutionary patriots, military and civil. But I well remember the smile on his face and the twinkle of his black eye when he said: 'The old fox was too cunning for Us.'"

70. Green, "Jefferson's Papers," 309.

71. Waldman, *Founding Faith,* 162.

72. Sixth Annual Address, Nov. 19 1794, *CMPP* 1:168.

73. Church, *So Help Me God,* 99.

74. *PJM: Retirement* 1:390–91n4.

75. Ibid. In his autobiography, Madison described Hamilton's approach as evidence of "the danger of mingling political & even party views with such Proclamations" (Adair, "Madison's Autobiography," 208).

76. Church, *So Help Me God,* 102.

77. Ibid.

78. Bentley, *Diary of William Bentley,* 2:129.

79. Gilbert, *Farewell Address,* 124–25.

80. Alexander Hamilton to George Washington, July 30, 1796, *PAH* 20:170.

81. Hamilton kept much of Madison's introductory language and conclusion, but added an extensive middle section discussing many of the contemporary political issues, such as the desirability of maintaining neutrality during the conflict between England and France (*PAH* 20:170).

82. Washington, "Farewell Address," *CMPP* 1:227. Hamilton's draft read: "Nor ought we to flatter ourselves that morality can be separated from religion. Concede as much as may be asked to the effect of refined education in minds of a peculiar structure—can we believe—can we in prudence suppose that national morality can be maintained in exclusion of religious principles?"

83. Boller, *Washington and Religion,* 162.

84. J. West, *Politics of Revelation and Reason,* 39–40.

85. Church, *So Help Me God,* 148.

86. Adams, Inaugural Address, Mar. 4, 1797, *CMPP* 1:232.

87. Alexander Hamilton to Timothy Pickering, Mar. 22, 1797, *PAH* 20:545.

88. Adams depicted Hamilton's plan as recommending "a national Fast not only on account of the intrinsic propriety of it but because we should be very unskilful if we

neglected to avail ourselves of the religious feelings of the people in a crisis so difficult and dangerous" (Adams, "Correspondence from Boston Patriot" [1809], *WJA* 9:289–91).

89. Ibid.

90. A. Green and J. Jones, *Life of Ashbel Green,* 270–71.

91. Hitchcock, *Supreme Court and Religion,* 30.

92. A. Green and J. Jones, *Life of Ashbel Green,* 623.

93. Ibid., 270.

94. Adams, Proclamation, Mar. 4, 1797, *CMPP* 1:285.

95. John Mitchell Mason, "The Voice of Warning to Christians" (1800), in Sandoz, *Political Sermons,* 2:290.

96. Waldman, *Founding Faith,* 164.

97. Art. 11, Treaty of peace and friendship, between the United States of America and the Bey and subjects of Tripoli of Barbary, Nov. 4, 1796 (emphasis added), *Public Statutes at Large of the United States of America,* 8:155.

98. Wolcott, *Administrations of Washington and Adams,* 421. See also Lyman, *Diplomacy of the United States,* 382–83: "We are embarrassed to understand, not the meaning, but the object of the eleventh article. A Jew, Turk or Hindoo, Atheist or the Heathen may hold any office of trust, honour or profit under the federal constitution. But if the government of this country is not founded on the christian religion, on what religion is it founded?"

99. Press, *How the Republicans Stole Religion,* 51.

100. Ibid. (emphasis in original). See also Nussbaum, *Liberty of Conscience,* 113 ("In rejecting a nonpreferential Christian understanding of the nation, it is overwhelmingly likely that Adams and others were rejecting nonpreferentialism itself").

101. The most likely source is Joel Barlow, the diplomat who negotiated the treaty and translated it from Arabic (Church, *So Help Me God,* 206).

102. Treaty of peace and amity, between the United States of America, and the Bashaw, Bey, and subjects of Tripoli, in Barbary, June 4, 1805, in Elliot, *American Diplomatic Code,* 1:61.

103. Foster, *Practice of Diplomacy,* 252.

104. See, e.g., Rodda, *Liars for Jesus,* 320.

105. There is one religious preamble; during the Adams administration, the phrase "God is infinite" was used in a 1799 treaty with Tunis (Elliot, *American Diplomatic Code,* 1:508).

106. See generally Hertslet, *Map of Europe by Treaty.* Some examples include the Definitive Treaty of Peace between Great Britain, etc. (Austria, Portugal, Prussia, Russia, Spain, Sweden), and France, May 30, 1814 (1:2–3); Convention between Great Britain and the Netherlands, Aug. 13, 1814 (1:42); Treaty between Great Britain, Austria, Prussia, and Russia, and the Netherlands, May 21, 1815 (1:179); General Treaty between Great Britain, Austria, France, Portugal, Prussia, Russia, Spain and Sweden, June 9, 1815 (1:211); Convention between Great Britain and the Netherlands, Aug. 12, 1815 (1:296); Treaty of Accession of Great Britain, to the Territorial Treaty between Saxony and Prussia (Austria and Russia), May 18, 1815 (1:145); Treaty between Great Britain and Austria, Prussia and Russia, respecting the Ionian Islands, Nov. 5, 1815 (1:337); Treaty of Alliance and Friendship between Great Britain, Austria (Prussia, and Russia), Nov. 20, 1815 (1:372); Treaty between Great Britain, France, and Russia, for the Pacification of Greece. Signed at London, July 6, 1827 (769); Treaty between Great Britain, Austria, France, Prussia, and Russia, on the one part, and The Netherlands, on the other, Apr. 19, 1839 (2:992). It should be noted that many of England's treaties, such as those with Spain, Portugal, and Denmark, did not contain a religious preamble.

107. 1818 treaty with Sweden and Norway, *Treaties and Other International Agreements,* 11:868.

108. Convention of St. Petersburg, Elliot, *American Diplomatic Code,* 1:284. The last time the phrase appeared in an American treaty was for a treaty with Paraguay in 1859.

109. See, e.g., Rodda, *Liars for Jesus,* 320.

110. John Mitchell Mason, "The Voice of Warning to Christians" (1800), in Sandoz, *Political Sermons,* 2:1453.

111. Waldman, *Founding Faith,* 168.

112. Linn, *Considerations on the Election of a President,* 24.

113. Jefferson, *Notes on the State of Virginia,* 265.

114. Linn, *Considerations on the Election of a President,* 19.

115. Ibid., 24.

116. Mason, "The Voice of Warning to Christians," in Mason, *Complete Works of John Mason,* 4:556.

117. Lambert, "God—and a Religious President," 770.

118. Ibid., 771.

119. Waldman, *Founding Faith,* 170.

120. Duane, "Federalism vs. Republicanism," Oct. 14, 1800, reprinted in Humphrey, *Revolutionary Era,* 344–45.

121. Miller, "From Covenant to Revival," in J. W. Smith and A. Jamison, *Religion in American Life,* 357.

122. John Adams to Benjamin Rush, June 12, 1812, *OFL,* 392.

123. According to Adams, all the different groups he named believed "let us have Jefferson, Madison, Burr, any body, whether they be Philosophers, Deists, or even Atheists, rather than a Presbyterian President" (ibid., 392–93).

124. Alexander Hamilton to John Jay, May 7, 1800, *PAH* 24:465.

125. Note, *PAH* 24:467.

126. Alexander Hamilton to James Bayard, April 1802, *PAH* 25:605–8.

127. Ibid.

128. James Bayard to Alexander Hamilton, Apr. 25, 1802, *PAH* 25:613.

129. Chernow, *Alexander Hamilton,* 659.

130. John Adams to Benjamin Rush, Sept. 4, 1812, *OFL,* 423.

131. Ibid.

132. This statement is an interesting analogue to his more famous phrase from this inaugural: "We are all Republicans; We are all Federalists." In both, he strives to find the unity behind the philosophical differences.

133. Jefferson, Second Annual Message, Dec. 15, 1802, *CMPP* 1:342.

134. Jefferson, Fifth Annual Message, Dec. 3, 1805, *CMPP* 1:383.

135. Thomas Jefferson to Charles Clay, Jan. 29, 1815, *WTJ* (Wash.): 5:415.

136. Thomas Jefferson to Nehemiah Dodge, Ephraim Robbins, and Stephen S. Nelson, a committee of the Danbury Baptist association in the state of Connecticut, Jan., 1, 1802, *PTJ* 36:258.

137. *Reynolds,* 98 U.S. at 164.

138. *Everson,* 330 U.S. at 16 (internal quotation marks omitted). In 1878, in a case upholding the prosecution of a Mormon for bigamy, the Supreme Court quoted the "wall of separation" and said that "it may be accepted almost as an authoritative declaration of the scope and effect of the amendment thus secured (*Reynolds,* 98 U.S. at 164). That case, however, focused mostly on the defendant's interest in the free exercise of religion.

139. Ironically, in *Everson,* after stating the wall metaphor, the Court upheld the use of governmental funds to pay the bus fares of parochial school pupils along with those of public schools students.

140. *Wallace,* 472 U.S. at 92 (Rehnquist, J., dissenting).

141. Ibid., at 107 (Rehnquist, J., dissenting).

142. Ibid., at 92 (Rehnquist, J., dissenting).

143. Fleet, "Madison's Detached Memoranda," 554–60.

144. Thomas Jefferson to James Madison, Mar. 15, 1789, *PTJ* 14:659.

145. Nehemiah Dodge, Ephraim Robbins, and Stephen S. Nelson, a committee of the Danbury Baptist association in the state of Connecticut, to Thomas Jefferson, reprinted in Dreisbach, "'Sowing Useful Truths and Principles,'" 455.

146. The committee noted that Jefferson had faced hostility from other Connecticut clergymen because of his refusal to "assume the prerogative of Jehovah and make Laws to govern the Kingdom of Christ."

147. Thomas Jefferson to Levi Lincoln, Jan. 1, 1802, *PTJ* 36:256.

148. Jefferson acknowledged that the Baptist letter did not directly raise this issue; their letter, he wrote Lincoln, "to be sure does not point at this, and its introduction is awkward" (ibid).

149. Ibid.; emphasis added.

150. In 1998, the Library of Congress requested an FBI computer analysis of his draft; see Hutson, "'A Wall of Separation.'" The analysis revealed that Jefferson had blotted out language stating, "confining myself therefore to the duties of my station, which are merely temporal, be assured that your religious rights shall never be infringed by any act of mine and that." The analysis showed that he had also written and crossed out "Adhering to this expression of the supreme will of the nation in behalf of the rights of conscience" before his statement "I shall see with friendly dispositions the progress of those sentiments which tend to restore to man all his natural rights, convinced that he has no natural rights in opposition to his social duties."

151. Levi Lincoln to Thomas Jefferson, Jan. 1, 1802, *PTJ* 36:256.

152. Levi Lincoln also suggested that Jefferson could add a phrase indicating that the thanksgiving proclamations were subject to "the particular situations, usages & recommendations of the several States, in point of time & local circumstances" (ibid.).

153. Thomas Jefferson to Nehemiah Dodge, Ephraim Robbins, and Stephen S. Nelson, a committee of the Danbury Baptist association in the state of Connecticut, Jan., 1, 1802, *PTJ* 36:258.

154. *Wallace,* 472 U.S. at 92 (Rehnquist, J., dissenting). See Hutson, "'A Wall of Separation'": "The edited draft of the letter reveals that, far from being dashed off as a 'short note of courtesy,' as some have called it, Jefferson labored over its composition."

155. Hutson, "'A Wall of Separation.'"

156. Dreisbach, "'Sowing Useful Truths and Principles,'" 474.

157. *JCC* 6:1014, Dec. 9, 1776.

158. Thomas Jefferson to the Rev. Samuel Miller, Jan. 23, 1808, *WTJ* 9:175.

159. Jefferson was similarly ambiguous in explaining why he did not follow the practices of Washington and Adams: "I am aware that the practice of my predecessors may be quoted. But I have ever believed that the example of state executives led to the assumption of that authority by the general government, without due examination, which would have discovered that *what might be a right in a state government,* was a violation of that right when

assumed by another" (emphasis added). By saying what "might" be right, Jefferson leaves open the possibility that such calls also might not be right.

160. Gallatin, *Writings of Albert Gallatin*, 1:227.

161. James Madison to Thomas Jefferson, Feb. 8, 1805, *WTJ* 8:342.

162. Second Inaugural Address, *CMPP* 1:378.

163. Emphasis added.

164. "Notes of a Draft for a Second Inaugural Address," *WTJ* 9:476.

165. "Mercury & New-England Palladium (Boston) Jan. 22, 1802," in Dooley, *Early Republic*, 101–2.

166. Ibid.

167. Manasseh Cutler to Dr. Joseph Torrey, Jan. 4, 1802, in Withington, "Cutler and the Ordinance of 1787," 505.

168. Kramnick and Moore, "Baptists, the Bureau, and the Missing Lines," 817–22.

169. See, e.g., Hutson, "James H. Hutson Responds," 823–24: "That [Jefferson] chose to begin worshiping in the House two days after calling for a wall of separation between church and state shows that this phrase did not pertain to religious activities on public property (always provided that they were voluntary and nondiscriminatory) and that he had no intention of proscribing such activities."

170. See Hutson, "'Wall of Separation.'"

171. Kramnick and Moore, "Baptists, the Bureau, and the Missing Lines," 821.

172. P. Scott and J. Lee, *Buildings of the District of Columbia*, 262.

173. In fact, services continued in the building until after the Civil War; see Sandoz, *Republicanism, Religion, and America*, 82. These services were not, however, formal "sessions" of the House. The House leadership opened the building for services, and many, though not all, members of Congress attended.

174. When he was president, James Madison also attended religious services in the Capitol building (ibid.).

175. Rodney A. Grunes, "Jefferson, Lincoln, and Religious Freedom," in Pederson and Williams, *Presidential Triumvirate*, 98.

176. Purcell, *Early National Period*, 135.

177. Treaty with the Kaskaskia, art. 3, 7 Stat. 78 (ratified Nov. 24, 1803).

178. Cord, "Founding Intentions," 51.

179. Robert Cord has argued that the grant of money to specifically pay for a Catholic priest was "not favoritism to the Catholic Church . . . because they were working with the Indians there" (Cord, *Separation of Church and State*, 47). Such an argument is functionally the same as that used by Massachusetts and Connecticut in using "neutral" rules of majority vote to fund the preexisting, favored Congregationalist churches. The fact that other religious organizations may have received money to teach Native Americans (63–79) would no more make the policy nondiscriminatory than the fact that other denominations received some money from Massachusetts and Connecticut.

180. Nussbaum, *Liberty of Conscience*, 148.

181. Mann, *Legalities of Early America*, 41.

182. Witheridge, "No Freedom of Religion," 6.

183. Beneke, *Beyond Toleration*, 198.

184. Thomas Jefferson to James Jay, Apr. 7, 1809, *PTJ: Retirement* 1:110.

185. Thomas Jefferson to James Pemberton, Nov. 16, 1807, *WTJ* (Wash.) 5:212–13. In both these letters, Jefferson criticized groups that focused solely on religion, whose teachings, he wrote to Pemberton, resulted "either in effecting nothing, or ingrafting bigotry

on ignorance, and setting them to tomahawking and burning old women and others as witches, of which we have seen a commencement among them."

186. James Madison to Thomas Jefferson, Washington, Oct. 1, 1803, in James M. Smith, *Republic of Letters*, 2:1297–98.

187. Third Annual Message to Congress, Oct. 17, 1803, *CMPP* 1:359.

188. James Madison, First Inaugural Address, Mar. 4, 1809, *PJM: Presidential* 1:18. Interestingly, he did not use any religious imagery in his second inaugural; see James Madison, Second Inaugural Address, Mar. 4, 1813, *PJM: Presidential* 6:85–87.

189. "A Memorial and Remonstrance," June 20, 1785, *PJM: Congressional* 8:303.

190. Hickey, *War of 1812*, 16.

191. Benjamin Rush to John Adams, June 4, 1812, in John Schultz and D. Adair, *Spur of Fame*, 242. According to Rush, the exhortations of the Continental Congress were answered, since God "blessed both their councils and their arms."

192. Presidential Proclamation, July 9, 1812, *PJM: Presidential* 4:581.

193. James Madison to Edward Livingston, July 10, 1822, *WJM* 9:101–3.

194. Presidential Proclamation, July 23, 1813, *PJM: Presidential* 6:458–59. In his autobiography, Madison described his proclamation as calling for "a voluntary concurrence of those who approved a general union on such an occasion" (Adair, "Madison's Autobiography," 208).

195. Epstein, "Rethinking Ceremonial Deism," 2115.

196. His last two religious proclamations had similar, though less eloquent, disclaimers. His 1814 proclamation recommended that a day be set aside "on which all may have an opportunity of voluntarily offering at the same time in their respective religious assemblies their humble adoration to the Great Sovereign of the Universe" (Proclamation, Nov. 16, 1814, *CMPP* 1:558). His final proclamation recommended that the people "of every religious denomination may in their solemn assemblies unite their hearts and their voices in a free-will offering to their Heavenly Benefactor of their homage of thanksgiving and of their songs of praise" (Proclamation, Mar. 4, 1815, *CMPP* 1:561).

197. Fleet, "Madison's Detached Memoranda," 534–36.

198. Ibid., 560.

199. Madison spelled the word "erroneous" as "erronious."

200. Fleet, "Madison's Detached Memoranda," 560–61.

201. Ibid., 561.

202. Ibid.

203. Veto, Feb. 21, 1811, *CMPP* 1:489.

204. Interestingly, when he cited the establishment clause, he misquoted it as "Congress shall make no law respecting a religious establishment," instead of the actual text: "Congress shall make no law respecting an establishment of religion."

205. An Act to Incorporate the Trustees of the Presbyterian Congregation of Georgetown, 2 Stat 356, 9 Cong. Ch. 16 (1806).

206. Sections 2 and 4, An act incorporating the Protestant Episcopal Church in the town of Alexandria, in the District of Columbia, in *DPC* 22:995–98.

207. Section 8, An act incorporating the Protestant Episcopal Church in the town of Alexandria, in the District of Columbia, in *DPC* 22:995–98. The actual law authorized aid only for the "support of the poor of the said church," but Madison's veto message described the law as providing for the support of the poor without limitation.

208. Veto, Feb. 21, 1811, *CMPP* 1:490.

209. Section 6, *Annals* 22:982–85.

210. McLemore, *Mississippi Baptists*, 46.

211. Baptist Churches in Neal's Creek to James Madison, Apr. 27, 1811, *PJM: Presidential* 3:292–93. A second Baptist Church wrote Madison to simply state its agreement with the Black Creek letter (Baptist Church on Black Creek to James Madison, Apr. 27, 1811, *PJM: Presidential* 3:293).

212. James Madison to the Baptist Churches in Neal's Creek and on Black Creek, North Carolina, June 3, 1811, *PJM: Presidential* 3:323.

213. Feb. 23, 1811, *DPC* 22:995–98.

214. Mar. 2, 1811, ibid.

215. Feb. 23, 1811, *DPC* 22:995–98.

216. *Muzzy*, 1 N.H. (1 Smith) (1803), printed in *Decisions of the Superior and Supreme Courts*, 12–13.

217. Feb. 23, 1811, *DPC* 22:995–98.

218. *Senate Journal* 1:10 (Apr. 7, 1789).

219. *House Journal* 1:12 (Apr. 9, 1789).

220. *Senate Journal* 1:12 (Apr. 15, 1789).

221. *Senate Journal* 1:16–17 (Apr. 25, 1789).

222. *House Journal* 1:24–26 (May 1, 1789).

223. Act of Sept. 22, 1789, ch. 17, sec. 4, 1 Stat. 70.

224. Marsh v. Chambers, 463 U.S. 783, 788–92 (1983). See also McConnell, "Reading the Constitution," 362, saying that Madison "did not consider legislative chaplains to violate the Establishment Clause."

225. Cord, *Separation of Church and State, 32–33*.

226. As president, he did sign a bill solely limited to fixing the chaplain's salaries: An Act fixing the compensation of the chaplains of Congress, 14 Cong. Ch. 170; 3 Stat. 334, Apr. 30, 1816. By that point, the chaplains had been part of Congress for more than a quarter century and it is not surprising that Madison would have acquiesced rather than risk political repercussions.

227. James Madison to Edward Livingston, July 10, 1822, *WJM* 9:100–103.

228. Fleet, "Madison's Detached Memoranda," 554–60.

229. James Madison to Edward Livingston, July 10, 1822, *WJM* 9:100–103. In his autobiography, Madison said that he "disapproved also of Chaplains to Congress paid out of the public Treasury—as a violation of principle. He thought the only legitimate and becoming mode would be that of voluntary contribution from the members (Adair, "Madison's Autobiography," 204).

230. James Madison to Edward Livingston, July 10, 1822, *WJM* 9:100–103. In his Detached Memoranda, he also said that the legislative chaplaincies could be dismissed as "Maculis quas aut incuria fudit, aut humana parum cavit natura," which means "a few blots which a careless hand has let drop, or human frailty has failed to avert" (Olree, "Madison and Legislative Chaplains," 221n309).

231. D. Davis, *Religion and the Continental Congress, 79*.

232. According to Ashbel Green, a congressional chaplain from 1792 to 1800, "about one third of the members in congress in each house were commonly present at prayers" (A. Green and J. Jones, *Life of Ashbel Green, 263*). While such attendance belies the notion of a legislature unified by prayer, it does not negate the significance of the prayers for those who attended.

233. Boudinot, *Addresses and Letters of Elias Boudinot, 1:21*.

234. Act of March 3, 1791, ch. 28, sec. 5, 1 Stat. 222.

235. Ch. 20, Art. 2, 2 Stat. 359 (1806).

236. Act of January 18, 1815, ch. 23, sec. 14, 3 Stat. 186, 190 (1815). When Congress assumed responsibility for governing Washington, D.C., it continued preexisting tax exemptions for church property; see, e.g., Act of July 9, 1798, sec. 8, 1 Stat. 585.

237. Sec. 9, 2 Stat. 592 (Apr. 30, 1810); reenacted, sec. 11, 3 Stat. 102 (Mar. 3, 1825). See generally J. West, *Politics of Revelation and Reason.*

238. "11th Congress, 3rd Session, Remonstrance Against the Delivery of Letters, Papers, and Packets, at the Post-Office on the Sabbath," communicated to the House of Representatives, Jan. 31, 1811, *ASP* 177. See generally John, "Taking Sabbatarianism Seriously."

239. "13th Congress, 3rd Session, Sunday Mails," communicated to the House of Representatives, Jan. 20, 1815, *ASP* 46.

240. "13th Congress, 3rd Session, Sunday Mails, Friday, February 10, 1815," *ASP* 185–86.

241. Ibid.

242. Jan. 16, 1815, 48 Annals of Cong. 1074–75. See also Fuller, *Morality and the Mail,* 15.

243. Niles, "Sunday Mails," *Niles' Weekly Register* 35 (Jan. 24, 1829), 352.

244. Leland, "Transportation of the Mail," *WJL,* 566.

245. Ibid., 565. In a letter of support to Senator Johnson, Leland warned that if the religious forces prevailed in stopping Sunday mail, then, "encouraged by success, they would next proceed to have the days of Christmas, and Easter, and their associations and synods exempted in the same way, and where would it end?" (Leland to Richard Johnson, Jan. 8, 1830, *WJL,* 562).

246. Public Law Appropriations, Postal Service, 37 Stat 539, 543 (Aug. 24, 1912).

247. Mead, "Neither Church nor State," 350.

248. Jasper Adams, *Relation of Christianity to Civil Government,* 12.

249. James Madison to Jasper Adams, September 1832, *WJM* 9:485.

250. For an interesting discussion of the two metaphors, see M. Hall, "Jeffersonian Walls and Madisonian Lines," 563.

251. See, e.g., McBrien, *Caesar's Coin,* 66–67: "Theoretical appeals to the 'wall of separation' notwithstanding, the Court has adopted, in practice, the Madisonian rather than the Jeffersonian metaphor."

252. Some have argued that, in practice, legislative chaplains have been sectarian and divisive. See Marsh v. Chambers, 463 U.S. 783, 800n10 (1983), "Legislative Chaplain" article. In that case, the wall of separation may be the appropriate response.

253. See, e.g., Dreisbach, "'Sowing Useful Truths and Principles,'" 497: "It would be a mistake to construe his 'line of separation' as support for something less than a separation between church and state."

CHAPTER 7. ORIGINAL WISDOM

1. Whittington, "New Originalism," 599. See also Kesavan and Paulsen, "Constitution's Secret Drafting History," 1128.

2. Bork, *Tempting of America,* 144.

3. Balkin, "Abortion and Original Meaning," 304–5. Adherents of this approach have been dubbed "new new originalists" (P. Smith, "Originalism and Non-Originalism," 709.)

4. P. Smith, "Originalism and Non-Originalism," 710.

5. Bailyn, "Political Experience and Enlightenment Ideas," 350.

6. D. Davis, *Religion and the Continental Congress,* 225. As Noah Webster wrote in

1787 when Pennsylvania replaced its more "Christian" test oath with one requiring a belief in God: "This is a prelude to wiser measures; people are just awaking from delusion. The time will come (and may the day be near!) when all test laws, oaths of allegiance, abjuration, and partial exclusions from civil offices, will be proscribed from this land of freedom" (Webster, *Collection of Essays*, 151–53).

7. Curry, *First Freedoms*, 219.

8. Ibid., 221.

9. *Everson*, 330 U.S. at 11.

10. Drakeman, *Church, State, and Original Intent*, 330.

11. Ibid.

12. Ibid., 328.

13. Rakove, "Thinking like a Constitution," 16.

14. Ibid., 18.

15. 5 U.S. 137 (1803).

16. Drakeman, *Church, State, and Original Intent*, 328.

17. See, e.g., B. Brown, Emerson, Falk, and Freedman, "Equal Rights Amendment," 912–22.

18. Thomas Jefferson to James Madison, Mar. 15, 1789, *PTJ* 14:659.

19. Wood, "Without Him, No Bill Of Rights."

20. Carroll, "To John Fenno of the Gazette of the United States," June 10, 1789, in Hanley, *John Carroll Papers*, 368.

21. Madison made this same point in *Federalist* 51, asserting: "In a free government the security for civil rights must be the same as that for religious rights. It consists in the one case in the multiplicity of interests, and in the other in the multiplicity of sects." Madison's biographer William Rives noted that Madison was fond of quoting Voltaire's statement that "if one religion only were allowed in England . . . the government would possibly become arbitrary; if there were but two, the people would cut each other's throats; but, as there are such a multitude, they all live happy and in peace" (Rives, *Life and Times of Madison*, 2:220–21n1).

22. Finke and Stark, *Churching of America*.

23. Ibid.

24. Article 3, Constitution of Massachusetts, Mar. 2, 1780, in Poore 1:956; Art. 38, Constitution of South Carolina, Mar. 19, 1778, in Poore 2:1620; Constitution of Georgia, Feb. 5, 1777, art. 56, in Poore 1:383; Constitution of Maryland, Nov. 11, 1776, arts. 33 and 35, in Poore 1:817; New Hampshire Constitution of 1784, part 1, art. 6, in Poore 2:1281; Vermont Constitution of 1777, ch. 1, sec. 3, in Poore 2:1859. Vermont was not technically a state in 1777; it did not officially join the union until 1791.

25. See, e.g., S. Green, "Second-Class Constitutional Right?" 1454–57.

26. See, e.g., Jegley v. Picado, 349 Ark. 600, 631 (Ark. 2002): "We have recognized protection of individual rights greater than the federal floor in a number of cases."

27. State v. Hershberger, 462 N.W.2d 393 (Minn. 1990). The court in *Hershberger* noted that the language of the Minnesota constitution protecting religion "is of a distinctively stronger character than the federal counterpart" (397).

28. Church of Lukumi Babalu Aye v. City of Hialeah, 508 U.S. 520, 523–24 (1993).

29. J. Underwood, *Religious Freedom in South Carolina*, 61.

30. Brevard, *Public Statute Law of South-Carolina*, 1:xviii.

31. Art. 8, sec. 1.

32. J. Underwood, *Constitution of South Carolina*, 42–43.

33. W. Cooper and T. Terrill, *American South*, 1:267.

34. Ramsay, *History of South-Carolina*, 2:137.

35. Ibid., 139.

36. D. Davis, *Religion and the Continental Congress* 36 (quoting Stephen Smith, "Prelude to Article VI"). See generally Dreisbach, "Forgotten Religion Clause," 272–73.

37. Art. 22, Delaware Constitution, 1776, in *FSC* 1:566.

38. Art. 1, sec. 2, Delaware Constitution, 1792, in *FSC* 1:582.

39. Art. 4, sec. 10, Georgia Constitution (1789); art. 1, sec. 3, Indiana Constitution (1816); art. 7, sec. 4, Illinois Constitution (1818); art. 1, sec. 3. Maine Constitution (1819) (Thomas, *Strictures on Religious Tests*, 23). In 1793, Vermont deleted its requirement that representatives take an oath acknowledging "the scriptures of the Old and New Testament to be given by divine inspiration; and own and profess the Protestant religion" (ch. 2, sec. 12, Vermont Constitution, 1788); see Djupe and Olson, *Encyclopedia of American Religion and Politics*, 374.

40. Sec. 10, Pennsylvania Frame of Government (1776), modified by art. 9, sec. 4, Pennsylvania Constitution of 1790, in Poore 2:1554.

41. Tennessee Constitution (1796), art. 11, sec. 4, and art. 8, sec. 2, in Poore 2:1674, 1672.

42. "The Jew Bill—From a Correspondent," 12.

43. Torcaso v. Watkins, 367 U.S. 488, 495 (1961). At the time *Torcaso* was decided, Arkansas, Mississippi, North Carolina, Pennsylvania, South Carolina, Tennessee, and Texas had similar constitutional provisions; see Schowgurow v. State, 213 A.2d 475 (Md. 1965).

44. Massachusetts Constitutional Convention, *Journal of Debates and Proceedings*, 461. The proposal was formally made by Ward Nicholas Boylston on Adams's behalf. Adams was undecided on the advisability of maintaining the constitutional provision requiring public funding of religious institutions. As he wrote to a friend, "An abolition of this law would have so great an effect in this State that it seems hazardous to touch it. However, I am not about to discuss the question at present. In Rhode Island, I am informed, public preaching is supported by three or four wealthy men in the parish, who either have, or appear to have, a regard for religion, while all others sneak away, and avoid payment of any thing. And such, I believe, would be the effect in this State almost universally; yet this I own is not a decisive argument in favor of the law. Subjudice lis est. [The matter is still undecided]" (John Adams to Henry Channing, Nov. 3, 1820, *WJA* 10:393).

45. 1780, chap 6, art. 1, *Official Report of the Debates and Proceedings*, 365.

46. Art. 11, Massachusetts Constitution (1833), *Acts and Resolves Passed by the General Court*, 35.

47. John Adams to Mordecai Manuel Noah, July 31, 1818, in "The Jew Bill—From a Correspondent," 10 (emphasis added).

48. George Washington's Letter to Roman Catholics in America, March 1790, *PGW: Presidential* 5:299.

49. As James Madison wrote in 1820, "Among the features peculiar to the political system of the United States, is the perfect equality of rights which it secures to every religious sect" (James Madison to Jacob de la Motta, August 1820, *LWJM* 3:178–79.

50. This approach is similar to that offered in Dworkin, *Taking Rights Seriously*, 340, but instead of creating a theory that is better "from the standpoint of political morality" (Dworkin, *Law's Empire*, 256), I will try to create a theory that is closest to the framers' political philosophy.

51. Balkin, "Understanding Legal Understanding," 117.

52. James Madison to Thomas Jefferson, Washington, Oct. 1, 1803, in James M. Smith, *Republic of Letters*, 1297–98.

53. "Jefferson and Madison often recognized that minor accommodations, while inconsistent with principles of religious freedom, might be unavoidable as a political matter when greater issues were at stake. . . . While one should seek to avoid interpretations that are inconsistent with pervasive or major restrictions, some flexibility in analysis is needed" (Ragosta, "Jefferson's Statute for Religious Freedom," 29).

54. *Lee*, 505 U.S. 624n5 (1992) (Souter, J., concurring).

55. James Madison, First Inaugural Address, *WJM* 8:49.

56. Leland, "Government of Christ," *WLJ*, 279.

57. James Madison to Edward Everett, Mar. 19, 1823, *WJM* 9:124.

58. The full text of Jefferson's quotation reads: "I have sworn upon the altar of God, eternal hostility against every form of tyranny over the mind of man" (Thomas Jefferson to Benjamin Rush, Sept. 23, 1800, *PTJ* 32:166).

59. George Washington to George Mason, Oct. 3, 1785, *PGW: Confederation* 3:293.

60. George Washington to Edward Newenham, June 22, 1792, *PGW: Presidential* 10:493.

61. Nussbaum particularly objected to Justice Breyer's concurring opinion in refusing to order the removal of a monument containing the Ten Commandments that had stood on the ground of the Texas Capitol for forty years without previous complaint (*Liberty of Conscience*, 264). According to Breyer, the four decades without incident showed that "this display is unlikely to prove divisive," but the "removal of longstanding depictions of the Ten Commandments from public buildings across the Nation [could] create the very kind of religiously based divisiveness that the Establishment Clause seeks to avoid" (Van Orden v. Perry, 545 U.S. 677, 704 [2005] [Breyer, J., concurring]).

62. Nussbaum, *Liberty of Conscience*, 314.

63. George Washington to the United Baptist Churches of Virginia, May 1789, *PGW: Presidential* 2:424.

64. John Adams to Thomas Jefferson, Apr. 19, 1817, *WJA* 10:254.

65. George Washington to The Clergy of Different Denominations Residing In And Near The City Of Philadelphia, Mar. 3, 1797, *WGW* 12:245.

66. Washington, "Farewell Address," *CMPP* 1:227. Hamilton's draft read: "Nor ought we to flatter ourselves that morality can be separated from religion. Concede as much as may be asked to the effect of refined education in minds of a peculiar structure—can we believe—can we in prudence suppose that national morality can be maintained in exclusion of religious principles?"

67. "Outline of Argument in Support of His Resolutions," *PTJ* 1:538.

68. Leland, "Transportation of the Mail," *WJL*, 566.

69. Alexander Hamilton to James Bayard, April 1802, *PAH* 25:605–8.

70. Alexander Hamilton to Timothy Pickering, Mar. 22, 1797, *PAH* 20:545.

71. Fleet, "Madison's Detached Memoranda," 561. Madison added that a far "better proof of reverence for that holy name wd be not to profane it by making it a topic of legisl. Discussion."

72. J. Miller, *Federalist Era*, 265n34.

73. William Duane, "Federalism vs. Republicanism," Oct. 14, 1800, in Humphrey, *Revolutionary Era*, 344–45.

74. Lambert, *Founding Fathers and Religion*, 283.

75. Lambert, "God—and a Religious President," 770–71.

76. Stone, "One Nation Under God?" The percentage who so characterize the country has varied from 71 percent in 2005 to 62 percent in 2009.

77. Barton, "Is President Obama Correct?"

78. T. Hall, "Sacred Solemnity," 59–60: "To assert that the United States is a Christian nation is not simply to remark abstractly on the features of American religious demographics. Such an assertion claims dominion and attempts to justify the exercise of political power. It does not simply acknowledge sociological facts any more than observing that the United States is a white nation would amount to a mere recitation of certain facts about racial demographics."

79. Dreisbach, *Founders on God and Government,* 264.

80. Brent, *Biographical Sketch of John Carroll,* 97.

81. Leland, "Virginia Chronicle," *WJL,* 107.

82. Ibid.

83. Leland, "The Mosaic Dispensation" (1832), *WJL,* 670.

84. *Church of the Holy Trinity,* 143 U.S. at 471. Several years after writing his *Church of the Holy Trinity* decision, Brewer tried to explain his meaning of the term "Christian nation." In a lecture at Haverford College, Brewer first stressed that despite his belief that the country was a Christian nation, "the government as a legal organization is independent of all religions" (Brewer, *United States a Christian Nation,* 12). Instead, Brewer stated, the United States should be classified as a "Christian nation" because "Christianity came to this country with the first colonists; has been powerfully identified with its rapid development, colonial and national, and to-day exists as a mighty factor in the life of the republic" (40). Other than some ambiguity over what it means to say that Christianity has been "powerfully identified with" the country's "rapid development," his statement is probably true. But if those few generalities constitute the meaning of "Christian nation," the exclusionary potential of the phrase probably makes it not worth the effort to justify its use.

85. *Church of the Holy Trinity,* 143 U.S. at 465–67.

86. See ibid. at 467–68.

87. See ibid. at 468.

88. He also describes his view of "American life as expressed by its laws, its business, its customs and its society," and notes: "The form of oath universally prevailing, concluding with an appeal to the Almighty; the custom of opening sessions of all deliberative bodies and most conventions with prayer; the prefatory words of all wills, 'In the name of God, amen;' the laws respecting the observance of the Sabbath, with the general cessation of all secular business, and the closing of courts, legislatures, and other similar public assemblies on that day; the churches and church organizations which abound in every city, town and hamlet; the multitude of charitable organizations existing every where under Christian auspices; the gigantic missionary associations, with general support, and aiming to establish Christian missions in every quarter of the globe" (*Church of Holy Trinity,* 143 U.S. at 471). Note that most of these are local and state practices and do not implicate the federal government of the framing period.

89. The Presbytery of the Eastward to George Washington, Oct. 28, 1789, *PGW: Presidential* 4:276n1.

90. George Washington to the Presbytery of the Eastward, Nov. 2, 1789, *PGW: Presidential* 4:274.

91. A. Green, "Jefferson's Papers," 305.

92. George Washington to the Presbyterian Ministers of Massachusetts and New Hampshire, Nov. 2, 1789, *WGW* 12:245.

93. George Washington to the Members of the New Jerusalem Church of Baltimore, Jan. 27, 1793, *PGW: Presidential* 12:53.

94. See, e.g., Simpson v. Chesterfield County Board of Supervisors, 404 F.3d 276, 280

(4th Cir. Va. 2005), upholding a county policy of limiting prayers at board of supervisors meetings to "non-sectarian invocations [that] are traditionally made to a divinity that is consistent with the Judeo-Christian tradition."

95. Silk, "Judeo-Christian Tradition in America," 69. See also B. Murray, *Religious Liberty in America*, 20: "Following World War II and the horror of the Holocaust, Jews were embraced by the American mainstream. . . . What began as Protestant pluralism, over time becomes Christian pluralism, to 'Judeo-Christian.'"

96. Recognizing the Importance of Christmas and the Christian Faith, H.R. Res. 847, 110th Cong. (2007).

97. John Adams wrote, "Our Constitution was made only for a moral and religious people. It is wholly inadequate to the government of any other" (Adams to the Officers of the First Brigade of the Third Division of the Militia of Massachusetts, Oct. 11, 1798, *WJA* 9:229).

98. Fleet, "Madison's Detached Memoranda," 561.

99. Ibid.

100. James Madison to the Baptist Churches in Neal's Creek and on Black Creek, North Carolina, June 3, 1811, *PJM: Presidential* 3:323.

101. George Washington to the Presbytery of the Eastward, Nov. 2, 1789, *PGW: Presidential* 4:274.

102. First Inaugural Address, *PJM: Presidential* 1:15.

103. *CMPP* 1:290.

104. Curry, *First Freedoms*, 219.

105. Virginia Statute for Religious Freedom, in Virginia General Assembly, *Collection of All Such Acts*, 29.

106. Story, *Commentaries on the Constitution*, sec. 1868, 3:726.

107. In a footnote, Story cites "2 Lloyd's Deb 195, 196," which corresponds to 1 Annals of Cong. 730–31.

108. Sekulow, *Witnessing Their Faith*, 26.

109. Vidal v. Philadelphia, 43 U.S. 127, 198–199 (1844).

110. Ibid. at 127.

111. Updegraph v. Commonwealth, 11 Serg. & Rawle 394, 400 (Pa. 1824). The New York courts reached a similar conclusion, holding that Christianity was part of New York State's common law. See also People v. Ruggles, 8 Johns. 290 (N.Y. 1811): "Nor are we bound, by any expressions in the constitution, as some have strangely supposed, either not to punish at all, or to punish indiscriminately the like attacks upon the religion of Mahomet or of the Grand Lama; and for this plain reason, that the case assumes that we are a Christian people, and the morality of the country is deeply ingrafted upon Christianity, and not upon the doctrines or worship of those impostors. Besides . . . imputation of malice could not be inferred from any invectives upon superstitions equally false and unknown."

112. Vidal, 43 U.S. at 198 (emphasis added).

113. Ibid.

114. Story, *Commentaries on the Constitution*, sec. 1871, 3:701 (emphasis added).

115. *McCreary County*, 545 U.S. at 880–81 (O'Connor, J., concurring).

116. Newmyer, *Justice Joseph Story*, 183, quoting Story, *Commentaries on the Constitution* 3, sec. 1867.

117. Finkelman and Cobin, introduction to *Blackstone's Commentaries* 1.

118. Cornell, "Tucker and the Second Amendment," 1127.

119. Hardy, "Lecture Notes of St. George Tucker," 1528.

120. Tucker, *Blackstone's Commentaries* 1:app. 7 (quoting Richard Price).

121. Ibid., 10.

122. Ibid., 7.

123. Cornell, "Tucker and the Second Amendment," 1123, 1124–25.

124. Hardy, "Lecture Notes of St. George Tucker," 1527. Tucker was also a friend of both Jefferson and Madison. Jefferson referred to Tucker as among his "earliest and best friends" (Thomas Jefferson to St. George Tucker, Sept. 10, 1793, in *PTJ* 8:41). Tucker also wrote a biography of Jefferson, which he dedicated to Madison (Tucker, *Life of Jefferson*, ix). Madison's acknowledgment of the dedication was the last letter he wrote before his death.

125. George Washington to the Hebrew Congregation in Newport Rhode Island, Aug. 18, 1790, *PGW: Presidential* 6:285.

126. See Nussbaum, *Liberty of Conscience*, 3.

127. Backus, *Church History of New-England*, 225.

128. *CMPP* 1:490. Madison actually misquotes the First Amendment here as "Congress shall make no law respecting a religious establishment," instead of the actual language, "Congress shall make no law respecting an establishment of religion." Madison also misquoted the First Amendment in his first veto message as "Congress shall make no law respecting a religious establishment."

129. Mar. 2, 1811, 11th Cong., 3rd sess., *DPC* 22:995–98.

130. Garry, "Religious Freedom Deserves More," 3. See also, Cord, "Church-State Separation," 138, stating that the First Amendment only prevents "the establishment of a national church or religion, or the placing of any one religious sect, denomination, or tradition, into a preferred legal status."

131. Bradley, *Church-State Relationships*, 135, 145. This was also the view of Justice Rehnquist, who wrote that when the First Amendment was drafted, "the evil to be aimed at, so far as those who spoke were concerned, appears to have been the establishment of a national church, and perhaps the preference of one religious sect over another; but it was definitely not concerned about whether the Government might aid all religions evenhandedly" (*Wallace*, 472 U.S. at 99 [Rehnquist, J., dissenting]).

132. Leland, "Government of Christ," *WJL*, 476.

133. Laycock, "'Nonpreferential' Aid to Religion," 922–23.

134. This was also the position James Madison had argued in his Memorial and Remonstrance, warning that "the same authority which can force a citizen to contribute three pence only of his property for the support of any one establishment, may force him to conform to any other establishment in all cases whatsoever" (*PJM: Congressional* 8:303).

135. *Colonial Records of Georgia*, 19:395.

136. According to one account, "the obnoxious act was repealed in the fall of 1785" (Boykin, *Baptist Denomination in Georgia*, 1:263). One author has found a single newspaper advertisement from Jan. 26, 1786, indicating an attempt to get the "Episcopalians in Chatham County to register with their church wardens so that their numbers might be determined for collecting the public tax from the treasury" (J. Nichols, "Religious Liberty in the Thirteenth Colony," 1727). This may indicate that repeal occurred in early 1786, since, "there is no known application other than this" (ibid.).

137. "Remonstrance of the Georgia Baptist Association," May 16, 1785, in Boykin, *Baptist Denomination in Georgia*, 1:262.

138. "Resolution of the First and Second Baptist Churches of Groton, January 6, 1817," and "Resolution of Baptists, Methodists and Episcopalians in Andover, April 1, 1817," in McLoughlin, *New England Dissent*, 2:1040–41 (emphasis in the original).

139. One-third was allocated to the Congregationalists, one-seventh to Episcopalians, one-eighth to the Baptists, one-twelfth to the Methodists, one-seventh to Yale, and "the remaining one-sixth was to remain in the treasury" (ibid., 1034).

140. "Resolution of the Methodist Society in Burlington, December 25, 1816," in ibid., 1038. William McLoughlin termed the funding bill "the worst blunder [they] could possibly have made" (1034).

141. The legislative committee that drafted the funding bill had anticipated this complaint and said that money had been "left unappropriated [so] that the Legislature may have it in its power to supply any such omission when it shall be discovered" (ibid., 1035).

142. Ibid., 1036.

143. "Resolution of the Methodist Society in Burlington, December 25, 1816," in ibid., 1038.

144. "Resolution of the First and Second Baptist Churches of Groton, January 6, 1817," in ibid., 1040. The Methodists ultimately did take their share of the money. The Baptists did as well, but only in 1820, after the formal disestablishment of the Congregationalists in Connecticut (1041–42).

145. McConnell, "Free Exercise Revisionism," 1118. There were other exemptions as well. As Martha Nussbaum noted, "North Carolina and Maryland exempted Quakers from the requirement to remove their hats in court. William Penn was actually imprisoned in England for his refusal to remove his hat, and the scandal created by this incident redoubled the determination of the colonists to do things differently" (Liberty of Conscience, 123–24).

146. Vizzard, Shots in the Dark, 53.

147. Employment Division v. Smith, 494 U.S. 872, 878 (1990).

148. Ibid., at 894 (O'Connor, J., concurring).

149. Ibid., at 888.

150. See generally E. West, "Religion-Based Exemptions in Early America," 380.

151. The first time "compelling interest" was used was in 1958: NAACP v. Alabama, 357 U.S. 449, 463 (1958), using the phrase "the subordinating interest of the State must be compelling," quoting Sweezy v. New Hampshire, 354 U.S. 234, 265 (1957) (Frankfurter, J., concurring).

152. PJM: Congressional 1:175.

153. James Madison to Edward Livingston, July 10, 1822, WJM 9:100.

154. "The Answer of the President of the United States to the Address of the Religious Society Called Quakers," October 1789, PGW: Presidential 4:267n1.

155. Justice Scalia, noting that Washington had referred to his own "wish and desire," stated that Washington's opinion on accommodation of religion reflected only his view "of the 'proper' relationship between government and religion, but not . . . of the constitutionally required relationship" (City of Boerne v. Flores, 521 U.S. 507, 542 [1997] [Scalia, J., concurring]).

156. This is similar to the Court's analysis in a case striking down a Connecticut law granting employees the absolute right not to work on their particular Sabbath as violating the establishment clause of First Amendment (Estate of Thornton v. Clador, 472 U.S. 703 [1985]). As Justice O'Connor noted in concurrence, this absolute provision indicated an "endorsement" of Sabbatarian beliefs; in contrast, the civil rights laws that require only a reasonable accommodation of religious practices would be perceived by an objective observer "as an anti-discrimination law rather than an endorsement of religion or a particular religious practice" (at 712). Many leading scholars have proposed similar tests. For example, Christopher Eisgruber and Lawrence Sager suggested that governments must be required

to accommodate the "serious interests of minority religious groups or individuals" when it would have accommodated comparable "serious mainstream religious or secular interests" (Eisgruber and Sager, *Religious Freedom and the Constitution,* 90). Michael McConnell would require that "the claims of minority religions should receive the same consideration under the Free Exercise Clause that the claims of mainstream religions receive in the political process" (McConnell, "Free Exercise Revisionism," 1147). Rodney Smolla proposed that "the flexible standard of intermediate judicial scrutiny should be adopted," adding, "Laws of general applicability that place substantial burdens on the free exercise of religion should be justified by substantial governmental interests and should be narrowly tailored to achieve those interests" (Smolla, "Free Exercise of Religion," 937).

157. Chalifoux v. New Caney Independent School District, 976 F. Supp. 659, 671 (S.D. Tex. 1997).

158. See Goldman v. Weinberger, 475 U.S. 503 (1986), holding that a ban on an orthodox Jewish military officer from wearing his yarmulke was not unconstitutional.

159. Fraternal Order of Police v. City of Newark, 170 F.3d 359 (3d Cir. 1999).

160. The *Chalifoux* court ruled that because the wearing of the rosaries combined free exercise of religion and free speech interests, "this Court must perform a balancing test to determine whether the school's regulation places an 'undue burden' on Plaintiffs' religious exercise and whether the regulation bears more than a 'reasonable relation'" to the school's objectives (*Chalifoux,* 976 F. Supp. at 671). The Court ruled that the school did not meet this burden.

161. See Mintz v. Roman Catholic Bishop, 424 F. Supp. 2d 309, 311 (D. Mass. 2006). The church won its lawsuit, based on the Religious Land Use and Institutionalized Persons Act of 2000, which prohibits a government from imposing "a land use regulation in a manner that imposes a substantial burden on the religious exercise of a person, including a religious assembly or institution, unless the government demonstrates that imposition of the burden on that person, assembly, or institution—(A) is in furtherance of a compelling governmental interest; and (B) is the least restrictive means of furthering that compelling governmental interest" (42 USC § 2000cc(a)(1)).

162. Justice Scalia has made this same point, except that he would extend this to acknowledge the right of government to give public aid to all religions on a nondiscriminatory basis. According to Scalia, the principle that "the government cannot favor one religion over another . . . is indeed a valid principle where public aid or assistance to religion is concerned, or where the free exercise of religion is at issue, but it necessarily applies in a more limited sense to public acknowledgment of the Creator" (*McCreary County,* 545 U.S. at 893 [Scalia, J., dissenting]).

163. According to Martha Nussbaum, there are four factors that identify truly nondenominational public language: "The first is history and ubiquity: how old is the reference, how well embedded in tradition, and how widespread? . . . The second is absence of worship or prayer: the observance should not demand that people join in an act of worship. The third criterion is absence of reference to particular religion. . . . The final criterion is minimal religious content. The reference should be 'highly circumscribed,' so that people who want to avoid it can easily do so" (*Liberty of Conscience,* 271–72).

164. Adams, Proclamation, Mar. 4, 1797, *CMPP* 1:285.

165. John Adams to Benjamin Rush, June 12, 1812, *OFL,* 392.

166. Thomas Jefferson to the Rev. Samuel Miller, Jan. 23, 1808, *WTJ* 9:175.

167. Fleet, "Madison's Detached Memoranda," 560.

168. Thomas Jefferson to Rabbi Mordecai Manuel Noah, May 28, 1818, *ASP,* 195–97.

169. Thomas Jefferson to Jared Sparks, Nov. 4, 1820, *WTJ* 7:186.

170. Trollope, *Domestic Manners of the Americans,* 99.

171. Fleet, "Madison's "Detached Memoranda."

172. *McCreary County,* 545 U.S. at 894 (Scalia, J., concurring).

173. For example, 45 percent of U.S. Catholics supported legalized abortion in a 2009 survey. See Pew Research Center for the People and the Press, *Support for Abortion Slips* (Oct. 1, 2009), http://pewforum.org/uploadedfiles/Topics/Issues/Abortion/abortion09.pdf.

174. It also ignores "Hindus and Buddhists, rapidly growing segments of American society, [who] are very upset about some displays that denigrate them" (Nussbaum, *Liberty of Conscience,* 269). Nussbaum also points out, *"Even Muslims, Jews, and Roman Catholics, moreover, would not approve of the Protestant version* of the commandments, which is the one in question here" (emphasis in original).

175. See U.S. Census Bureau, *Statistical Abstract of United States 2004,* 55.

176. Stark and Finke, "American Religion in 1776," 49.

177. "The answer of the President of the United States to the Address of the Religious Society called Quakers," October 1789, *PGW: Presidential* 4:265–66 (emphasis added).

178. George Washington to the Members of the Volunteer Association, Dec. 2, 1783, *WGW* 27:254.

179. Rousseau, *On the Social Contract,* 96.

180. Bellah, "Civil Religion in America."

181. D. Davis, *Religion and the Continental Congress,* 219.

182. Bellah, "Civil Religion in America," 18.

183. Mirsky, "Civil Religion and the Establishment Clause," 1251.

184. D. Davis, *Religion and the Continental Congress,* 215.

185. Ibid.; see also Linder, "Civil Religion in Perspective," 416.

186. *McCreary County,* 545 U.S. at 893 (Scalia, J., concurring). See also Corbin, "Nonbelievers and Government Religious Speech."

187. Ibid.

188. Jefferson, *"Autobiography," WTJ* 1:62.

189. Fleet, "Madison's Detached Memoranda," 554–60.

190. Jefferson, *"Autobiography," WTJ* 1:62.

191. While the actual characterization of the Hindu religion as polytheistic is somewhat controversial, that is undoubtedly how the English and colonial governments saw it; see Nussbaum, *Liberty of Conscience,* 311.

192. According to a leading dictionary of Jefferson's time, the word "infidel" meant "an unbeliever, a miscreant, a pagan one who rejects Christianity" (Johnson, *Dictionary of the English Language,* 584).

193. Thomas Jefferson to Thomas Leiper, Jan. 21, 1809, *WTJ* 9:238. Jefferson thought far more highly of the moral branch. As he added, "The former [moral branch] instructs us how to live well and worthily in society; the latter are made to interest our minds in the support of the teachers who inculcate them" (ibid.).

194. Jeffrey Schultz, J. West, and I. MacLean, *Religion in American Politics,* 281.

195. Lynch v. Donnelly, 465 U.S. 668, 688 (1984) (O'Connor, J., concurring).

196. Richard Berke, "Religion Center Stage in Presidential Race," *New York Times,* Dec. 15, 1999.

197. Hanna Rosin, "Bush's 'Christ Moment' Is Put to Political Test by Christians," *Washington Post,* Dec. 16, 1999.

198. As of June 2011, the advertisement, titled "'Home Invasion': Vote NO on Prop 8," was available at http://www.youtube.com/watch?v=q28UwAyzUkE.

199. Feldman, *Divided by God*, 58.

200. Thomas Jefferson to the Society of the Methodist Episcopal Church at New London, Feb. 4, 1809, *WTJ* 8:147.

201. B. Murray, *Religious Liberty in America*, 3.

202. Prothero, *Religious Literacy*, 55.

203. Haynes and Thomas, "Religion in the Public School Curriculum," 90.

204. Ibid.

BIBLIOGRAPHY

Abrams, Douglas E. "America's Founding Editors." *Precedent* 2 (Summer 2008): 12.

Acts and Resolves Passed by the General Court of Massachusetts in the year 1863. Boston: Wright and Potter, 1916.

Adair, Douglass, ed. "James Madison's Autobiography." *William and Mary Quarterly,* 3rd ser., 2 (1945): 191–209.

Adams, Arlin M., and Charles J. Emmerich. "A Heritage of Religious Liberty." *University of Pennsylvania Law Review* 137 (1989): 1559–1671.

Adams, Herbert Baxter, ed. *The Life and Writings of Jared Sparks.* Vol. 2. Cambridge, Mass.: Houghton, Mifflin, 1893.

———. *Thomas Jefferson and the University of Virginia.* Washington, D.C.: Government Printing Office, 1888.

Adams, Jasper. *The Relation of Christianity to Civil Government in the United States.* Charleston, S.C.: Miller, 1833.

Adams, Samuel. *The Writings of Samuel Adams, 1773–1777.* Edited by Harry Alonzo Cushing. New York: Putnam's Sons, 1907.

Amar, Akhil Reed. *The Bill of Rights: Creation and Reconstruction.* Harrisonburg, Va.: Donnelly and Sons, 1998.

American Historical Association. *Annual Report for the Year 1899.* 2 vols. Washington, D.C.: Government Printing Office, 1900.

Anderson, James S. M. *The History of the Church of England, in the Colonies and Foreign Dependencies of the British Empire.* London: Francis and John Rivington, 1845.

Antieau, Chester James, Arthur T. Downey, and Edward C. Roberts. *Freedom from Federal Establishment: Formation and Early History of the First Amendment Religion Clauses.* Milwaukee, Wis.: Bruce, 1964.

Backus, Isaac. *An Abridgment of the Church History of New-England: From 1602 to 1804*. Boston: Lincoln, 1804.

———. *The Diary of Isaac Backus*. Edited by William G. McLoughlin. Providence, R.I.: Brown University Press, 1979.

———. *A History of New England, with Particular Reference to the Denomination of Christians Called Baptists*. Newtown, Mass.: Backus Historical Society, 1871.

Bailyn, Bernard, ed. *The Debate on the Constitution*. 2 vols. New York: Library of America, 1990.

———. "Political Experience and Enlightenment Ideas in Eighteenth-Century America." *American Historical Review* 67 (1992): 339–51.

———. *To Begin the World Anew: The Genius and Ambiguities of the American Founders*. New York: Random House, 2004.

Bainton, Roland Herbert. *The Reformation of the Sixteenth Century*. Boston: Beacon, 1985.

Baird, Robert. *Religion in the United States of America; or, An Account of the Origin, Progress, Relations to the State, and Present Condition of the Evangelical Churches in the United States; With Notices of the Unevangelical Denominations*. New York: Harper and Brothers, 1844.

Balkin, Jack M. "Abortion and Original Meaning." *Constitutional Commentary* 24 (2007): 291–352.

———. "Understanding Legal Understanding: The Legal Subject and the Problem of Legal Coherence." *Yale Law Journal* 103 (1993): 105–74.

Bancroft, George. *History of the United States of America: From the Discovery of the Continent [to 1789]*. 10 vols. New York: Appleton, 1896.

Barrett, Jay Amos. *Evolution of the Ordinance of 1787*. New York: Putnam's Sons, 1891.

Barrington, Linda. *The Other Side of the Frontier: Economic Explorations into Native American History*. Boulder, Colo.: Westview, 1999.

Barton, David. "Is President Obama Correct: Is America No Longer a Christian Nation?" WallBuilders.com, April 2009. http://www.wallbuilders.com/LIBissuesArticles.asp?id=23909.

———. *Original Intent*. Aledo, Tex.: WallBuilder, 2003.

Bates, Frank Greene. *Rhode Island and the Formation of the Union*. New York: Macmillan, 1898.

Becker, Carl. *The Declaration of Independence*. New York: Harcourt, Brace, 1922.

Beeman, Richard. *Plain, Honest Men: The Making of the American Constitution*. New York: Random House, 2010.

Bellah, Robert N. *Beyond Belief: Essays on Religion in a Post-Traditional World*. Berkeley: University of California Press, 1991.

———. "Civil Religion in America." *Daedalus* 96 (1967): 1–21.

Benedict, David. *A General History of the Baptist Denomination in America and Other Parts of the World.* New York: Colby, 1848.

Beneke, Chris. *Beyond Toleration: The Religious Origins of American Pluralism.* New York: Oxford University Press, 2006.

Bentley, William. *The Diary of William Bentley D.D., Pastor of the East Church, Salem, Massachusetts.* Vol. 2. Salem, Mass.: Essex Institute, 1907.

Bickford, Charlene Bangs, Kenneth R. Bowling, and Helen E. Veit, eds. *Debates in the House of Representatives.* Baltimore: Johns Hopkins University Press, 1992.

Billingsley, Amos Stevens. *The Life of the Great Preacher, Reverend George Whitefield.* Philadelphia: Ziegler, 1878.

Blakely, William Addison, and Williard Allen Colcord, eds. *American State Papers Bearing on Sunday Legislation.* Washington, D.C.: Religious Liberty Association, 1911.

Blomquist, Robert F. "The Presidential Oath, the American National Interest, and a Call for Presiprudence." *University of Missouri–Kansas City Law Review* 73 (2004): 1–51.

Boller, Paul F. *George Washington and Religion.* Dallas: Southern Methodist University Press, 1963.

———. "George Washington and Religious Liberty." *William and Mary Quarterly,* 3rd ser., 17 (1960): 486–506.

Book of Common Prayer. Oxford: Wright and Gill, 1771.

Boorstin, Daniel J. "The Mythologizing of George Washington." In *The Americans: The National Experience.* New York: Vintage, 1965.

Bork, Robert. *The Tempting of America: The Political Seduction of the Law.* New York: Touchstone, 1991.

Boston, Rob. *Why the Religious Right Is Wrong about Separation of Church and State.* Buffalo, N.Y.: Prometheus, 1993.

Botein, Stephen. "Religious Dimensions of the Early American State." In *Beyond Confederation: Origins of the Constitution and American National Identity,* edited by Richard Beeman, Stephen Botein, and Edward C. Carter, 315–30. Chapel Hill: University of North Carolina Press, 1987.

Boudinot, Elias. *The Life, Public Services, Addresses and Letters of Elias Boudinot.* Boston: Houghton, Mifflin, 1896.

Boyd, Julian P. *The Declaration of Independence: The Evolution of the Text.* Princeton, N.J.: Princeton University Press, 1945.

Boykin, Samuel. *History of the Baptist Denomination in Georgia.* 2 vols. Atlanta: Harrison, 1881.

Bradley, Gerard V. *Church-State Relationships in America.* New York: Greenwood, 1987.

————. "The No Religious Test Clause and the Constitution of Religious Liberty: A Machine That Has Gone of Itself." *Case Western Reserve Law Review* 37 (1986–87): 674–747.

Brant, Irving. *James Madison the Nationalist, 1780–1787*. New York: Bobbs-Merrill, 1948.

Brent, Daniel, ed. *Biographical Sketch of the Most Rev. John Carroll: First Archbishop of Baltimore*. Baltimore: Murphy, 1843.

Brevard, Joseph. *An Alphabetical Digest of the Public Statute Law of South-Carolina*. Charleston, S.C.: Hoff, 1814.

Brewer, David J. *The United States a Christian Nation*. Philadelphia: Winston, 1905.

Brinsfield, John Wesley. *Religion and Politics in Colonial South Carolina*. Greenville, S.C.: Southern Historical Press, 1983.

Brown, Barbara A., Thomas I. Emerson, Gail Falk, and Ann E. Freedman. "The Equal Rights Amendment: A Constitutional Basis for Equal Rights for Women." *Yale Law Journal* 80 (April 1971): 871–985.

Browne, William H., et al., eds. *Archives of Maryland*. Baltimore: Maryland Historical Society, 1906.

Buckley, Thomas E. *Church and State in Revolutionary Virginia, 1776–1787*. Charlottesville: University of Virginia Press, 1977.

Bushman, Richard L. *The Great Awakening: Documents on the Revival of Religion, 1740–1745*. Chapel Hill: University of North Carolina Press, 1989.

Butterfield, Lyman H., ed. *The Letters of Benjamin Rush*. Princeton, N.J.: Princeton University Press, 1951.

Byrd, Robert. *The Senate, 1789–1989: Addresses on the History of the United States Senate*. Washington, D.C.: Government Printing Office, 1988.

Carson, John Fleming. *Is the American Republic a Christian State?* New York, 1908.

Chandler, Thomas Bradbury. *An Appeal to the Public in Behalf of the Church of England in America*. New York: Parker, 1767.

Channing, Edward. *A History of the United States*. New York: Macmillan, 1905.

Chernow, Ron. *Alexander Hamilton*. New York: Penguin, 2004.

————. *Washington*. New York: Penguin, 2010.

Church, Forrest, ed. *The Separation of Church and State: Writings on a Fundamental Freedom by America's Founders*. Boston: Beacon, 2004.

————. *So Help Me God*. Orlando, Fla.: Harcourt, 2007.

Clarke, John. "Ill Newes from New-England." Reprinted in *Collections of the Massachusetts Historical Society,* 4th ser., 1:1–113. Boston: Massachusetts Historical Society, 1852.

Clement, Maud Carter. *The History of Pittsylvania County, Virginia*. Baltimore: Clearfield, 2001.

Cloud, Matthew W. "One Nation, Under God: Tolerable Acknowledgement of Religion or Unconstitutional Cold War Propaganda Cloaked in American Civil Religion." *Journal of Church and State* 46 (2004): 311–40.

Clune, Mary Catherine, ed. "Joseph Hawley's Criticism of the Constitution of Massachusetts." In *Smith College Studies in History*, 3:54. Northampton, Mass.: Department of History of Smith College, 1917.

Cobb, Sanford H. *The Rise of Religious Liberty in America: A History.* New York: Macmillan, 1902.

Cogliano, Francis. *No King, No Popery: Anti-Catholicism in Revolutionary New England.* Westport, Conn.: Greenwood, 1995.

Coleman, Leighton. *A History of the American Church to the Close of the Nineteenth Century.* New York: Gorham, 1906.

Collingwood, Robin George. *Religion and Philosophy.* London: Macmillan, 1916.

The Colonial Laws of New York from the Year 1664 to the Revolution. New York: Lyon, 1894.

The Colonial Records of the State of Georgia. Atlanta: Franklin, 1911.

The Compact, Charter and Laws of the Colony of New Plymouth. Boston: Dutton and Wentworth, 1836.

Conley, Patrick T., and Robert G. Flanders, Jr. *The Rhode Island State Constitution: A Reference Guide.* Westport, Conn.: Praeger, 2007.

Connor, Robert D. W. *History of North Carolina.* 3 vols. Chicago: Lewis, 1919.

Conway, Moncure Daniel. *Omitted Chapters of History Disclosed in the Life and Papers of Edmund Randolph.* New York: Putnam's Sons, 1888.

Cooper, William James, and Tom E. Terrill. *The American South: A History.* Lanham, Md.: Rowman and Littlefield, 2008.

Corbin, Caroline Mala. "Nonbelievers and Government Religious Speech." *Iowa Law Review* 97 (2011).

Cord, Robert L. "Church-State Separation: Restoring the 'No Preference' Doctrine of the First Amendment." *Harvard Journal of Law and Public Policy* 9 (1986): 129–72.

———. "Founding Intentions and the Establishment Clause: Harmonizing Accommodation and Separation." *Harvard Journal of Law and Public Policy* 10 (1987): 47–52.

———. *Separation of Church and State: Historical Fact and Current Fiction.* New York: Carlson, 1982.

Cornell, Saul. "St. George Tucker and the Second Amendment: Original Understandings and Modern Misunderstandings." *William and Mary Law Review* 47 (2006): 1123–54.

"Correspondence between John Adams and Mercy Warren." In *Collections of the Massachusetts Historical Society*, 5th ser., 4:317–491. Boston: Massachusetts Historical Society, 1878.

Cross, Arthur Lyon. *The Anglican Episcopate and the American Colonies*. New York: Longmans, Green, 1902.

Crosskey, William Winslow, and William Jeffrey. *Politics and the Constitution in the History of the United States*. Chicago: University of Chicago Press, 1980.

Cunningham, Noble E. *Jefferson and Monroe: Constant Friendship and Respect*. Chapel Hill: University of North Carolina Press, 2003.

Currier, John J. *"Ould Newbury": Historical and Biographical Sketches*. Boston: Damrell and Upham, 1896.

Curry, Thomas J. *Farewell to Christendom: The Future of Church and State in America*. New York: Oxford University Press, 2001.

———. *The First Freedoms: Church and State in America to the Passage of the First Amendment*. New York: Oxford University Press, 1986.

Davis, Derek H. *Religion and the Continental Congress, 1774–1789: Contributions to Original Intent*. New York: Oxford University Press, 2000.

Davis, James Calvin. *The Moral Theology of Roger Williams: Christian Conviction and Public Ethics*. Louisville, Ky.: Westminster John Knox, 2004.

Dearden, Robert Rowland. *The Bible of the Revolution*. San Francisco: Grabhorn, 1930.

The Debates and Proceedings in the Congress of the United States. Washington, D.C.: Gales and Seaton, 1834.

Decisions of the Superior and Supreme Courts of New Hampshire from 1802 to 1809, and from 1813 to 1816. Boston: Little, Brown, 1879.

De Pauw, Linda Grant, ed. *The Documentary History of the First Federal Congress of the United States of America*. Baltimore: Johns Hopkins University Press, 1972.

"Disestablishment in New England." *British Quarterly Review* 63:61–71. London: Hodder and Stoughton, 1876.

Djupe, Paul A., and Laura R. Olson, eds. *Encyclopedia of American Religion and Politics*. New York: Facts on File, 2003.

Dodd, William Edward. *American Statesmen: James Madison*. Boston: Houghton, Mifflin, 1898.

Donaldson, Thomas. *The Public Domain: Its History, with Statistics*. Washington, D.C.: Government Printing Office, 1880.

Dooley, Patricia L., ed. *The Early Republic: Primary Documents on Events from 1799 to 1820*. Westport, Conn.: Greenwood, 2004.

Drakeman, Donald L. *Church, State, and Original Intent*. New York: Cambridge University Press, 2010.

Dreisbach, Daniel L. "The Constitution's Forgotten Religion Clause: Reflections on the Article VI Religious Test Ban." *Journal of Church and State* 38 (1996): 261–95.

———. *The Founders on God and Government*. Lanham, Md.: Rowman and Little-field, 2004.

———. *A Godless Constitution? A Response to Kramnick and Moore*. Leadership U. http://www.leaderu.com/common/godlessconstitution.html.

———. "In Search of a Christian Commonwealth: An Examination of Selected Nineteenth-Century Commentaries on References to God and the Christian Religion in the United States Constitution." *Baylor Law Review* 48 (1996): 927–1000.

———. *Religion and Politics in the Early Republic: Jasper Adams and the Church-State Debate*. Lexington, Ky.: University Press of Kentucky, 1996.

———. Review of *The Godless Constitution: The Case against Religious Correctness*, by Isaac Kramnick and R. Laurence Moore. *Journal of Church and State* 38 (1996): 644–46.

———. "'Sowing Useful Truths and Principles': The Danbury Baptists, Thomas Jefferson, and the Wall of Separation." *Journal of Church and State* 39 (1997): 455–501.

———. "Thomas Jefferson and Bills Number 82–86 of the Revision of the Laws of Virginia, 1776–1786: New Light on the Jeffersonian Model of Church-State Relations." *North Carolina Law Review* 69 (1990): 159–211.

Dreisbach, Daniel L., Mark David Hall, and Jeffry H. Morrison, eds. *The Forgotten Founders on Religion and Public Life*. Notre Dame, Ind.: University of Notre Dame Press, 2009.

Duncan, Jason K. *Citizens or Papists? The Politics of Anti-Catholicism in New York, 1685–1821*. New York: Fordham University Press, 2005.

Dwight, Timothy. *A Discourse in Two Parts, Delivered July 23, 1812, on the Public Fast*. New Haven, Conn.: Howe and Deforest, 1812.

———. *Theology: Explained and Defended in a Series of Sermons*. New York: Carvill, 1828.

Dworkin, Ronald. *Law's Empire*. Cambridge, Mass.: Harvard University Press, 1986.

———. *Taking Rights Seriously*. Cambridge, Mass.: Harvard University Press, 1978.

Eckenrode, H. J. *Separation of Church and State in Virginia*. Richmond: Virginia Public Printing, 1910.

Eisgruber, Christopher L., and Lawrence G. Sager. *Religious Freedom and the Constitution*. Cambridge, Mass.: Harvard University Press, 2007.

Eliot, Charles W., ed. *American Historical Documents from 1000–1904*. New York: Collier and Son, 1910.

Elliot, Jonathan. *The American Diplomatic Code*. Vol. 1. Washington, D.C.: Jonathan Elliot, 1834.

Ellis, George E. *The Puritan Age and Rule in the Colony of the Massachusetts Bay, 1629–1685*. Cambridge, Mass.: Riverside, 1888.

Ellis, Joseph J. *His Excellency: George Washington*. New York: Vintage, 2005.

Epstein, Steven B. "Rethinking the Constitutionality of Ceremonial Deism." *Columbia Law Review* 96 (1996): 2083–174.

Esbeck, Carl H. "Uses and Abuses of Textualism and Originalism in Establishment Clause Interpretation." *Utah Law Review* 2011, no. 2.

"The Federal Parade of 1788." *American Jewish Archives* 7 (January 1955): 65–66.

Federer, William J. *America's God and Country: Encyclopedia of Quotations*. St. Louis: Amerisearch, 2000.

Feiler, Bruce S. *America's Prophet: Moses and the American Story*. New York: Morrow, 2009.

Feldman, Noah. *Divided by God: America's Church State Problem and What We Should Do about It*. New York: Farrar, Straus and Giroux, 2006.

Fenton, Elizabeth. "Birth of a Protestant Nation." *Early American Literature* 41 (March 2006): 29–57.

Ferguson, Robert. "The Commonalities of Common Sense." *William and Mary Quarterly*, 3rd ser., 57 (July 2000): 465–504.

Fielding, Henry. *Tom Jones*. In *The Miscellaneous Works of Henry Fielding*, vol. 1. New York: Derby, 1861.

Finke, Roger, and Rodney Stark. *The Churching of America, 1776–2005: Winners and Losers in Our Religious Economy*. New Brunswick, N.J.: Rutgers University Press, 2005.

Finkelman, Paul, and David Cobin. Introduction to *Blackstone's Commentaries: with Notes of Reference, to the Constitution and Laws, of the Federal Government of the United States; and of the Commonwealth of Virginia*, edited by St. George Tucker. 5 vols. 1803. Reprint, Clark, N.J.: Lawbook Exchange, 1996. Available at http://www.constitution.org/tb/tb-0000.htm.

Fitzpatrick, John Clement. *George Washington Himself*. Indianapolis: Bobbs-Merrill, 1933.

———. *The Spirit of the Revolution: New Light from Some of the Original Sources of American History*. Boston: Houghton Mifflin, 1924.

Fleet, Elizabeth. "Madison's Detached Memoranda." *William and Mary Quarterly*, 3rd ser., 3 (1946): 534–68.

Ford, Paul Leicester. *Essays on the Constitution of the United States*. Brooklyn, N.Y.: Historical Printing Society, 1892.

————. *Pamphlets on the Constitution of the United States.* Brooklyn, N.Y., 1888.

Foster, John Watson. *The Practice of Diplomacy.* Boston: Houghton, Mifflin, 1906.

Franklin, Benjamin. *The Autobiography* [1793]. New York: Penguin, 1961.

————. *Memoirs of the Life and Writings of Benjamin Franklin.* London: Colburn, 1818.

————. *The Works of Benjamin Franklin.* Edited by Jared Sparks. Boston: Tappan, 1844.

Fredrickson, George M. "The Coming of the Lord: The Northern Protestant Clergy and the Civil War Crisis." In *Religion and the American Civil War,* edited by Randall M. Miller, Harry S. Stout, and Charles Reagan Wilson, 110–30. New York: Oxford University Press, 1998.

Freeman, Douglas Southall. *George Washington: A Biography.* New York: Scribner, 1957.

Frost, J. William. *A Perfect Freedom: Religious Liberty in Pennsylvania.* University Park: Pennsylvania State University Press, 1993.

Fuller, Wayne Edison. *Morality and the Mail in Nineteenth-Century America.* Urbana: University of Illinois Press, 2003.

Furman, Richard. "An Address to the Residents between the Broad and Saluda Rivers Concerning the American War for Independence, November, 1775." In *Richard Furman: Life and Legacy,* edited by James A. Rogers, 269. Macon, Ga.: Mercer University Press, 2001.

Gales, Joseph, ed. *The Debates and Proceedings of the Congress of the United States.* Washington, D.C.: Gales and Seaton, 1853.

Gallatin, Albert. *The Writings of Albert Gallatin.* Vol. 1. Philadelphia: Lippincott, 1879.

Garry, Patrick M. "Religious Freedom Deserves More than Neutrality: The Constitutional Argument for Nonpreferential Favoritism of Religion." *Florida Law Review* 57 (2005): 1–52.

Gilbert, Felix. *To the Farewell Address: Ideas of Early American Foreign Policy.* Princeton, N.J.: Princeton University Press, 1961.

Gillies, John, and George Whitefield. *Memoirs of Rev. George Whitefield.* New Haven, Conn.: Whitmore and Buckingham, 1834.

Goen, C. C. *Revivalism and Separatism in New England, 1740–1800: Strict Congregationalists and Separate Baptists in the Great Awakening.* New Haven, Conn.: Yale University Press, 1969.

Gould, William D. "The Religious Opinions of Thomas Jefferson." *Mississippi Valley Historical Review* 20 (September 1933): 191–208.

Green, Ashbel. "Review of Jefferson's Papers." *Christian Advocate* 8 (1830): 78–83, 251–310.

Green, Ashbel, and J. H. Jones. *The Life of Ashbel Green.* New York: Carter, 1849.

Green, Steven K. "Federalism and the Establishment Clause: A Reassessment."
    Creighton Law Review 38 (2005): 761–97.

———. "A Second-Class Constitutional Right? Free Exercise and the Current
    State of Religious Freedom in the United States; Religious Liberty as a
    Positive and Negative Right." *Albany Law Review* 70 (2007): 1453–71.

———. *The Second Disestablishment: Church and State in Nineteenth-Century America.*
    New York: Oxford University Press, 2010.

———. "A 'Spacious Conception': Separationism as an Idea." *Oregon Law Review*
    85 (2006): 443–80.

Greene, Nathanael. *The Papers of General Nathanael Greene.* Chapel Hill: University
    of North Carolina Press, 2005.

Griffin, Martin I. J. *Catholics and the American Revolution.* Vol. 1. Ridley Park,
    Pa.: Griffin, 1907.

Griswold, Rufus Wilmot. *The Republican Court; or, American Society in the Days
    of Washington* [1854]. Reprint, New York: Appleton, 1856.

Grizzard, Frank E. *George Washington: A Biographical Companion.* Santa Barbara,
    Calif.: ABC-CLIO, 2002.

———. *The Ways of Providence: Religion and George Washington.* Buena Vista,
    Va.: Mariner, 2005.

Grossman, Cathy Lynn. "No Proof Washington Said 'So Help Me God'; Will
    Obama?" *USA Today,* Jan. 7, 2009. http://www.usatoday.com/news/religion/
    2009-01-07-God-oath_N.htm.

Guelzo, Allen C. "God's Designs: The Literature of the Colonial Revivals of
    Religion, 1735–1760." In *New Directions in American Religious History,* edited
    by Harry S. Stout and Darryl G. Hart, 141–72. New York: Oxford University
    Press, 1997.

Guilday, Peter. *The Life and Times of John Carroll: Archbishop of Baltimore, 1735–1815.*
    New York: Encyclopedia Press, 1922.

Hall, David D., ed. *The Antinomian Controversy, 1636–1638: A Documentary History.*
    2nd ed. Durham, N.C.: Duke University Press, 1990.

Hall, Mark David. "Jeffersonian Walls and Madisonian Lines: The Supreme
    Court's Use of History in Religion Clause Cases." *Oregon Law Review* 85
    (2006): 563–614.

Hall, Timothy L. "Roger Williams and the Foundations of Religious Liberty."
    Boston University Law Review 71 (1991): 455–524.

———. "Sacred Solemnity: Civic Prayer, Civil Communion, and the Establish-
    ment Clause." *Iowa Law Review* 79 (1993): 35–92.

Hallahan, William H. *The Day the American Revolution Began: 19 April 1775.* New
    York: HarperCollins, 2000.

Haltigan, James. *The Irish in the American Revolution, and Their Early Influence in the Colonies.* Washington, D.C.: Patrick J. Haltigan, 1908.

Hamburger, Philip A. "A Constitutional Right of Religious Exemption: An Historical Perspective." *George Washington Law Review* 60 (1992): 915–48.

Hamilton, Alexander, James Madison, and John Jay. *The Federalist.* Edited by Jacob E. Cooke. Middletown, Conn.: Wesleyan University Press, 1961.

Hanley, Thomas O'Brien, ed. *The John Carroll Papers.* Notre Dame, Ind.: Notre Dame University Press, 1976.

Hardy, David T. "The Lecture Notes of St. George Tucker: A Framing Era View of the Bill of Rights." *Colloquy: Northwestern University Law Review* 103 (2008): 272–85.

Hastings, Hugh, ed. *Ecclesiastical Records, State of New York.* 6 vols. Albany, N.Y.: Lyon, 1905.

Hawkins, Ernest. *Historical Notices of the Missions of the Church of England in the North American Colonies.* London: Fellowes, 1845.

Hawks, Francis L. *A Narrative of Events Connected with the Rise and Progress of the Protestant Episcopal Church in Virginia.* New York: Harper and Brothers, 1836.

Haynes, Charles C., and Oliver Thomas. "Religion in the Public School Curriculum: Questions and Answers." In *Finding Common Ground: A Guide to Religious Liberty in the Public Schools,* 97–110. Nashville: First Amendment Center, 2001.

Hazard, Samuel, ed. *The Register of Pennsylvania.* Vol. 1: January–July 1828. Philadelphia: Geddes, 1828.

Heimert, Alan. *Religion and the American Mind: From the Great Awakening to the Revolution.* Cambridge, Mass.: Harvard University Press, 1966.

Henry, Patrick. *Patrick Henry: Life, Correspondence and Speeches.* New York: Scribner's Sons, 1891.

Hertslet, Edward. *The Map of Europe by Treaty.* Vols. 1 and 2. London: Butterworths 1875.

Hickey, Donald R. *The War of 1812: A Short History.* Urbana: University of Illinois Press, 1995.

Hills, George Morgan. *History of the Church in Burlington, New Jersey.* Trenton, N.J.: Sharp, 1885.

Hills, Margaret T. "The First American Bible, as Published by Robert Aitken." *Bible Society Record* 113 (January 1968): 2–5.

"His Majesty's Most Gracious Speech to Both Houses of Parliament, on Friday, October 27, 1775." Philadelphia: Hall and Sellers, 1776. Available through the Rare Books and Special Collections Division, Library of Congress, *An American Time Capsule: Three Centuries of Broadsides and Other Printed Ephemera,* http://memory.loc.gov/ammem/rbpehtml/.

Hitchcock, James. *The Supreme Court and Religion in American Life.* Princeton, N.J.: Princeton University Press, 2004.

Holmes, Abiel. "Repeal of the Clause in the Act of the Assembly of Rhode Island excepting Roman Catholics from the Privileges of Freemen." *Collection of the Massachusetts Historical Society* 5:243–44. Boston: Massachusetts Historical Society, 1836.

Holmes, David L. *The Faiths of the Founding Fathers.* New York: Oxford University Press, 2006.

Holmes, J. T. *The American Family of Rev. Obadiah Holmes.* Columbus: Stoneman, 1915.

Hooker, Richard J. "John Dickinson on Church and State." *American Literature* 16 (May 1944): 82–98.

Hopkinson, Francis. *The Miscellaneous Essays and Occasional Writings of Francis Hopkinson.* Philadelphia: Dobson, 1792.

Hoskins, Joseph A. *President Washington's Diaries, 1791 to 1799.* Summerfield, S.C., 1921. Reprint, Charleston, S.C.: Forgotten Books, 2010.

Houghton, Raymond C. *A Revolutionary War Road Trip on US Route 9W.* Delmar, N.Y.: Cyber Haus, 2004.

Hovey, Alvah. *A Memoir of the Life and Times of Isaac Backus.* Boston: Gould and Lincoln, 1858.

Howard, Seymour. "Thomas Jefferson's Art Gallery for Monticello." *Art Bulletin* 59 (December 1977): 583–600.

Hoyt, Albert Harrison. *Sketch of the Life of the Rev. Thomas Bradbury Chandler.* Boston: Clapp and Son, 1873.

Hulber, Archer Butler, ed. *The Records of the Original Proceedings of the Ohio Company.* Marietta, Ohio: Marietta Historical Commission, 1917.

Humphrey, Carol Sue, ed. *The Revolutionary Era: Primary Documents on Events from 1776 to 1800.* Westport, Conn.: Greenwood, 2003.

Hunt, Gaillard. *The Seal of the United States: How It Was Developed and Adopted.* Washington, D.C.: U.S. Department of State, 1892.

Hutchinson, Thomas, ed. *A Collection of Original Papers Relative to the History of the Colony of Massachusetts-bay.* Boston: Fleet, 1769. Reprint, Carlisle, Mass.: Applewood, 2009.

Hutson, James. "James H. Hutson Responds." *William and Mary Quarterly,* 3rd ser., 56 (1999): 823–24.

———. *Religion and the Founding of the American Republic.* Washington, D.C.: Library of Congress, 1998.

———. "'A Wall of Separation': FBI Helps Restore Jefferson's Obliterated Draft." *Library of Congress Information Bulletin* 57 (June 1998): 136–39.

Irvin, Benjamin H. *Samuel Adams: Son of Liberty, Father of Revolution*. New York: Oxford University Press, 2002.

Irving, Washington. *Life of George Washington*. New York: Putnam, 1856.

Isaac, Rhys. *The Transformation of Virginia, 1740–1790*. Chapel Hill: University of North Carolina Press, 1982.

Isaacson, Walter. *American Sketches*. New York: Simon and Schuster, 2009.

———. *Benjamin Franklin: An American Life*. New York: Simon and Schuster, 2003.

Jackson, Gregory S. "America's First Mass Media: Preaching and the Protestant Sermon Tradition." In *A Companion to the Literatures of Colonial America*, edited by Susan P. Castillo and Ivy Schweitzer, 402–25. Malden, Mass.: Blackwell, 2005.

Jackson, Kenneth T., and David S. Dunbar, eds. *Empire City: New York through the Centuries*. New York: Columbia University Press, 2002.

Jackson, Samuel Macauley, ed. *The New Schaff-Herzog Encyclopedia of Religious Knowledge*. New York: Funk and Wagnalls, 1911.

James, Charles F., ed. *Documentary History of the Struggle for Religious Liberty in Virginia*. Lynchburg, Va.: Bell, 1900.

Jefferson, Thomas. *Autobiography of Thomas Jefferson, 1743–1790*. Edited by Paul Leicester Ford and George Haven Putnam. New York: Putnam's Sons, 1914.

———. *Notes on the State of Virginia*. London: Stockdale, 1787.

"The Jew Bill—From a Correspondent." In supplement, *Niles' Weekly Register* 15 (1819).

John, Richard R. "Taking Sabbatarianism Seriously: The Postal System, the Sabbath, and the Transformation of American Political Culture." *Journal of the Early Republic* 10 (1990): 517–67.

Johnson, Samuel. *A Dictionary of the English Language*. Dublin: Jones, 1768.

Johnson, Thomas Cary. *Virginia Presbyterianism and Religious Liberty in Colonial and Revolutionary Times*. Richmond, Va.: Presbyterian Committee of Publication, 1907.

Jones, Newton B., ed. "Writings of the Reverend William Tennent, 1740–1777." *South Carolina Historical Magazine* 61 (July–October 1960): 197–204.

Journals of the Provincial Congress, Provincial Convention, Committee of Safety and Council of Safety of the State of New York 1775–1777. Albany, N.Y.: Weed, 1842.

Kennedy, Paul McClure, ed. *Documents of the Canadian Constitution, 1759–1915*. Toronto: Oxford University Press, 1918.

Kesavan, Vasan, and Michael Stokes Paulsen. "The Interpretive Force of the Constitution's Secret Drafting History." *Georgetown Law Journal* 91 (2003): 1113–214.

Kidd, Thomas S. *The Great Awakening: The Roots of Evangelical Christianity in Colonial America*. New Haven, Conn.: Yale University Press, 2007.

Kirschke, James J. *Gouverneur Morris: Author, Statesman, and Man of the World.* New York: St. Martin's, 2005.

Knight, Edgar W. *Public School Education in North Carolina.* Boston, Mass.: Houghton Mifflin, 1916.

Kramnick, Isaac, and R. Laurence Moore. "The Baptists, the Bureau, and the Case of the Missing Lines." *William and Mary Quarterly,* 3rd ser., 56 (1999): 817–22.

———. *The Godless Constitution: The Case against Religious Correctness.* New York: Norton, 1996.

Labunski, Richard. *James Madison and the Struggle for the Bill of Rights.* New York: Oxford University Press, 2006.

Lambert, Frank. *The Founding Fathers and the Place of Religion in America.* Princeton, N.J.: Princeton University Press, 2003.

———. "God—and a Religious President [or] Jefferson and No God: Campaigning for a Voter-Imposed Religious Test in 1800." *Journal of Church and State* 39 (1997): 769–89.

Langston, Paul. "'Tyrant and Oppressor!' Colonial Press Reaction to the Quebec Act." *Historical Journal of Massachusetts* 34 (2006): 1–17.

Lash, Kurt T. "The Second Adoption of the Establishment Clause: The Rise of the Nonestablishment Principle." *Arizona State Law Journal* 27 (1995): 1085–153.

Laycock, Douglas. "'Nonpreferential' Aid to Religion: A False Claim about Original Intent." *William and Mary Law Review* 27 (1986): 875–923.

Lee, Richard Henry. *Memoir of the Life of Richard Henry Lee.* Philadelphia: Carey and Lea, 1825.

Leibiger, Stuart E. *Founding Friendship: George Washington, James Madison, and the Creation of the American Republic.* Charlottesville: University of Virginia Press, 1999.

Lengel, Edward G. *Inventing George Washington: America's Founder, in Myth and Memory.* New York: HarperCollins, 2011.

Leonard, Lewis Alexander. *Life of Charles Carroll of Carrollton.* New York: Moffat, Yard, 1918.

Levinson, Sanford. *Wrestling with Diversity.* Durham, N.C.: Duke University Press, 2003.

Levy, Leonard W. *The Establishment Clause: Religion and the First Amendment.* 2nd ed. Chapel Hill: University of North Carolina Press, 1994.

Lillback, Peter A. *George Washington's Sacred Fire.* Bryn Mawr, Pa.: Providence Forum, 2006.

Limbaugh, David. *Persecution: How Liberals Are Waging War against Christianity.* New York: Perennial, 2004.

Linder, Robert. "Civil Religion in Historical Perspective: The Reality That Underlies the Concept." *Journal of Church and State* 17 (1975): 399–421.

———. *The Reformation Era*. Westport, Conn.: Greenwood, 2008.

Linn, William. *Serious Considerations on the Election of a President: Addressed to the Citizens of the United States*. New York: Furman, 1800. Reprint, Chicago: Library Resources, 1971. Available at http://candst.tripod.com/pol1800.htm#Serious.

Locke, John. *A Letter Concerning Toleration* [1689]. Edited by J. Cockin. Huddersfield, UK: Brook, 1796.

Lippy, Charles H. "The 1780 Massachusetts Constitution: Religious Establishment or Civil Religion?" *Journal of Church and State* 20 (1978): 533–49.

Longmore, Paul K. *The Invention of George Washington*. Berkeley: University of California Press, 1988.

Low, Sidney J., and Frederick Sanders Pulling. *The Dictionary of English History*. London: Cassell, 1884.

Lucas, Stephen E. "Justifying America: The Declaration of Independence as a Rhetorical Document." In *American Rhetoric: Context and Criticism,* edited by Thomas W. Benson, 67–130. Carbondale: Southern Illinois University Press, 1989.

Lyman, Theodore. *The Diplomacy of the United States*. Boston: Wells and Lilly, 1828.

Maclay, Edgar S., ed. *Journal of William Maclay*. New York: Appleton, 1890.

Maier, Pauline. *American Scripture: Making the Declaration of Independence*. New York: Knopf, 1997.

———. *From Resistance to Revolution: Colonial Radicals and the Development of American Opposition to Britain, 1765–1776*. New York: Norton, 1991.

———. *Ratification: The People Debate the Constitution, 1787–1788*. New York: Simon and Schuster, 2010.

Madison, James. *Letters and Other Writings of James Madison, 1769–1793*. Vol. 1. Philadelphia: Lippincott, 1865.

Malone, Dumas. *Jefferson and His Time: Jefferson and the Ordeal of Liberty*. Boston: Little, Brown, 1962.

Mann, Bruce H. *Legalities of Early America*. Chapel Hill: University of North Carolina Press, 2001.

Mapp, Alf J., Jr. *The Faiths of Our Fathers: What America's Founders Really Believed*. Lanham, Md.: Rowman and Littlefield, 2005.

Marshall, Christopher. *Passages from the Diary of Christopher Marshall*. Edited by William Duane. Philadelphia: Hazard and Mitchell, 1849.

Marshall, Maria Newton. "An Episode in Madison's Career." *Green Bag* 12 (1900): 339–41.

Mason, John. *The Complete Works of John Mason*. New York: Baker and Scribner, 1849.

Massachusetts Constitutional Convention. *Journal of Debates and Proceedings in the Convention of Delegates, Chosen to Revise the Constitution of Massachusetts.* Boston: Daily Advertiser, 1853.

Mayer, Brantz. "Introductory Memoir." In Charles Carroll, *Journal of Charles Carroll of Carrollton: During His Visit to Canada in 1776.* Baltimore: John Murphy for the Maryland Historical Society, 1876.

McBrien, Richard P. *Caesar's Coin.* New York: Macmillan, 1987.

McClellan, James. *Liberty, Order, and Justice: An Introduction to the Constitutional Principles of American Government.* Indianapolis: Liberty Fund, 2000.

McConnell, Michael W. "Free Exercise Revisionism and the Smith Decision." *University of Chicago Law Review* 57 (1990): 1109–153.

———. "On Reading the Constitution." *Cornell Law Review* 73 (1988): 359–63.

———. "The Origins and Historical Understanding of Free Exercise of Religion." *Harvard Law Review* 103 (1990): 1409–517.

McKinley, Albert Edward. *The Suffrage Franchise in the Thirteen English Colonies in America.* Philadelphia: University of Pennsylvania Press, 1905.

McLemore, Richard Aubrey. *A History of Mississippi Baptists, 1780–1970.* Jackson: Mississippi Baptist Convention Board, 1971.

McLoughlin, William G. *New England Dissent, 1630–1833: The Baptists and the Separation of Church and State.* 2 vols. Cambridge, Mass.: Harvard University Press, 1971.

Meacham, Jon. *American Gospel: God, the Founding Fathers, and the Making of a Nation.* New York: Random House, 2007.

Mead, Sidney E. "Neither Church nor State: Reflections on James Madison's 'Line of Separation.'" *Journal of Church and State* 10 (1968): 349–63.

———. *The Old Religion in the Brave New World.* Berkeley: University of California Press, 1977.

Metzger, Bruce Manning, and Michael David Coogan, eds. *The Oxford Companion to the Bible.* New York: Oxford University Press, 1993.

Middlekauff, Robert. *The Glorious Cause: The American Revolution.* 2nd ed. New York: Oxford University Press, 2005.

Miles, Geoffrey. *Classical Mythology in English Literature: A Critical Anthology.* London: Routledge, 1999.

Miller, John C. *The Federalist Era, 1789–1801.* New York: Harper and Row, 1963.

Miller, William Lee. *The First Liberty: America's Foundation in Religious Freedom.* Washington, D.C.: Georgetown University Press, 2003.

Mirsky, Yehudah. "Civil Religion and the Establishment Clause." *Yale Law Journal* 95 (1986): 1237–57.

Mitchell, James T., et al., eds. *The Statutes at Large of Pennsylvania from 1682–1801.* Philadelphia: Busch, 1896.

Morgan, George. *The True Patrick Henry*. Philadelphia: Lippincott, 1907.

Morison, Samuel Eliot. *A History of the Constitution of Massachusetts*. Boston: Wright and Potter, 1917.

———. "The Struggle over the Adoption of the Constitution of Massachusetts." *Proceedings of the Massachusetts Historical Society* 50 (1916–17): 353–412.

Muñoz, Vincent Phillip. "Religion and the Common Good: George Washington on Church and State." In *The Founders on God and Government*, edited by Daniel L. Dreisbach, Mark D. Hall, and Jeffry H. Morrison. Lanham, Md.: Rowman and Littlefield, 2004.

Murray, Bruce T. *Religious Liberty in America*. Amherst: University of Massachusetts Press, 2008.

Murray, John. *The Life of Rev. John Murray*. Boston: Marsh, Capen and Lyon, 1832.

Myers, Denys P. *Massachusetts and the First Ten Amendments to the Constitution*. Washington, D.C.: Government Printing Office, 1936.

Nathan, Joan. *Jewish Cooking in America*. New York: Knopf, 1998.

National Reform Association. *Proceedings of the National Convention to Secure the Religious Amendment of the Constitution of the United States. Held in Pittsburg, February 4, 5, 1874*. Philadelphia: Christian Statesman Association, 1874.

Nelson, John K. *A Blessed Company: Parishes, Parsons, and Parishioners in Anglican Virginia, 1690–1776*. Chapel Hill: University of North Carolina Press, 2001.

Nevins, Allan. *The American States during and after the Revolution, 1775–1789*. New York: Macmillan, 1924.

Newmyer, R. Kent. *Supreme Court Justice Joseph Story: Statesman of the Old Republic*. Chapel Hill: University of North Carolina Press, 1985.

Nichols, Joel A. "Religious Liberty in the Thirteenth Colony: Church-State Relations in Colonial and Early National Georgia." *New York University Law Review* 80 (2005): 1693–772.

Nichols, Thomas Low. *Religions of the World*. Cincinnati: Nicholson, 1855.

Niles, Hezekiah, ed. *Niles' Weekly Register*. Vol. 35: September 1828–March 1829. Baltimore: Niles, 1829.

Norwood, Stephen Harlan, and Eunice G. Pollack, eds. *Encyclopedia of American Jewish History*. Santa-Barbara, Calif.: ABC-CLIO, 2008.

Novak, Michael. *On Two Wings: Humble Faith and Common Sense at the American Founding*. San Francisco, Calif.: Encounter Books, 2002.

Novak, Michael, and Jana Novak. *Washington's God: Religion, Liberty, and the Father of Our Country*. New York: Basic Books, 2006.

Nussbaum, Martha. *Liberty of Conscience: In Defense of America's Tradition of Religious Equality*. New York: Basic Books, 2008.

Nybakken, Elizabeth I., ed. *The Centinel: Warnings of a Revolution*. Cranbury, N.J.: Associated University Presses, 1980.

O'Callaghan, Edmund B., and Berthold Fernow. *Documents Relative to the Colonial History of the State of New York*. 15 vols. Albany, N.Y.: Weed, Parsons, 1883.

The Official Report of the Debates and Proceedings in the State Convention. Boston: White and Potter, 1853.

O'Gorman, Thomas. *A History of the Roman Catholic Church in the United States*. New York: Christian Literature, 1895.

Olree, Andy G. "James Madison and Legislative Chaplains." *Northwestern University Law Review* 102 (2008): 145–21.

O'Malley, Deborah. *"The Dictates of Conscience": The Debate over Religious Liberty in Revolutionary Virginia*. Ashland, Ohio: Ashbrook Center, 2006. Available at http://www.ashbrook.org/publicat/thesis/omalley/omalley.pdf.

"An Originalist Analysis of the No Religious Test Clause." *Harvard Law Review* 120 (2007): 1649–69.

Paine, Thomas. *Common Sense* [1776]. Reprint, Ontario, Canada: Broadview, 2004.

———. *Rights of Man: Being an Answer to Mr. Burke's Attack on the French Revolution*. London: Jordan, 1791.

Patterson, Richard S., and Richardson Dougall. *The Eagle and the Shield: A History of the Great Seal of the United States*. Washington, D.C.: Government Printing Office, 1978.

Paulsen, Michael A. "Religion, Equality, and the Constitution: An Equal Protection Approach to Establishment Clause Adjudication." *Notre Dame Law Review* 61 (1986): 311–70.

Pederson, William D., and Frank J. Williams. *The Great Presidential Triumvirate at Home and Abroad: Washington, Jefferson, and Lincoln*. New York: Nova Science, 2006.

Penn, William. "The Great Case of Liberty of Conscience Once More Briefly Debated and Defended by the Authority of Reason, Scripture, and Antiquity" [1670]. In *The Select Works of William Penn*, 3:1–52. London: William Phillips, 1825.

Perry, William Stevens, ed. *Historical Collections Relating to the American Colonial Church*. Hartford, Conn.: Church Press, 1873.

Peters, Thomas Nathan. "Religion, Establishment, and the Northwest Ordinance: A Closer Look at an Accommodationist Argument." *Kentucky Law Journal* 89 (2000): 743–80.

Peters, William Edwards. *Ohio Lands and Their Subdivision*. Athens, Ohio: Peters, 1918.

Peterson, Merrill D. *Thomas Jefferson and the New Nation*. New York: Oxford University Press, 1970.

Pew Forum on Religion and Public Life. *U.S. Religious Landscape Survey—Religious Affiliation: Diverse and Dynamic*. Washington, D.C.: Pew Research Center, 2008. Available at http://religions.pewforum.org/pdf/report-religious-landscape -study-full.pdf.

Pfander, James E. "So Help Me God: Religion and Presidential Oath-Taking." *Constitutional Commentary* 16 (1999): 549–53.

Pólya, George. *Mathematics and Plausible Reasoning: Induction and Analogy in Mathematics*. Princeton, N.J.: Princeton University Press, 1990.

Press, Bill. *How the Republicans Stole Religion*. New York: Random House, 2010.

Preston, Howard W., ed. *Documents Illustrative of American History, 1606–1863*. New York: Putnam's Sons, 1886.

Proceedings of the Massachusetts Historical Society, 1873–1875. Boston: Massachusetts Historical Society, 1875.

Prothero, Stephen R. *Religious Literacy: What Every American Needs to Know—and Doesn't*. New York: HarperCollins, 2008.

Purcell, Sarah J. *The Early National Period*. New York: Facts on File, 2004.

Quincy, Edmund. *Life of Josiah Quincy of Massachusetts*. Boston: Ticknor and Fields, 1867.

Quincy, Eliza Susan Morton. *Memoir of the life of Eliza S. M. Quincy*. Boston: Wilson and Son, 1861.

Ragosta, John A. "Jefferson's Statute for Establishing Religious Freedom: How We Got It, What We Did with It, and Implications for the First Amendment Debate." Paper presented at the conference "John Adams and Thomas Jefferson: Libraries, Leadership, and Legacy," Boston and Charlottesville, Va., June 27, 2009. Available at http://www.adamsjefferson.com/papers/ Ragosta_final_7_09.pdf.

———. *Wellspring of Liberty: How Virginia's Religious Dissenters Helped Win the American Revolution and Secured Religious Liberty*. New York: Oxford University Press, 2010.

Rakove, Jack N. *The Beginnings of National Politics: An Interpretive History of the Continental Congress*. Baltimore: Johns Hopkins University Press, 1982.

———. *Revolutionaries: A New History of the Invention of America*, Boston: Houghton Mifflin Harcourt, 2010.

———. "Thinking Like a Constitution." *Journal of the Early Republic* 24 (2004): 1–26.

Ramsay, David. *The History of South-Carolina*. 2 vols. Charleston, S.C.: Longworth, 1809.

Randall, Jaynie. "Sundays Excepted." *Alabama Law Review* 59 (2008): 507–37.

Rapport, Leonard. "Printing the Constitution: The Convention and Newspaper Imprints, August–November 1787." *Prologue* 2 (Fall 1970): 69–89.

"Rethinking the Incorporation of the Establishment Clause: A Federalist View." *Harvard Law Review* 105 (1992): 1700–1719.

Rice, Charles E. *The Supreme Court and Public Prayer: The Need for Restraint.* New York: Fordham University Press, 1964.

Richardson, James D. *A Compilation of Messages and Papers of the Confederacy.* Nashville: United States Publishing, 1905.

Rives, William Cabell. *History of the Life and Times of James Madison.* Vol. 1. Boston: Little, Brown, 1859.

Rodda, Chris. *Liars for Jesus: The Religious Right's Alternate Version of American History.* North Charleston, S.C., 2006.

Rosenbach, A. S. W. *Dedication of the New Synagogue of the Congregation Mikve Israel.* Philadelphia: Cahan, 1909.

Ross, Tara, and Joseph C. Smith, Jr. *Under God: George Washington and the Question of Church and State.* Dallas: Spence, 2008.

Rousseau, Jean-Jacques. *On the Social Contract* [1762]. Reprint, Mineola, N.Y.: Dover, 2003.

Rowland, Kate Mason. *The Life of George Mason, 1725–1792.* New York: Putnam's Sons, 1892.

Sandoz, Ellis, ed. *Political Sermons of the American Founding Era.* 2nd ed. 2 vols. Indianapolis: Liberty Fund, 1998.

———. *Republicanism, Religion, and the Soul of America.* Columbia: University of Missouri Press, 2006.

Sanford, Charles B. *The Religious Life of Thomas Jefferson.* Charlottesville: University of Virginia Press, 1984.

Saunders, William L., ed. *The Colonial Records of North Carolina.* Raleigh, N.C.: Hale, 1886.

Scarberry, Mark S. "John Leland and James Madison: Religious Influence on the Ratification of the Constitution and on the Proposal of the Bill of Rights." *Penn State Law Review* 113 (2009): 733–800.

Scharf, John Thomas. *History of Maryland: From the Earliest Period to the Present Day.* 3 vols. Baltimore: Piet, 1879.

Schragger, Richard C. "The Role of the Local in the Doctrine and Discourse of Religious Liberty." *Harvard Law Review* 117 (2004): 1810–92.

Schultz, Jeffrey D., John G. West, and Iain S. MacLean, eds. *Encyclopedia of Religion in American Politics.* Phoenix: Oryx, 1999.

Schultz, John A., and Douglass Adair, eds. *The Spur of Fame: Dialogues of John Adams and Benjamin Rush, 1805–1813.* Indianapolis: Liberty Fund, 1999.

Schwartz, Bernard. *The Great Rights of Mankind: A History of the American Bill of Rights.* New York: Oxford University Press, 1977.

Scott, Pamela, and Antoinette Josephine Lee. *Buildings of the District of Columbia*. Oxford: Oxford University Press, 1963.

Scott, W. W. *A History of Orange County, Virginia*. Richmond, Va.: Waddey, 1907.

Sedgwick, Theodore. *A Memoir of the Life of William Livingston*. New York: Harper, 1833.

Seixas, Gershom Mendes. *A Religious Discourse* [1789]. Reprint, New York: Jewish Historical Society of New York, 1977.

Sekulow, Jay. *Witnessing Their Faith: Religious Influence on Supreme Court Justices and Their Opinions*. Lanham, Md.: Rowman and Littlefield, 2006.

Semple, Robert B. *A History of the Rise and Progress of the Baptists in Virginia*. Richmond, Va.: Pitt and Dickinson, 1894.

Sewel, William. *The History of the Rise, Increase, and Progress of the Christian People Called Quakers*. London: Sowle, 1722.

Seymour, Aaron Crossley Hobart. *Memoirs of the Life and Character of the Late Rev. George Whitefield*. Philadelphia: Probasco, 1820.

Shakespeare, William. *Much Ado about Nothing* [1598]. Cambridge: Cambridge University Press, 2003.

Silk, Mark. "Notes on the Judeo-Christian Tradition in America." *American Quarterly* 36 (1984): 65–85.

Smith, James Morton, ed. *The Republic of Letters: The Correspondence between Thomas Jefferson and James Madison, 1776–1826*. New York: Norton, 1995.

Smith, James Ward, A. Leland Jamison. *Religion in American Life*. Princeton, N.J.: Princeton University Press, 1961.

Smith, Peter J. "How Different Are Originalism and Non-Originalism?" *Hastings Law Journal* 62 (2011): 707–36.

Smith, Rogers M. *Civic Ideals: Conflicting Visions of Citizenship in U.S. History*. New Haven, Conn.: Yale University Press, 1999.

Smith, Stephen A. "Prelude to Article VI: The Ordeal of Religious Test Oaths in Pennsylvania." In *1992 Free Speech Yearbook*, edited by Dale A. Herbeck, 1–106. Carbondale: Southern Illinois University Press, 1993.

Smith, Steven D. *Foreordained Failure: The Quest for a Constitutional Principle of Religious Freedom*. New York: Oxford University Press, 1995.

Smolla, Rodney A. "The Free Exercise of Religion after the Fall: The Case for Intermediate Scrutiny." *William and Mary Law Review* 39 (1998): 925–43.

Smyth, Albert Henry, ed. *The Writings of Benjamin Franklin*. 10 vols. New York: Macmillan, 1906.

Spalding, Matthew. "Attestation Clause." In *The Heritage Guide to the Constitution*, edited by Edwin Meese III, 301–2. Washington, D.C: Heritage Foundation, 2005.

Sparks, Jared, ed. *Correspondence of the American Revolution: Being Letters of Eminent Men to George Washington*. Boston: Little, Brown, 1853.

———. *The Life of Gouverneur Morris*. Boston: Gray and Bowen, 1832.

Sprague, William Buell. *Annals of the American Pulpit: Presbyterian*. New York: Carter and Brothers, 1858.

Stark, Rodney, and Roger Finke. "American Religion in 1776: A Statistical Portrait." *Sociological Analysis* 49 (1988): 39–51.

Steiner, Franklin. *The Religious Beliefs of Our Presidents*. Amherst, N.Y.: Prometheus, 1995.

Steiner, Rachel C. "One Nation Indivisible: In Liberty We Trust." *Wisconsin Law Review* (2003): 937–76.

Stiles, Ezra. *The Literary Diary of Ezra Stiles*. Edited by Franklin B. Dexter. 3 vols. New York: Scribner's Sons, 1901.

Stone, Daniel. "One Nation under God?" *Newsweek,* Apr. 7, 2009. Available at http://www.thedailybeast.com/newsweek/2009/04/06/one-nation-under -god.html.

Story, Joseph. *Commentaries on the Constitution*. 3 vols. Boston: Hilliard, Gray, 1833.

Stout, Harry S., and Peter Onuf. "James Davenport and the Great Awakening in New London." *Journal of American History* 70 (December 1983): 556–78.

Strickland, William Peter. *History of the American Bible Society from Its Organization to the Present Time*. New York: Harper and Brothers, 1849.

Sweet, William Warren. *Religion in Colonial America*. New York: Cooper Square, 1965.

Talcott, Mary K., ed. *The Talcott Papers: Correspondence and Documents (Chiefly Official) during Joseph Talcott's Governership of the Colony of Connecticut, 1724–41*. Vol. 5 of *Collections of the Connecticut Historical Society*. Hartford: Connecticut Historical Society, 1896.

Thomas, Abel C. *Strictures on Religious Tests*. Philadelphia: Richards, 1838.

Treaties and Other International Agreements of the United States of America, 1776–1949. Washington, D.C.: Department of State Publishing, 2010.

Trollope, Frances Milton. *Domestic Manners of the Americans*. New York: Whittaker, Treacher, 1832.

Trumbull, Benjamin. *A Complete History of Connecticut*. Vol. 2. New Haven, Conn.: Maltby, Goldsmith, 1818.

Tucker, George. *The Life of Thomas Jefferson*. Philadelphia: Carey, Lea and Blanchard, 1837.

Tucker, St. George, ed. *Blackstone's Commentaries: with Notes of Reference, to the Constitution and Laws, of the Federal Government of the United States; and of the Commonwealth of Virginia*. 5 vols. 1803. Reprint, Clark, N.J.: Lawbook Exchange, 1996. Available at http://www.constitution.org/tb/tb-0000.htm.

Underhill, Edward Bean, ed. *The Bloudy Tenent of Persecution for Cause of Conscience Discussed: And Mr. Cotton's Letter Examined and Answered.* London: Haddon, 1848.

Underwood, B. F. "Was Washington a Christian?" *Chicago Tribune,* May 4, 1889.

Underwood, James L. *The Constitution of South Carolina: Church and State, Morality and Free Expression.* Columbia: University of South Carolina Press, 1986.

———. *The Dawn of Religious Freedom in South Carolina.* Columbia: University of South Carolina Press, 2006.

———. "The Dawn of Religious Freedom in South Carolina: The Journey from Limited Tolerance to Constitutional Right." *South Carolina Law Review* 54 (2002): 124–80.

U.S. Bureau of the Census. *Statistical Abstract of United States, 2004.* Washington, D.C.: Government Printing Office, 2004.

U.S. Department of State. Bureau of Public Affairs. *The Great Seal of the United States.* Washington, D.C.: U.S. Department of State, 2003. Available at www .state.gov/documents/organization/27807.pdf.

Van Tyne, Claude H. *The Causes of the War of Independence.* Bethesda, Md.: Simon, 2001.

Vile, John R. *The Constitutional Convention of 1787: A Comprehensive Encyclopedia of America's Founding.* Santa Barbara, Calif.: ABC-CLIO, 2005.

———. *James Madison: Philosopher, Founder, and Statesman.* Athens: Ohio University Press, 2008.

Virgil. *Publii Virgilii Maronis Opera; or, The Works of Virgil.* Edited by Joab Goldsmith Cooper. New York: Pratt, Oakley, 1858.

Virginia General Assembly. *A Collection of All Such Acts of the General Assembly of Virginia, of a Public and Permanent Nature, as Are Now in Force.* Richmond: Pleasants and Page, 1803.

Vizzard, William J. *Shots in the Dark: The Policy, Politics, and Symbolism of Gun Control.* Lanham, Md.: Rowman and Littlefield, 2000.

Waldman, Steven. *Founding Faith: Providence, Politics, and the Birth of Religious Freedom in America.* New York: Random House, 2008.

Ward, Nathaniel. "The Simple Cobler of Aggawam in America" [1647]. Reprinted in *Tracts and Other Papers Relating Principally to the Origin, Settlement, and Progress of the Colonies in North America from the Discovery of the Country to the Year 1776,* edited by Peter Force. Vol. 3. Washington, D.C.: Force, 1844.

Webster, Noah. *A Collection of Essays and Fugitive Writings on Moral, Historical, Political and Literary Subjects* [1790]. Reprint, Delmar, N.Y.: Scholars' Facsimiles and Reprints, 1977.

Wells, William V. *The Life and Public Services of Samuel Adams.* Boston: Little, Brown, 1865.

West, Ellie M. "The Right to Religion-Based Exemptions in Early America: The Case of Conscientious Objectors to Conscription." *Journal of Law and Religion* 10 (1993–94): 367–401.

West, John G., Jr. *The Politics of Revelation and Reason.* Lawrence: University Press of Kansas, 1996.

White, Henry Clay. *Abraham Baldwin.* Athens, Ga.: McGregor, 1926.

Whittington, Keith E. "The New Originalism." *Georgetown Journal of Law and Public Policy* 2 (2004): 599–613.

Williams, Peter W. *America's Religions: From Their Origins to the Twenty-First Century.* Chicago: University of Illinois Press, 2008.

Wills, Garry. *Cincinnatus: George Washington and the Enlightenment.* Garden City, N.Y.: Doubleday, 1984.

Winship, Michael P. *The Times and Trials of Anne Hutchinson: Puritans Divided.* Lawrence: University Press of Kansas, 2005.

Winthrop, John. "Modell of Christian Charity" [1630]. Reprinted in *Collections of the Massachusetts Historical Society,* 3rd ser., vol. 7. Boston: Little and Brown, 1838.

Witheridge, David E. "No Freedom of Religion for American Indians." *Journal of Church and State* 18 (1976): 5–19.

Withington, Nathan N. "Manasseh Cutler and the Ordinance of 1787." *New England Magazine* 24 (1901): 494–509.

Witte, John, Jr. "The Theology and Politics of the First Amendment Religion Clauses: A Bicentennial Essay." *Emory Law Journal* 40 (1991): 490–507.

Wolcott, Oliver. *Memoirs of the Administrations of Washington and John Adams.* Edited by George Gibbs. New York: Van Norden, 1846.

Wolfe, Alan, and Ira Katznelson. *Religion and Democracy in the United States: Danger or Opportunity?* Princeton, N.J.: Princeton University Press, 2010.

Wood, Gordon S. "Without Him, No Bill of Rights." *New York Review of Books,* Nov. 30, 2006.

Young, Norwood. *George Washington, Soul of the Revolution.* New York: McBride, 1932.

Zubly, John J. "A Sermon on American Affairs." 1775. In *"A Warm & Zealous Spirit": John J. Zubly and the American Revolution; A Selection of His Writings,* edited by Randall M. Miller, 123–31. Macon, Ga.: Mercer University Press, 1982.

INDEX